HISTORY OF
RUSSIAN MUSIC

VOLUME I

History of Russian Music

BY

GERALD R. SEAMAN

VOLUME I

From Its Origins to Dargomyzhsky

FREDERICK A. PRAEGER, Publishers

New York · Washington

BOOKS THAT MATTER

Published in the United States of America in 1967
by Frederick A. Praeger, Inc., Publishers,
111 Fourth Avenue, New York, N.Y.10003

© Gerald Seaman 1967

*

Library of Congress Catalog Card Number 67–21754

Printed in Great Britain

Folk-songs are a living and vivid history of the people. . . . The historian must not search in them for any indications of the date of a battle, nor for any exact account of it. . . . But if he desires to learn about the everyday life of the people, the elements of its character, the subtle shades of its feelings, its emotions, sufferings and amusements, if he wishes to inquire into the spirit of a past age, the nature of the people as a whole, and of each individual separately, then he will be fully satisfied: the history of the people will be revealed to him in all its grandeur. . . .

GOGOL

Contents

List of Plates

Foreword

One of the pleasures of an academic life is that, as you grow older, you find your 'young men' tackling the jobs you have neglected to do yourself. For at least thirty years I have been telling myself that one day I must get down to the writing of a concise but comprehensive history of Russian music. Fate, in various disguises, decided otherwise. Often distracted from Russian music altogether, I never found time for anything more than dictionary articles and studies of limited subjects. And now my half-namesake has done the work instead and it is a pleasure to welcome it.

The existing non-Russian histories of Russian music in general are either too short (like Calvocoressi's little Penguin *Survey*), hopelessly out-of-date, or compilations from other Western sources. Until Findeisen published his great *Outlines of the History of Russian Music* in 1929, the pre-Glinka period was largely unknown even to most Russian musicians—and probably thought not worth knowing; the book was admirably translated by S. W. Pring for the American Council of Learned Societies but, inexplicably, never published. Twenty years later R. A. Mooser came along with his *Annales de la musique et des musiciens en Russie au XVIIIe siècle* which was at least accessible to Western readers, like Dieter Lehmann's *Russlands Oper und Singspiel in der zweiten Hälfte des 18ten Jahrhunderts* in 1958. But all these studies end with the early nineteenth century, admittedly the period to which Russian musical scholars have devoted most of their best work since the Second World War, and none is available in English. Dr. Seaman, knowing Russian and the Russian sources (both musical and musicological), has covered the whole ground and the English-reading lover and student of Russian music has reason to be deeply grateful to him.

GERALD ABRAHAM

xi

Preface

The writer of a history of Russian music is faced with an unusual problem—the virtual absence of any reliable contemporary literature in the English language, giving a comprehensive picture of the evolution of Russian music. Of the existing histories those of Rosa Newmarch and Montagu-Nathan are of value only in their accounts of nineteenth-century music, commencing with Glinka. The works of Abraham and Calvocoressi are likewise concerned with developments in Russian musical history over the last hundred years, though Abraham has made some brief excursions into the eighteenth century in his chapter on vocal music in *A History of Song* (ed. Denis Stevens), London, 1960. Martin Cooper's volume *Russian Opera* likewise deals mostly with the nineteenth century. The only recent histories of Russian music are those of Calvocoressi (1944), R. A. Leonard (1956) and James Bakst (1966). These are written primarily for the non-specialist and, with the exception of the Calvocoressi, do not contain music examples. Other volumes in English are translations of Pougin's *History of Russian Music*, published in 1915, and Asafyev's *Russian Music from the Beginning of the Nineteenth Century*, 1930, translated by Swan. Some comments on the latter book will be found in Chapter Five of the *Sources* section at the conclusion of this work. It should be pointed out that none of the above-mentioned works makes reference to the investigations by R.-A. Mooser into Russian music of the eighteenth century. Though articles on various aspects of Russian folk and ecclesiastical music have appeared in musical periodicals, much has been left unsaid. Nor is reference literature readily available. Useful, but not definitive, bibliographies have appeared in *Notes, Fontes Artis Musicae, Basic Russian Publications* (ed. Paul L. Horecky), *Acta Musicologica* and in A. Olkhovsky's *Music Under the Soviets*, London, 1955. Russian writings apart, the best existing introduction to early Russian music is probably the long article *Russland* in the

encyclopaedia *Die Musik*, which contains an extensive bibliography. This, however, employs German transliterations, which
are sometimes difficult to decipher. A contributor to the encyclopaedia and the compiler of the bibliography, Dieter
Lehmann, has made a number of surveys of eighteenth-century
Russian music, drawing heavily on Soviet sources. The most
reliable and meticulous scholar, is, of course, R.-A. Mooser,
whose *Annales* and other publications are a *sine qua non* for any
investigator into Russian music before 1800. In some cases
Mooser, who spent many years in painstaking research in
Russian archives, has discovered information apparently not
known to Soviet scholars. Mooser, however, does not include
music examples in his studies, being more concerned with
factual detail than music *per se*.

It is the aim of the present History to attempt to bring about
a deeper understanding of Russian music and to reveal the
extent to which it has been influenced by the folk element. It
does not pretend to be all-embracing—indeed, such a task
would be impossible in face of the vast quantities of new
material and interpretations (mostly in Russian) constantly becoming available—but, if nothing else, it is hoped that it will
serve perhaps as a basis for future research.

This History is an amplification of a doctoral thesis completed in 1961 entitled *The Influence of Folk-Song on Russian Opera
in the Eighteenth Century up to and including the Time of Glinka*,
materials for which were obtained during the course of a year's
study in the U.S.S.R. from 1960–61. Although the author has
relied largely on the histories of Pekelis, Keldysh and Tumanina,
Ginzburg, Rabinovich and Findeisen, every attempt has been
made to secure verification of facts. Wherever possible this has
been achieved by personal consultation of autograph materials
in Leningrad, Moscow, Kiev and elsewhere. The author has
also had recourse to the published researches of Mooser.

Much of the present work originated in the form of articles
in *Music and Letters*, *The Music Review*, *The Monthly Musical
Record*, the Supplementary Volume to the Fifth Edition of
Grove, and *The Slavonic and East European Review*, and I am
grateful to the Editors for allowing them to be reprinted here.
However, these were all monographs written at the commencement of the writer's research career and have been subjected

influence of Graeco-Roman culture, connected more or less directly with the music of the Eastern and Western Slavs, is the *Kolyady*—the ritual sacred songs. Ritual songs similar in content and form to the Russian, Ukrainian and White-Russian exist also among the Western and Southern Slavs (such are the Serbian, Czech, Bulgarian and Slovak *Kolyadki*, the so-called *Koleda*), and also among the Roumanians—the *Colinda*, and the Albanians—the *Colendre*. It has now been established beyond any doubt that all these names spring from a common root—the name of the Graeco-Roman New Year festival, the *Kalanda* or *Calendae*. If the customs and rituals of the Graeco-Roman winter festivals are compared with those of the Eastern Slavs (from the point of view of the mummers, the songs, &c.), the resemblances are even more apparent.

Still further influences on the music of the Eastern Slavs are described in some of the ancient *byliny* (the old Russian ballads) and in the Mediaeval chronicles (e.g. in the *Povest vremennikh let* of the eleventh century). From these accounts it is learnt that the repertoire of the ancient Russian *gusli*-players[1] was extremely varied, and that it included, apart from stories of the exploits of Russian *bogatyrs*,[2] melodies brought by pilgrims from Jerusalem, Byzantium and Venice, and, finally, Jewish chants, which might well have been borrowed from the Jewish population in Kiev. There is no doubt that in a big trading centre such as Novgorod these influences would be still stronger.

FOLK GENRES: BYLINY

Of the various Russian folk genres outstanding are the *byliny* or *stariny*—the name given to the ancient epic ballads, which first arose about the tenth and eleventh centuries. The content of the *byliny* is most diverse and embraces about a hundred different subjects. Often these deal with the exploits of the *bogatyrs*. In many of the *byliny* of the 'Kiev cycle' the subject matter frequently centres round the struggle of the young Russian state with its enemies—the Steppe nomads, the Polovtsians, and, most of all, the Tartars. Among the best known of the *byliny* characters is the *bogatyr* ploughman Mikhail Selyaninovich, who is remarkable for his tremendous physical strength. One of the

---

[1] *Gusli*—a favourite bowed stringed instrument.
[2] *Bogatyr*—a heroic Russian warrior.

best-known *byliny* is 'O Volge i Mikule' (Mus. Ex. 1) the melody of which was written down by Musorgsky and used subsequently in his opera *Boris Godunov*. The *bylina* describes how the young Prince Volga Svyatoslavovich goes out into the meadow, discovers a plough, but neither he nor his bodyguard together can move it. Mikhail Selyaninovich, however, is able to manipulate it with only one hand.

Another famous *bylina* character, Ilya Muromets, is often represented as a symbol of courage and defiance against oppression. Other characters such as Dobrynya Nikitich, Alësha Popovich, Sadko, Vasiliy Buslaev, are historical and are mentioned in the ancient chronicles. (1) At the same time the *byliny* also record the names of Russia's foes, particularly the dreaded Polovtsian Khans of the twelfth century—Konchak and Atrak. In one *bylina* the Polovtsian Tugor-Khan, who lived at the end of the eleventh century, is transformed into the legendary monster Tugarin Zmievich, who was conquered by the *bogatyr* Alësha Popovich.

The struggle between Russia and the Tartars left a deep mark on the *byliny* epos, almost to the extent of completely obliterating the memory of all her battles with her former enemies —the Pechenegs and the Polovtsians. Thus, the battle of the River Kalka in 1223 was commemorated in the *bylina* 'O Kalskom poboishche', the invasion of Khan Batu in 1234 and his destruction of Kiev in the *bylina* 'Vasiliy-pyanitsa i Batyga'. As may be expected the main theme of the Russian *byliny* of this later period is the defence of the Russian land, the struggle with its enemies, and the desire for State unity.

STRUCTURE OF BYLINY

The *byliny* themselves fall into two categories—the *odnogolosnaya* or *solnaya* ('monophonic' or 'solo'), and the *mnogogolosnaya* or *khorovaya* ('polyphonic' or 'choral'). The first of these is generally referred to as the 'Northern' *byliny* epos, the second as the 'Southern' or 'Donskoi', as the choral *byliny* are most frequently found among the Don Cossacks. The texts of the Northern *byliny* are strictly metrical and consequently influenced the nature of the music, which follows precisely the natural accents of the words. It is by no means uncommon, however, for the same tune to be used for several other texts of a similar verse structure, and often a ballad-singer will know only two or three *byliny* melodies. The tunes of the Northern *byliny* are laconic and usually consist of only one or two phrases forming a single verse (see Mus. Ex. 1):

Mus. Ex.1
Moderato
R-K, No.2

Zhil Svya-to-slav de-vya-no-sto let,   zhil Svya-to-slav, da pe-re-sta-vil-sya, o-sta-
-va-los ot ne-vo cha-do_ ma-lo-e,   mo-lo-doy Vol-ga Svya-to-sla-vo-vich.

In the choral *byliny*, however, words and melody are inseparable, both being of equal importance. Consequently each choral *bylina* possesses its own melody. Mus. Ex. 2, which describes how Ilya Muromets sets out into the wilds of the steppe, is a typical illustration (Mus. Ex. 2):

Mus. Ex.2
Slowly ♩=58
Women's voices
ILYA MUROMETS, No.25

Men's voices
Ai - - - da ne go-ry to sy go - ra - -
- mi - sy-kho di - - li - sya
ei, da ne le-sy to sy le-soch - ka
- mi sy-klo - nya - li - sya.

Characteristic of both types of *byliny* is the use of hyperbole, the 3-fold repetition of description or events, and, in the course of performance, the employment of a pause at the end of each verse. Often a *bylina* will be introduced by a so-called '*zapev*'—a 'prelude' having no direct connection with the main context. The melodies of the Northern *byliny* are quiet, majestic and of a recitative-like nature. The texts are occasionally of great length, in some cases exceeding 400 verses.

COMIC BYLINY

Apart from the *byliny* categories mentioned above, there is yet a third type—the comic ballad, which is of a more animated nature. These are known as *byliny-novelly* and are concerned not with *bogatyrs* (though in some cases the traditional figures of Dobrynya and Alësha are encountered) but with the pranks of *skomorokhs*, deceived husbands, and other popular objects of humour. Sometimes the comic ballads contain elements of social satire directed against the Tsar, the clergy, or authority in general.

SUMMARY

The *byliny* were essentially the property of the *skomorokhi*, who played a vital part in their composition, performance and preservation. It is interesting to note that the greater part of the *byliny* collected have been found not in Kiev or Novgorod, as might be expected, but in the far North—on the shores of the White Sea and the banks of the Rivers Pinega, Pechora and Mezen in the former Provinces of Arkhangelsk and Olonets. The reasons for this are that the Northern regions were far less subject to attacks by Steppe raiders, so that there was a general movement to the North, and secondly that the repressive measures taken by the Church and State against the *skomorokhi* in the seventeenth century compelled them to take refuge in these areas as the only means of escape.

HISTORICAL SONGS

The second great folk-song genre is that of the Historical Song ('Istoricheskaya pesnya'). These are known among the peasants as 'stariny' or 'starinki', although they distinguish them from the *byliny* or *stariny* of the 'Kiev' and 'Novgorod' cycles. The earliest historical songs relate to events of the fourteenth century; however, their real flourishing occurs in the second half of the sixteenth century during the reign of Ivan the Terrible. The principal difference between *byliny* and historical songs lies in their texts, those of the historical songs giving a less fanciful, more factual account of occurrences and events. The texts are shorter and the three-fold repetition, characteristic of the *byliny*, is employed less consistently. Like the epic ballads most of the historical songs reflect the historical past.

A special part in the historical songs is played by the peasant uprisings and the Polish intervention at the beginning of the seventeenth century. Among the favourite heroes are Mikhail Vasilevich Skopin-Shuysky, a young prince who defeated the Polish invaders in 1610, and Minin and Pozharsky, the saviours of Moscow. At the end of the sixteenth and seventeenth centuries a large number of historical songs were written among the Cossacks. Outstanding in the seventeenth century is the figure of Stepan Razin, leader of a famous rebellion. An analogous figure is Emelyan Pugachëv a hundred years later. An interesting light is thrown upon the life of the nineteenth century by the fact that when historical songs were first being collated, many folk-singers feared to give them to collectors on account of censorship, or, if they did so, they changed the names so that they became ordinary 'robbers' songs or songs of the Volga *burlaki*.[1] Such is the remarkable song 'Ne shumi ty, mati zelënaya dubrovushka'. Up to the time of Pushkin there still prevailed a legend that this was a favourite song of Pugachëv, the notorious rebel leader in the reign of Catherine the Great, and Pushkin included it as such in his story *The Captain's Daughter*. The melody is an excellent example of its kind (Mus. Ex. 3).

Of the other figures mentioned in the historical songs a favourite is Peter the Great.

During the nineteenth century the genre deteriorated, though a number of songs were written about the Napoleonic War.

---

[1] *Burlaki*—'haulers', were the poorest of the poor, the equivalent of Irish navvies in Victorian England, who spent their lives hauling barges up the Volga. These, of course, are the famous Volga boatmen, whose melodies were collected by Balakirev (see Plate 9).

Mus. Ex. 3

LOPATIN and PROKUNIN Vol. II

Steadily

Ne shu - mi   ty   i   mat   ze - lĕ -

na - ya - - - du - bro - - - vush - ka,

du - bro - vush - ka,   ne

me - shay mne, dob - ru   mo ː lod - tsu,

du - mu   du - - - - - ma - ti.

Historical songs also came into their own in the 1917 Revolution when many were written about Lenin, Stalin, Chapaev and others, and again during the Second World War.

RITUAL SONGS

By far the oldest songs are the so-called 'obryadovye pesni' or 'ritual songs', many of which preserve traces of pagan symbolism. The melodies likewise show the remains of archaic musical structures. The ritual songs may be divided roughly into 'seasonal' or 'calendar' songs (e.g. 'kolyadki', 'vesnyanki', &c.), and ritual bytovye[1] songs (e.g. funeral laments, lamentations, &c.). Of particular importance in the texts of the ritual songs is the use of metaphor borrowed from the world of nature. Thus, a girl is compared to a white swan or a birch tree (berëza); a youth to a hawk, falcon, or stoat; a married woman to a grey duck; a husband to a dove-coloured drake; unexpected guests to a suddenly arising wind; a widow or orphan to a cuckoo[2]; the yearning woman to trampled-down grass. The guelder-rose and the red-currant bush are both symbols of the virgin bride, while knotted flowers, the drooping branches of a tree, or the troubled waters of a river are all personifications of sorrow and grief. The following lament—a literal translation—conveys

[1] Bytovoy—an untranslatable term, but having the sense of anything pertaining to everyday life. In some cases it has the meaning of 'secular'.

[2] In Russia the cuckoo is always associated with sadness.

some idea of the manner in which this symbolism is employed:

> Through the currant bushes
> There flowed a stream,
> What time my mother
> Bare me, the unhappy one.
> Having chosen unwisely,
> She gave me in marriage,
> To go to a distant,
> Unknown home.
> My father-in-law
> Scolds me for nothing;
> My mother-in-law,
> For every trifle.
> I will flee, dart away;
> In a cuckoo's shape:
> I will fly to my home,
> To my father's home.
> In his garden green
> Will I take my place,
> On the apple-tree
> My mother loves.
> I will cuckoo cry,
> I will sadly wail,
> Till my wailings sad
> Make all eyes weep,
> Till the garden is drowned
> In bitter tears. (2)

The ritual songs themselves, however, have come down to us largely in a modified form, mostly as a result of the work of the Church, which often incorporated pagan festivals into the Christian year. (3)

The calendar songs reveal the peasant's continual care for the coming harvest and are best represented by the *kolyadki*, with their traditional pleas for prosperity in the New Year. The following is typical:

> Afield, afield, out in the open field!
> There a golden plough goes ploughing,
> And behind that plough is the Lord himself.
> The holy Peter helps Him to drive,
> And the Mother of God carries the seed corn,
> Carries the seed corn, prays to the Lord God,
> 'Make, O Lord, the strong wheat to grow,

> The strong wheat and the vigorous corn!
> The stalks there shall be like reeds!
> The ears shall be [plentiful] as blades of grass!
> The sheaves shall be [in number] like the stars!
> The stacks shall be like hills,
> The loads shall be gathered together like black clouds.' (4)

The approach of spring with the thoughts of work in the fields following the departure of winter is accompanied by a whole host of different rituals. Such are the 'passing of Maslenitsa', with the traditional burning of the strawman, and, to a greater extent, the ancient ritual of 'calling in the Spring', (5) concluding in the singing of 'vesnyanki' ('*vesna*' = 'Spring') by girls at dawn. A good example of a *vesnyanok* is the melody 'Vyidi, vyidi, Ivanku, zaspivay nam vesnyanku', which was written down in the Starodubsky district in the Province of Chernigov, and used by Tchaikovsky in the finale of his Piano Concerto in B♭ Minor. Other rituals in the spring cycle are the Spring *khorovods* (round dances), lasting seven weeks, the 'semitskie', 'troitskie' and 'rusalnye' songs, and finally the pagan festival of Ivan Kupala, with its picturesque rituals of the lighting of bonfires, the manufacture of strawmen, and other customs. (6)

The summer field works, culminating in the burden of harvesting, are reflected in the *zhnivnye* (i.e. 'harvest' or 'reaping') songs, which accompany the rituals of 'zazhinki' and 'dozhinki', which are widespread in the districts bordering Belo-Russia and the Ukraine. Of especial interest are the so-called 'dozhinochnye' songs, connected with the harvest festival and the ritual blessing of the last sheaf. This is adorned with flowers and is triumphantly carried to the peasant's home, or to the house of the landowners if the work is in the nature of a *corvée*. It is this rite which is celebrated in Tchaikovsky's *Evgeniy Onegin*.

WEDDING SONGS

A unique place in Russian folklore is occupied by the peasant wedding. The ancient Russian wedding was a complex business lasting several days. Besides choruses of young people, especially invited professional mourners took part, and, at a later date, even *skomorokhi*. The ceremony was opened by the 'compact' (sometimes being preceded by a 'looking-over' of the bride), which was accompanied by the bride's traditional laments. If the bride were unable to sing herself, a professional *plakalsh-chitsa* (mourner) would do it for her. The 'shaking of hands' took place a week before the marriage. On the eve of the wedding was the *devichnik*, when the bride was visited by her girl friends and relatives for the last time. During this period of otherwise general rejoicing, supported by festive songs and games, the fiancée, with veiled face, would spend her time in lamentation, bidding farewell to her girlish freedom. Later she would visit the homes of all her relatives, performing before each a special lament. On the evening before the wedding the girl was obliged to go to the cemetery to bewail her grief before the graves of her deceased ancestors. The ritual custom of washing the bride, the unplaiting of her hair and the preparation for receiving the crown was likewise accompanied by mournful songs. On the other hand, the ritual songs performed during the wedding feast in the house of the bridegroom were notable for their gaiety and liveliness, the active role passing from the *plakalshchitsa* to the *svatushka* (matchmaker)—to the jester with his pert witticisms. It is worth noting that separate episodes from the ancient Russian wedding were often represented in Russian operas of the eighteenth and nineteenth centuries—in *The Miller-magician* of Sokolovsky and Fomin, in Dargomyzhsky's *Rusalka*, and in several operas of Rimsky-Korsakov, to mention only a few. An outstanding modern example is Stravinsky's *Les Noces*.

Apart from the wedding cycle the lament was also used at funerals and for any manifestation of grief. Later they were used by recruits compelled to join the army against their will. In all cases the element of improvization played a vital part and though certain standard melodies would be handed down from generation to generation, a gifted folk-singer would often create music in the folk idiom on the spur of the moment.

MELODIC CHARACTERISTICS

The text and melody of Russian folk-songs are inseparable. As one collector has observed: 'For the folk-singer the text is meaningless without the melody, and the melody without the text'. This applies especially to the oldest *genres*—the epic ballads, the laments, the historical songs, all of which are connected with the intonations of spoken speech. The tunes of the

heroic *byliny* of the 'Kiev cycle', and also the funeral laments,
are not really melodies in the proper sense of the word. Thus
the basis of the laments is often a short characteristic refrain,
usually within the limits of a third or fourth. The laments
themselves, which are born from the intonations of excited
human speech, and usually characterized by a striking opening,
consist of fragmentary motives which are repeated time and
time again, and possess neither clearly expressed tempo nor
clearly defined pitch. Between each verse could be inserted a
sob or cry. The laments of the far North make use of chromaticism, of which Mus. Ex. 4, depicting the grief of a bride, is a good
illustration (Mus. Ex. 4): (7)

An example of a fragmentary melody, originating in spoken
words, is the primitive children's folk-song 'Dozhdik, dozhdik,
pushche', a Spring incantation to rain (Mus. Ex. 5):

Many ritual songs are based on the pentatonic scale and
numerous instances of these are found in wedding, *khorovod*
(round dance) and game songs ('*igrovye pesny*'), and in the Ukrainian and White-Russian *kolyadki* and *vesnyanki*. The pentatonic is not found everywhere, however, although it is a
peculiarity of the folk music of the Kazan Tartars, the Bashkirs,
the Chuvashes and the Mari. Nor, for that matter, does the
fact that a melody is pentatonic mean that it has necessarily
lost all significance. Mus. Ex. 6—a pentatonic wedding melody
—is a particularly beautiful illustration (Mus. Ex. 6):

BYTOVYE SONGS

Bytovye songs are songs connected with the everyday working life of the Russian people. The sharp contrast between the 'heart-felt longing' and the 'wild revelry' of Russian folk-songs was noticed by Pushkin in his poem 'Zimnyaya doroga' (The Winter Road), and, indeed, *bytovye* songs cover an exceedingly wide range, embracing both humorous, satirical and dance songs. Particularly interesting are the singing games, in which a common factor is the combination of spoken dialogue with a choral refrain. (8)

The satirical songs often parody ecclesiastical chants. Thus, according to the testimony of one collector, a so-called 'Monasheskaya pesnya' (Monastery song), written in the former Province of Tver, was sung to the chant 'Tebe, Boga khvalim' (We praise Thee, O God). In Russian classical music this device of folk parody was first employed by Musorgsky for his amusing characterization of the Church in his song 'The Seminarist' and in his operas *Boris Godunov* and *Sorochintsy Fair*.

An important place in the *bytovye* songs is occupied by the *khorovods*, though these sometimes fall under the classification of ritual songs as well. The *khorovods* (round dances) are most varied, both in structure, genre, melody and rhythm (time signatures of 5/4 or 7/4 are not uncommon), though sometimes they are symmetrical in design, often forming an AABB pattern. The *khorovod* is a collective song and is usually performed in a slow tempo. In the spring singing-game 'A my proso seyali' (a *khorovod* used by Rimsky-Korsakov in his opera *Snegurochka*), the melody and movement of the dance are closely related (Mus. Ex. 7):

Mus. Ex.7
Steadily   R-K, No. 48
First Chorus

A my se-chu chi-sti-li, chi-sti-li, oy Did La-do, chi-sti-li, chi-sti-li.

Second Chorus

A my pa-shnyu pa-kha-li, pa-kha-li, oy Did La-do, pa-kha-li, pa-kha-li.

Dance songs ('plyasovye pesny') are often associated with solo performance and are closely connected with the movements of the dance. Typical of this genre are short laconic melodies with strong accents on the final beat and clearly expressed rhythms of which Mus. Ex. 8 is a good illustration (Mus. Ex. 8):

Mus. Ex. 8
Lively

LVOV - PRACH, No. 96

[Kak] u 'nash-ikh u vo - rot, [kak] u 'nash-ikh u vo - rot,

Lyu - li, lyu - li, u vo - rot, Lyu - li, lyu - li, u vo - rot.

It may be noted that all genres of songs connected with movement may possess independent existence and be performed without choreographic action.

LYRICAL SONGS

The lyrical songs (called by the people 'dolgie', 'protyazhnye' or 'progolosnye') also relate to everyday life and are extremely varied in content. Indeed, one of the most striking features of the lyrical protracted song ('liricheskaya protyazhnaya pesnya') is its diversity. The lyrical songs are the crowning achievement of Russian folk music and are acknowledged as such in the works of Tolstoy, Turgenev, Chekhov, Nekrasov, Pushkin, Gogol, and others. (9) Very often one song is found in different variants over a wide area; often each song is sung in its own way in a style peculiar to that district. The subject matter of the lyrical songs is equally manifold, ranging from love songs, agricultural songs, 'robbers' songs', to songs of oppression, recruiting songs (stemming from the period of Peter the Great onwards), and revolutionary songs. This diversity makes it almost impossible to seize on any particular one as a representative example. However, typical of the melodies of all historical periods are the slow tempi, the sustained development of the content, and the completeness of the text. This last factor is important, for dance songs, for instance, sometimes break off in the middle of a word or sentence when the dance is completed: a lyrical song, on the other hand, is always a complete entity. Frequently encountered in the 'haulers' ', 'robbers' ' or 'coachmen's' songs is the same poetic imagery—the dense forest, the wide steppe, the distant road, Mother Volga, the dark night and the red sun.

Characteristic of the more ancient melodies are the briefness of the text, the limited range of the melody (often being only of a fourth, fifth or sixth), and the absence of 'raspev' (melismata or ornamentation). In Mus. Ex. 9 one may clearly see a resemblance to many calendar and ancient wedding songs. The melody consists of only three notes in the limits of a fourth and is made up entirely of variations of the opening phrase. This 'variation development' is a typical feature of lyrical songs as a whole, and in the course of performance an experienced folk-singer would vary the melody considerably according to his or her ability. This element of variation is another consideration which differentiates lyrical song from the more archaic forms such as the *byliny* or the laments, where wholesale repetition is an essential requirement.

Mus. Ex. 9
Slowly
POPOVA, Vol. II, p.108

1. Po - duy, po - duy, ne - po-go - du - shka, bu - en ve - te - rok. 2. Bu - en ve - te - - rok. Raz - duy, raz - duy ty ka - li - - nu - shku, la - zo - re - vy tsvet.

During the fifteenth–sixteenth centuries a desire arose to give greater range to melodies and text, in consequence of which several notes began to be sung to more than one syllable (often taking the form of an initial 'Akh!' or 'Ekh!'), and words to be repeated.

The real flourishing of the lyrical protracted song, however, took place in the sixteenth–seventeenth centuries, and in the greatness of its range, its breadth and freedom, the spontaneity of its development, and its melodic richness, it may be regarded as a purely Russian phenomenon, having no parallel in the music of other Slav races. Of particular importance in the lyrical song are the intervals of the fifth and sixth, the former being associated with moderate feelings, the latter with

ebullience and decisiveness.[1] In Mus. Ex. 10 notable are the
wide range, the smooth-flowing nature of the melody, typical
rhythms and cadences, and the descending movement. Characteristic, too, is the repetition of individual syllables of the words
of the text (e.g. bb. 6–8 'Mozdo step Mozdokskaya'), and the
entry of the chorus in the middle of a word (b. 4). In this particular instance the first three bars are virtually the basis of
the whole song. The accenting of the words is likewise somewhat arbitrary.

Mus. Ex. 10

LOPATIN and PROKUNIN No. IV (15) p. 292

Each protracted song has its own text, so that, therefore,
there is the closest connection between words and music. This
factor also differentiates the lyrical protracted song from most
other forms of folk creation.

[1] Glinka wrote on one occasion: 'The fifth is the soul of Russian music'.

PLATE I

THE BOGATYRS by V. M. VASNETSOV (1848–1926), painted 1881–1898

PLATE 2

PEASANT WEDDING by A. PETROV

from an early nineteenth-century water-colour

FOLK POLYPHONY

From the musical illustrations given above it will be noticed that one of the most striking characteristics of the lyrical protracted song is its polyphonic ('*mnogogolosnaya*') setting, although in this respect the lyrical protracted song is not alone. Basically, folk polyphony consists of free imitation of a single melodic line ('zapev') from which other voices ('*podgoloski*') diverge in accordance with established conventions. In style the '*podgolosnaya polifoniya*' (lit. 'underpart polyphony') offers a parallel to the earliest known Western polyphony, successions of parallel seconds, fourths, sevenths and ninths being of possible occurrence. It must be observed, however, that in folk polyphony each part is of equal importance—a fact that was realized by investigators only at the turn of the century when the task of recording melodies was facilitated by the employment of the phonograph. (10)

MODAL STRUCTURE OF FOLK-SONG

Manifest in the lyrical protracted melodies are the basic principles of modal harmony underlying Russian folk-song. It will be noted that if the earliest folk tunes belonging to the calendar cycle are neither major nor minor but consist only of a simple succession of notes within a narrow gamut (c.f. Mus. Ex. 4 and 5), then the folk-songs of a later period clearly fall into the categories of either the natural major or the natural minor, with the addition of certain characteristic intervals, e.g. a flattened second in the minor mode, a flattened sixth in the major mode, &c. Also encountered are the sharpened fourth in the major and the sharpened sixth in the minor. Certain Siberian harmonicas are constructed so that they play only these notes.

Mus. Ex. 11

At a moderate pace

BAL, No. 20

Ka-ten- ve-sě-la-ya, Ka-tya cher-no-bro-va-ya,

Proy-di, Ka-tya go-ren-koy, top-ni, ra-dost, no-zhen-koy!

The '*lad*' or mode of a melody may frequently be determined

C

by the final note of a folk-song, though it is by no means rare
for a folk-song to conclude on another degree (e.g. on the
dominant or sub-dominant). Sometimes a melody will seem to
begin in one mode and conclude in another—a phenomenon
known as '*peremennost*' (mutation). In Mus. Ex. 11, for instance,
a possible interpretation (and that followed by Balakirev in his
harmonization of the tune) is that the first half of the melody
is in B minor and the second half in the key of D, the relative
major. Another interpretation is that the whole melody is in
the natural major, beginning on D with its final on E. Another
peculiarity sometimes encountered is the simultaneous employment of major and minor. Folk melodies from the far North,
in particular, are noted for their unusual intervals, chromaticisms, and modal irregularities. It must be stressed, however,
that even to this day there is considerable difference of opinion
as to the precise nature of the Russian modal system.

RUSSIAN FOLK INSTRUMENTS:
STRINGED INSTRUMENTS

Russian folk instrumental music in most cases is connected
directly with folk-song. The only exceptions are the military
fanfares and the hunting signals of ancient Russia (mentioned
in the chronicles and other literature) and the music played by
shepherd's pipes, *dudkas*, *zhaleykas*, *rozhki*, and a few other
instruments to be discussed below.

The Russian folk instruments are many and varied, and the
ancient Russian chronicles describe how even in distant antiquity the Eastern Slavs had their own stringed, wind, and percussion instruments—the *gusli*, *truby*, *roga*, *dudki*, *sopeli*, *svireli*,
sipovochki, and, later, in the sixteenth–seventeenth centuries, the
gudok and the *domra*. A Russian folk percussion instrument
which has survived to the present day is the *lozhki* (lit. 'spoons'),
which is often embellished with small bells, and may be regarded as an individual kind of Russian castanet. In recent
archaeological excavations a number of primitive clay ocarinas
have been discovered.

The most popular stringed instrument of the Eastern Slavs
was the *gusli*, and descriptions of performances on it are often
found in folk-songs and *byliny*. In particular the *gusli* was favoured by the *skomorokhi* and it is frequently represented in

miniatures and frescoes of Ancient Russia. The *gusli* was most diverse in form, being oval, triangular, trapeziform, or even alated. The number of strings varied from 5 to 7, later from 10 to 17. Precise details of the tuning are not known.

Of later origin than the *gusli*, but no less prevalent, was another bowed instrument—the *gudok* (which was also adopted by the *skomorokhi*). It is asserted by investigators that the *gudok* made its appearance in Russia about the fourteenth–fifteenth centuries together with a number of other instruments of Oriental origin such as the *domra, surna,* &c. In literature the term '*gudok*' is met with only in the seventeenth century; the term '*gudenie*', which is found much earlier, seems to have been a general expression having the meaning of playing on any kind of instrument. A parallel between this term and the word 'organizing' in Western Mediaeval music is immediately apparent. The *gudok* maintained its place in folk life up to the nineteenth century. According to preserved evidence, the highest string was used by performers for playing the melody, while the other two strings, tuned a fifth below, provided the bass.

A third category is occupied by the *domra* and the *balalaika*, both of which are plucked instruments, consisting of a body and a neck. It seems that the *domra* (which was played with a plectrum) was acquired by the *skomorokhi* from the Asiatic nomads during their occupation of Russia. Instruments of a similar type and even nomenclature (e.g. *dumbra, domr*) are found among Asiatic peoples even at the present day. In the eighteenth century the *domra* was supplanted by the *balalaika* (mostly in its two-stringed form), since its triangular body was more suitable for hand-made mass production. The *balalaika* (which is plucked with the fingers) is one of the most widespread and popular instruments of the Russian people today and is used for accompanying both song and dance. Imitations of the sound of *balalaikas* are frequently encountered in Russian classical music, outstanding examples being in Glinka's *Kamarinskaya*, Balakirev's *Overture On Three Russian Themes*, Serov's *Vrazhya sila*, and elsewhere.

WIND INSTRUMENTS

Among the Russian folk wind instruments may be mentioned the *roga, truby* and *rozhki*, many diverse instruments of the flute type such as the *dudki, svireli, sipovochki, kuvichki,* and finally the reed instrument, the *zhaleyka*.

The *zhaleyka* is an instrument belonging to the clarinet family, made out of reed or wood, and furnished with a single vibrating tongue. The shepherd *zhaleykas* sometimes have bells of natural cow horn, as a result of which they are often confused with the *rozhok*—an embouchure instrument. The *zhaleyka* can either be 'single twin', consisting of two pipes with identical finger holes, or 'double', in which case it is made up of two pipes with differently placed finger apertures, thus enabling the playing of two-part harmony. The *zhaleyka* is used primarily as a solo instrument on which may be performed not only pastoral music but also 'protracted' and dance melodies. Sometimes the *zhaleyka* accompanies a choral ensemble, joining the chorus with the entry of the '*podgoloski*' after the opening '*zapev*'. Imitation of the sound of the *zhaleyka* is occasionally found in Russian opera, a striking instance being in Rimsky-Korsakov's *Snegurochka*.

A reed instrument of the clarinet family is the *volynka*—a kind of bagpipe—which is constructed from a whole goat's or calf's skin, with two or three tubes. One or two of these provide a continual drone, while the melody is played on the remaining pipe. The *volynka* however is by no means encountered over a wide area.

Of the instruments of the flute type of greatest interest is the many-stemmed *svirel*, which is of great antiquity, being known in literature as the syrinx or 'Pipes of Pan'. In the 1860's such an instrument was discovered in the Province of Kursk under the name of *kuvichki*. The *kuvichki* consist of a group of five (or sometimes three) cane *dudochki* (pipes), each of which is shorter than the other, and in no way connected. The person playing the *kuvichki* first arranges the pipes according to their height and, holding them with his hands in front of his lips, quickly moves them from one corner of his mouth to the other, alternating the performance with shouts. To perform upon the *kuvichki* is no easy task and demands considerable practice, and it is a curious fact that it is played only by women. A common combination is that of *kuvichki* and *dudki* (pipes).

The Russian embouchure instruments comprise various species of shepherds' pipes and horns. These include the natural aurochs[1] horns, formerly in great use among the ancient Eastern

---

[1] Aurochs—the urus or wild ox.

Slavs. A magnificent example of one of these, mounted in silver, was found in a *kurgan* [tumulus] in Chernigov. Descriptions of performance on aurochs horns are encountered occasionally in songs and *byliny*. At a later date when the aurochs became extinct, there was a tendency to make the horns of wood, though their former shape was still retained. Such wooden horns, bound round with birch bark, are still preserved in the folk life of the North. An interesting fact is that, apart from their employment in the hunt and in the communal life of ancient Russia (e.g. in military music), trumpets and horns were used at various rituals—e.g. the 'burial of Kostroma' (the 'seeing-off' of summer). This is described in the texts of several wedding songs.

Horns (*rozhki*) were used both for solo and ensemble work. In the latter case, the horns were of different length (varying from 30 cms. to a metre), the one being a small horn (or, as it was called, a *vizgunok*), the other a bass horn, twice its size, sounding an octave lower. Often for local performances two small horns and a bass horn formed an adequate combination, but frequently ensembles assumed larger dimensions. One of the most famous ensembles was that of the Vladimir horn-players, directed by Nikolay Vasilevich Kondratev, who toured Russia and abroad about 1900. Mus. Ex. 12 is a phonographic record

Mus. Ex.12
Lively
Solo
LINEVA Vol. I, No. 23

Tutti

of 'Kamarinskaya', as performed by the Vladimir horn-players, which was made by Elizaveta Linëva—a pioneer in the scientific recording of folk music. Apart from its intrinsic merit it also gives a good insight into Russian folk instrumental polyphony, which is analogous in all respects to the choral. The performance is introduced by a solo '*zapev*', which is then taken up by the remainder of the instruments (Mus. Ex. 12).

INSTRUMENTAL ENSEMBLES

Folk instrumental ensembles are sometimes mixed. Thus, the *khorovods* of the Kursk district are accompanied by a large ensemble of *dudkas* and *kuvichki*. In 1937 a group of research workers from the Moscow Conservatory wrote down a whole series of songs (mostly dance songs) in the same district, which were performed by four *kuvichki* (five-stemmed and three-stemmed), played by women, two *zhaleykas*, and a violin.

The favourite mass instrument of the present era is the accordion (*garmon*). Produced in the former Province of Tula in the 1850's, the accordion quickly acquired widespread popularity. Of the countless models available, the most common variety is the so-called two-tier accordion (the 'German' and the 'Viennese'). Apart from its role as a solo and accompanying instrument the accordion is also important for its use in connection with the *chastushka*—lively folk verses of a humorous or satirical nature. The guitar likewise is very popular.

THE CHASTUSHKA

Although the *chastushka* was specially favoured in the second half of the nineteenth and the first half of the twentieth centuries, it is at the same time a genre with roots in the ancient past, being connected with dance songs, with the *skomorokh byliny*, with the patter songs of parodied wedding refrains. Evidence for this is provided in the first place by the separate records of dance songs at the end of the eighteenth century, which are very close in metre and rhythm to contemporary *chastushki*, and, secondly, the fact that in some Northern districts *chastushki* texts are performed to the melodies of ancient dance songs (such as 'Kamarinskaya', for instance).

A characteristic feature of the *chastushka* is the loose relationship between text and music, for, whereas in certain genres of folk-song, text and music are inseparable, in most Russian villages hundreds or even thousands of verses of *chastushka* texts will be sung to three or four unchanged melodies. However, it would be unfair to regard *chastushkas* as a purely literary genre. The accompaniments of *chastushkas* are often endlessly varied and subject to all manner of ingenious transformations.

In performance, literary improvization usually alternates with musical interludes, which occasionally results in quite complex musical compositions. Usually the *chastushka* melodies are short and 'catchy', falling into two symmetrical sections. The texts themselves are of a witty, satirical nature. Typical of the genre is the combination of folk-song turns in the accordion accompaniments with conventional West-European harmonizations.

SUMMARY

Such then is a brief outline of Russian folk music—its genres and instruments. It is worthy of record that in the Soviet era interest in folk-song is constantly stimulated and that the writing of ballads about Soviet achievements or Soviet heroes is encouraged by the State. Such are the lament about Lenin, 'Kamenna Moskva vsya proplakala' (All Stone Moscow Wept)[1] by the White-Sea ballad-singer M. S. Kryukova, the description of Kirov's death 'Kak uznala ya pro smert Sergey Mironycha' by the Mordovian ballad-singer E. P. Krivosheeva, and, more recently, ballads about the first Soviet cosmonauts.

FOLK-SONG CREATORS AND PERFORMERS

It is, of course, true that a great deal of folk art is purely oral and that much of its success depends on skilful improvization. In this task the part played by individuals cannot be underestimated, and nowhere is this better illustrated than in the case of the Ryabinin family, generations of whom lived in the region of Lake Onega and who passed their music from father to son. The first classical ballad-singer who is really known to us is Trofim Grigorevich Ryabinin, who was 'discovered' by the *byliny* collectors Rybnikov and Hilferding in the second half of the nineteenth century. The following is a condensed account of Trofim Grigorevich's life, compiled by Hilferding at the end

[1] In folk-lore Moscow is invariably referred to as 'Moscow built of white stone'.

of the 1860's. Being deprived of his mother and father at an early age the young Trofim was raised by the village orthodox community.

> When he grew up, so that he should not beg and be a burden to other people, he began to wander through the neighbouring villages, to repair nets, traps, and other fishing appliances. In the course of this he chanced to work for a long time with Ilya Elustafev, a poor old man from Volkh-ozer, the village of Shlyaminskaya . . . This man (who died 40 years ago in his nineties) knew a great many *byliny* and sang them while working, and Ryabinin of course picked them up.

Later Hilferding describes in detail when and from which ballad-singer Ryabinin acquired his art:

> Apart from agriculture his main task was fishing. Not being tied to a trade near home he went forty times with other peasants from Zaonezh to fish in Lake Ladoga. He went twice to St. Petersburg but only for a very short time in order to sell his produce. He considered fishing an extremely good profession, though not one of the most remunerative. Of his four sons two were called up as soldiers and died on active service; the other two lived with their father and partly learned to sing *byliny* from him.

Ryabinin was brought to St. Petersburg by Hilferding on several occasions and performed his *byliny* to a large audience. Musorgsky, who was present at his performances, took down two *byliny* melodies, including 'O Volge i Mikule' which he used in the 'scene near Kromy' for the song of Varlamov and Misail in *Boris Godunov*. Ryabinin's name is also associated with the opera *Sadko*, and Rimsky-Korsakov tells us in his memoirs that the recitatives in the opera, written in the style of *byliny*, were based on Ryabinin's melodies.

Trofim's fame was perpetuated by his son, Ivan Trofimovich, who performed frequently in Russia and abroad in the 1890's. His heir was his stepson, Ivan Grigorevich Ryabinin-Andreev (who also performed in Petersburg not long before the October Revolution), who in turn passed on *his* skill to his son, Peter Ivanovich, who lives to this day in the same village of Garnitsy, in the Kizhsky region of Lake Onega. Peter Ivanovich is also a writer of contemporary ballads.

Among the many ballad-singers of recent times (among

whom may be mentioned V. P. Shchegolenok, from whom Tolstoy, who knew him personally, borrowed the subjects of some of his stories), outstanding is the famous A. M. Kryukova, a singer from the White Sea region, from whom were written nearly sixty *byliny* and who passed on her art to her daughters. One of them, Marfa Semënovna Kryukova, was an outstanding contemporary singer and apart from the vast store of ballads retained in her memory (more than a hundred *byliny* have been taken down from her) she also created new ballads.

Among the Soviet singers, notable is the celebrated 'lamentress' Irina Andreevna Fedosova. A peasant of the former province of Olonets, this remarkable woman, who lived to the age of about 100, had great influence on the work of the poet Nekrasov. Gorky, too, wrote of her with great enthusiasm in 1896. Not the least remarkable of her many gifts was her phenomenal memory and E. V. Barsov, a collector of folk lore, wrote down from her more than 30,000 verses of wedding songs, recruit songs and funeral laments, which were published in his book *Prichitaniya Severnovo kraya* (Laments of the Northern Region), St. Petersburg, 1872. At the age of 30 Irina Andreevna was already famed as a 'mourner' all over Zaonega. Meeting her when she was 50, Barsov relates that she was an extremely plain woman, of short stature, grey and lame, but with great spiritual forces, and a poetic disposition of the highest order. Her speech was lively and witty, proverbs and colloquialisms flowing from her tongue. Apart from laments she also knew *byliny*, historical and lyrical songs, but in these she was less talented.

CONCLUSION

It will be seen, therefore, that Russian folk-song is a subject of remarkable diversity and complexity. With the spread of industrialization and urbanization in the nineteenth century, however, peasant song began to decline in Russia just as it did in England, Germany, and other countries. Today, while peasant song still continues to exist in certain remote areas of Russia, special efforts are being made to record ancient songs by scientific methods from the few folk-singers who survive. Courses in folk-song and the playing of folk instruments are available to students at all Soviet Conservatories.

CHAPTER 2

The Music of
Kiev, Novgorod, and Moscow
up to 1700

INTRODUCTION

The origins of Russian music are to be found in the folk-song
creation of the Eastern Slavs, whose ancestors were agricultural
tribes inhabiting Russian territory about 4000 B.C. Judging
from archaeological remains and other evidence the ancient
Slavs lived a sedentary life, dwelling not only in villages but in
well-fortified settlements. With the course of time the Slavs
divided into three independent branches: the Western branch,
which lived to the East of the Visla and along the Baltic, from
whom are derived the Czechs, Poles, and Polabian Slavs settled
along the Elbe; the Southern branch, from whom are descended
the modern Bulgarians, Serbians, and Croatians; and the Eastern branch, which consisted of a number of tribes (including
the Antes), who later constituted the population of the vast territory of Kiev. Antic tribes lived in the Steppes round the Black
Sea and the forest belt between the Dnepr and the Dnestr in
the first few centuries A.D. and some of their customs have been
described by Byzantine historians (including Procopius of
Caesarea), who praised their honourable character, hospitality,
and humane attitude towards captives and slaves. A detailed
examination of the complex movement of tribes and races,
which eventually led to the formation of the Kievite State, is
beyond the scope of this chapter. Let it suffice to say, however,
that by the end of the ninth century A.D. the Kievite State had
come into being.

KIEVITE RUSSIA: CULTURAL BACKGROUND

The State of Kiev was the largest of all contemporary States in

Europe, its boundaries stretching from the upper reaches of the Volga and Oka to the Danube, from the Black Sea to the Baltic. Connected by trade links with Byzantium and the West, at the height of its power (in the tenth–eleventh centuries) it was one of the most flourishing and culturally advanced States in Europe. Specially strong were the ties between Kiev and Byzantium, and during the tenth century, in particular, Russian goods such as honey, tar, wax and furs were exchanged for Byzantine silks, wine, spices and gold. Cargoes of slaves were also delivered for sale in the Constantinople slave-markets. (1) At the end of the tenth century the religion of Byzantine Orthodoxy was introduced into Russia by Prince Vladimir Svyatoslavich—an action which not only brought about temporary political unity in the feudal State, but also encouraged ties with Greek, Southern Slav, and other West-European peoples.

Other developments in the Kiev period were the appearance of written literature, the creation of an original style of architecture, and a school of painting. Although, according to Soviet scholars, some kind of literature had existed among the Eastern Slavs in about the seventh–eighth centuries—a factor which is established from agreements between Russian Princes and Byzantine Emperors, evidence from foreign sources and various archaeological discoveries (in particular the so-called 'birch letters' found during excavation at Novgorod)—it was not until the beginning of the eleventh century that an independent and original literature was created in Kiev. (2) Translations of Greek scriptures and liturgies were made together with stories from the Old Testament, Lives of the Saints, sermons and teachings, while an important part was played also by the historical chronicles (*Letopisi*), travels, historical legends and heroic military narratives. In the *Povest vremennykh let* (Annals) describing the evolution of the Russian land, which was compiled by the monks of the Kiev Pechersky Monastery, mention is made of the geographical distribution of the various Eastern Slav races, of the internal structure of ancient Slav society prior to the formation of the Kiev State, and of the position of Kiev in world history. (3) In a number of cases the Chroniclers turned to folk legends in order to supplement their material. That architecture, too, reached a high standard of craftsmanship is confirmed from examination of the numerous stone churches and cathedrals preserved from the eleventh–twelfth centuries in Kiev, Vladimir, Chernigov, Smolensk, Novgorod, and in remains in ancient towns, e.g. fortresses in Ladoga, the Golden Gates of Kiev, the Golden Gates of Vladimir, &c. The greatest architectural achievement among the preserved edifices of the eleventh century is the magnificent Cathedral of Saint Sophia in Kiev, modelled on that of Constantinople, with its great marble columns, mosaics and frescoes. Among the frescoes notable are the portraits of Prince Yaroslav and his family, especially the female group, in which are charmingly reproduced the majestic profiles of the Russian Princesses as they walk graciously along with tapers in their hands. The wall of the staircase leading into the galleries is covered with paintings representing scenes from everyday life; among the murals is a vivid depiction of a Royal hunt and a group of Court musicians. That the Cathedral must have produced a powerful impression on the minds of visitors, completely in accordance with Kiev's political might, cannot be doubted (see Plate 4).

Other artistic monuments of the same period are the five-chaptered Cathedral of the Assumption at Vladimir-Zalessky, and many fine monuments in Novgorod the Great.

Metal work, glass work and enamel work also flourished.

MUSIC IN KIEV: THE BYLINY

From Kiev and Novgorod stems the first written music—that of the divine service books, which made use of neumatic notation. Unfortunately the neumes are still undecipherable and provide only the haziest idea of the nature of ecclesiastical music in the eleventh–fourteenth centuries. Of military music, instrumental music and music in everyday life we know much more from the poetry of the period, from paintings and frescoes, and from the ancient Chronicles. Judging from the quantity of evidence preserved, military music was particularly important, doubtless as a result of the almost continuous warfare which was maintained against the streams of invaders from the Steppes. The Chronicles constantly make mention of trumpets and tambourines (*bubny*), while miniatures in the ancient manuscripts frequently depict horns and trumpets. (4) Ballad-singers also play a prominent part in the life of the times, and the greatest epic of Mediaeval Russia, the *Slovo o polku Igoreve* (The Epic of Igor's Host), written in the twelfth century, opens with the venerable figure of the minstrel Boyan. (5) Like many *byliny* of the period the *Slovo o polku Igoreve* has as its main theme the plea for national unity in the face of the common enemy, and was probably sung to the accompaniment of the *gusli*—one of the oldest Russian instruments, counterpart of the Western psaltery. As mentioned in Chapter 1, the *guslis* were diverse in form: over the wooden frame were stretched the strings, which were plucked by the player with both hands, the instrument resting on his knees. Apart from its literary merits, the *Slovo* is also of interest in that it contains several references to pagan symbolism. An example is the moment when Yaroslavna, in her lament on the ruined walls of Putivl, turns to the wind, the Dnepr, the sun, even comparing herself with the cuckoo, the eternal personification of sadness in Russian folk poetry. (6)

At the same time that the *Slovo o polku Igoreve* was written, there came into being the Kiev cycle of *byliny*—ballads about Ilya Muromets, Dobrynya Nikitich, and many others, though, it must be remembered, they have all come down to us in much later versions (not earlier than the seventeenth–eighteenth centuries) and have inevitably lost much of their original flavour. The *byliny* themselves often describe singers, *gusli*-players, and music at State festivities, the favourite setting being the Court of Prince Vladimir (tenth century). The following lines are typical:

> Then out spake the great Kievite Vladimir:
> 'Now young Dobrynyushka Nikitich,
> Take up your lusty *gusli*,
> Play us something doleful, something moving,
> Then play us something gay!'

In the course of time the individual traits of the historical characters appearing in the epic ballads were obliterated and the *bogatyrs* became attributed with the best features of the Russian people in general.

Together with the *bogatyr byliny* dealing with the subject of war in the twelfth–fourteenth centuries, of importance also are the narratives concerned with social and domestic life. The actors of such *byliny* are not *bogatyrs* but epic personages such as Dyuk Stepanovich, Churila Plenkovich, Solovey Budimirovich,

Khoten Bludovich, Staver, and Sadko and Vasiliy Buslaev in
the Novgorod *byliny*. Some of these ballads give an excellent
insight into the life of Russia at that period. Thus, one ballad
about Dyuk Stepanovich has as its theme the rivalry between
a Kievite Prince and a Prince (or merchant) of the Kingdom of
Galycia-Volynya during the latter's sudden development in
the twelfth and early thirteenth centuries.

Apart from the *gusli*, the *byliny* also mention 'golden trumpets' and reed pipes, while the Chronicles speak of tambourines
and *sopeli* (wind pipes or wooden whistles). Of particular interest
in this respect is a fresco in St. Sophia's Cathedral depicting a
group of *skomorokhi* of clearly non-Russian origin. Dressed in
jesters' costumes they are entertaining the Royal Court with
music, dancing, and acrobatics. Some of them hold in their
hands Mediaeval instruments characteristic of both East and
West—the transverse flute, the oboe, a plucked stringed instrument of the lute family with an oval body and an extremely
long neck, the trapeziform harp, and cymbals—all of which
attest to the fact that groups of foreign musicians, jesters and
buffoons were participants in the musical life of the Kiev Court.
There is no doubt that instruments of Oriental provenance such
as the harp and the lute were adopted into Kiev, where they
underwent further development. Generally speaking, the
musical life of Kiev was by no means of a provincial character;
Kievite Princes visited Byzantium, and their own Royal music
was without question formed under the influence of the elegant
Byzantine Court. There were also innumerable foreign merchants in Kiev and they too would doubtless introduce their
own musical customs. In one didactic fable, the *Slovo o bogache
i Lazare* (The Tale of the Rich Man and Lazarus), a vivid
picture of a feast in the house of a rich man is portrayed, complete with sycophants, priests, gossipers, *gusli*-players and
buffoons.

SECULAR MUSIC

Secular music in Kiev was represented not only by the ballad-
singers but by the *skomorokhi*—the singers, jesters, animal-train-
ers, and actors, who were essential participants in the numerous
popular festivals. Their art was most diverse, comprising acting,
acrobatics, dancing, music and poetry. Like the *jongleurs*,

Spielmänner, and other peripatetic musicians of the West, they continued the traditions of the syncretic actors of antiquity, combining sacred and profane in a highly original manner. At a somewhat later date, particularly in the Novgorod period, the *skomorokhi* acquired even greater significance.

ECCLESIASTICAL MUSIC

Undoubtedly one of the greatest events in Russian history was the conversion in the year 988 of Russia to Christianity. Not only was a Russian Prince married to the sister of the Byzantine Emperor, but Byzantine chant was introduced into Russia by imported Greek and Bulgarian singers. They were accompanied by a whole stream of builders, architects, artists and masters of the art of mosaics, all of which left their imprint on Russian culture. Russia also became familiar with the eight Church modes (the so-called Octoechos) and after a few years special schools were set up in monasteries for the training of singers (who were named *demestiki* or *golovshchiki*) in the performance and reading of the neumatic notation. Although the issue is far from clear, it seems that within a comparatively short while the Byzantine chant began to be transformed under Russian influences and to acquire a Slavonic nature. Even the neumes (which themselves were originally of Oriental provenance) began to be modified and later acquired the name of *znameni* ['*znamen*' = a sign], later termed '*kryuki*'. The most ancient form of Orthodox music is the so-called *znamenny* chant. During the Kiev period this was performed chorally in unison and, as far as can be ascertained, was of a limited compass and of a quiet, majestic character (Mus. Ex. 1).

In its early stage of development the notation employed, like that of Byzantine music, to which it shows close similarity, was ecphonetic—in other words, merely demonstrated the general rise and fall of the melody and in no way indicated the precise pitch.

In addition to the *znamenny* chant there was also a melismatic vocal form, more florid than the *znamenny*, known as *kondakarnoe* chant (preserved from the eleventh–fourteenth centuries). As opposed to the *znamenny* chant, the *kondakarnoe* was used mostly in festival hymn celebrations [the *kondaks* is a short hymn of praise to the glory of the Saviour, the Virgin Mary, or a

Mus. Ex.1

D.V. RAZUMOVSKY
'Tserkovnoe penie v Rossii'

Tvo — ya po — be — di — tel — na — ya   des — ni — tsa bo —

-go — le — pno vkre — po — sti pro — sla — vi — sya,

ty   bo bes — smer — tne, ya — ko vse — mo — gu — shcha — ya

pro — ti — vny — ya so — tri iz — ra — il —

— tya — nam put   glu — bi — ny no — vo so — de — lav — sha — ya.

Saint]. These hymns were not included in the usual services and were performed only on special occasions. The *kondakarnoe* chant, like the *znamenny*, also had its own notation, but this has still not been deciphered.

THE DECLINE OF KIEV

The unity of Kiev lasted some considerable time, but from the second half of the eleventh century the State began to be divided into a number of isolated principalities. Kiev became ever more susceptible to attacks from the Steppe raiders and less capable of defending herself, especially in the Southern regions, and foreign trade deteriorated. However, in the eleventh–twelfth centuries political and cultural centres such as Galich, Vladimir-Volynsky, Turov, Polotsk, Smolensk, Vladimir-Zalessky and others began to play an ever-increasing part. Despite the isolated nature of these principalities, all were united in a common religion and language. Local variants of the *znamenny* chants were produced in religious centres such as Novgorod, Pskov, Vladimir, Rostov and Yaroslavl.

THE RISE OF NOVGOROD

With the gradual dissolution of Kiev the cultural and musical life of Russia in the thirteenth–fourteenth centuries was continued by the city of Novgorod, which, at the same time, con-

PLATE 3

THE SPENDING OF MASLENITSA by A. VASNETSOV

PLATE 4

AN ELEVENTH-CENTURY FRESCO IN ST. SOPHIA CATHEDRAL, KIEV showing musicians playing (clockwise) a flute, oboes, a lute, harp and cymbals

tributed new features of her own. (7) However, long before this there had been contact between the two cities. Many fine buildings were erected and Novgorod's own Cathedral of St. Sophia, which came into being about the middle of the eleventh century, was modelled on the larger Cathedral of the same name in Kiev. In the Novgorod libraries were preserved some of the most valuable records of ancient Russian literature. The Novgorod school of icon painting, which reached its zenith in the last two decades of the city's independence at the end of the fifteenth century, was also of a very high standard. Novgorod was especially fortunate in her geographical location, being situated in the far north not far from the upper reaches of the Volga, and thus on the line of one of the oldest trading routes. Her ties with the West and her membership of the Hanseatic league were likewise of significance and were factors in contributing to her prosperity.

Undoubtedly one of the most remarkable aspects of Novgorod was her highly individual political structure. Although originally subservient to Kiev, as the result of her great wealth Novgorod gradually became autonomous, her power being held not in the hands of the Princes but in those of the mayor (the *posadnik*) and a ruling council. A prominent role was played by the *veche*—the city popular assembly—which, though found in other principalities in the Kievite period (e.g. Pskov), was quite unique in its authority. The *veche*, consisting of the entire male population of the city, was summoned to attendance by the ringing of the great bell of St. Sophia in Yaroslavl Square, after which important questions were settled by shouting or fighting. The community itself consisted of *boyars*, rich merchants, the clergy, and the workmen and peasants, between which battles frequently raged. The conflicts between the rich merchants and the town poor are often referred to in ancient Novgorodian literature.

The Novgorod land covered a very large area, two of its principal regions being the so-called 'Zavoloche', situated between Beloozero and the River Sukhona, and the Dvinskaya Land along the coast of the Northern Dvina. It is this last-named area, especially round the Rivers Pinega and Mezen, that has been very fruitful in the preservation of Novgorod folk music down to the present day.

D

FOLK MUSIC IN NOVGOROD

The lively street life, the ties between Novgorod and the West
at the dawn of the Renaissance, the animated bustle of the
prosperous town, with its soldiers, sailors and foreign visitors,
inevitably had a profound effect on folk music, and nowhere is
this better seen than in the Novgorod *byliny*, in which, apart
from the *skomorokhi*, the favourite personages are Sadko and the
reckless Vasiliy Buslaev. Both are musicians; indeed, as one
bylina expresses it:

> there are no singers amongst us
> In the whole of Mighty Novgorod
> Better than Vasiliy Buslaev.

Peculiarities of the northern *byliny* are their diatonic nature and
the use of tritones—diminished fifths and augmented fourths—
which distinguish the North Russian melodies from those of
Central Russia. A good illustration of this is the folk-song 'Ay,
polno li, solnyshko', which is taken from A. Kolotilova's collection *Pesni severa* (Songs of the North) (Mus. Ex. 2):

Mus. Ex. 2
Protractedly   A. KOLOTILOVA 'Pesni severa'

Ay, pol - no li, so - - - - - olny - shko...

SKOMOROKHI BALLADS OF THE NOVGOROD CYCLE

A special place in the folk music of Novgorod is played by the
skomorokhi, and in some ballads the *skomorokhi* even appear as
actors. In one amusing *bylina* entitled 'Pro gostya Terentishcha'
the *skomorokhi* help a rich Novgorod visitor discover his young
wife's infidelity, though at the same time they scoff at his
jingling money-bags (Mus. Ex. 3).

In another *bylina*, from Pinega, which was written down from
M. D. Krivopolenova, a remarkable ballad-singer, the *skomorokhi* appear in the guise of the Saints Kosma and Damian and
are endued with miraculous powers. Together with Vavila, a
peasant lad, they set out on a long journey in order to fight the
bloodthirsty Tsar-Dog, and having conquered him, they place
Vavila on the throne in his stead.

Mus. Ex.3

Characteristic of the *skomorokhi* ballads are the short lines (on the average of about 8 to 11 syllables), with 2, 3, or even 4 stresses. The melodies are simple and concise and are performed at a fairly rapid tempo.

The *skomorokhi* enjoyed a different social status in Novgorod from all other cities, for instead of being renegades and hounded by Church and State, they enjoyed full legal rights, even having their own quarters. *Skomorokhi* villages were founded all over the Novgorod lands and traces of them, discernible either in the names of settlements or in family-names derived from the word '*skomorokh*', survive to this day.

Apart from the traditional *byliny*, another aspect of the *skomorokh* ballad is revealed in the humorous song 'Vavila', which was written down by Elizaveta Linëva. The song is set in the form of a comic dialogue between a village priest and an old country-woman, who has decided to celebrate the memory of her deceased husband—a *skomorokh*—but has forgotten his name. Use is made of patter and there is also a parody of an ecclesiastical chant. The dialogue concludes with an animated dance in the manner of 'Kamarinskaya' performed by the country-woman in which she tries to demonstrate to the priest the kind of song her husband sang when he was alive.

FOLK INSTRUMENTS IN NOVGOROD

The instrument most often mentioned in the *byliny* is, of course, the *gusli*, drawings and representations of which even found their way into the ecclesiastical writings. Trumpets also were in general use, trumpeters (as in the West) serving as town watchmen. (8) Apart from these, however, the folk instrumentalists would also know the *gudok* (a three-stringed bowed instrument, the players of which were called *gudoshniki*—such are the *skomorokhi* Skula and Eroshka in Borodin's *Prince Igor*), probably the *domra* (a plucked instrument of Eastern provenance, played with a plectrum), *surna* (a simple wind instrument of cane or reed, also of Eastern origin), and the *bubny* (a percussion instrument resembling the tambourine and used in conjunction with the *surna* in military music).

ECCLESIASTICAL MUSIC

An important development in ecclesiastical music in Novgorod was the founding of the Novgorod Choir School, from which there emerged a number of singers whose names have been preserved. These singers not only upheld the standard forms but created new chants and it is quite possible that in Novgorod originated the first polyphonic ecclesiastical singing—the so-called '*strochnoe penie*'.

SACRED DRAMA

In Novgorod in the fifteenth–sixteenth centuries were performed a number of sacred dramas, including that of 'The Procession on the Ass', which depicted Christ's entry into Jerusalem and which was performed annually on Palm Sunday in the Cathedral Square. On the ass sat the Archbishop himself making the sign of the cross to left and right. In front of him went a group of singers performing appropriate chants, while another group of singers, accompanied by palm-bearers, brought up the rear. A detailed description of this rite is preserved in the *Chinovnik* (service book) of St. Sophia, Novgorod. A similar procession was staged at a later date in Moscow.

A more developed spectacle was the 'Drama of the Stove', based on the Biblical story of the three pious boys, who were thrown into a burning oven by the heathen King Nebuchadnezzar, but were miraculously rescued by an angel descending from Heaven. The 'Drama of the Stove' was given on the last Sunday before Christmas and performed inside the Church where a mock oven was erected. The *dramatis personae*, or, more accurately, the *occupantes furnum*, consisted of three boys (Ananius, Azarius, and Misail) and two simpletons (played by *skomorokhi*), the whole being accompanied by sacred chants.

This drama was likewise performed with great pageantry in the Moscow Cathedral of the Assumption.

THE RISE OF MOSCOW

In the fourteenth century the Muscovite Principality began to acquire significance, the Muscovite Princes gradually gathering under their power different districts of feudal Russia. Although the greater part of Russia paid tribute to the Mongols, a union of the lands around Moscow produced an army of 150,000 men, which, under the leadership of Prince Dmitry Donskoy (1359–89), succeeded in at last defeating the Tartar forces at the battle of Kulikovo Field in 1380. Although this was by no means the end of Tartar dominion—Moscow was sacked again two years later, and it was not till the mid-fifteenth century that the Mongol power decisively waned—nevertheless, it did dispel the legend of the Mongols' invincibility. (9) The historical events of the fourteenth century connected with the growth of power of Muscovite Russia found their reflection in folk ballads, such as the *byliny* about 'the slaughter of Mamay', and in many others, such as the *Zadonschchina*, written by the priest Sophonia of Ryazan, a factor which gives some idea of the immense part played by the Church in the fostering, creation and preservation of early Russian culture. The fifteenth century saw the gradual formulation of the Russian State and from this time onwards the phrase 'Moskva belokamennaya' (lit. 'Moscow built of white stone') becomes the symbol in folk-song of Russia's unity. And not only was that expression used in the newly-composed songs, but it was applied to the already existing *byliny* of the 'Kiev' cycle with the result that even such figures as Dobrynya Nikitich found themselves not in Kiev but in 'Stone Moscow'!

CULTURAL DEVELOPMENTS IN MUSCOVITE RUSSIA

The unification of the Muscovite lands provided suitable conditions for cultural development, and from the middle of the fifteenth century Moscow became a centre for musical, literary, architectural and artistic activities.

Particularly successful in this period was the development of Russian architecture and even at the end of the fourteenth century building operations had begun to take place. In 1367, under Dmitry Donskoy, white stone walls were erected round the

Kremlin in place of the former wooden ones. Under Ivan III
(1462–1505) great edifices such as the Cathedral of the Assumption and the Granovitaya Palata came into being and for these
works were enlisted the best Russian builders from Novgorod,
Suzdal, Rostov, and other towns, along with foreign architects
(including the brilliant Italian, Aristotle Fioravanti, who arrived in 1475). (10) It was through the Italians that the Italian
Renaissance first made its impact on Muscovite architecture.
By the end of the fifteenth–sixteenth centuries a distinctive style
of Russian Church architecture had come into being, in which
characteristic is the tower-like shape of the main section of the
building, which is surmounted by a cupola or pyramid. These
edifices are given the generic name of 'tent' churches. Opinions
differ as to whether the Muscovite style was an adaptation of
the wooden buildings of North Russia, or whether it was influenced by the architecture of India and Asia. However, the
originality of the buildings cannot be doubted. One of the first
examples of the new architectural style was the Church of the
Ascension in the village of Kolomenskoe, near Moscow, a
favourite Royal residence from the times of Ivan III, completed
in 1532 and attributed to Aloisio Novi.

The most outstanding architectural work of the period is the
famous Cathedral of St. Basil in Red Square, Moscow, which
was erected in 1555–60 during the reign of Ivan IV (Ivan the
Terrible) to commemorate the capture of Kazan. The builders
of this remarkable edifice were the Russian craftsmen Barma
and Postnik Yakovlev, the latter from Pskov.

A connection with the folk art of the period is seen in various
forms of woodwork, and some fine wood carving similar to that
of peasant huts may be found on gate pillars, in surrounds on
windows and doors in *boyars'* palaces and mansions, or in the
form of interior decoration. One of the most valuable relics of
the period is the magnificent carving of the Royal throne in the
Uspensky Cathedral in the Kremlin.

At the end of the fourteenth and beginning of the fifteenth
centuries icon-painting reached unprecedented heights, crea-
tively developing the traditions of the Vladimir-Suzdal culture
of the thirteenth–fourteenth centuries. An important part in
this was played by Theophanes the Greek, who spent the last
thirty years of his life in Russia. The greatest Muscovite artist

of the period was Andrey Rublëv (*d. c.* 1428), who, like his friend and associate Daniel Chërniy, was a monk of the Troitse-Sergieva (Trinity) Monastery. Rublëv's best works—the decoration of the Uspensky Cathedral in Vladimir and icons in the Troitse-Sergieva Monastery—are remarkable for their life and movement, the inspired beauty of their faces and the felicitous blending of colours. Probably his greatest work is the icon 'The Old Testament Trinity', which is now housed in the Tretyakov Gallery, Moscow. The art of Rublëv forms the consummation of a long line of development. Rublëv created a whole school of gifted masters and with his name are associated the finest artistic achievements of the period. Continuing the traditions of Rublëv was the great Russian painter Dionysius, a Muscovite who is famed for his wall paintings at the St. Therapont Monastery near Beloozero.

Russian painting in the second half of the sixteenth century also saw a number of innovations, notable being the attraction of Russian iconographers towards large and complex compositions. The icon 'The Church Militant' in the Golden Room of the Kremlin, which was painted to mark the capture of Kazan, is of huge dimensions, depicting a Russian cavalry detachment leaving the burning stronghold to return to the holy city of Moscow. Of importance towards the end of the century is the so-called 'Stroganov School' of iconography.

The chief Russian painter in the second half of the seventeenth century was Simën Ushakov, whose work was influenced by Western models.

The fifteenth–sixteenth centuries likewise saw developments in literature and a whole number of works came into being during the reign of Ivan the Terrible (1533–84). A curious document of a didactic nature was the so-called *Domostroy* (lit. 'House-orderer'), which set out in Church Slavonic the principles by which the head of the family was to rule his wife, children, and serfs. Ivan himself was a prolific writer, and though his prose style relies largely on scriptural sources, his works (especially his correspondence with Kurbsky) are among some of the finest literature of its kind in Russian history.

In the second half of the fifteenth and in the sixteenth centuries was undertaken the gigantic task of compiling a single all-Russian historical chronicle. The vast mass of heterogeneous materials contained in the ancient chronicles were re-examined and supplemented with the aid of folk legends, the underlying idea of the whole being the representation of the greatness of the Muscovite Tsardom, as if prepared by all fore-going history. (11) This huge work, the *Nikonovskiy litsevoy svod*, which consisted of about 20,000 pages with 16,000 well-drawn illustrations, was completed some time during the 1570's. The *Svod*, which included all previous historical narratives, with the addition of a number of materials concerning the struggle with the Mongols, was brought up to the middle of the reign of Ivan IV. (12)

Other literary compositions were the great *Menelogion* or Saint's Calendar, which was the work of Macarius, Metropolitan of Moscow, who died in 1563 (this remained the official calendar of the Russian Church until the time of Peter the Great), and the *Stepennaya kniga* (The Book of Degrees), which derived its name from the fact that the Russian Princes and Tsars were grouped according to generations.

Of particular importance was the appearance of printing, which was a very necessary requirement for the correction of the numerous errors which had found their way into MS copies of the Divine service books. In 1563 a printing house was established in Moscow and the first work (*The Acts of the Apostles*) was published by the Russian typographers Ivan Fëdorov and Pëtr Mstislavets. Owing to the heavy costs of printing, however, it was not till after the time of Peter the Great that mass publishing became a practical proposition. Among the early publications are a book of travels by Ivan Peresvetov and the ecclesiastical writings of Maxim the Greek.

The early seventeenth century, the epoch of Russian history known as 'The Time of Troubles', served as the basis for many historical tales in which the events of the period are explained away as God's punishment on mankind for its sins. Later the historical tale became popular, but the master-piece at the end of the century is the novel *Frol Skobeev*, which is remarkable for its realism.

MUSIC IN MUSCOVITE RUSSIA: SECULAR MUSIC

Music firmly existed in Muscovite Russia at the end of the fifteenth century, a particular part in the musical life of the country being played by the *skomorokhi*. Apart from their role at Court, for Ivan employed the *skomorokhi* to satirize the *boyars* (indeed, at his Coronation large numbers of them were brought specially from Novgorod for service at the Royal Court and elsewhere), they were essential elements in any kind of popular festivity, and in their wandering from village to village they performed a unique task in preserving and creating folk music. A valuable contribution of the *skomorokhi* was the construction of the puppet-theatre, whose hero, Petrushka, embodied the essential characteristics of the *skomorokh*-buffoon. The puppet-theatre made ample use of music in the form of singing, and playing on the *domra* and *gusli*, and its popularity has lasted down to the present day.

During the fifteenth–sixteenth centuries the struggle between the Muscovite Church and the *skomorokhi*—the embodiments of paganism—reached unprecedented heights. *Ukaz* was followed by *ukaz* till, in the middle of the seventeenth century, the Moscow Patriarch ordered the destruction of all folk instruments that could be found in the city. Cartloads of instruments were burned on the banks of the River Moskva and there was no alternative left to the *skomorokhi* but to flee. By the beginning of the eighteenth century their ranks had grown thin, but their places were taken by the newly emerged professional musicians —representatives of the new town culture, versed in West-European techniques. In the minds of the people, however, the memory of the *skomorokhi* never faded, and their ribald humour, their lively satire, continued to live on in the puppet-theatre, the *byliny*, and the historical songs.

MUSIC AT THE MUSCOVITE COURT

In the reign of Ivan III (1462–1505), a ruler who called himself 'Prince of all Russia' and who regarded his State as 'The Third Rome', cultural ties were formed between Moscow and the West. In the desire for the strengthening of the power of the State and the elevation of Moscow, the whole order of Court life was changed. The marriage of Ivan III to the Greek princess Sofia Paleologus, niece of the last Byzantine Emperor, was of special significance in this respect and in Moscow appeared not only Italian architects and doctors, but, in 1490, an organist named Giovanni Salvatore. The Court ceremonial acquired an unprecedented elaborateness and solemnity (being based on the Byzantine model), and music, which hitherto had served only the Church, was given a new role. A special choir of State Singing Clerks was instituted for the needs of the Court Chapel and various festivities, and this choir was always in attendance on the Tsar himself. Indeed, foreign observers were struck by the fact that, whereas music at Western Courts was invariably instrumental, that of the Russian Court was essentially vocal. It was this choir, which, subsequently expanded and modified as regards the composition of the voices, eventually became the famous *Pridvornaya pevcheskaya kapella*— the Choir of the Imperial Chapel. At the end of the sixteenth and beginning of the seventeenth centuries another choral body came into being known as the Choir of Patriarchal Singing Clerks, which was associated with the establishment of the Patriarchate in Moscow in 1589—an event of considerable political importance, since it decisively confirmed Moscow as the capital of Russia. In 1721 the Choir of Patriarchal Singing Clerks was renamed the Moscow Synodal Choir.

In 1586, during the reign of Tsar Theodore I (1584–98), the English Queen Elizabeth sent as a present to Tsaritsa Irene, his wife, gilded clavichords, and according to the testimony of the English envoy, crowds gathered in their thousands round the windows of the palace to hear how it sounded. Theodore's successor, the ill-fated Boris Godunov (1598–1605), is of importance in that he was the first of the Moscow rulers to send young Russians abroad for education, though this well-meaning intention misfired since none of his emissaries ever returned to Russia. A few foreign musicians arrived in Moscow during the reign of the False Dmitry I (1605–6), while the travels of Russians abroad also furthered the development of cultural ties. Finally, the forming of the foreign quarter in Moscow—the so-called *Nemetskaya sloboda* (lit. 'German suburb')—also played its part, for from its inhabitants the Muscovites could make the acquaintance of Western musicians and musical instruments.

In the second half of the seventeenth century, not only were there organs and an instrumental ensemble at the Court of Tsar Alexis, but, in the homes of the most progressive Muscovite nobility—Nikita Romanov, Artamon Matveev, Ilya Miloslavsky—there arose an ever-increasing interest in music, and professional musicians began to be acquired from abroad. A foreign traveller visiting Moscow in 1672 observed that 'intelligent Russians have Polish musicians in their homes, who teach them to play on different instruments, and also instruct them in singing'. This preoccupation with secular music was viewed with suspicion and anxiety by the Church, which considered such innovations as 'sinful'.

DEVELOPMENT OF ECCLESIASTICAL MUSIC IN MUSCOVITE RUSSIA

The first developments in professional music in Muscovite Russia (particularly as regards the *znamenny* chant) were connected with the old established cultural centres such as Kiev, Novgorod, Vladimir, and Suzdal. It was the aim of the Moscow Princes, however, and later the Tsars, to raise ecclesiastical singing to the highest possible level, and with this in mind the most talented performers and singers from other towns were summoned to Moscow.

In the fifteenth century was undertaken the vast task of inspecting, checking and systematizing the entire body of Orthodox chants. The result of this work was the so-called *Obikhod*— a collection of the most important and most generally used *znamenny* melodies, which was set out in a definite order in accordance with the various kinds of divine services in the Church's year. Though repeatedly supplemented by new chants, the collection retained its value over the succeeding centuries.

Particular attention was paid to ecclesiastical music during the reign of Ivan the Terrible, who, when sober, was a connoisseur of *znamenny* melodies. Indeed, to him are attributed the composition of two *stikhir* [a *stikhira* is a hymn, song, canticle or hymn of thanksgiving] written in *kryuki* notation. In 1551 Ivan created the *Stoglavniy sobor* [the title comes from the fact that the resolutions thus made were set out in 100 chapters and published under the title of '*stoglav*' or '*stoglavnik*'], whereby, with the assistance of the higher dignitaries of the Church, were made a series of important decisions affecting the Orthodox belief, and how improvements could be made in iconography

and ecclesiastical music. The *Sobor* sought means for the correcting of morals and the life of the people, the restoration of true
Orthodox practice, and the insistence upon Church 'decency'.
Many of the resolutions were directed against the old folk
customs (particularly the pagan agricultural festivals and the
songs accompanying them) and against the participation of
skomorokhi in weddings and funerals. The various chapters of the
Sobor dealing with the ancient folk customs and folk music are
the most important source of information for the period.

From the fifteenth century Moscow became one of the chief
centres of Church music and from a coalescence of many local
variants a specific style of Muscovite chant was formed. The
Moscow *znamenny* chant at its height was characterized by
broad-flowing melody and a wealth of ornament. Between different syllables of the text were inserted melismatic passages. In
some cases syllables were included for no particular reason.
Each of the inserted passages (*razvody*) had a strictly defined
melodic formula which was indicated by a special sign. Performance of *znamenny* melodies with these *razvody* demanded
great skill from the singer and was rated very highly. Many
divine texts were given new settings by singers, some of whose
names have been preserved. Thus from Novgorod we know of
Savva and Vasiliy Rogov, Markel Bezborodny, and Stefan
Golysh. In the Sovereign's Choir of Singing Clerks outstanding
were Ivan Nos and Fëdor Khristianin, while equally famous
was the singer Loginov from the Troitse-Sergieva monastery,
who was renowned for his ability to perform every Church
chant in five or six, or even ten melodic variants.

Of particular importance in the sixteenth century was the
evolution of the so-called *strochnoe penie* (lit. 'line chant'), a polyphonic chant, which acquired its name from the fact that each
part was written one above the other on separate lines. Examination of the chant suggests that it was influenced by the polyphony of Russian folk-song, for the parts diverge and converge
in exactly the same manner. Usually *strochny* chants are written
in three or four parts, though two-part works are sometimes
encountered. Examples belonging to the early seventeenth
century even make use of four parts. In the three-part works
the chant is entrusted to the middle voice (the '*put*'), the upper
and lower voices being termed '*verkh*' and '*niz*' respectively. In

Mus. Ex. 4 (the opening of the chant 'Kreste khristov'), the lowest voice often moves in unison or in fourths with the *'put'*, while the upper voice is sometimes in unison with the *'put'* or moving in parallel seconds. The resultant effects, as already stated, may be compared with Russian folk polyphony, or, to some extent, in the movement of parallel fourths and fifths, with Western organum (Mus. Ex. 4):

Mus. Ex.4   TIRM I, p. 59

Apart from the *znamenny* chant, of importance was the so-called *demestvenny* chant.[1] The *demestvenny* chants were not in-cluded in the *obikhod* and were almost secular in their nature, being used on official occasions in the life of the Moscow Court, such as the departure of the Tsar, the procession of his Suite to prayer, the rejoicing over a military victory. To this period also belong the *dukhovnye stikhi* or religious poems, corresponding roughly in form to the *byliny*, which were sung by the *kaliki*, itinerant singers. In the *Stepennaya kniga*, where mention is made of the unison *znamenny* chant and the three-part *strochny* chant, the *demestvenny* is referred to by contemporaries as being 'the most beautiful', while in the introduction to the *Stikhiria*, the well-known singer of the sixteenth century, Vasiliy Rogov, is described as 'a singer and creator' both of '*znamenny, troestrochny*

[1] According to several written sources the *demestvenny* chant existed as far back as Kievite Russia, although it reached its zenith in Muscovite Russia in the fifteenth-sixteenth centuries. Remains of four-part *demestvenny* chants are found in the second half of the sixteenth century.

and *demestvenny* chants'. Outstanding features of the *demestvenny* chant were its abundance of ornament and its lesser dependence on the modes. The *demestvenny* chant of the fifteenth–sixteenth centuries was also polyphonic, though it differed from the *strochny* chant in that the upper voice was called a '*demestvo*'. The '*demestvo*' was a melodic variant of the '*put*' and at times doubled it precisely. At first the chant was written down by means of *znamenny* or *kryuki* symbols, but towards the end of the sixteenth century the four-part *demestvenny* chant made use of a new, more complicated notation in which the old *kryuki* signs were used in different combinations with new meanings.

Of the various attempts to modify and clarify notation, one of the most important was that of a Novgorod clerk named Ivan Shaydurov, who devised a system of 'cinnabar marks', in which red signs were employed in addition to black ones in order to attain greater accuracy. Though this system was a slight improvement, it was not till the middle of the seventeenth century that the *znamenny* notation was replaced by the five-line European and it is interesting to note that the old *znamenny* notation has been retained by the Old Believers to the present day.

ECCLESIASTICAL MUSIC IN THE SEVENTEENTH CENTURY

The seventeenth century was the scene of violent battles between the guardians of ecclesiastical traditions, represented by the Old Believers, and the supporters of reform, headed by the Patriarch Nikon, which culminated in the schism in the Russian Church. Among the factors which contributed to the schism were the making of the sign of the cross with two fingers and saying Alleluia twice, instead of the Greek three fingers and treble Alleluia. So intense were the people's feelings, that thousands of people preferred self-immolation rather than accept the reforms proferred by Nikon. One of the strongest supporters of the Old Believers was the priest Avvakum, whose sturdy autobiography is one of the finest literary works of the century. It is this period which forms the background to Musorgsky's opera *Khovanshchina*. In the sixties of the seventeenth century it was decreed that all services should be conducted in accordance with the actual pronunciation of the texts, and a special commission, consisting of experts on *znamenny* chant, was set up to examine and amend all the Church singers' books. This formidable task was undertaken by a young monk from the Zvenigorod Monastery, a White Russian by origin, named Alexander Mezenets. Apart from correcting many texts by removing meaningless syllables, the commission also suggested the publishing of fresh music-books, while Mezenets himself compiled a systematic handbook for the reading of the *znamenny* notation, entitled *Azbuka znamennovo peniya* (The ABC of Znamenny Chant), which had wide circulation. (13)

A significant part in the formation of a new vocal style was played by the union of the Ukraine and White-Russia with Moscow in 1654. As a result of the treaty of Lublin (1569) all the West of Russia had come under the direct rule of Poland. The Poles, under the organization of the Jesuits, started a campaign against the Orthodox faith and Russian nationality. To counteract Catholic influence the Russian Church began vigorous activities in the realm of education. In the seventeenth century Ukrainian choral music reached quite a high standard, largely as a result of the thorough training provided in the Church schools, and Ukrainian singers became known all over Muscovite Russia. In the second half of the century, despite considerable opposition, a new polyphonic style, originating in the Ukraine, became known in Moscow under the title of '*partesnoe penie*' or 'part-song'. As opposed to *znamenny* chant, which had been formulated gradually over the ages, the principles of the 'part-song' were set out from the very beginning in theoretical treatises, of which the chief was a work entitled *Musikiyskaya grammatika* (Musical Grammar) (1679) by the Kievite composer Nikolay Diletsky. Diletsky's treatise deals with the spiritual power of music and its ability to summon forth varying emotions. Mention is made of the expressive forces of major and minor and descriptive methods are even recommended for a visual transmission of the content of the texts! A defender of the new music was the Muscovite deacon, Ivan Korenev, who wrote a long introduction to Diletsky's treatise entitled '*Musikiya*'. In this Korenev attacks those 'unreasoning' people, who contend that 'Music is from the devil, and Church chant is not from Music'. In his opinion there are no differences between various kinds of music, for they are all given to man by God. Instrumental music, which had long been anathemized by the Church and regarded as 'a devilish lure', Korenev regards as equal to vocal music, perhaps even greater since it had existed before it.

The development of the part-song on Russian soil was aided by the existence of the State choirs. A number of composers emerged who were capable of writing polyphonic music and by the end of the seventeenth century and the beginning of the eighteenth century a considerable choral literature had appeared, running into hundreds of liturgical works in the new style. All these compositions were written in the Kiev 'square' notation [*kvadratnaya notatsiya*], which was a variant of the five-line European, and the choirs themselves were re-organized into four sections—discant, alto, tenor and bass.

An innovation at the end of the seventeenth century were the so-called '*dukhovnye kontserty*' (spiritual concertos)—sacred polyphonic compositions performed during the service but differing from the simple *obikhod* chants by their greater complexity. Characteristic of these works was the imitative concertato style of writing, *tutti* alternating with solo sections. Although the concertos were undoubtedly founded on Western models and written in a diatonic language, unlike their Western prototypes they were invariably performed *a cappella*. Into one of the middle voices was often introduced a *znamenny* chant by way of a *cantus firmus*. The hey-day of the spiritual concerto occurred in the beginning of the eighteenth century, when 8-, 12-, or even 24-part works were written. Among the composers of these were Vasiliy Titov, Nikolay Kalachnikov, Nikolay Babykin, and others, the works of Titov, perhaps, being of the greatest value.

RISE OF SACRED AND SECULAR DRAMA

As in the West, though at a much later date, ecclesiastical music also played its part in the religious plays and 'mysteries' which were performed with great ceremony in Moscow in the seventeenth century. Reference has already been made to the 'Drama of the Stove' and the 'Procession of the Ass'. In the latter not only the Patriarch took part but the Tsar himself and according to contemporary accounts, the drama was concluded with the sounds of choral singing and the ringing of bells.

The last third of the seventeenth century saw the rise of theatrical productions at the Moscow Court, in which music

played a prominent role.[1] The first performance took place in
1672 in the village of Preobrazhensky—a suburb of Moscow—
in a mansion built specially for the occasion. Up to this time
only the puppet-theatre had existed in Russia, while in the
South-Western part of the country (and especially in the
Ukraine) there had been the spiritual theatre, where pupils of
the monasteries and ecclesiastical schools performed so-called
'school' or 'ecclesiastical' dramas. (14) The text of a Nativity
play has come down to us, for instance, together with even some
of the music, which is written in a very simple three-part form
known as a *kant*. The following excerpt from the Nativity Play
gives a good idea of the music (Mus. Ex. 5):

The first theatrical performances at the Court of Tsar Alexey
Mikhailovich (1645–76) were similar in their subject matter to
the Sacred Dramas. However, the solemnity of the action was
disrupted by the insertion of all manner of comic and *buffo*
scenes. Some plays were clearly secular in nature—e.g. *Malaya
komedia Bayazet i Tamerlan* (A short Comedy Bayazit and
Tamerlane), or the ballet *Orfeo*. The first organizers of this
theatre were Simën Polotsky, a gifted monk, poet, and writer

[1] This arose from the Tsar's friendship with A. S. Matveev, a widely travelled
cavalry officer and a lover of the theatre in whose house the Tsar's second wife
had been raised. With the blessing of his confessor, who cited precedents set by
other Christian Emperors, especially those of Orthodox Byzantium, the Tsar was
urged to arrange a comedy to mark the birth of his son, Peter.

from the Ukraine (who later became tutor to Tsar Theodore III), and a Lutheran pastor, Dr. Johann Gregory. From the very first the theatre was closely connected with music, and as soon as the idea of theatrical entertainment arose, a special envoy was sent abroad to bring back a trumpeter and four other instrumentalists. Before they returned, however, the first theatrical performance of a drama *Esfir, ili Artaksersovo deystvo* (Esther, or The Adventures of Artaxerxes) took place in 1672 in German with the assistance of those musicians that could be found in Moscow.

A special role in these performances was occupied by vocal music, which took the form of solo songs (e.g. the comic song of the soldier Susakim in *Judith*), or final choruses, but apart from that there are directions in the texts of the plays for instrumental music. Judging from the character of the texts, it seems most likely that the vocal numbers were set in the form of *kants*. The instrumental numbers were of the simplest possible nature, or perhaps consisted of dance suites imported from the West. That dance music played a part is attested by the performance in 1673 of the ballet *Orfeo*, the music of which has been lost, but was possibly written by the German composer, Heinrich Schütz. In any case it is known that several musicians were acquired from abroad, and that instrumentalists (e.g. an organist) from the Nemetskaya sloboda (and also amateur singers) augmented the theatrical ensemble. It is quite understandable that, bearing in mind Russia's improved political and economic position, Tsar Alexis should not wish to lag behind the rulers of other European nations in the field of culture, though, having in the Russia of that time neither actors nor professional musicians, he was obliged to borrow from other nations. Apart from that, any surviving organists and harpsichordists (brought originally from Poland and Holland), or their descendants, that had been enlisted for Tsar Mikhail Fëdorovich's 'Pleasure Palace', founded in 1613, could also take part in the performances. Thus, at the Court of Tsar Alexis, there gradually came into being a considerable band of mostly foreign instrumentalists.

The Court Theatre survived in Moscow only for a short while, for in 1676, on the decease of Alexis, it was closed down as the result of the intrigues of those groups that were opposed to any form of Western influence. However, the four-year existence of a theatre in Moscow had not been without effect. It left an unforgettable impression in the minds of the Muscovite people and introduced new elements into Russian culture, of which not the least important was that of music. Indeed, just as the appearance of Florentine opera proved a turning point in the history of Western music, so did the Russian theatre play a considerable part in the development of secular music.

KANTS AND PSALMS

In the seventeenth century a special kind of religious chant known as the *kant* was created in Poland and the Ukraine, which was performed by clergy, monks, and by the pupils of Church schools. *Kants* were distributed over a wide area and are found in many MSS and other sources of the period, together with folk-songs. Indeed, it was in the style of the *kant* that the first folk tunes were written down in the middle of the eighteenth century. Arriving in Moscow in the second half of the seventeenth century it soon acquired great popularity. Generally speaking, the *kant* is symmetrical in structure, often following the pattern A—A'—B—A''. Essentially major or minor, it betrays the influence of Western harmony. Usually it is set in three parts, the two upper voices often moving in parallel thirds, while the lowest voice forms the bass. At first it was performed by a choir or small vocal ensemble *a cappella* as in Mus. Ex. 5. Very occasionally two-part *kants* are found, and even at a later date four-part, but these are exceptional.

A special form of religious chant was the *psálmy* or *psalmý*, which were related to the *kants*. In 1680 a verse translation in Russian of the Psalms was published in Moscow by Simën Polotsky, who, as previously mentioned, had studied at the Kiev spiritual academy and later was appointed Court Poet and teacher of the Royal children in Moscow. Polotsky's work was based on Polish translations and his psalms were set to music by Vasiliy Polikarpovich Titov, who was one of the best Russian composers of the period. Titov's settings acquired great popularity, and were soon imitated by other composers. Although Titov's *Psalms* are close to Western music of the same period, they do occasionally show some national colouring. His

Twenty-seventh Psalm is particularly expressive with its false relations and pathetic intonations (Mus. Ex. 6):

Mus. Ex.6   PIRM I, pp.97-98

Gos - po - di, k te - be sle - zno vzy - va - yu,
dazhd svya-ty so - vet to - go o - zhi - da - yu

a shche ty bo - zhe, a shche ty bo - zhe glas svoy

u - der - zhi - shi v grob mya vse - li - shi

Titov's *Psalms* are important for a number of reasons: on the one side they succeeded in bridging the gap between liturgical and secular music, and on the other they laid the foundations of the Russian vocal lyric.

FOLK-SONG IN THE MUSCOVITE ERA

During the Muscovite era folk-song continued to play a prominent part. In the North the majority of the oldest historical songs, dealing with events of the sixteenth–seventeenth centuries, were called *stáriny* by the peasants and were often sung to the same melodies as the *byliny* of the Kiev and Novgorod cycles or to melodies showing close resemblance to them. In Central and South Russia the historical songs were called '*protyazhnye*' and '*doselnye*' and were similar in style to the protracted lyrical songs. The majority of the oldest historical songs to come down to us are connected with the period of Ivan the Terrible and in them are described the principal historical events of the second half of the sixteenth century (e.g. the capture of Kazan and Astrakhan) as well as the commanding and dreaded figure of Ivan himself.

A favourite hero of the sixteenth century was the Cossack

ataman (chieftain) Ermak Timofeevich, the conqueror of Siberia, and in the many songs surrounding his name is pictured the carefree life of the Cossack.

Towards the end of this period, along with the epic and historical songs, the lyrical protracted song underwent particular development. Many of the lyrical songs are filled with protest against oppression or the severe burden of family life. Similar themes are found in the satirical songs of the seventeenth century, where favourite subjects are mockery of the aged husband, ridicule of secular or spiritual power, hatred of monasticism and the desire for personal freedom. An important part, too, was played by the comic songs, the dance songs and the *khorovods*. Whereas the *khorovods* had in former times been performed only in spring, in Muscovite Russia they began to be sung and danced all the year round. The peasant wedding ritual reached fulfilment, being performed with regional variants.

Although the seventeenth century was a time of general expansion and development, it was accompanied by considerable internal unrest, manifest in revolutionary outbreaks between 1598 and 1613—the period known as 'The Time of Troubles'. The cleft between the leaders of the ruling class, the internecine struggle and rivalry of the feudal nobility, resulting in almost total exhaustion, opened the road for foreign intervention on the part of Sweden and Poland, and it was through the efforts of a butcher and cattle-dealer named Kuzma Minin, who was mayor of Nyzhny-Novgorod, and Prince Dmitry Pozharsky, a local *boyar*, that Moscow was liberated in 1612 from its Polish occupants and Mikhail Romanov elected Tsar by the National Assembly (*Zemsky Sobor*), an event which is celebrated in Glinka's *A Life for the Tsar*. In the second half of the seventeenth century the Muscovite State was overrun by another series of uprisings, the most spectacular of which was that of Stepan Razin in 1670-1, whose daring and ruthless exploits along the River Volga captivated the popular imagination, causing his name to be surrounded in Russia with a romantic aureole. All these turbulent events were preserved in the folk memory in the form of revolutionary songs, those about Razin depicting the main events in his life, beginning with his appearance among the Cossack 'poor', and concluding with his death in Moscow. Together with the 'Razin' cycle there are also a group of melodies known as 'songs of freedom', composed mostly by fugitives from serfdom or the army, who took refuge in the Steppes.

During the seventeenth century no attempt was made to write down the music of folk-songs, though a number of texts were recorded individually.

SUMMARY

The seventeenth century was dominated by two important factors: the decline of the part played by the Church in Russian culture, and the ever-increasing influence of the West. From the musical point of view the century marks the last appearance of such age-old figures as the *skomorokhi* and the emergence of the new school of professional musicians. The end of the seventeenth century was dominated by a figure of truly titanic proportions, whose draconian measures radically transformed the whole of Russia's personality—Peter the Great.

CHAPTER 3

Russian Music in the Reigns of Peter, Anna, Elizabeth, and Catherine the Great

INTRODUCTION

From the point of view of cultural development, the eighteenth century may well be regarded as the most remarkable in the whole of Russia's pre-Revolutionary history. In less than a hundred years, resulting from the measures inaugurated by Peter the Great (1682–1725), Russia was transformed in the hands of the Empresses Anna (1730–40), Elizabeth (1741–62), and Catherine II (1762–96) from an undeveloped feudal power into a highly civilized state, complete with universities, an Academy of Arts (founded in St. Petersburg in 1757), theatres and concert halls. The Petersburg Court (particularly in the time of Catherine the Great) became the meeting point of some of Europe's most illustrious artists, sculptors, architects, composers and performers, and was famous throughout the West for its brilliance, opulence, and splendour. For much of the eighteenth century Russia was indebted to West-European (especially Italian) culture. The efforts of architects such as the Italians Rossi and Rastrelli, or the Scotsman Cameron, sculptors such as the Italian Canova, and many others, are still to be seen as permanent monuments in Leningrad and its environs to this day. This influx of foreign talent was particularly noticeable in the realms of music, St. Petersburg being visited by many of the outstanding musicians of the time. By the end of the century, however, there worked side by side with the foreign artists Russian craftsmen, many of them of serf extraction, who proved skilful imitators of their mentors and who, in some cases, succeeded in producing works of definite national colouring and originality. Such are the Russian artists Levitsky, Borovikovsky and Rokotov, the sculptors Shubin and Kozlovsky, the architects Bazhenov and Kazakov, the composers Pashkevich, Matinsky, Khandoshkin, Fomin, and Bortnyansky. The eighteenth century likewise saw the appearance of a distinctive Russian literature, at first entirely dependendent on West European models, but later acquiring unmistakably Russian characteristics. In a word, the eighteenth century was a period of imitation and assimilation, the culmination of which appeared in a series of artistic creations at the end of the century by indigenous artists.

PETER THE GREAT (1682–1725)

The reign of Peter the Great coincides with the end of the seventeenth century and the culmination of the Muscovite period in the evolution of Russian music. With the beginning of the new century the musical culture was transferred to the new capital (founded in 1703), where it was developed on entirely different lines. (1)

Unlike his father, Tsar Alexis, Peter had no artistic instincts. Music did not attract him, and although a clavichord was included among his childish amusements, it is not known who played upon it. When in 1697 he went abroad for the first time, the *Kurfürstin* of Hanover and Brandenburg proposed to entertain him with Italian singers, but Peter frankly admitted that he did not care for music: 'I would rather go on the sea and let off fireworks', he said. During his visit to Paris in 1717 he was invited to the opera by the Duke of Orleans (the regent), but could not sit out the performance. Both instances, especially Peter's reply to the Princess, reveal a fundamental trait in his character. He attached only a utilitarian significance to music and the theatre, preferring the pyrotechnical art to the musical. The Russian fondness for fireworks and ingenious set pieces and illuminations, supplemented by music, dates from this time.

Peter was a remarkably expert performer on the drum, but apart from that, his only interest in music was church singing, inherited, no doubt, from his father. Of the Tsar we have various accounts by foreigners. Bergholtz (who was a member of the suite of Karl Friedrich, Duke of Holstein—the future husband of the Tsarevna, Anna Petrovna) records in his diary that

Peter had little liking for music but was fond of drinking and compelled others to join him. (2) At the rejoicings over the Treaty of Nystadt he was exceedingly merry, drinking heavily and even dancing on the tables. But during banquets he frequently stopped the music, because it interfered with the 'conversation'. His attitude to church singing, however, was quite different. He often sang in the choir, preferably the bass parts; the vocal scores for his use, legibly copied out, bound in parchment, and inscribed: 'The Emperor Peter Alekseevich deigned to sing from this music', were preserved in the Moscow Arsenal.

The Imperial singers often accompanied him on his travels. One of his favourite servants was a singer named Vasiliy; another was Stepan Belyaev, a singing clerk who became his choir master in 1713. In 1712 Belyaev was granted a plot of land in the Kolomna district: (3) Peter also liked to have choral singing at the celebrations of his victories, and for this he utilized the form of the *kant*.

PETER'S RELATIONS WITH THE WEST

The first years of Peter's reign saw the establishment of closer relations with the West. It became customary to enlist foreigners in the Russian service, and embassies and Russian missions were sent abroad more frequently and assumed an entirely different character, as may be gathered from reports by ambassadors and communications from other contemporaries of Peter, which are far more interesting than those received in the time of Alexis. Previously the people of Moscow had been merely astonished at the cunning devices of the West and had held aloof from foreigners, fearing infection by some heresy; in the eighteenth century, however, that same West became an object of admiration and imitation. (4) Peter's reign saw the beginning of assemblies, and fanfares at meals became customary in the houses of the wealthy; in the second half of the eighteenth century the capitals had public theatres, concerts, and even performances of oratorios.

On the other hand, foreign visitors to Moscow, especially ambassadors, brought with them musicians and musical instruments. Some of the foreigners kept record of these 'music-makings' and of their impressions of the social life of Muscovy.

For fullness of detail, the diaries of Johann Korb and Kammer-junker Bergholtz are outstanding. Johann Georg Korb, secretary to the Imperial ambassador Gvarient has some particularly interesting things to say in his *Diary of a Traveller in Muscovy* (1698–9). (5) According to Korb, musicians were in the service not only of foreigners occupying the highest administrative posts, but also of Russian aristocrats.

THE FIRST RUSSIAN THEATRE

In the course of his frequent travels, Peter observed the social life of other countries, though he took no pleasure in their music. Nevertheless soon after his first journey (1697–8), from which he returned with a zeal for reforms, he introduced music and the theatre to the inhabitants of Moscow. Instructions were given for the organization of assemblies with music and dancing; new musicians and actors were brought from abroad, and a public theatre was established. The management of the theatre was entrusted to foreign 'principals' imported for the purpose; but, apart from them, theatrical performances were also staged at the Moscow Slavo-Graeco-Latin Academy and, later on, at the Surgical School under the direction of Doctor Bidloo. Plays were produced before the Court in the Preobrazhenskoe village, where the theatre was revived by the Tsarevna Natalya Alekseevna (Peter's sister); and afterwards at the residence of Tsaritsa Praskovya Fëdorovna in the village of Izmailovo. Copies have been preserved of pieces performed at the Kiev Ecclesiastical Academy; in the metropolitan of Rostov's Krestovaya chamber; and even at Novgorod. The repertory of these enterprises falls into three main categories: (i) Mysteries and school performances of a similar character; (ii) Comedies and *intermezzi*; and (iii) Theatrical pieces with political undertones. Music undoubtedly played some part in these productions. It is an interesting factor that theatrical music in these productions had now become completely secularized, for in the plays of Peter's time we find an 'Officer's Dance', as well as love songs and priests' songs satirizing the Russian clergy, &c.

The public theatre was opened in Moscow in 1702 under the management of Johann Kunst, a German actor from Danzig, who was succeeded shortly afterwards by Otto (Artemius) Fürst. Its repertoire, comprising thirty plays, differed little from those of contemporary French and German theatres. Most of them were translated in the office of the Moscow embassy, but there were a few original Russian *intermezzi* of a local character. These plays were also given at both Court theatres. Though the actual music has not been discovered, it seems fairly certain that vocal and instrumental numbers were employed to add variety to the dramatic action.

Productions at Fürst's theatre ended shortly after the removal of the Court to the new capital. In 1707 the comedy hall was dismantled and the 'properties' were transferred to the Preobrazhenskoe village for theatrical performances at the Tsarevna Natalya Alekseevna's Court. But Moscow still had its theatre, since the students at Dr. Bidloo's Surgical School began to produce plays in the great hospital building, and this went on until the 1740's.

VISITS OF FIRST FOREIGN MUSICIANS

The foreign actors in Moscow were followed by foreign musicians. On 5 August 1702 a small wind orchestra was engaged through the agency of Popp Bros., Hamburg, consisting of seven musicians, plus a conductor (Kapellmeister Sienknechter), and this was the beginning of a constant stream of foreign performers who were summoned to serve in Russia.[1] Often they were also made responsible for the training of young Russian musicians and it not infrequently happened that boy-singers, who had formerly been choristers, changed their vocation to that of secular singers. Thus, in Moscow, and afterwards in St. Petersburg, there were soon plenty of serving musicians, trained regimental oboists (by an *ukaz* of 1711, each division of Peter's army was equipped with a small wind orchestra), trumpeters, and drummers, and members of the Court orchestra. The last-named was apparently formed after the removal of the Court to the new capital, where the most thoroughly Europeanized nobles made a practice of maintaining private orchestras and musicians. To speak of the existence of a special theatre orchestra would be premature. In Peter's theatres there were no operas, the choral numbers were sung *a cappella*, and the solos might, as formerly, be accompanied by a clavichord or a small organ. Until the 1720's we hear only of individual performers

[1] All dates are given according to the 'Old Style' or Julian Calendar.

and bands consisting entirely of oboes, horns and trumpets. Occasionally, when the band included musicians capable of playing both the violin and a wind instrument, strings might be added to the wind; a case in point was Hübner, a famous violinist-conductor, who was originally a brilliant horn-player.

MUSIC IN PETER'S TRIUMPHS

The use of vocal music in the social life of Moscow also became more frequent. The triumphal celebrations of fresh conquests and victories were attended with the ceremonial dearly loved by Peter, which gradually became more complicated and was of longer duration; to the salvoes of guns and the special *kants* were added theatrical performances, illuminations, fireworks, and even masquerades. On Kunst's arrival in Moscow, an embassy order required him to prepare as quickly as possible a new comedy based on the Tsar's victory and the surrender of Oreshko. The MSS of many of the *kants* composed for such occasions have come down to us.

The first of these triumphs was apparently organized in 1696 to celebrate the fall of Azov. On that occasion, following the example of the West, triumphal arches were erected, decorated with symbolical emblems and inscriptions, through which the victors rode to the sounds of music and the singing of *kants*. Other celebrations, each more brilliant than its predecessor, took place in 1702, marking the first victory over the Swedes with the capture of Schlüsselberg, after the fall of Narva and Dorpat in December 1704, the victory of Poltava in 1709 (for which there still exists the score of a 13-part concerto 'Na primirenie Poltavskoy batalii', written for discant, 2 altos, 8 tenors, and 2 basses), and, most of all, after the signing of the Peace of Nystadt, which brought to an end the long war in the North. On 18 December 1721 Peter made a triumphal entry into Moscow, where he was received by Theodosius, Archbishop of Novgorod. There were numerous triumphal arches, trumpet fanfares and perhaps marches, and vocal choruses by the Singing Clerks and the students of the Slavo-Graeco-Latin Academy, whose songs were in various languages.

The Peace of Nystadt gave rise to a considerable number of *kants*. One of them, 'Raduysiya Rosko zemle' (Rejoice, Land of Russia), was probably sung when Peter was received by Prince

Menshikov or some other participant in the conquest of the 'Swedish Lion' (Charles XII). This is suggested by the repeated 'vivats' and the reference to the Peace Treaty in the final verse: (Mus. Ex. 1)

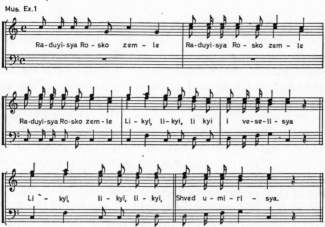

Mus. Ex.1

The word 'vivat' frequently appears in the *kants* of this period; indeed, sometimes it is the only word. This was a custom borrowed from the Polish Court and was evidently used to greet the procession at the triumphal arches. This form of *kant* proved to be the forerunner of the works of Sarti and his contemporaries, the authors of Catherine's triumphal cantatas, who supplemented the salvoes of guns and the ringing of bells with horn music and even fireworks.

The public musical and theatrical performances described above began to be more frequent in Moscow during the second half of the reign: St. Petersburg became the capital and the centre of government, but the 'ancient imperial city' was preferred as the stage for great functions such as the coronation and the victory celebrations.

PETER'S REFORMS AND THE BEGINNING OF THE ST. PETERSBURG PERIOD

Towards the beginning of the eighteenth century considerable changes were made in Court and social life—changes so violent and decisive as to destroy any hope of a return to the old, traditional ways. The *terem* in which the Tsaritsas and Tsarevnas had been secluded from the public gaze, and in which the Russian woman was protected generally, was thrown open. In 1699, for the first time in Moscow, there was music at a funeral —that of the Tsar's favourite, General Lefort (who, incidentally, had his own band). The Tsar himself arranged the ceremonial, in which three Guards regiments, each headed by nine flautists, took part. According to Korb: 'The air was filled with the soft sound of mournful tunes'. In December 1699 an edict was issued altering the chronology, which henceforth was to date from the birth of Christ and not from the creation of the world. Following the European custom New Year's Day was to be 1 January instead of 1 September, and the celebrations were to be continued for a week, with salvoes of guns, the firing of rockets, the lighting of tar barrels, and the decoration of the houses. Then followed a series of edicts, which caused considerable agitation among the people—the shaving of beards, the wearing of clothes cut in the German fashion, the organizing of assemblies, &c. In October 1700 Adrian, the last of the Moscow Patriarchs, died, and in 1721 the patriarchate was abolished in Russia, its place being taken by the Holy Synod, an ecclesiastical body subservient to the Crown. St. Petersburg, founded in 1703, soon became Peter's favourite residence, and the laying-out of the new capital was one of his chief occupations. (6) Yet another innovation was the Table of Ranks, which divided all the armed services and Civil Servants into fourteen *chiny* or grades. This was the start of bureaucracy in Russia. The year 1703 saw the foundation of the first Russian newspaper, the *Moskovskiya vedomosti* (Moscow News).[1] All these factors, combined with the heavy taxation imposed to meet the cost of the war and other of Peter's undertakings, compulsory military service, &c., to say nothing of the institution of serfdom, profoundly affected the inner life of the country and brought about a complete and sudden change in the social conditions.

With the new capital was also associated a new period—the St. Petersburg period—in the history of Russian music, the outcome of an intense admiration for and imitation of Western Europe. The assemblies instituted by Peter's edict accomplished far more than might be imagined. Everything that had been dear to ancient Moscow, that reminded her of her former, self-

---

[1] The Academy of Sciences was founded in 1725.

contained existence, was now out of place. Dress, manners, amusements, and even the external appearance, had to bear a different stamp and to comply unfailingly with the example set by the West. Peter's orders were always strict enough: the disobedient were fined, flogged, or sent to the galleys.

Orchestral music now began to play a considerable part in everyday life. Thus, according to a description of St. Petersburg and Kronshlot (Kronstadt) published in 1710–11, following the custom of German cities, a band of twelve trained German trumpeters and kettle-drummers from time to time played at noon in the upper gallery of the newly-erected Post-house. (7)

An interesting document from the point of view of the music of the period is the diary of Kammer-junker Bergholtz, to which reference has already been made, and which was written in 1721–5. Despite the fact that he pays little attention to Russian folk music, which also played its part at Court and in everyday life in the form of *bandurists* (a performer on the Ukrainian *bandura*), folk dancers and folk-singers, his diary contains information about orchestras, serenades, shows, dances, masquerades, and other Court and social amusements. (8)

The assemblies introduced by Peter were an important factor in training the people to observe the rules of social behaviour. Special regulations were drawn up, from which some idea may be formed of the life of the period. Music played no small part, as dancing was a feature of public and family gatherings. The dances then in vogue included a German dance (probably the *Grossvater*, in which the Tsar took part; it was generally used to open the ball); the minuet; and Polish and English dances. (9)

Bergholtz describes how many Russian grandees and distinguished foreign visitors kept their own bands, among them Tsaritsa Catherine Alekseevna; Admiral F. M. Apraksin (*d.* 1728); Prince A. D. Menshikov (exiled in 1727), who had trumpeters and kettle-drummers; Count A. Stroganov, whose orchestra consisted of eight musicians; General-prokuror P. I. Yaguzhinsky (*d.* 1736), a great lover of music and performer on the clavichord, who had his own horn-players, and who sold his music library to the Duke of Holstein; Princess Marya Yurevna Cherkasskaya (*d.* 1747), daughter of Prince Y. Y. Trubetskoy, who had her own *bandurist*, and an orchestra of ten good musicians, including Germans and Swiss; and many others. (10) So great in fact was the growth of interest in music that soon the first musical amateurs began to order harpsichords and clavichords from abroad.

Of the foreigners, the Duke of Holstein's orchestra was famous, and consisted originally of two horn-players imported from Vienna by the Duke in 1721. Both had to play during the Duke's dinner, as well as on ceremonial occasions, and Bergholtz gives vivid descriptions of these activities. (11)

The table music and serenades began to be supplemented by regular concerts, first in Moscow and then in St. Petersburg. In the autumn of 1722 the Duke acquired from Count Kinsky and some Russian notabilities a quantity of music whereby his band, which Bergholtz now calls an orchestra, was furnished with 'many beautiful pieces'. (12) This facilitated the arrangement of concerts, which were usually given on Wednesdays after dinner and attracted many hearers from embassy circles in the Nemetskaya sloboda.

All these outward forms embodying Peter's musical innovations affected Russian social life only and did not concern the masses of the people, who remained faithful to, and fought for, their ancient customs. Nevertheless, that Peter's harsh and determined measures were not taken kindly by the mass of the people is revealed by many texts of folk-songs and in popular drawings, woodcuts, and etchings. The imagination of the people even identified the great Tsar with antichrist. The new ideas and vexatious edicts affecting the old way of life contributed powerfully to the diffusion of numerous rumours concerning the end of the world. Many Old Believers fled to the outlying regions of the Empire. At the same time, Peter's reign left its trace on folk-song, which extols many events of the period.

THE INTERIM PERIOD AND THE REIGN OF ANNA (1730–40)

The reigns of Catherine I (1725–7) and Peter II (1727–30) were too brief to permit the appearance of any new and outstanding musical features in Russia, though we do know that Peter II played the violin. In Anna Ivanovna's reign, however, Italian opera was established in the capital—a sign of a more serious musical culture.

Whereas music in Peter's time had served a purely utilitarian purpose, Peter accepting it as a means of elevating the social manners, under his successors, particularly at the beginning of Anna's reign, music became indispensable to the life of the Court—an embellishment and a distraction. One fact must be noted: during Peter's reign Western music had not succeeded in producing a purely Russian creative style, unless it was in the 'concerto style', which produced a more florid ecclesiastical music. The reign of Anna, however, succeeded in producing an independent, though entirely imitative musical literature, brought about partly by the large numbers of foreign musicians present in Russia and the gradual arising of a 'Court intelligentsia'.

Anna's accession to the throne in 1731 was greeted by Vasiliy Trediakovsky (a future academician, but then a student) with a triumphal *kant* composed by him in Hamburg in 1730:

> Long live the Empress Anna...
> More beautiful than sun and stars...

The music, which was possibly not by Trediakovsky himself, was probably sung by the Court singers, since Trediakovsky returned to Russia in the autumn of 1731 and published it. The first strophe was printed with the music, and the *kant* itself was subsequently included in a MS collection of three-part vocal *kants*. It may be regarded as the first musical work printed in Russia. The music was engraved on copper in the printing office of the Academy of Sciences. (13)

The new Empress (the daughter of Tsar Ivan Alekseevich— Peter I's brother—and the Tsaritsa Praskovya Fëdorovna) lived, prior to her election to the Russian throne, at Mittau, where the modest ducal household was probably copied from the Court establishments of the German princes. Now, however, Anna had ample resources and, according to one source, she made use of them to impart unusual splendour to her Court. Within a year of her accession she had Court singers and an orchestra, eminent virtuosi were engaged, and brilliant operatic performances were given.

ANNA'S HABITS AND CHARACTER

Nevertheless, despite her efforts to equal the magnificence of European Courts, Anna's amusements and distractions were an astonishing mixture of contraries. On the one hand one finds

the organization of Italian opera and Court concerts and the
introduction of outstanding Western artists: on the other the
pranks of debased jesters, so profitable that some of the professional Court musicians preferred to join their ranks; *khorovods*
in Court apartments by guardsmen and their wives; or, lastly,
the amazing rudeness with which Anna treated her German
maids. When she felt bored, they had to sing to her: 'Now,
girls, sing!' she would shout, and, when she was tired of them,
'That's enough!' She rewarded the weary girls with a box on
the ears, or sent them to the laundry to wash clothes. In all these
contradictions one may see a propensity for the old Muscovite
'grandfatherly customs' combined with an increasing desire to
pass for an 'enlightened Empress'. Surrounding herself with
Western luxury and amusing herself with riding and cards,
Anna believed at the same time in oil from the image lamps and
wore a scarf round her head when in her private apartments.

Music was often required for Court functions and State occasions, indeed, contemporary accounts are filled with descriptions of dinners and balls with music and illuminations, which
replaced the triumphal entries and processions with *kants* of the
days of Peter. (14)

A Court orchestra was organized at the beginning of Anna's
reign for permanent and extra concerts and theatrical performances. It was built up gradually and was composed originally
of musicians who remained in the service of the Court after the
deaths of Peter I and Catherine I, and of others who had
belonged to the Duke of Holstein's orchestra, the Duke having
been banished to Kiel in 1727 owing to his quarrel with the
all-powerful Prince Menshikov.

VISITS OF FOREIGN OPERA COMPANIES

The year 1731 saw the visit to Moscow of two foreign opera
companies, one headed by T. Ristori, the other (recruited by
J. Hübner) by Johann Kayser, whose repertoire appears to
have consisted largely of *intermezzi*. According to Mooser, who
has corrected a number of errors occurring in Findeisen's
Ocherki and in the works of other scholars in the field, a three-
act *opera buffa: commedia per musica* entitled *Calandro* has the distinction of being the first opera to be performed in Russia, and

not Araja's *Forza dell'amore e dell'odio*, as is generally assumed (see MOOS, I, pp. 50–1, 80–1).

In 1732 Hübner was again sent on a mission, to Venice, which he accomplished with even greater success, bringing with him to Russia three excellent violinists—Luigi Madonis, Madonis's brother Antonio, and Pietro Mira—and an Italian company, which arrived in 1733. (16) This company performed several comedies and *intermezzi* (short plays with musical episodes) in St. Petersburg, which were translated into Russian and German where appropriate, till it left Russia in 1735. Although the texts of these pieces have been preserved, (17) very little of the music has survived, though some materials have been discovered by Mooser. (18) In 1734 the clown Pedrillo (Pietro Mira) was sent abroad to recruit an opera troupe, a mission that he completed most satisfactorily. In the summer of 1735 the capital was visited by a brilliant company of performers, headed by the composer Francesco Araja (1700–67[?]). Araja remained in St. Petersburg till 1759, and on 29 January 1736 his opera *La forza dell'amore e dell'odio* (The Power of Love and Hate) was given at the St. Petersburg Court. The opera was performed in Italian by Italian singers, but the libretto was printed in Russian in a translation by the poet Trediakovsky. (19) Between the acts of the opera were inserted decorative ballets. Like any other Neapolitan opera of the time the principal musical number was the aria, while the action, which abounded in all manner of stage effects, pageantry and dramatic situations, was advanced by the recitatives. (20) In the succeeding years a further two operas were performed by Araja—*Il finto Nino, overo la Semiramide riconosciuta* (The Mock Nino, or Semiramide Revealed) being given in 1737, and *Artaserse* (Artaxerxes) in 1738. Both libretti were by Metastasio. Generally speaking, performances of foreign operas in the first half of the eighteenth century were a comparatively rare event—possibly due to the excessive cost of production—and were reserved only for special occasions of State. (21)

After Araja's *Artaxerxes* the opera company, together with many members of the Court orchestra, left Russia. No operas were staged during the last two years of Anna's reign, though Araja's services were retained. (22) It is possible that Court audiences first made the acquaintance of German *Singspiel* from

the visit of Neuber's German dramatic company, imported in
the spring of 1740, though with little success.

FOREIGN COMPOSERS AT THE RUSSIAN COURT

Whilst Araja was resident in Russia there were also a number
of foreign composers and musicians such as the violinists Giovanni Verocai, (23) Luigi Madonis, (24) Domenico dall'Oglio,
(25) and Pietro Mira, (26) who wrote mostly instrumental music.

Whereas dall'Oglio specialized in the writing of chamber
trios (his *XII Sonate a Violino e Violoncello o Cimbalo* were published
in Amsterdam, 1738), Madonis specialized in the writing of
violin sonatas and his *12 Different Symphonies for Violin and Bass*
(each of which is subtitled 'Sonata') were written in 1738 and
dedicated to Anna. The period from 1735–8 also saw the publication of *12 Sonatas for Violin Solo with Bass* by Giovanni Verocai. (27) These may be regarded as the first secular instrumental
pieces to be composed in Russia and were certainly among the
first editions to be engraved by Russian publishers. The sonatas
by Madonis were apparently not the only ones to be engraved
by Russian publishers, nor were they the only ones to be written
by him, for Stählin informs us that he composed 'a pair of
sonatas based on Ukrainian themes'. (28) That he should
choose Ukrainian melodies for his inspiration is explained by
the fact that the music was written for Anna's successor—the
Empress Elizabeth—whose lover, the famous Count Razumovsky (nicknamed 'the nocturnal Emperor'), was himself of
Ukrainian origin, as well as being a gifted singer. Madonis's
'Symphonies' are violin sonatas in the sense in which the term
was then understood, with a figured bass accompaniment. Consisting of several short movements—an introductory *Adagio*,
sarabandes, sicilianas, minuets, gigues, &c., they contain elements of both the sonata and the suite. Of particular interest is
that in some cases may perhaps be detected the influence of
Russian folk music. The following representative figures, for
instance, are typical of Russian dance songs (Mus. Ex. 2):

Mus. Ex. 2

Capriccio

FOUNDATION OF FIRST MUSIC SCHOOL

Anna's reign also saw the development of musical education. In 1740 an Imperial *ukaz* ordered the foundation of a small music school under J. Hübner, the purpose of which was to train young Ukrainian singers as Court musicians. (29) Another school was opened at Glukhov in the Ukraine in 1741. (30)

DEVELOPMENT OF MUSICAL LIFE

Another of Anna's new musical enterprises was the construction of a great organ in the Lutheran St. Petri-Kirche in St. Petersburg, and the *Sanktpeterburgskie vedomosti* (The St. Petersburg Gazette) describes the consecration, which took place on 27 December 1737. (31) The first organist was apparently Joachim Bernard Wilde, who was a manufacturer and dealer in musical instruments. Before this period musical instruments had been imported from abroad. Another maker was Johann Christian Förster (*c.* 1733).

The publication in 1739 of academician Leonard Euler's treatise *Tentamen novae theoriae musicae* was likewise a significant event in Anna's reign. Not only was the Academy of Sciences the first academy to have its own printing office—it published the first libretti of *intermezzi* and operas as well as books on music—but it printed music from its own type. Its bookshops in St. Petersburg and Moscow were the first to sell music and obtain it from abroad. Especially important was its work in the way of translation, composition of verses and laudatory odes. Of the members outstanding were Vasiliy Kirillovich Trediakovsky (1703–68), Jakob von Stählin (1712–85), who did much in the way of musical journalism, composition of poetry and dramatic productions, and Professor Leonard Euler (*b.* Basle 1707, *d.* St. Petersburg 1783), who studied the question of musical acoustics.

ACCESSION OF ELIZABETH

The Coronation of the Empress Elizabeth in 1742, which took place in Moscow after 375 days of political catastrophes and intrigues, was marked by celebrations of unusual splendour. A Prologue (with text by Jakob von Stählin and music by dall' Oglio) bore the title *La Russia afflitta e riconsolata* (After Sorrow Russia Rejoices). This was followed by an opera *La Clemenza di*

Tito (The Clemency of Titus), with music by Hasse, a German composer of some standing and a devotee of the Italian tradition. For the occasion, a theatre was specially constructed on the banks of the River Yauza. There were also two ballets staged by J.-B. Landé, who in 1734 had been given the task of teaching ballet to the Cadet Corps. In 1738 he founded a choreographic school, the ancestor of the Petersburg Theatrical School (established 1783) (MOOS, I, p. 152).

ELIZABETH'S CHARACTER

Like Anna, Elizabeth was fundamentally a simple person. She liked folk-songs and was herself a performer. Unlike her predecessor, however, she believed in the protection of Russia against foreigners and the restoration of the rights of Russian citizens. During her reign, and even more so in the time of Catherine, her successor, may be seen an ever-increasing sense of national awareness. The 1750's witnessed the emergence of the first Russian scientist, Lomonosov. The Rossiyskiy Teatr (Russian Theatre) was opened in St. Petersburg in 1756 by Volkov, (32) Sumarokov being appointed its director, while the Locatelli Theatre came into being in Moscow in 1759.

NATURE OF COURT MUSIC

As regards the character of the music performed at Court, there was little change. Italian vocal and instrumental music was oligatory at dinners, suppers, and masquerades; on the Empress's birthday, name day, (33) accession, and Coronation. To add to the splendour of these functions, some of them were accompanied by performances of new operas, others by French plays, which had begun to be fashionable. Music's share in all this became increasingly important and the Court orchestra had to be considerably enlarged. (34)

APPEARANCE OF FIRST OPERA TO A RUSSIAN TEXT

An outstanding musical event from the point of view of the history of Russian music was the performance in 1755 of the first opera to a Russian text—*Tsefal i Prokris* (Cephalus and Procris) with music by Francesco Araja and libretto by Sumarokov. From surviving documents it is learnt that the soloists were made up of young Russian and Ukrainian vocalists, (35) while the chorus consisted of the Court singers. To all intents and purposes, however, *Cephalus and Procris* is still essentially an Italian *opera seria*, the plot, taken from Ovid, describing the hopeless love of the Goddess Aurora for the young Cephalus, resulting in his subsequent death. Araja's treatment of the theme is conventional and the opera is void of almost any national colouring. (36)

ACCESSION OF CATHERINE II (1762–96)

Of the three Empresses governing Russia in the eighteenth century, Catherine II was by far the most remarkable. Not only did her political and economic schemes prove a great success but also, under her reign, cultural life rose to an impressive level. Like her predecessor, Catherine ascended the throne after a revolution. In her early years the fundamental principle in her manifesto was 'the protection of the Russian faith and nationality', which had been threatened with destruction in the brief reign of Peter III. Although commencing her reign with liberal ideas, her last years were marked by a period of reaction —the result of the French Revolution and such domestic troubles as the rebellion of Pugachëv (1773–5).

CATHERINE'S MUSICAL TASTES

Whereas in Elizabeth's reign 'Italian music with concertos and cantatas provided a continuous accompaniment' to a gala supper, (37) Catherine, according to many of her contemporaries, was in general rather indifferent to musical performances, which at her Court assumed the character of brilliant but intelligent diversions. (38) In the 1750's Russia made the acquaintance of Italian *opera buffa* and, later, French *opéra comique*.

VISITS BY FOREIGN COMPOSERS

A host of foreign composers took up the capital as their temporary abode—Manfredini, Galuppi (1765–8), Traetta (1768–75), Paisiello (1776–84), Sarti (1784–1802), Cimarosa (1787–91), and many others. (39) French *opéra comique* became the fashion and works by Philidor, Monsigny, Dalayrac, and later Grétry, were performed with Russian translations and given in private houses.

Of the foreign musicians resident in Russia, Galuppi took a far more active part in musical life than Araja and apart from operas such as *Didone abbandonata, Ifigenia in Tauride*, &c., he often performed his harpsichord sonatas at Court. In this he was one of the first representatives of the new harpsichord technique in Russia. In his capacity of Director of the Imperial Chapel he had great influence on Church music, which from this period began to become more Italianate in style. His work in this field was developed by his pupil Dmitriy Stepanovich Bortnyansky.

Paisiello was also active in the realms of opera and *The Barber of Seville* (with libretto by Beaumarchais), which was specially written for the St. Petersburg Court in 1782, was one of the most successful *opera buffa* of its day. Undoubtedly the humour, effortlessness and formal perfection of Paisiello's music were of influence on the young generation of Russian composers then coming into being. Paisiello also wrote a number of piano concertos, compositions for violin and piano, and *divertissements* for wind instruments.

No less remarkable was the work of Sarti, whose wide activities ranged from *opera buffa* and *opera seria* to his grandiose cantatas and oratorios. He also did research into musical acoustics (for which he was elected a member of the Academy of Sciences) and was one of the directors of the Ekaterinoslavskaya Academy of Music.

DEVELOPMENT OF CONCERT LIFE AND SERF ORCHESTRAS

The last third of the eighteenth century saw the development of concert life (40) as well as domestic music-making. (41) (42) Certain wealthy nobles, such as Count Sheremetev or Count Vorontsov, had their own theatres and serf orchestras and in the magnificence of their performances sought to rival those of the Court, whose musical activities they imitated. Sheremetev had an opera troupe of serf artists and a large orchestra of musicians, who often took part in Moscow concerts. Gradually the local nobility took an interest in opera, and opera companies of varying strength and ability were set up in country estates. Towards the end of the century operatic performances in private houses became the fashion. From Sheremetev's serfs emerged at the beginning of the nineteenth century the Russian composer S. A. Degtyarëv, author of the patriotic oratorio *Minin i Pozharsky ili osvobozhdenie Moskvy* (Minin and Pozharsky or the Liberation of Moscow), and the singer P. I. Kovalëva (Zhemchugova), who later became Sheremetev's wife. Catherine's diary for 1764 gives many descriptions of her travels in different parts of Russia and her musical experiences which provide a valuable insight into the provincial music life of the time. (43)

CONDITION OF SERF MUSICIANS

Conditions for the serf musicians were far from good. In some cases musicians to train serfs were procured in the same way as cooks, (44) while the serf musicians themselves were put up for sale together with fowl and pigs. (45) The fate of indigenous artists and composers seems to have been a hard one, depending entirely on the nature of their owner or patron. There are no surviving memoirs of any Russian composer of the period and even the dates of their biographies are frequently unknown.

THE RUSSIAN HORN BAND

One of the most remarkable musical phenomena in the second half of the eighteenth century was the Russian horn band, in which each serf musician played only one note, the size of the horns varying in length from 98 inches (with a 9-inch bell) to 3 inches (with a ½-inch bell). Such bands had a total compass of 4½ octaves with all the chromatic intervals. One of the most famous was that developed by Anton Maresch,[1] a Bohemian by origin, for Prince Naryshkin. According to Hinrichs, (46) author of the only printed treatise on horn bands of the period, between 1753 and 1796 there were no less than nine of these bands in St. Petersburg, while there were others in Moscow and the provinces. Apart from their use in adding colour to State occasions and other festivities, (47) they were sometimes employed in theatrical productions, e.g. in Fomin's melodrama *Orfey*. (48)

REPERTOIRE OF SERF ORCHESTRAS

In 1774–5 Johann Kerzelli published four parts of his *Muzykalnye uveseleniya*, the first journal of printed music in Russia, which included, amongst other things, 'Russian songs', and

[1] One source identifies him as Jan Antonín Mareš (see V. Štěpánek and B. Karásek, *An Outline of Czech and Slovak Music*, Part I. Prague, 1964, p. 32).

sacred and secular music. The latter give some idea of the music of the serf orchestras, while in some cases they performed overtures and symphonies of Haydn, Mozart, Beethoven, Cherubini, and Rossini. Copies of these works, and of others by Western and Russian composers, reached the country estates and were incorporated in the latest programmes of the serf orchestras to which Glinka makes reference in his memoirs. The number of serf musicians in Russia by the end of the century must have been considerable. Opera and ballet performances, given by the Institute for Daughters of the Nobility, took place at the Smolnyi Convent from 1770.

DOMESTIC MUSIC-MAKING

In the homes of the nobility people studied the harp and the harpsichord, performed sentimental songs, quartets and chamber works. During the 1790's and the early nineteenth century the guitar was very popular. (49) Wind ensembles, consisting of flutes, oboes, and horns, were performed on boats on the Rivers Neva, Moskva, and elsewhere.

APPEARANCE OF NATIVE ARTISTS

By the end of the eighteenth century quite a number of outstanding Russian artists and performers had made an appearance—the Russian singers Sandunova and Vinogradov; Khandoshkin, the gifted violinist; (50) Daniel Kashin, the pianist; and others. Sometimes concerts would be given consisting entirely of Russian works: thus Sandunova in 1795 announced that her concert would consist 'for the most part of Russian arias, and one never sung here before at a concert of Russian song'. Occasionally, performances of oratorios, &c., demanded several hundred participants, with the result that musicians had to be imported from neighbouring districts. (51)

FIRST MUSIC CLUBS

At the end of the century, the growth of musical life was reflected in the founding of various musical societies, circles, and clubs. One of these, which was formed in Moscow in 1800 by wealthy Muscovites and members of the aristocracy, received the name of the 'Musical Academy', although it was nothing more than a club which gave musical performances.

An earlier venture, though modelled on the same lines, was founded in St. Petersburg in 1772, and stayed in existence for five years.

FIRST MUSICAL PUBLICATIONS

The last three decades also saw the emergence of three important music manuals (all of them translations of foreign works)— Löhlein's *Klavikordnaya shkola* (Clavichord School) (1773), Kellner's *Vernoe nastavlenie v sochinenii General-Basa* (Reliable Instruction in the Writing of Thorough-bass) (1791), and Vever's *Metodicheskoy opyt* (A Methodical Attempt). There were also a guitar journal and a journal of piano and keyboard music, all of which contained popular operatic arias, arrangements of operatic excerpts, dances, and arrangements of Russian folksongs. Of interest in 1795 and 1796 were the publication of two music-lover's pocket books (*Karmannye muzykalnye knigi*) by Gerstenberg, whose publishing firm, founded in the 1790's, was the first real Russian music publishers in our sense of the word. Besides the ordinary calendar, the first issue contained a literary section divided into (i) short biographies of eminent musicians; (ii) a musical dictionary; (iii) musical inventions, Descriptions of the Glass Harmonica; (iv) musical anecdotes; (v) musical dice, or a method of composing minuets and trios for the clavichord by means of two tables and figures and a pair of dice; (vi) music supplements; (vii) 'Catalogue de Livres de Musique gravés et imprimés chez J. D. Gerstenberg et Comp.' (52)

Mention should be made of a *Sobranie nailuchshikh rossiyskikh pesen* (Collection of the best Russian Songs) issued by the bookseller Meyer at St. Petersburg in 1781, in five parts, each containing six songs, all of which were anonymous.

OUTSTANDING MAKERS OF MUSICAL INSTRUMENTS

Finally, the end of the eighteenth century (from 1775 onwards) saw the appearance of a whole number of Russian makers of musical instruments. In particular may be mentioned the violins of Ivan Andreevich Batov (*b.* 1767, pupil of Vladimirov, the Moscow craftsman), whose violins were reckoned among the finest in the world.

DEVELOPMENT OF VOCAL MUSIC

The middle part of the eighteenth century saw the development of vocal music, the most prominent form being the *kant*, large numbers of which are preserved in anonymous collections, presumably written by talented amateurs. As opposed to the crudeness of the melodies of Peter the Great's time greater freedom may be observed in the *kants'* melodic lines, while there are also elements of sentimentality. The words, often flowery in nature, were sometimes settings of poems by pseudo-Classical writers such as Sumarokov, Trediakovsky, and Lomonosov.

GRIGORIY NIKOLAEVICH TEPLOV (1711–79)

The first Russian composer to pay attention to vocal music was Grigoriy Nikolaevich Teplov (1711–79), who is chiefly remembered for his volume *Mezhdu delom bezdelye* (Leisure 'midst Labour), consisting of seventeen songs and published in 1759 (though there is evidence to suggest that it was first published ten years earlier). Teplov was a prominent State official, who received his education in Thübingen and Paris and later became a distinguished member of the Petersburg Academy of Sciences. He had a good voice, played the harpsichord and violin, frequently took part in public concerts and conducted comic operas. Whereas the texts of most of the songs of the period are anonymous (with the exception of settings of Trediakovsky and Lomonosov), the words of Teplov's songs are all borrowed from well-known contemporaries—Sumarokov, Elagin, and others. In their refinement, elegance, and artificiality, they reflect the tastes of the Court and are the perfect counterpart to the sophisticated gavottes, minuets, and sarabandes then in fashion. (53) In some cases there is a strong contrast between the fervency of the words (usually expressing hopeless love) and the very mundane (almost instrumental) nature of the melody. National colouring is almost entirely absent. Sometimes, though, as in the following example—a setting of Sumarokov's 'K tomu li ya toboy, k tomu li ya plenilas' (Why am I drawn to you, Why am I enraptured?)—Teplov is capable of lyrical emotion (Mus. Ex. 3):

Mus. Ex. 3

Teplov's collection achieved great popularity and was reprinted several times. From the point of view of style his music marks the transition from the *kant* to the early Russian *romance*.[1] Although still in three parts (like the *kant*) it differs in that the bass has a definite instrumental nature; Teplov's songs, in fact, are chamber lyrics with instrumental accompaniment.

[1] The term *romance* (Russian *romans*) was first used in Russia to denote songs with French words, though, later, it is used in a much wider sense.

DEVELOPMENT OF THE RUSSIAN ROMANCE

The 1760's to 1780's saw the development of the Russian *romance*, of which the outstanding composers were Fëdor Mikhailovich Dubyansky (1760–96) and Józef Kozłowski (1757–1831). The music of both composers was closely connected with the growth of sentimental poetry at the end of the eighteenth century and lyrical writers such as Dmitriev, Neledinsky-Meletsky, and Kapnist provided many of their words.

FEDOR MIKHAILOVICH DUBYANSKY (1760–96)

Dubyansky was an amateur composer of military parentage, a well-educated man, a violinist, and a friend of Dmitriev and Derzhavin. A *habitué* of literary circles (he was by profession an adviser to the Board of Directors of the Loan Bank) in 1795 he produced six 'Russian songs' which were published anonymously in the already-mentioned *Music-lover's Pocket Book for 1795* printed by Gerstenberg. The songs are simple, tuneful and sincere. Indeed, one could hardly expect great music from such words as:

> Moans the grey-hued little dove
> Moans he day and night.
> His little friend has long departed,
> Long departed on his flight!

Dubyansky's setting of these verses by Dmitriev gives a good idea of his general style. This song 'Stonet siziy golubochek' proved a great favourite, its popularity lasting well into the middle of the nineteenth century (Mus. Ex. 4).

Among other songs by Dubyansky may be mentioned the mournful elegy 'Uzhe so tmoyu noshchi' (Now with the Darkness of Night), to words by Kapnist, and the sentimental *romance* 'Byvalo, ya s prekrasnoy podrugoy' (It Happened that Once With a Beautiful Friend). (54)

RUSSIAN SONG

All these pieces are excellent illustrations of 'Russian song'[1] in which characteristic are the sentimental subject matter, the

[1] By the term 'Russian song' is understood a vocal composition, imitating certain melodic features of peasant folk-song or dance, though written with conventional West-European harmonies.

Mus. Ex. 4

minor key (frequently leading into the relative major) and the imitation of folk intonations. It is not an exaggeration to claim that in these songs of Dubyansky, the subject matter of which echoes the 'pseudo-pastoral' style fashionable at Court, may be found resemblances to the early *romances* of Glinka.

JÓZEF [OSIP ANTONOVICH] KOZŁOWSKI (1757–1831)

A different circle of moods is revealed in the 'Russian songs' of Kozłowski. Born in Warsaw in 1757 he studied as a boy at the Cathedral, where he sang in the choir and played the organ. Later he became a private teacher of music, entered military service in the Russian army during the 80's and retired in 1796 with the rank of major. From 1799 he was attached to the Imperial Theatres in St. Petersburg, first in the capacity of 'inspector' of music, later as 'director', his tasks being the supervision of all the theatre orchestras and the training of orchestral musicians in the Theatrical *uchilishche*.[1] Kozłowski began to compose while he was still in the army and rose to fame particularly after the writing of his Polonaise *Grom pobedy, razdavaisya*

[1] *Uchilishche*—a training school for musicians, dancers, &c.

(The Thunder of Victory now Resound!) in 1791.[1] During
the 1790's he arranged music for every conceivable form of
Court festivity, writing polonaises, a requiem, marches and
other compositions. (55) Apart from his 'Russian songs' he
was also the composer of incidental music. Despite the fact that
they are called 'Russian songs', Kozłowski's compositions in this
genre (which were written at the end of the 1790's) have all the
properties of *romances*, both in their subject matter and their
musical content. Though lacking the control and restraint of
Dubyansky, they are more varied and dynamic and have
many of the characteristics of pre-Romanticism. Typical are
the light-hearted pastoral 'Milaya vechor sidela' (My Darling
sat in the Evening), to words by Neledinsky-Meletsky, in which
Kozłowski depicts musically the song of the nightingale; the
slow pathetic song 'Prezhestokaya sudbina' (Too Cruel Fate),
which out of a total of 42 bars has 24 bars of piano introduction
and epilogue (the song, incidentally, is marked *Largo lamenta-
bile*); and the turbulent, dramatic composition 'Gde, gde, akh,
gde ukrytsya' (Where, Where, oh, Where to Hide!), in which
the introduction represents a storm, complete with peals of
thunder, flashes of lightning and gusts of wind. In many cases
the piano accompaniment is given particular prominence and it
is refreshing to encounter for the first time in the work of a
Russian vocal composer truly pianistic figurations.

OTHER COMPOSERS OF ROMANCES

Among the other composers of *romances* may be mentioned a
naval officer, A. S. Kozlyaninov (1777–1831), and one, A.
Shaposhnikov, who is of some importance as the composer of a
satirical song 'Filosofy pyanye i trezvye' (The intoxicated and
sober Philosophers), to words by Derzhavin, which was published in a set of 'Anacreontic songs' in 1816.

IMPORTANCE OF DUBYANSKY AND KOZŁOWSKI

Dubyansky and Kozłowski were the founders of the Russian
romance and although their music was still limited in its range,

[1] A polonaise in this sense of the word was an eighteenth century triumphal
dance procession, performed by soloists, chorus and orchestra, given on State
occasions. Tchaikovsky includes one of Kozłowski's polonaises in *The Queen of
Spades*. Kozłowski is reputed to have introduced this form into Russia, and his
settings are not only for voice, but for piano, and orchestra.

it is nevertheless of importance in that it paved the way for the greater creations of Glinka in the early nineteenth century.

INSTRUMENTAL WORKS BY RUSSIAN COMPOSERS

Reference has already been made to the instrumental compositions of foreign composers resident in Russia. The eighteenth century also saw the appearance of the first instrumental works by Russian composers, though these take second place to vocal music both in quality and quantity. (56) The main genres of instrumental composition by Russian composers encountered in the eighteenth century are dances, and variations on Russian themes. An interesting example of early variations, written in 1780, is by Trutovsky (compiler of the celebrated collection of folk-songs), in which the entire development consists of changes in scoring, the harmonies remaining unaltered. The whole cycle concludes with a repeat of the theme in its basic form.

WORKS BY BORTNYANSKY (1751–1825)

Another important composer is Bortnyansky, who, apart from his operas and ecclesiastical music, was also an outstanding composer of chamber and symphonic music. He was the first Russian composer to make use of complex sonata forms, and his works—most of which were written for the Tsarevich Paul for performance at the Palaces of Gatchina and Pavlovsk (57) —include overtures, a symphony for chamber ensemble, a quintet, a quartet, sonatas for violin and piano, the first Russian piano concerto, and sonatas and miscellaneous pieces for piano solo. The Quintet in C major for Harp, Piano, and Strings and the Symphony in B♭ major are outstanding and compare favourably with the Viennese-Italian classical school in their spontaneity, melodiousness and formal perfection.

The piano sonatas of Bortnyansky (which occasionally show folk influence) are also of interest and are obviously designed for domestic music-making. The slow movements have much in common with the lyrical themes of his ecclesiastical concerti (Mus. Ex. 5):

G

Mus. Ex. 5
Adagio

IVAN EVSTAFEVICH KHANDOSHKIN (1747–1804)

The greatest Russian instrumental composer of the eighteenth century, however, is Ivan Evstafevich Khandoshkin (1747–1804), a gifted violinist and composer, apparently of serf origin. From the few biographical details available it seems that he was originally a violinist in the Court Theatre, and subsequently gave concerts in Russia and abroad, his playing showing comparison with some of the finest violinists in the whole of Europe. A man of diverse talents—he was also a guitarist and an excellent pianist—he was lauded by poets and critics and his works were published in many countries.

Most famous of Khandoshkin's compositions are his variations on the themes of Russian folk-songs, which are frequently written as duets for two instruments, e.g. for two violins, or for violin and viola. These employ all the subtleties of string technique, such as double-stopping, rapid alternations of *arco* and *pizzicato*, harmonics, rapid leaps, &c.

In some cases Khandoshkin draws his inspiration from folk music. Thus, in the Variations on the Theme 'Akh po mostu, mostu' (Trutovsky No. 35) the dance theme is developed with chromatic turns characteristic of Glinka. The *pizzicato* sixth variation is reminiscent of *balalaika* playing, while the eighth variation, with its ethereal harmonics, recalls the pastoral sound of a flute or a *svirel*.

Khandoshkin's unaccompanied violin sonatas are outstanding in their colour and expressiveness as well as in the diversity of effects employed, and undoubtedly owe something to Bach. Each sonata commences with a slow introduction of an improvizatory character, though the subsequent order of movements is varied. The finale of the First Sonata, for instance, is a theme and variations; of the Second, a rondo. Similarly, in the First Sonata, the slow introduction is followed by the usual sonata *Allegro*; in the Second and Third Sonatas it is followed by minuets.

Some idea of the nature of Khandoshkin's music is provided by the opening of the last movement of his Sonata No. 1 in G minor for unaccompanied violin—an *Andante con variazione*. The other movements consist of a slow introduction in the form of a funeral march and an impassioned *Allegro* (Mus. Ex. 6):

Mus. Ex. 6
[Andante]

RUSSIAN SYMPHONIC MUSIC

Russian symphonic music in the eighteenth century is best represented by the overture—the programme overture to an opera, tragedy or melodrama. Such are Fomin's overture to the melodrama *Orfey* and the elegant overtures of Bortnyansky and Alyabyev. However, of prime interest from the point of view of the history of Russian music are the overtures to national operas such as *The Miller-magician*, *The St. Petersburg Bazaar*, and a number of others, all of which will receive consideration in the following chapter.

ECCLESIASTICAL MUSIC IN THE EIGHTEENTH CENTURY

About the middle of the eighteenth century ecclesiastical compositions were influenced by secular music, the chief form being the spiritual concerto. Of importance are the concertos of Maxim Sozontovich Berezovsky (1745–77). Like so many Russian composers of the eighteenth century Berezovsky was born in the Ukraine, where he was a pupil of the Kiev Ecclesiastical Academy. As a youth he was taken to St. Petersburg, where he joined the Imperial Boy's Chapel. So outstanding were his musical gifts, that he was sent almost immediately to Italy, where he studied under the celebrated Padre Martini and was elected academician. After the successful performance of his opera *Demofoonte* he returned to Russia, but in St. Petersburg he received so little recognition and encouragement (perhaps as the result of his attempted reforms) that he committed suicide. Berezovsky's best Russian composition is the spiritual concerto in D minor *Ne otverzhi mne vo vremya starosti* (Do Not Spurn Me In My Old Age). In the final section of the work a concentrated *Adagio* serves as an introduction to an animated fugato, of which the following is part of the exposition (Mus. Ex. 7):

Mus. Ex.7

This concerto may well be considered one of the best classical productions of Russian choral music in the eighteenth century.

The dominating figure towards the end of the century is D. S. Bortnyansky, the majority of whose work consisted of unaccompanied choral compositions. Indeed, among his 100 or so *a cappella* works there are 35 4-part concertos and 10 concertos for double chorus. Occasionally in Bortnyansky's compositions may be detected phrases with a national colouring close to Russian and Ukrainian folk-song, but the greater part of his music consists of elegiac themes of a dreamy, contemplative

nature. This is revealed in his Thirty-second Concerto in
C minor; Tchaikovsky (who edited all Bortnyansky's ecclesiastical compositions) claimed that it was 'the best of all the 35'.
An important part in the concerto is played by the wistful
opening phrase, which culminates in a rhetorical pause—a
device often employed by Tchaikovsky himself (Mus. Ex. 8):

Mus. Ex.8

Bortnyansky's skill as a contrapuntist is seen in the concluding
movements of his concertos, which are sometimes written in the
form of a fugue. The subject of the last movement of his Thirty-
first Concerto shows some resemblance to folk-song (cf. the opening of *A Life for the Tsar*) (Mus. Ex. 9):

Mus. Ex.9

Apart from his ecclesiastical compositions, of some interest are
the patriotic works written during the Napoleonic Wars, such
as *Pesnya ratnikov* (Soldiers' Song), *Marsh opolcheniya* (March of

the Militia), and the cantata *Pevets vo stane russkikh voinov* (The Singer in the Camp of the Russian Warriors), which was written to words of Zhukovsky. In all these compositions Bortnyansky paved the way for later developments, and his influence on composers such as Glinka and Tchaikovsky was not inconsiderable.

CHAPTER 4

Russian Music in the
Eighteenth Century (Continued)
First Folk-song Collections
Rise of Russian Opera

APPEARANCE OF FIRST FOLK-SONG COLLECTIONS

Interest in folk-song was manifest throughout the whole of the eighteenth century. The first transcriptions of folk-songs are found in manuscripts together with psalms and *kants*. Generally speaking melodies are absent in these manuscripts, but by the end of the century folk-songs became more prevalent. (1) These early collections were entirely the work of musical amateurs and were concerned for the most part with town folk-songs.

CHULKOV'S COLLECTION

The first printed collection of the texts of Russian folk-songs was that of Chulkov, divided into four parts which first began to appear from 1770 to 1774 under the title *Sobranie raznykh pesen*. (2) Chulkov's collection, though containing a mass of material, was unsystematic in nature and made no attempt to divide the folk-songs into separate genres. Altogether there were some 800 texts, of which 400 examples of peasant songs were either taken from already existing manuscripts or were written down by him in person. The collection was reprinted in 1780–1 by N. I. Novikov in six parts, (3) and yet again in 1788. Chulkov's collection established the pattern for future folk-song collections during the remainder of the eighteenth century and all subsequent compilers of folk-song collections turned to it as a source of information.

TRUTOVSKY'S COLLECTION

Trutovsky may be regarded as the first real collector of folk-songs. (4) His *Sobranie russkikh prostykh pesen s notami* (Collection of Simple Russian Songs with Music) appeared in four parts between 1776 and 1795 and consisted of eighty songs. (5) The first part of the collection was issued in three editions (1776, 1782, 1796), the second part in 1778, the third in 1779, and the fourth in 1795. The folk-songs in Trutovsky's collection, with the exception of the third edition of the first part (1796) and the fourth part of the collection (1795), consist simply of melody and bass, the words being written between the two staves. The songs are intended for practical performance and were written down in the manner in which they were sung in the town. No attempt is made to classify the melodies, soldiers' songs alternating with dance songs, epic with lyrical songs, &c. Of interest are the protracted songs and the historical songs. The collection also includes thirteen Ukrainian folk-songs.

Trutovsky's collection is prefaced by an introduction, which is of interest on account of the light thrown on the attitude of composers and musicians to the folk-song of the period:

> Lovers of folk-song have long wished that they might be published with music according to the rules, but hitherto no one has undertaken the task of reducing them to order and adding a bass underneath. To the satisfaction of many music lovers, I have finally decided to publish these Russian songs collected by myself for solo voice as they are usually sung, but by retaining the bass part they can be harmonized and so played or sung [*sic*]. I should point out that this gave me no little trouble, since in almost every case I found that the text needed correction, and I was sometimes obliged to lengthen or curtail it in order to adapt it to the music. As for the tunes, after listening to many of them, I discovered that everywhere they were sung differently, and I have therefore tried to preserve their accuracy and have followed the simplest forms. (6) If this small collection of Russian songs is favourably received, I shall do my best to find and publish others. Should anyone discover mistakes, I hope that he will be lenient and take into consideration that although I may not have achieved perfection, I have done my utmost to bring order out of disorder.

From this it may be seen that Trutovsky completely misunderstood the nature of Russian peasant song. Not only did he deliberately change the melodic outline of the melody in some cases, but he also introduced sharps and flats into otherwise modal tunes and gave them harmonic accompaniments. It may be observed, however, that since in his own words he wrote down folk-songs 'as they are usually sung', he was merely perpetuating a popular practice, since the way in which peasant songs were performed in the country was quite different from the way in which they were performed in the town. This is illustrated in the following example, where the melody is written in the mixolydian mode, the peculiarity of which is the interval of a flattened seventh. Trutovsky has not realized this and has employed a key signature of one sharp. Furthermore, throughout the piece he has attemped to harmonize the tune with conventional European harmonies, conducting the melody through various keys (e.g. into C, G, C, F, C, and finally back to G), instead of drawing the harmonization from the basic triads of the natural scale on which the melody is based (as is done in the best folk-song arrangements of the next century) (Mus. Ex. 1):

Mus. Ex.1

In those cases where the folk-song is of town origin Trutovsky's arrangements are more suitable; however, his harmonizations of peasant genres are far from satisfactory.

COLLECTION OF LVOV-PRACH

The celebrated collection of Lvov-Prach appeared in the year 1790 under the title *Sobranie narodnykh russkikh pesen s ikh golo-sami. Na muzyku polozhil Ivan Prach* (Collection of Russian Folk-songs with their parts. Set to Music by Ivan Prach). (7) (8) The first edition was composed of 100 songs and was divided into six sections: (i) Protracted songs; (ii) Dance or 'Fast' songs; (iii) Wedding songs; (iv) Khorovods; (v) Christmas ('Svyato-chnye') Carols; (vi) Ukrainian songs. The first edition included sixty new arrangements of Russian folk-songs, the remaining forty being taken from Trutovsky, mostly in fresh variants. In 1806 the volume was re-edited with an additional fifty-two songs, thus making a total of 150, since two were omitted from the previous collection.

Prach may be regarded as the first Russian musician to attempt to make a systematic classification of folk-songs. (9) Many of the songs arranged by him were borrowed from Trutovsky, sometimes with only minor changes to the accompaniment. However, like Trutovsky, Prach failed to recognize the true properties of folk-songs (10) and the criticisms made of Trutovsky are equally applicable. Prach's harmonizations are more skilful and elaborate than those of Trutovsky, the voice part being written on a separate stave with a separate piano accompaniment. However, the deficiencies of both arrangers, in comparison with the skill of such figures as Balakirev and Rimsky-Korsakov are revealed in the following example. The melody lies in the natural minor, with the final note on A. Trutovsky has treated this as if it were A minor. Prach, on the other hand, has used a fuller, richer harmonization, but has followed Trutovsky's key plan almost identically. The G sharps are inappropriate and destroy the modal nature of the melody. However, even Rimsky-Korsakov cannot resist the temptation of introducing colourful harmonies into his accompaniment— the dominant seventh chord in bar 1, the augmented fifth in bar 2 (Mus. Ex. 2):

Mus. Ex. 2

(TRUTOVSKY)

(a) Ya si-de-la li-bo den, li-bo dva, Pod o ko-she-chkom si-ro-to-chka od-na.

(PRACH)

(b) Ya si-de-la li-bo den, li-bo dva,

Pod o-ko-shech-kom si-ro-toch-ka od-na.

(RIMSKY-KORSAKOV)

(c) Ya si-de-la li-bo den, li-bo dva, Pod o-ko-shechkom si-ro-tochka odna.

Pod o-koshech kom si-ro-toch-ka od-na, posmo-tri-tko ty, moy mi-ly na menya!

Like Trutovsky the best arrangements, with a few isolated exceptions, are those of town songs.

COLLECTION OF GERSTENBERG AND DITMAR

The third volume of folk-songs to appear at the end of the eighteenth century was that of I. D. Gerstenberg and F. A. Ditmar—*Pesennik, ili polnoe sobranie starykh i novykh rossiyskikh i prostykh pesen dlya fortepiano, sobrannye izdatelyami* (Song-book, or a Complete Collection of Old and New Russian and Simple Songs for Pianoforte, Compiled by the Publishers), (11) which was issued in three parts between the years 1797–8. In all there were 140 melodies which were set out in piano arrangement, the first verse of each text being written between the staves. The majority of the songs were of town origin, but there were also peasant tunes (e.g. 'A my proso seyali'), and Ukrainian melodies. Sometimes the arrangements were reminiscent of *kants* in their three-part harmonizations, but on other occasions they were more elaborate. The collection was uneven in quality. Most of the melodies were taken from manuscript sources and no attempt was made to relegate them to separate genres.

COLLECTION OF KIRSHA DANILOV

The most curious volume of folk-songs relating to the eighteenth century is that of Kirsha Danilov (*Drevnie rossiyskie stikhotvoreniya* —Ancient Russian Verses), (12) which was written by an unknown author in Western Siberia about the middle of the eighteenth century. (13) Danilov's collection is important as the first record of *byliny* and historical songs, and contains about seventy texts with melodies of epic songs and ballads together with a number of humorous and satirical songs. It was first published (without music) in 1804, but a fuller edition (with music) appeared in 1818. A peculiarity is that the collection, unlike all other folk collections of the eighteenth century, was probably designed not for amateur music-making, but for the erudite reader interested in folk poetry. The melodies are without accompaniment and are set in too high a register for the voice, possibly being intended for some folk instrument. In several cases, as is typical of the Northern tradition, there is only one melody to several texts.

RISE OF RUSSIAN OPERA

Opera first appeared in Russia in the 30's of the eighteenth century. From 1731 onwards St. Petersburg and Moscow were visited by a constant stream of Italian opera companies performing *intermezzi*. In 1736, as already mentioned above, a full scale Italian opera *La forza dell'amore e dell'odio* (The Power of Love and Hate), with music by Francesco Araja, was given at St. Petersburg with great success and this was only one of many operas of a similar nature, in which characteristic were the virtuosity of the vocal parts, the abundance of stage effects and the elaborateness of the productions. These operas were all sung in Italian and it was not till 1755 that an opera was given in the Russian language and performed by young Russian artists. This was *Cephalus and Procris*, with words by Sumarokov. However, since the music was again written by Araja, it differed in no way from Italian opera and made little or no use of national elements. In the subsequent years Russia was visited by a whole host of foreign composers, among them Galuppi, Traetta, Cimarosa, Sarti, Manfredini, and Paisiello, who produced not only *opera seria* but (as in the case of Cimarosa and Paisiello) *opera buffa*. Although the operas were given primarily at Court, they were later staged with Russian translations at the public theatres, Locatelli's Theatre opening in Moscow in the 1750's (followed soon after by Maddox's Theatre), and Knipper's 'Free' Theatre in St. Petersburg. The 1750's to 1760's also saw productions of French *opéras comiques*. Such performances were undoubtedly of value in acquainting the future composers of Russian national opera with the basic elements of operatic composition.

Russian opera in the strictest sense of the word arose in the last third of the eighteenth century and from its first appearance showed links with Russian folk lore and folk music. About 100 operas were written in the course of the last years of the eighteenth century, but of these the music of 30 or so operas (surviving mostly in the form of manuscript scores and orchestral parts) (14) have come down to us, of which 15 make use of Russian or Ukrainian folk music. (15) These operas employed a total of about 55 identifiable folk-songs. (16) Although several of the composers of Russian opera in the eighteenth century were foreigners, they too made use of folk material in order to give their music national colouring. At first folk-song was employed literally in the form of simple quotations, but by the end of the century composers were able to write freely in the folk idiom and imbue their characters with national features. Character- ization of folk figures is especially prominent in the first three Russian operas of importance to come down to us, all of which were written in 1779; *Melnik-koldun, obmanshchik i svat* (The Miller-magician, Deceiver and Matchmaker) by Sokolovsky, *Sanktpeterburgskiy gostinny dvor* (The St. Petersburg Bazaar) by Matinsky, and *Neschastye ot karety* (The Misfortunes of Having a Carriage) by Pashkevich.

The underlying principle of all Russian opera of the eigh- teenth century is simplicity, the reason for which being that the operas were for the most part performed by amateur actors and vocalists, who were incapable of undertaking anything of a complex nature. As opposed to the brilliant vocal pyrotechnics of the Italian opera, coloratura is almost entirely absent, the only exceptions being in Matthias Stabhinger's operas *Baba Yaga* and *Schastlivaya Tonya*. The chief vocal form is the aria, though ensembles and choruses are also employed, a favourite device being the introduction of the chorus to form an opera's closing number. The orchestral writing is likewise of the simplest construction and is scored for conventional forces. An essenti- ally Russian feature, however, is the occasional employment of *pizzicato* strings to suggest the sound of *balalaikas*, a good illus- tration being that of the Miller's aria 'Uzh kak shli starik so starukhoy' in *The Miller-magician*. The principal themes of the libretti, which, with the exception of Matinsky's, were written by established *littérateurs* such as Fonvizin, Novikov, Krylov, Radishchev, Nikolev and Knyazhnin, may be divided very roughly into five categories;

    (i) A play with music to stipulated folk tunes (e.g. *Rozana i Lyubim*)

    (ii) Grotesque buffonade (e.g. *Neschastye ot karety*)

  (iii) Folk vaudeville (e.g. *Melnik-koldun*)

  (iv) Satirical comedy (e.g. *Skupoy*)

   (v) Fantastic opera (e.g. *Ivan Tsarevich*).

Very often such operas (all of which consisted of musical items interpolated with spoken dialogue) were concerned with some kind of satire, a typical example being that of Gallomania (i.e. an exaggerated enthusiasm for all things French) in *The Misfortunes of Having a Carriage*, or the exposure of the rapacity of merchants in *The St. Petersburg Bazaar*.

FIRST RUSSIAN OPERAS: ANYUTA (1772)

The first Russian opera by a native composer appeared in the year 1772. This was *Anyuta* with libretto by M. Popov, (17) which was first performed by the Court Singers at Tsarskoe selo on 26 August 1772. (18) The music is lost. The plot of *Anyuta* is as follows:

The scene opens in a field in a village, surrounded by forest. Miron is cutting wood and bewailing the hard life of the peasant. He and his wife have one helper, Anyuta, their adopted daughter, who was brought to them mysteriously by a servant long before. Anyuta believes herself to be their real child. Miron's labourer, Filat, wishes to marry Anyuta, and Miron is quite agreeable to this, since it means that Filat will remain in the family. Anyuta, however, loves Victor, a nobleman and spurns Filat, vowing that she will remain faithful to her beloved. A tense scene ensues between Victor and Filat in which words are exchanged. Anyuta fears the anger of her supposed father. However, Victor proposes a solution: he is willing to give Miron a large sum of money in order to hire labourers, if he will release Anyuta. Miron is annoyed by Anyuta's stubbornness and threatens to beat her. But at the last moment Victor reveals that Anyuta is really the daughter of Colonel Tsvetkov, who had been forced to leave home by his enemies, and now wishes to have his daughter restored. By way of gratitude he presents Miron with a purse. All are satisfied and the opera concludes with the motto, that the happiest man is the one contented with his lot.

Anyuta is not a critical caricature of the times in the manner of Radishchev, (19) for both the good and bad qualities of the protagonists are highlighted. Serfdom, as such, is not the main contention and the peasants speak a coarse perverted dialect. From a study of the libretto it appears that a number of the vocal items in *Anyuta* begin with quotations from folk-song, which suggests that the opera probably employed folk music, but the majority of the musical numbers, judging from the verse metres and structure of the ensembles were composed without reference to existing melodies. Of the several candidates suggested as the composer of the opera, Pashkevich is the most likely. (20)

LYUBOVNIK KOLDUN (1777)

The libretto of *Lyubovnik koldun* (The Lover Magician) was also based on a subject which enjoyed great popularity in the eighteenth century—the theme of feigned magic. As in most plots of this nature cunning enables the pair of young lovers to unite. The scene of *The Lover Magician* is laid in the domain of a small noble landowner, and although folk melodies are employed, they in no way reveal the character of the persons with whom they are associated. It has been established by Mooser that the librettist was N. P. Nikolev (1758–1815) and that the music (unfortunately lost) was by M. F. Kerzelli. Its première took place in Moscow about 1777. (21) With regard to the music of *Lyubovnik koldun* one can form a clearer impression than in *Anyuta*, thanks to the fact that the greater part of the songs (14 out of a total of 24) are specifically marked '*golosa*'—in other words are set to established folk tunes or popular melodies. The other vocal numbers, which are not allotted definite folk tunes, could easily be fitted to similar folk melodies according to their structure.

ZORIN'S PEREROZHDENIE (1777)

The first Russian opera to be preserved in its entirety is Zorin's *Pererozhdenie* (The Rebirth), (22) which was given its first performance on 8 January 1777 in Moscow. (23) The libretto appeared in 1779 and was later published in a volume of *Rossiyskiy teatr* (The Russian Theatre) (24) and has been attributed by some authorities, with, however, possibly insufficient justification, to Matinsky. There is evidence that the libretto was a translation, but in any case its artistic value is negligible. As a composer Zorin was not without powers of invention but was handicapped by poor technique. The overture to *The Rebirth* is of an extremely simple structure and is written in miniature sonata form. Between the exposition and the development are inserted eleven bars marked *Andante* in 6/8—a perfect example of the eighteenth century Italian operatic 'symphony' overture, of which Mozart's overture to *Die Entführung* is a good illustration. The remainder of the work is of interest in that it is the first example of a Russian opera with surviving music to be based partly on folk melodies. The first folk-song occurs in Act I No. 3 (chorus) and is based on the well-known folk tune 'Vo lesochke komarochkov' (25) (Mus. Ex. 3):[1]

Mus. Ex. 3

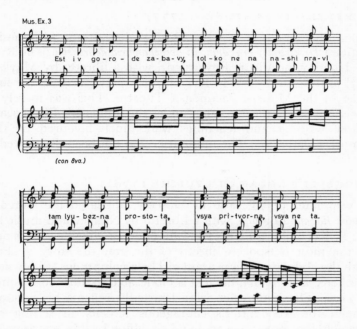

In comparison with the song as it later appears in Prach, apart from the difference in key (two flats instead of one sharp), the melody is almost identical. The arrangement is typical of the methods employed by the early compilers of folk-song collections. On the other two occasions that he introduces folk melodies the composer succeeds either in continuing the music in a similar style or in devising simple variations. Zorin is not a good composer, however, and like most of the early arrangers of

---

[1] There is a misprint in bar 4 of Rabinovich's version of Mus. Ex. 3 (RODG, p. 44), which the author has corrected from the 1779 score preserved in TSMB.

H

folk-song had difficulty in fitting words to existing tunes. This perhaps explains the fact that although a folk tune is sometimes stipulated in the libretto, he uses an entirely different melody. A curiosity of the orchestration is that No. 11 (a chorus) is accompanied by a 'band' (*secondo orchestro sul teatro*) consisting of 2 flutes, 2 clarinets, 2 horns, and a bassoon. No. 10 makes use of accompanied recitative.

DEREVENSKIY PRAZDNIK (1777)

About the same year (1777) (26) a 'pastoral drama with music' entitled *Derevenskiy prazdnik, ili uvenchannaya dobrodetel* (The Rustic Holiday, or Virtue Rewarded), with a libretto by Maykov (27) and music by M. F. Kerzelli, was performed for the first time in the Moscow Znamenka Theatre. This was merely a pseudo-pastoral piece written under the influence of Rousseau, whose writings and teachings were much favoured by the Empress Catherine. The music itself has not been discovered.

KERZELLI'S ROZANA I LYUBIM (1778)

A year later (1778), also in Moscow, appeared the four act opera *Rozana i Lyubim*, with a libretto by Nikolev and music by M. F. Kerzelli. (28) This youthful effort of Nikolev (29) is one of the most outspoken libretti of the era, the story dealing with the abduction of a peasant girl by a voluptuous landowner. But here, as in *Anyuta*, the text is moderated to show both points of view. The landowner wholeheartedly repents his actions; Semën the woodcutter's courageous ferocity in setting off through the forest, axe in hand, is offset by his boorishness, drunkenness and venality. The libretto also demands attention on account of the abundance of directions given by the librettist to the composer. (30) Unfortunately Kerzelli was unequal to the task confronting him and made not the slightest attempt to realize Nikolev's precise instructions. Although the opera is specifically termed 'a drama with folk tunes', the folk element plays a very insignificant role and the greater part of the music falls into the realms of the conventional harmonies and figurations of the period. That Nikolev intended his work to have national colouring cannot be doubted.

OTHER LIBRETTI BY NIKOLEV

Nikolev was responsible for a further four libretti during the years 1778–84. These were *Prikashchik* (The Clerk), with music by Darcis (31); *Finiks* (The Phoenix); *Tochilshchik* (The Knife-grinder); and *Opekun-professor ili lyubov khitree krasnorechiya* (The Guardian-professor, or Love is More Cunning than Eloquence). The composers of the last three are unknown. These productions were capably written (from the literary point of view, at least) and would have lent themselves well to musical composition. Unfortunately, none of the music has survived.

According to Rabinovich, the scene of *The Phoenix* is set in Turkey. The action takes place in the Sultan's garden and is fitted 'with all the embellishments corresponding to the Asiatic taste'. There are many curious musical directions in the opera. There is a 'recitative', a 'voice blending into the chorus' [*sic*], Turks on the tower 'playing musical trumpets'. In one duet a eunuch counts his money, constantly stammering and making mistakes, in a manner that anticipates Varlaam in the inn scene in *Boris Godunov*. The composer was possibly one of the Kerzellis.

The opera *The Knife-grinder* closely resembles Philidor's *Le Bûcheron* (1763) (based on Pérrault's story *Les trois souhaits*), and is chiefly remarkable for its mixture of fantasy and reality. There are some interesting onomatopoeic interjections, as, for example, the refrain 'Ru, ru, ru chiki, chiki' in the Knife-grinder's song, the lament 'Hi, hi, hi' &c. (32)

Of the seven operas performed in the years 1772–8 *Lyubovnik-koldun* and *Rozana i Lyubim* were especially popular.

IMPORTANCE OF THE YEAR 1779

The most important year in early Russian opera is that of 1779, since it saw the appearance of three operas of some quality— *The Miller-magician*, *The St. Petersburg Bazaar* of Mikhail Matinsky, and *The Misfortunes of Having a Carriage* by V. A. Pashkevich, all of which make use of folk music.

THE MILLER-MAGICIAN (1779)

The Miller-magician enjoys the distinction of being the first Russian opera to achieve really prolonged success (33) and was performed for the first time at the Moscow Znamenka Theatre on 20 January 1779. (34) The text of the opera was written by Alexander Ablesimov, (35) a gifted playwright whose work in the Russian theatre has been compared with that of Favart. (36) Ablesimov himself determined to a large extent the musical form of *The Miller* by stipulating the employment of a number of well-known folk-songs, which were sung to his words. The subject of the opera is very simple (37) and obviously owes something to Rousseau's *Le Devin du Village*. (38)

The Miller-magician consists of three short acts and, like all Russian operas up to the time of Glinka, employs spoken dialogue (written in this case in verse). Quantitatively this predominates over the musical items. The music was arranged in the first instance (in accordance with Ablesimov's directions) by Sokolovsky, a violinist of the Moscow Russian Theatre, but has come down to us only in a version by Fomin. The action includes a *devichnik* scene, (39) which gives opportunity for the employment of authentic folk material. This connection with peasant ritual and ancient customs is a common feature of early Russian operas and is often employed to underline their national character. The precise part played by Fomin in the writing or re-writing of the opera is far from clear. (40) However, it seems fairly certain that his principal contribution lay in improvements to the orchestration and in the composition of the ensembles. (41)

The Miller-magician is of prime interest in that the greater part of the music is based on folk-songs, most of which appear in the collections of Prach, Trutovsky and Gerstenberg. The numbers not making use of authentic folk-songs are written either in imitation of town song or in the general light-hearted musical style typical of the eighteenth century. Generally speaking, a folk-song rarely appears in a developed form. Usually the folk melody is used literally in the first part of an aria, being then followed by a second section, sometimes in a quicker tempo, which is related to the first half by the use of identical musical figures. In other words the composer continues the folk melody in a similar style. A good illustration is Anyuta's song 'Kaby ya mlada, uverena byla' (Mus. Ex. 4):

Mus. Ex. 4

*Accompaniment omitted.

Here the first part of the aria (the *Andante*) is almost identical with the folk-song 'Kak u nashevo shirokovo dvora' as it later appears in Trutovsky (No. 28), though being preceded by a short introduction of six bars. The *Allegretto* section, however, is clearly written by the composer in imitation of town dance songs. The whole of the *Andante* section is a typical example of a 'pro-tracted' song, as sung in the town, in which characteristic are the clearly expressed harmonic basis, the presence of sharps and flats (e.g. the F♯ in bar 3) and the system of contrasting tonalities (e.g. the modulations from tonic to relative major and the return to the tonic) which is foreign to authentic peasant song. On other occasions the composer has had difficulty in making a modal folk-song fit an orthodox harmonization, or sometimes has been obliged to amend a folk-song's uneven structure. However, some of the songs show surprising freedom in this respect, the first song of the Miller, for instance, dividing up into two 5-bar phrases, while the Miller's second song is divisible into 3 + 4 bars. (42)

The Miller-magician, like several other Russian operas of the eighteenth century, also includes a *devichnik* scene which occurs at the beginning of Act III, and consists of three wedding songs arranged for two-part female chorus. (43) Whether the melodies are genuine folk-songs it is impossible to tell, but it is likely that they are representative of peasant wedding songs as they were sung at the time. Of particular interest is the first chorus, which contains several typical folk features, outstanding being the breaking into unison at the cadence, a practice common in folk polyphony. Characteristic also of folk polyphony is the abundance of parallel thirds (Mus. Ex. 5):

Mus. Ex.5
Andante   Allegretto

Chto bez bu - ri, bez vi-kho - rya vo - ro - ta ot-pi-ra - li - sya, v te - rem

dve - ri, v te - rem dve - ri ot vor - rya - li — sya.

Notable in the opera are the use of songs written in the town idiom in the form of 'Russian song', while the composer has endeavoured occasionally to imitate the sound of *balalaikas*. (44)

Aloof from the rest of the work stands the overture, which for a long period was attributed to Fomin. However, thanks to the discovery recently by B. Volman of a 'Russian symphony on Ukrainian songs' contained in the October number (1790) of a *Journal de musique, dédié aux dames*, it seems probable that the real composer was Baron Vančura. (45) (46) The overture was added to the opera at a later date. The principal difference between the overture and the symphony as it appears in the *Journal de musique* lies in the change of key (from C major to D major) and in a number of slight improvements to the part writing and accompaniment figures of the original symphony. The overture is unique among Russian music of the period in that it is based upon two folk-songs, the first of which 'Molodka molodaya' is heard in the slow introduction. The most striking feature of the theme is its unison opening and its breaking into harmony in bars 3–4 in a manner suggestive of folk polyphony. The use of a folk-song in this way is highly original. (47) The second subject is based on a Ukrainian folk-song 'Oy, gai, gai, zelënenkiy'. In the recapitulation the second subject precedes the first. The overture also makes use of *pizzicato* strings to suggest the sound of *balalaikas*.

MATINSKY'S ST. PETERSBURG BAZAAR (1779)

The first version of the opera *Sanktpeterburgskiy gostinny dvor* (The St. Petersburg Bazaar) received its première in the capital on 26 December 1779 at Knipper's 'Free' Theatre. (48) Twelve years later the opera reappeared in a second version entitled *Kak pozhivësh, tak i proslyvësh* (As You Live, So Are You Judged) and was performed at Court on 2 February 1792. The music and libretto were written in probably both cases by the serf composer Mikhail Matinsky. (49) Of the two versions only the music of the second has come down to us. The principal difference between the two editions is that a number of scenes and songs have been interchanged in the first and third acts. The texts of the songs and ensembles are identical.

The St. Petersburg Bazaar is outstanding from both the literary and musical points of view, since it presents a vivid picture of

contemporary life, in which are used not only the everyday
language of the merchants and street-sellers but also their
musical cries. (50) The weakest aspect of the opera is the plot,
which is far too slender to support a musical entertainment
in three acts. (51) Considerable doubt exists as to the nature of
the music of the original version of the opera, and this also
applies to some extent to the score of 1792. According to the
Dramaticheskiy slovar (52) Matinsky wrote the music to his own
libretto, but as there is no reference to his work as a composer,
one is compelled to suspect that he was possibly not the composer in the generally accepted sense of the word but (like Sokolovsky in *The Miller-magician*) the arranger of folk-songs to fresh
texts. The use of folk-songs in the 1779 version is corroborated
by their presence in the later edition. However, not all the
numbers in the opera are based on folk material. This is particularly true of the ensembles, where the texts are of a complicated nature and would be unsuitable for folk melodies. There
is evidence to suggest that the music to the ensembles was composed not by Matinsky but by Pashkevich, who, in the course
of thirty years as a Court musician, often wrote music for a
variety of occasions. (53)

The St. Petersburg Bazaar is remarkable for the abundance of
folk material, the first example of which appears in the overture.
As the Soviet musicologist, A. S. Rabinovich, observes, the
overture betrays the presence of an experienced hand and was
probably written by Pashkevich. The first subject of the overture, though not based on any folk melody found in any of the
principal folk collections, is written in the folk idiom (see Mus.
Ex. 6), while the second subject is the folk-song 'Vo Donskikh
vo lesakh' (Prach No. 90):

Mus. Ex. 6

At the conclusion of the overture both melodies are combined
ingeniously. Treatment of folk melodies in this manner is unique
for the period. Folk melodies are also used extensively in the

remainder of the work, though on some occasions the composer has altered the melody of the folk tune, changed time values, lengthened certain notes, &c., as well as introduced fresh material.

Of particular interest in *The St. Petersburg Bazaar* are the seven wedding choruses, which are heard at the opening of Act II. The choruses, all of which appear to be based on original folk melodies, are peculiar in that not one of the tunes appears in any of the contemporary collections. The seven folk-songs, which are arranged for female voices, are for the most part in two-part harmony, though occasionally Matinsky has added a third part. (54) Some of the arrangements are reminiscent of the three-part traditions of the *kant*. Mus. Ex. 7 is an excellent example of a true peasant melody, especially with the characteristic B♭ in bar 6. However, the F♯ in bar 8 instantly marks the influence of town music (Mus. Ex. 7):

Mus. Ex.7

Le - tal go - lub vor - ko - val,   ko te - re - mu pri - pa - dal - *etc.*

PASHKEVICH'S THE MISFORTUNES OF HAVING A CARRIAGE

The third opera to appear in the year 1779 was *Neschastye ot karety* (The Misfortunes of Having a Carriage), which was performed for the first time in the Hermitage on 7 November 1779. The libretto was by Knyazhnin (55) and the music by Pashkevich. (56) As opposed to the opera *Anyuta* the peasants speak with a literary tongue. Folk music plays little part in the opera, its one and only appearance being in the overture, which is written in sonata form.

RAUPACH'S THE GOOD SOLDIERS (1779?)

Yet another opera to appear possibly in the same year was *Dobrye soldaty* (The Good Soldiers), with libretto by Kheraskov (57) and music by Hermann Raupach. Though the exact date of composition is not known, the première took place in Moscow on 26 February 1779. Its Petersburg première occurred on 17 February at Knipper's Theatre the next year. (58) The folk element plays a minor role in the opera, the only instances appearing in Burmin's aria in the form of a fragment from 'Kamarinskaya' and in the soldier's choruses (No. 26). A peculiarity of the latter is that, despite the fact that the performers are all soldiers, the music is written for mixed voices. (59)

FREULICH'S THE NEW HOUSEHOLD (1781)

The year 1781 saw the appearance of the opera *Novoe semeystvo* (The New Household) with libretto by Vyazmitinov and music by Freulich. However, the score is of little interest apart from an isolated instance of folk music and an unusually high soprano part, the opera obviously having been written with some particular singer in mind.

PASHKEVICH'S SKUPOY (1782) [1783?]

Pashkevich was responsible for the opera *Skupoy* (The Miser), written to a libretto by Knyazhnin and almost certainly modelled on Molière's *L'Avare*. The opera is notable for the monologue of Skryagin, which is set in *recitativo accompagnato*. In its faithful reflection of natural speech inflections it may be said to look forward to the works of Dargomyzhsky and Musorgsky, with whom it offers certain parallels.

BULLANDT'S SBITENSHCHIK (1784)

On a much higher level than the three preceding works stands *Sbitenshchik* (The *Sbiten*-seller)[1], an opera by Bullandt in four acts with a libretto by Knyazhnin. Several sources attest to the popularity of this production, which enables it to be compared with *The Miller-magician*. (60) A sequel to *Sbitenshchik* was written in 1793 with music by M. Kerzelli and libretto by Levshin. This was *Svadba Voldyreva* (The Marriage of Voldyrev). A. Bullandt was a Czech composer, who arrived in Russia in 1780, and was renowned as a bassoonist. He died in 1821. Findeisen and Rabinovich both confuse him with Jean Bullandt (see MOOS, II, pp. 368–70). Three copies are preserved of the score of *Sbitenshchik*, of which the oldest (apparently the autograph with the text written in Latin letters—a practice followed also by Sarti) is dated 1784. When he wrote the opera, Bullandt was still unacquainted with Russian grammar but had

[1] *Sbiten*—a hot Russian drink of water, spices and honey.

succeeded in grasping the elements of conversational speech (which was more than Araja did in twenty years!). The opera is well written, and capably orchestrated. However, the most interesting factor is that one comic aria is based on the cries of the *sbiten*-seller, a Slavonic counterpart, perhaps, of some of the programme *chansons* of Jannequin or Deering's *London Cries* (1599). This is yet another illustration of the manner in which Russian composers (or foreign composers resident in Russia) drew inspiration from their environment and sought to give realistic touches to their work by the employment of authentic melodies.

PASHKEVICH'S FEVEY (1786)

The third opera to come down to us by Pashkevich is *Fevey*, which was performed in 1786 with a libretto by Catherine II. (61) (62) The text was taken from a fairy story of the same name. *Fevey* is unusual in that there is more music than speech, the musical numbers comprising arias, ensembles, choruses and ballets. From the technical point of view it represents a considerable advance on previous Russian operas, besides incorporating folk music. Outstanding in this respect is Ledmer's song in Act II (No. 15) in which the melody (which shows similarity to the folk-song 'Akh ty dushechka'—Prach No. 16) is repeated incessantly against an ever-changing background; this is clearly an anticipation of the technique that Glinka was to develop more fully half a century later. A special place is occupied in Act IV by the so-called 'Kalmyk Chorus', in which Pashkevich has made a deliberate attempt to suggest something Eastern and exotic. (63)

STABHINGER'S SCHASTLIVAYA TONYA AND BABA YAGA (1786)

1786 saw the appearance of two operas by the Moscow kapellmeister Mathias Stabhinger—*Schastlivaya Tonya* (Lucky Tonya) and *Baba Yaga*, both with libretti by D. Gorchakov. *Baba Yaga* is a faultlessly written, if somewhat unimaginative, production and makes some use of folk music. Baba Yaga herself (a character from folklore) does not appear till late in the work, her part, which has no national colouring, being remarkable only in that it is entrusted to a baritone. (64) There is some attempt made at coloratura writing.

VANČURA'S AKHRIDEICH (IVAN TSAREVICH) (1787)

Another opera with libretto by Catherine II came into being in 1787. This was *Khrabryi i smelyi vityaz Akhrideich* (The Brave and Bold Knight Akhrideich), or, as it was later called, *Ivan Tsarevich*. The music was by Baron Vančura. The text is successful from both the literary and dramatic points of view and incorporates a number of folk characters and folk customs. (65) The composer likewise draws on several folk-songs for his inspiration (including the famous 'Vo pole berëza stoyala' employed by Tchaikovsky in his Fourth Symphony), and although his handling of them is somewhat uneven, he also succeeds in creating music in the folk idiom. In comparison with the arrangements of folk-songs published in contemporary collections, his accompaniments are characterized by enterprise and imagination.

MARTIN Y SOLER'S GORE-BOGATYR (1789)
AND PESNOLYUBIE (1790)

Another of Catherine's libretti was cast in the form of a massive allegorical pamphlet directed against the Swedish King Gustav III. This was *Gore-bogatyr Kosometovich* (Kosometovich, the Woeful Knight) (1789), the music of which was entrusted to the Spanish composer Martín y Soler (1754–1806) immediately on his arrival in Russia. Martín is best known as the composer of *Una cosa rara*, which had been produced at Vienna in 1785 with great success. Not knowing the Russian language, he was at a great disadvantage and his music, therefore, has little or no connection with the sense of the text. Martín, however, does employ three folk-songs in the overture and their choice gives a good insight into the method of approach of foreign composers incorporating folk melodies in their music. The folk tunes themselves (which appear later in Prach) are all similar in style and may be regarded as rather pallid specimens of Russian town dance songs. In selecting the melodies the composer made no attempt to achieve contrast, and his principal desire was to find themes which were well-proportioned, straightforward, or without unusual tempi or rhythms. When a melody failed to answer his requirements, he amended it accordingly. No effort is made to develop the music and the folk element is employed only in the overture.

Mention may also be made of Martín's opera *Pesnolyubie* (Love of Singing), written to a libretto by Khrapovitsky. This, too, makes some use of the folk idiom.

FEDUL AND THE CHILDREN (1791)

The year 1791 witnessed the appearance of another Imperial libretto. This was *Fedul s detmi* (Fedul and the Children), which purported to be representative of peasant life (for example, out of ten numbers in *Fedul* five begin with the repeated interjection 'Ekh! Ekh!'). Catherine endeavoured to give realism to her work by basing it on peasant characters and by employing rustic expressions. Though doubtless conceived in sincerity, some of these phrases have an amusing ring and the opera is not a true portrayal of peasant life. (66) The task of composing the music to *Fedul* was allotted to Martín and Pashkevich, both of whom employed folk music, none of which is in any way remarkable.

THE COLLECTIVE OLEG (1790)

Yet another opera by the indefatiguable Catherine enjoyed the elaborate title *Nachalnoe upravlenie Olega, podrazhenie Shakspiri bez sokhraneniya featralnykh pravil* (The First Government of Oleg, in Imitation of Shakespeare, Without Adherance to the Usual Theatrical Laws), i.e. without the observation of the unities of time, place and action. In essence *Oleg* is not an opera but a dramatic play with musical episodes, or, to be more precise, not even a drama but a political chronicle—an '*istoricheskoe predstavlenie*' or 'historical performance' as it is called in the preface. (67) The music was composed by Sarti, Canobbio (68) and Pashkevich in 1790 and makes use of folk elements. Notable is the difference in approach between Canobbio, a foreigner unfamiliar with Russian music, and Pashkevich—the former taking his material from contemporary collections (though, it must be admitted, on occasions showing signs of considerable originality in their treatment), the latter drawing folk music in the form of wedding choruses from its original source. However, although Pashkevich has attempted to write music in the folk idiom, his skill is still insufficient to do this in a convincing manner and the difference between the genuine folk material

and that of his own composition is clearly marked. Sarti's (69)
contribution to *Oleg* is of interest in that he attempted to underline the classical nature of the verse (taken from Pindar's *Odes*
and Euripides' *Alcestis*, which drama is performed in the Byzantine hippodrome in the course of the action) by writing his
music in the ancient modes, (70) although the final effect is no
different from music written in the usual major and minor keys.
In one scene Sarti imitates the lyre by means of harp and
pizzicato strings. Sarti's contribution to *Oleg* is also notable in
that the March in the Third Act (scored for 4 trumpets, 2
trombones, 2 serpents and triangle) is almost the sole surviving
march for wind instruments in Russian music of the eighteenth
century to come down to us in score.

OTHER OPERAS OF THE EIGHTEENTH CENTURY

Several other libretti made their appearance during the 1780's,
some of which made use of the *devichnik* rituals and wedding
ceremonies. These included I. Yukin's *Koldun, vorozheya i svatka*
(Magician, Fortune-teller and Matchmaker), and *Nevesta pod
fatoyu ili meshchanskaya svadba* (The Bride under the Veil or the
Bourgeois Wedding) by an unknown author. The music of these
pieces has not been preserved.

Mention should also be made of a group of operas with libretti
by Levshin, (71) which appeared, as far as one can tell from
the dates of the libretti, about 1793–4. The music of these productions, with the exception of the orchestral parts of *Svadba
Voldyreva*—the sequel to *Sbitenshchik*—has not been preserved.
Most interesting among Levshin's libretti is, perhaps, *Mnimye
vdovtsy* (The Mock Widowers), which is illustrative of both the
manner in which the literary and musical writers drew their
inspiration from foreign sources and transformed them into
something essentially Russian. In this opera there is one delightful scene, where, among other things, a talentless composer
struggles vainly to find 'a new harmony'. There is evidence to
suggest, however, that *The Mock Widowers* was not an original
production but a translation from the German, although the
original has not been discovered. If this were the case, the translation was a very free one. There is also an element of satire
and use of local colour in the form of street songs, peasant songs,
Polish melodies, *sbiten*-sellers, dairy maids, &c. (72)

THE OPERAS OF FOMIN (1761–1800)

The most important and most gifted Russian operatic composer at the end of the eighteenth century is Evstigney Ipatevich Fomin (1761–1800), in whose compositions are summed up the leading tendencies of the period. (73) Of significance in his work is the fact that he was able to create music freely and convincingly in the folk idiom. Like several other Russian musicians of his time Fomin was sent to Italy to consolidate his studies and immediately on his return to St. Petersburg began work on a small ballet-opera *Novgorodskiy bogatyr Boeslavovich* (Boeslavich, the Novgorod Hero), composed to a text of Catherine II. The libretto, which describes the adventures of the Knight Vasiliy Boeslavich, was based on authentic *bylina* material and was subtitled 'an opera compiled from fairy tales, Russian songs and other sources'. Examination of the surviving orchestral parts reveals that among the ballet numbers in Acts I, II, IV, and V, Fomin has employed several folk tunes in which notable is his skill in continuing the music in a similar style. (74)

Of Fomin's operas *Yamshchiki na podstave* (The Postdrivers) (1787), *Amerikantsy* (The Americans) (1788) and *Zolotoe yabloko* (The Golden Apple), *The Post-drivers* is the most outstanding and the only one to employ folk music.[1] The libretto was written by Lvov, the collaborator and patron of Prach. Notwithstanding the poorness of the plot (75) the opera's merits lie in the depiction of the coachmen, their customs, dialect, speech and, most of all, their songs. (76) Of the authentic folk melodies employed, all of which later appear in Trutovsky or Prach, outstanding is the treatment of the folk-song 'Vysoko sokol letaet', since it is the first serious attempt to reproduce the characteristic features of Russian folk polyphony by means of deliberately employed parallel fifths, octaves, open intervals, and long sustained notes (Mus. Ex. 8).

Though this bears only a slight resemblance to true folk choral polyphony, it is nevertheless of historical importance as a precursor of a practice that was later frequently employed in Russian opera, (77) though not fully understood till nearly a century afterwards. *The Post-drivers* is also notable for Fomin's

---

[1] The première of *The Americans* occurred on 8 February 1800, that of *The Golden Apple* on 15 April 1803, both in St. Petersburg.

Mus. Ex. 8 (Words and accompaniment omitted)

sympathetic and intelligent treatment of Russian protracted song.

Fomin's best work, however, is his 2-Act melodrama *Orfey i Evredika* (Orpheus and Euridice) (1791–2), which was based on a text by Knyazhnin. Apart from the adventurousness of the harmonic and melodic language, *Orpheus* abounds in musical innovations. There is a mysterious voice, which occurs three

PLATE 5

A RUSSIAN HORN BAND
from a contemporary engraving

PLATE 6

THE HERMITAGE THEATRE, ST. PETERSBURG

from a contemporary lithograph

times during the action, accompanying an Olympian pronouncement and which is performed by a chorus of bass voices behind the scenes; to represent Orpheus playing the lyre Fomin uses *pizzicato* strings and even anticipates the use of *Leitmotiv* by depicting Orpheus's absence by an expressive clarinet solo; lastly, especially effective is the employment of two groups of brass instruments (probably played by an ensemble of Russian horns) to augment the unseen bass voice chorus and to accompany the Dance of the Furies. Such an orchestral combination at the period must have sounded extremely imposing. (78)

OPERAS OF BORTNYANSKY

A unique part in Russian music of the eighteenth century is played by Dmitriy Bortnyansky, to whom reference has already been made in the previous chapter. After studying in St. Petersburg with Galuppi, Bortnyansky was sent to Venice, where he wrote three operas—*Creonte, Alcide* and *Quinto Fabio*. On his return he received an Imperial commission to write other operas, among them *Le Faucon* (1786) and *Le Fils Rival* (1787), (79) the libretti of which were by F.-H. Lafermière. Though impeccably written, elegant, and graceful, Bortnyansky's music is completely lacking in any national colouring and is the perfect musical counterpart of the sculptures of Canova, the structures of Rastrelli and Cameron and the prose of Karamzin. Significantly enough, both operas are written to French libretti. (80)

SUMMARY

The eighteenth century, therefore, was a decisive period in Russian music. Not only did the first folk-song collections come into being but Russian opera—an opera at first imitative of the West, but often unique in its employment of the folk idiom.

I

CHAPTER 5

Russian Music in the Early Nineteenth Century

HISTORICAL AND SOCIAL BACKGROUND

The reign of Paul I, following the death of Empress Catherine II, was marked by a period of reaction, in the course of which the Tsar introduced far-reaching reforms, intended to curb the moral laxity of the Russian (and particularly the Petersburg) population. Although, as Mooser informs us, musical and theatrical life was far from moribund, Paul's legislatory measures inevitably brought about a slowing-down of musical life. The number of private orchestras was reduced, all dramatic and operatic productions were subjected to censorship both before and during production, and restrictions were imposed on travel, publication and import of materials from abroad. In 1801 Paul was assassinated. The opening of Alexander's reign augured well for the future. His liberality had an invigorating effect on Russian literature (and consequently music) and the years 1801–12 were marked by an increase in the publication of books. Whereas the eighteenth century writers (unlike the composers) were mostly of noble birth (Lomonosov is an exception), the early nineteenth century writers sprung increasingly less from the aristocracy, the civil service or the army.

During the early years of the nineteenth century Russian music began to develop at a faster rate and to acquire a marked national colouring. The French Revolution, the Napoleonic Wars and the influence of Western Romanticism all left their imprint on Russian life and young Russians who had visited the West and come into contact with Western ideas returned to their native land with high ideals and the desire for reform. In Russian literature and music elements of sentimentalism and Romanticism began to make an appearance. The writer

Zhukovsky, for instance, author of numerous vaudevilles and operatic libretti, was particularly fascinated by German Romantic poetry, while the novels of Scott, the poetry of Byron and the Greek and Roman classics were widely read. Among the numerous writers to leave their imprint on the thought and literature of the period may be mentioned such diverse figures as Karamzin (1766–1826), Krylov (1769–1844), Zhukovsky (1783–1852), Zagoskin (1789–1852), and Griboedov (1795–1829). The titanic figure of the first decades of the nineteenth century was Alexander Pushkin (1799–1837), the creator and formulator of the modern Russian language. In music a similar function was performed by Mikhail Ivanovich Glinka. (1) By far the most important event in the early years of the nineteenth century was the Napoleonic War, as a result of which a large part of the young nobility not only visited Paris and other cultural centres but came into contact with the ordinary man and woman, a factor that cannot be sufficiently stressed. Despair at the backwardness of Russia in comparison with the achievements and cultural standards of the West, indignation at the fate of the peasants, anger at the growing reaction of Alexander I, resulted in the formation of numerous societies and aristocratic intellectual circles, culminating in the Decembrist rising of 1825—a revolutionary outbreak led by members of the young noble intelligentsia, which was crushed by Tsar Nicholas I (1825–55). The whole atmosphere of reaction and suppression, the world of bureaucracy, the growth of the merchant classes and the desire for reform and the abolition of serfdom are all vividly portrayed in the works of Gogol, Pushkin, Lermontov, and other writers of the period. Towards the end of the first half of the century realism becomes a stronger element in culture, notable in this respect being the paintings of Fedotov, the music of Dargomyzhsky, and the writings of Belinsky (1811–48), the Russian critic who sought above all 'truth of expression'.

DEVELOPMENT OF THE RUSSIAN THEATRE

It was only in the second quarter of the nineteenth century (i.e. from about the 1830's) that theatrical music became widespread in Russia. The Russian oratorio *Minin i Pozharsky* (1811) by Stepan Anikievich Degtyarëv (1766–1813), chorus-master of Count Sheremetev's private theatre, well illustrates the motleyness of construction typical of the productions of the period, and is clearly modelled on Italian prototypes. Like several other Russian composers of the time, Degtyarëv was first a pupil of Sarti (2) and then completed his training in Italy.

During the reign of Alexander I (1801–25) there were considerable developments in drama and writers such as Ozerov, Griboedov, Pushkin, Shakhovskoy, Khmelnitsky, Zagoskin, and others were responsible for the writing of works in many different genres—classical tragedies, Romantic tragedies, patriotic dramas based on national themes, sentimental dramas, comedies, melodramas and vaudevilles. On the stage appeared a whole number of distinguished Russian actors and actresses— Yakovlev, Bryansky, the Semënova sisters, Sandunova, Karatygin, Zlov, Samoylov, Chernikov, and others who infused life into many Russian productions. Drama also had influence on opera. Overtures, orchestral entr'actes, choruses, arias, duets, songs, melodramas, and ballets were all included in dramatic performances.

Up to 1836, when the rebuilt Bolshoy Theatre was opened in St. Petersburg for operatic productions, there had been no separate opera houses. (3) Before then there had been no difference between singers and actors, the roles in operas and dramas being taken by the same cast. Acting, singing, and ballet were studied at the *uchilishches* simultaneously. (4) Provincial theatres also existed at this period, especially on the big estates—e.g. that of the Yusupovs in Arkhangelskoe (near Moscow), of Kamensky in Orël, the Shakhovskoys in Nizhny-Novgorod, the Shepelevs on the Vyks. Some of the serf theatres (e.g. Kamensky's and Shakhovskoy's) became public and people were admitted for a small fee. The repertoire of these theatres consisted of plays, together with French, Italian and Russian operas, including works by Grétry, Monsigny, Salieri, Paisiello, Gluck, Martini. Sheremetev's serf theatres at Kuskovo and Ostankino were particularly magnificent. The best foreign and native talent was employed on the technical side (e.g. the Italian P. Gonzaga) and the repertoire was enormous, comprising some 116 pieces, including 73 operas (37 French, 23 Italian and 13 Russian). There was also an excellent ballet company.

RISE OF RUSSIAN VAUDEVILLE

The music composed for tragedies and epic dramas contained elements of the grandiose and the heroic, borrowed from the operas of Gluck and Cherubini. Such music was written by Aleksey Nikolaevich Titov (1769–1827), composer of numerous musical works such as *Andromeda and Perseus*, &c. Sentimental dramas, or dramas of low-life (by Kotzebue and other writers) and later (from the beginning of the 1820's) melodrama, were also popular. However, the most widespread form of all was that of vaudeville, a vaudeville being an indispensable element in every entertainment, whether ballet, opera, or drama. Certain writers, such as Shakhovskoy, Khmelnitsky, Pisarev, and others, specialized in the writing of vaudevilles, often adapting French models to the Russian taste; although the original satirical element was lost in Russian, it was replaced by other features. The subject matter of these vaudevilles was diverse, the favourite themes in the early decades of the nineteenth century being patriotism, fantasy, parody, and lower-class life. A special place in vaudeville was occupied by the solo couplet song, which, in most cases, had an unchanging verbal refrain. Usually the music was strongly rhythmic in nature, sometimes being set in a dance form such as a polonaise. Alternatively, in the case of a lyrical situation, a sentimental *romance* might be employed. Songs would sometimes be performed by two people. The vaudeville would invariably be introduced by an overture making use of the solo songs heard later in the work, and would often be concluded by an ensemble, each soloist singing a couplet to a general refrain. In some cases the subjects of vaudevilles would be taken from folk life and composers would give authenticity to their work by using folk themes. Thus, Cavos, in his music to Shakhovskoy's patriotic vaudeville *Kazak-stikhotvorets* (1812) employed Ukrainian melodies, one of which, amazing to relate, has even found its way down to the twentieth century in the form of a popular song entitled 'Yes, my darling Daughter!'

ROLE OF FOREIGN OPERA

About the same period French and German Romantic operas began to appear on the Russian stage, among which may be mentioned works by Cherubini and Spontini, and from 1824 Weber's *Der Freischütz*. In the beginning of the 1830's the operas of Meyerbeer made their appearance, *Robert le diable* having its first Russian performance in St. Petersburg in 1834. The same time saw the emergence of a number of outstanding Russian opera singers—Osip Afanasevich Petrov, the great Russian bass (1807–78) and Anna Yakovlevna Vorobëva (1816–1901), the contralto, who later became Petrov's wife. Petrov was a Ukrainian by origin and after having been several years with a provincial troupe was accidentally 'discovered' in Kursk by the *régisseur* of the St. Petersburg Theatres. He made his début in the autumn of 1830 at St. Petersburg in *Die Zauberflöte*. His later roles included Bertram in Meyerbeer's *Robert le diable* in 1834, Ivan Susanin in *A Life for the Tsar*, Farlaf in *Ruslan and Lyudmila*, the Miller in Dargomyzhsky's *Rusalka*, Varlaam in Musorgsky's *Boris Godunov*, Leporello in *Don Giovanni*, and others. Vorobëva-Petrova was also extremely gifted and created the roles of Vanya in *A Life for the Tsar* and Ratmir in *Ruslan*, to mention only a few. Glinka often sought their advice on musical matters.

In the first decade of the nineteenth century the Russian Court was dominated by French opera, largely as a result of the work of Boïeldieu, who himself was conductor of the Imperial Opera, St. Petersburg, from 1804–10. (5) In the early 1830's a German opera company attracted attention in the capital by giving performances of French and Italian operas. However, whereas Italian opera had completely dominated the Russian scene in the eighteenth century, its position in the early nineteenth century was far less secure. Although Italian productions were given from time to time in St. Petersburg, and attempts were made to form a private Italian opera theatre in Moscow in the 1820's, (a permanent opera theatre existed in St. Petersburg from 1829–31), Italian opera never regained its former position and from the beginning of the 1830's disappeared from St. Petersburg for more than ten years. However, in the spring of 1843 the famous Italian tenor, Giovanni Battista Rubini (1795–1854) arrived in St. Petersburg on a short visit and took part in a number of concerts and opera perfomances, which were extremely successful. In the autumn he again travelled to St. Petersburg but this time with an opera troupe among which were such famous singers as Pauline Viardot-Garcia, Antonio Tamburini, and others, and from then on Italian opera returned with new force, the Italian nightingales often being bombarded with flowers grown specially for the purpose by noble admirers in their own *orangeries*. Other distinguished visitors included Erminia Frezzolini, Guilia Grisi, Giovanni Matteo Mario (who married Grisi), Calzolari, and Luigi Lablache, though these were in Russia at a later date. At this period, it must be admitted, Russian operatic composers, even if their efforts had been given greater encouragement, were unable to offer any serious competition to the foreign masters. Rather they excelled in the miniature—in the comedy-vaudeville, the play with incidental music, the *divertissement*—examples of which were written by composers such as D. Kashin, Alyabyev, A. N. Titov, Cavos, Davydov, Verstovsky or A. F. Lvov. (6).

From autumn 1846 St. Petersburg was completely without Russian opera for three years, the troupe having been sent to Moscow, and it was only in the spring of 1849 that it returned to St. Petersburg on tour. Though it remained in St. Petersburg from 1850, even then it was deprived of a permanent stage. Nevertheless Russian operas continued to be performed, and a series of young Russian singers made their appearance—among them Bantyshev, Bulakhov, E. Semënova, Artemovsky, and others.

DEVELOPMENT OF CONCERT LIFE AND MUSICAL EDUCATION

From the beginning of the nineteenth century concert life began to develop on a wider scale, though still being centred almost exclusively in St. Petersburg and Moscow. Concerts were usually given at Lent and this tradition persisted for many decades. In the 1830's concerts became more frequent and more widespread as well as catering for a larger audience. *Abonnement* concerts were organized by singers and orchestral musicians in order to augment their wages. Usually the programmes of these were in no way remarkable and were often composed of items taken from the current theatrical repertoires. Foreign artists continued to visit Russia in ever-increasing numbers, including

John Field, Hummel, Bernhard Romberg, Angelica Catalani, Henselt, and, at a later date, Clara Schumann, Liszt, and others. Such visits were of the greatest value to young Russian musicians, not only in demonstrating new instrumental and vocal techniques, but in acquainting them with the latest forms of Western music. Hummel, for instance, had considerable influence on the development of Glinka. Several of the great virtuosi of the period, such as Field and Henselt, took up residence in Russia and settled down as teachers.

Musical education in the first half of the nineteenth century was almost entirely in the hands of foreigners, private lessons being given in the houses of the nobility and in the institutes of the privileged classes. Notable among the Moscow and St. Petersburg pedagogues, apart from those referred to above, were Charles Mayer (1799–1862), who was himself a pupil of Field, Franz Schoberlechner, Herke, and Miller the theoretician. The part played by John Field (1782–1837) was especially important, for not only did he create a new school of piano playing in Russia (the influence of which was felt in Moscow till the end of the nineteenth century through his pupil Dubuque), but had great influence on Russian music in general through the work of Glinka.

MUSICAL PERIODICALS

Another means of spreading musical knowledge was by the aid of almanachs and 'musical albums', which were prevalent in the 1820's and 30's in St. Petersburg and Moscow. The almanachs contained poems, prose and critical articles, together with music supplements in the form of *romances*, songs, or vaudeville couplets—the favourite musical form of the time. The 'musical albums' were even more popular, consisting of vocal and piano pieces, *romances*, 'Russian songs', piano variations on popular folk-songs, opera and *romance* melodies, and various dances for piano, most of which were by native composers. In the absence of any organized system of musical publication the albums were the most convenient way of propagating music on a wide scale and this method was used by Glinka himself. In 1829, together with N. Pavlishchev, who was a relative of Pushkin and a great lover of music, Glinka published a

'Lyrical Album' containing a number of his piano pieces and *romances*, and in 1839 he published independently five books of music under the title 'Collection of Music Pieces Compiled by M. Glinka'. These included songs and piano music by Glinka himself, along with works by other Russian composers.

Several publishers in St. Petersburg (though mostly foreigners) issued albums composed almost entirely of Western music, in which *salon* pieces were ranked alongside works by Beethoven, Haydn, and Mozart. In order to give difficult pieces the semblance of simplicity, publishers sometimes resorted to cunning. Thus, in the 'Album musicale pour l'Année 1828', published by I. Brief, Beethoven's Rondo in C major was included, but fearing to print the name of the formidable composer, the work was given instead the disarming title of 'Une soirée d'Eté au bord de la Newa'.

There were also a number of journals, which appeared intermittently, and from the very beginning of the nineteenth century publications such as *Journal d'Airs et Duos choisies dans les meilleurs opéras Français et Italiens donnés au Théâtre de St. Pétersbourg et arrangés pour Pianoforte*, *Journal pour la Guitarre*, *Severnaya arfa* (The Northern Harp), *Zhurnal dlya fortepiano* (Piano Magazine) were in regular circulation. In these were printed arrangements of operatic selections, variations, dances, and so on. The national tendencies prevalent at the period were likewise reflected in the musical publications. Thus, a *Zhurnal otechestvennoy muzyki* (Journal of National Music) was published by D. Kashin between 1806–7.

All these enterprises were short-lived, however, and it was not till 1839 with the publication of the musical journal *Nouvelliste*, that a periodical succeeded in firmly establishing itself. Indeed, the *Nouvelliste* stayed in existence till the beginning of the twentieth century. Until 1846 it appeared each month in music books containing four or five pieces, but after 1846 the number was increased to ten and to the musical section was added by N. Bernard, the publisher, a literary section, which up to 1878 was called the 'Literary Supplement'. In the journal were printed many works (mostly for piano or voice) by Russian composers—Alyabyev, Glinka, Varlamov, Dargomyzhsky, and others.

FURTHER DEVELOPMENT OF CONCERT LIFE

A special role in the development of concert life in the first half of the nineteenth century was occupied by concerts instituted for charitable purposes, most (if not all) of which were organized by the nobility. Often the performers in these were of humble origin, such as the singers Barteneva, Bilibina, Belenitsyna, for whom such concerts were a means of displaying their talents. Charitable aims also brought into being one of the first Russian musical concert organizations—the St. Petersburg Philharmonic Society, which was founded in 1802. From that year onwards the Philharmonic Society provided concerts in which place of honour was given to the performance of the great choral compositions—the oratorios of Handel, Haydn, Mozart's *Requiem*, works of Cherubini, &c. Beethoven's *Missa solemnis* was given its world première there in 1824.

In the middle of the century the demand for concert performances still further increased. Amateur societies sprang up, which at first were restricted mostly to the aristocracy, a typical example being the 'Society of Lovers of Music', which was inaugurated in the early 1840's. Although the Society's concerts were held in open concert halls, admission was available only through the personal recommendations of members.

A particularly interesting society was one known as 'Musical Rehearsals of Students of the Imperial University' (or 'University Concerts' as they were more generally termed), which arose likewise in the 1840's. These were amateur orchestral concerts which came into being on the initiative of one of the University inspectors, A. I. Fitztum von Ecstedt. The repertoire was mostly symphonic music and a good impression of the Society's activies is provided by D. V. Stasov in his *Musical Reminiscences*: 'In these rehearsals', he writes,

> the performers were actual students, former students and a number of amateurs, while any missing parts would be made up by inviting members of the theatre orchestra (e.g. trombones or horns, or a few other wind instruments). The orchestra consisted of 50–60 people, and the conductor was Karl Bogdanovich Schubert, an excellent cellist, soloist of the opera orchestra of the Imperial theatre, a great friend of Fitztum, a fine quartet-player, and a very kind man. These 'rehearsals' (called everywhere 'University

Concerts') were held on Sunday mornings, beginning at the end of November or the beginning of December (sometimes even in October) at 1.00. Usually there were ten in the winter in all, though sometimes (but very rarely) there were extra ones, and for that—i.e. for 10 concerts, one paid only 5 roubles! Although they were amateur concerts, played without rehearsals, nevertheless, thanks to the conductor, K. Schubert, and his skill in capturing the young people's enthusiasm and cooperation—and among them there were some very talented members—the performances were not at all bad. But the main thing was that any one wishing to get to know orchestral music was given the chance. The concerts were accessible to extremely poor people and when I went to them (from 1846–1856) the great University hall was always full; one had to get one's tickets beforehand. Only students were allowed in the gallery and they were let in free.

The pieces performed in these concerts were mostly by Haydn, Mozart and Beethoven, Schubert, Weber, and Mendelssohn. It is remarkable that several compositions of Schumann were given their first Russian performances there, including his Overture to *Manfred*. The whole of Glinka's incidental music to *Prince Kholmsky* was played by the Society after his death. During the 1850's both Balakirev and Anton Rubinstein were conductors of the University Orchestra. (7)

DEVELOPMENT OF MUSICAL CRITICISM

At the beginning of the nineteenth century musical criticism in Russia hardly existed as such. The few articles that did appear in journals and almanachs were concerned entirely with the life of a composer, his biography. At that time any assessment of the performance of artists of the Imperial Theatres in print was generally forbidden and it was only in the middle of the 1820's that F. Bulgarin, the publisher of the celebrated *Severnaya pchela* (The Northern Bee), began to agitate for permission to print in his own newspaper theatrical criticisms and articles, assuring in his petition that 'loyalty, and a noble, cheerful tone, neither coarse nor pedantic, will be the ideals for which my colleagues and I will strive in our undertaking'. From that time onwards the number of articles both in *The Northern Bee* and in contemporary publications such as the *Vestnik Evropy*, *Biblioteka dlya chteniya* (The Library for Reading), &c., began to increase. However, in most cases the reviews were written by unqualified persons, and the standard of musical criticism was not high.

VLADIMIR FËDOROVICH ODOEVSKY (1803[4?]–69)

The first serious attempts at musical criticism begin to appear at the beginning of the nineteenth century, the most outstanding writer being Prince Vladimir Fëdorovich Odoevsky. Odoevsky, who was a widely and diversely talented man, a scholar, writer and composer, paid much attention to music and in the beginning of the 1830's, following the example of Hoffmann, wrote two musical novels—*Poslednyi kvartet Betkhovena* (The Last Quartet of Beethoven) and *Sebastian Bach*, which were both skilful and imaginative studies. Despite the fact that Odoevsky himself was much influenced by German philosophy and Romanticism he was nevertheless a fervent patriot and a supporter of Russian culture. In an article in the *Vestnik Evropy* in 1824 he praised the ballads of Verstovsky and shortly after the appearance of *A Life for the Tsar* assessed the value of Glinka's music, speaking of it as an opera which 'has decided a question important for art in general and Russian art in particular—namely, the existence of Russian opera, Russian music'. Odoevsky also wrote articles on acoustics and musical education, as well as conducting researches into the questions of ancient *znamenny* chant and the properties of Russian folk-song. His publications at the end of his life on ecclesiastical music and folk music are among the best of the period.

VASILIY PETROVICH BOTKIN (1810–69)

A number of interesting articles on music, concerned mostly with criticism and the art of piano-playing, were written by Vasiliy Petrovich Botkin (1810–69), who was a friend of Turgenev and Belinsky. Influenced by German Romanticism, like Odoevsky, he was a man of wide culture and was concerned not so much with the superficial qualities of music but with its philosophical and aesthetic aspects. To Botkin, music was 'the art of those secret movements of the human soul, for the expression of which neither form nor word is sufficient'.

OSIP IVANOVICH SENKOVSKY (1800–58)

A curious figure in musical journalism was Osip Ivanovich Senkovsky (who wrote under the pseudonym 'Baron Brambeus') (1800–58). An outstanding orientalist, master of several Eastern languages, Senkovsky resigned his post as Professor at St. Petersburg University and dedicated himself to journalism and literature. Between 1834–44 he was the prolific editor of the popular journal *Biblioteka dlya chteniya*. Among his articles may be found many on various forms of music—on theory, acoustics, and aesthetics—though, generally speaking, his approach towards such questions tends to be conversational and somewhat superficial. Of importance is his article on *Ruslan and Lyudmila*, which was published in his journal shortly after the opera's première in 1842 and which showed great insight and understanding, a factor doubtless assisted by his oriental interests. Senkovsky was also a contributor (later editor) to a musical encyclopaedia, 14 volumes of which were published in Petersburg between 1835–8.

RISE OF RUSSIAN MUSICOLOGY

At the same period the first steps were made in Russian musicology. In 1826 Verstovsky published in the *Dramatic Album for Lovers of Theatre and Music for 1826* a short history of West-European opera entitled 'Fragments from the history of dramatic music'.

Also of importance was the appearance in 1843 of a three-volume biography of Mozart, in French, by Alexander Dmitrievich Ulybyshev (1794–1858), a Nizhny-Novgorod landowner and an ardent lover of music. Although it has some weaknesses and inaccuracies, it may be regarded as one of the first biographies of the composer. From 1813–24 he was editor of *Le conservateur impartial* and from 1825 of the *Journal de St. Pétersbourg*.

FURTHER DEVELOPMENT OF INSTRUMENTAL MUSIC

The early nineteenth century saw the continued growth of amateur music-making of which there are many accounts in the literature of the period. Such a musical gathering, for instance, is described by the poet Vyazemsky:

> The Moscow home of Princess Zinaida Volkonskaya was the elegant meeting-place of all the remarkable and select personalities

of contemporary society. Everything in that home bore the impression of service to art and thought. Readings took place there, concerts, and performances of Italian operas by amateurs and *dilettantes*. Chief among the artists was the hostess herself. Having heard her, one could not forget the impression produced by her full and resonant contralto and her inspired playing of the role of Tancredi in the opera of Rossini. It is still remembered and described how on the first day of her acquaintance with Pushkin and in his presence she sang his elegy, set to music by Genishta (8):

> *'The orb of day was now extinguished,*
> *The blue sea filled with evening mist.'*

Other memoirs describe the gatherings of Delvig, the intimate friend of Pushkin.

Commencing in the homes of the artistocracy, music-making slowly spread its way through society. Instrumental music was of special significance, the favourite instruments being the piano, harp and guitar, and the piano-*gusli* (*klavieroobraznye gusli*). (9) The harp and guitar were particularly fashionable and a certain Zhikarev recalls in his memoirs, for instance, how one distinguished Professor of Mathematics and Military Science in the University of Moscow used to practise fervently on the harp in his spare time! The guitar was also widespread and was used to accompany *romances*, 'Russian song', and dances, besides being the favourite instrument of gypsies. A key figure in its propagation was A. I. Sikhra (1773–1850), who arrived in St. Petersburg in the early 1820's, gave concerts, had many pupils and edited guitar journals. Among his disciples was Mikhail Stakhovich, compiler of the famous collection of folk-songs.

The favourite musical genres of the time were nocturnes, cradle-songs, songs without words, barcarolles, scherzos, capriccios, and the sparkling variations and *fantasies pot-pourris*. Variations on 'Russian songs' for piano, harp, or guitar were also popular. Among the piano variations those of Daniel Kashin were particularly well-known. Many virtuoso variations on folk themes were written by composers for the guitar such as Aksenov and Vysotsky. Dance music was also common, the favourite dances of the early nineteenth century being the waltz, the French quadrille, the polka, and mazurka. Quadrilles were written to themes from the operas *Robert le diable*, *Les Huguenots*,

A Life for the Tsar and *Ruslan,* and also to folk tunes, a 'French Quadrille on Asiatic melodies' even being composed by Alyabyev in 1834 using Circassian, Georgian, Azerbaijan, Kalmyk, and Persian melodies.

RISE OF THE BYTOVOY ROMANCE

A special place in domestic music-making was occupied by the *bytovoy romance,* which mirrored in its superficiality, refinement and emotional artificiality the social and aesthetic climate of the period. The principal factors leading to the formation of the *romance* were Russian town folk-song, the lyrical Italian aria, the elegant French arietta, the passionate gypsy song, as well as the influence, to a greater or lesser extent, of the German *Lied.* Other influences were the songs of Viennese *Singspiels* and the French opera and chamber *romances.* Nevertheless, despite its many varied sources, the *bytovoy romance* was something essentially Russian and became one of the most important factors in the formation of a national musical language. The *bytovoy romance* was not confined to vocal music but appeared also in opera-vaudevilles, besides having influence on opera itself. In Verstovsky's opera *Askold's Tomb* (1835) the first song of Nadezhda 'Gde ty, zhenikh moy nenaglyadniy' first appeared as a *bytovoy romance* in the almanach *Raduga* (Rainbow) in 1830 to the words 'Ne govori—ni da, ni net'. Glinka took for Antonida's *romance* in *A Life for the Tsar* 'Ne o tom skorblyu, podruzhenki' a song which he had written in 1829—'Ne osenniy chastiy dozhdichek' to words of Delvig. Dargomyzhsky, likewise, for a chorus of rusalkas in his opera of the same name, used a *romance,* which he had written earlier. It was fashionable at the period not only to be able to perform *romances,* but also to write them.

MIKHAIL YUREVICH VIELGORSKY (1788–1856)

One of the most colourful characters of the period, and one completely representative of his age, was Count Mikhail Yurevich Vielgorsky (1788–1856), an exceptionally well-educated man, who had studied first with Haessler, and then with Cherubini in Paris. Apart from *romances* he wrote many large-scale works (including an opera *The Gypsies*), symphonies and chamber ensembles. His *salon* was frequented not only by Russian celebrities but by those visiting from abroad—among them Liszt, Schumann, Clara Wieck, and Berlioz. Vielgorsky's brother, Matvey Yurevich (1794–1866), whose dates are sometimes given incorrectly as 1787–1863, was a first-rate cellist, and was one of the founders of the Petersburg branch of the Russian Musical Society (1859), and the Petersburg Conservatory in 1862.

OTHER COMPOSERS: CHARACTERISTICS OF ROMANCES

Other composers of *romances* were the two Titov cousins, Nikolay Alekseevich (1800–75), son of the theatrical composer, and Nikolay Sergeevich (1798–1843), and Nikolay Alekseevich's brother, Mikhail (1804–53). Characteristic of the *romances* is the prevalence of the minor key, the use of simple accompaniment figures, the bass part often comprising single notes, stereotyped cadences, limited modulations, a common transition being from the tonic minor to the relative major. More elaborate figures and the use of dance rhythms are found in *romances* of a slightly later date.

RUSSIAN SONG

An important phenomenon at the end of the eighteenth and beginning of the nineteenth centuries was that of 'Russian song' —the name given to vocal compositions written in the manner of folk-song, though usually folk-song in the form in which it appeared in the Russian towns. One of the first poets to compose verses in the spirit of folk poetry was Merzlyakov (10) (1778–1830), other poets following in his path being Delvig, Timofeev, Tsyganov, and Koltsov. Sometimes 'Russian songs' were composed to actual folk melodies, an example being a song of T. V. Zhuchkovsky (1785–1839) 'Dlya lyubvi odnoy priroda', which was based largely on the well-known folk tune 'Vo pole berëza stoyala'. 'Russian songs' may usually be classified into two groups—the lyrical, sad, 'protracted' type of song, and the more rhythmic, energetic variety. Often a 'Russian song' will fall into two divisions, a slow introduction leading into a lively *Allegro*. A good example of a 'Russian song' is A. Gurilëv's 'Prigoryunyus—li ya, prizadumayus', which is written in the manner of Russian dance songs (Mus. Ex. 1):

PLATE 7

D. S. BORTNYANSKY (1751–1825)

E. I. FOMIN (1761–1800)

PLATE 8

A MASQUERADE IN ST. PETERSBURG IN THE 1830's

from a contemporary lithograph

(NOTE MUSICIANS IN TOP RIGHT HAND CORNER)

Mus. Ex.1

Of importance also were the ballads of Zhukovsky, which were first set by his friend A. A. Pleshcheev (1775–1827).

FOLK COLLECTIONS IN THE EARLY NINETEENTH CENTURY: D. N. KASHIN

The chief collector of folk-songs at the beginning of the nineteenth century was Daniel Nikitich Kashin (1769–1841), a serf by origin who received musical education from Sarti. (11) Even during the 90's of the eighteenth century Kashin displayed a lively interest in folk music and from the commencement of the nineteenth century began to publish individual arrangements of folk melodies as well as composing songs in the folk idiom. In his declining years, in the early 1830's, Kashin published the fruits of his labours in the realms of folk music in the form of a three-volume collection entitled *Russkie narodnye pesni* (Russian Folk-songs) (1833–4), which were divided respectively into 'protracted', 'semi-protracted' and 'quick' songs.

K

Kashin's collection is valuable in that it gives a good insight into the attitude of composers towards folk-song in the first third of the nineteenth century. All the songs are set forth in a very simple diatonic manner, clearly influenced by the style of the *bytovoy romance*, the melodies having no superfluous adornments and the accompaniments being largely chordal in nature. That Kashin continues the traditions of Prach is illustrated by the following example (Mus. Ex. 2):

Mus. Ex. 2
Andante
Collection of D. KASHIN

Po - lu - chil pis - mo ot de - vi - tsy sey - chas;

stal chi - tat ya: po - li - lis slë - zy iz glaz.

The same synthesis between Western harmonies and Russian folk-song may be observed in other collections of Russian folk-song in the first half of the nineteenth century, all of which, to a greater or lesser extent, were influenced either by the sentimental harmonies of the pathetic *romance*, or, as in the case of the collections of Varlamov and Gurilëv, by the *fioriture* of the operatic aria.

Mention may also be made of Kashin's contemporary Aleksey Dmitrevich Zhilin (*c.* 1767 to *c.* 1848), a blind composer of some talent.

COLLECTION OF I. A. RUPIN

Another collection was that of Ivan Alekseevich Rupin (1789[?]–1850), consisting of twenty-four songs, which was published in 1831–3 in two parts. (12) Each song is given in two forms: firstly, for solo voice with a simple chordal accompaniment of a guitar-like nature, typical of the *bytovoy romance* of the 1820's to

30's; and secondly, in the form of a three-part choral or ensemble version similar to the three-part style of the *kant*. Rupin's
collection is of interest in that the lyrical songs are given in a
more complex form than in other collections of the time. The
songs are written down as they were performed. The texts of
Rupin's collection are considerably shorter than those of Prach
or Trutovsky.

COLLECTIONS OF VARLAMOV AND GURILËV

The 1840's saw the appearance of two further folk-song volumes
—*Russkiy pevets* (The Russian Singer), a collection by A. Varlamov, and *Izbrannye narodnye russkie pesni* (Selected Russian
Folk-songs), collected by A. Gurilëv. Both consist of free
arrangements of popular town folk-songs and are essentially
for concert performance (as is attested by the sometimes
lengthy piano preludes and postludes), some of them demand-
ing considerable virtuosity. No attempt is made to group the
songs into different genres.

ROLE OF ALYABYEV IN RUSSIAN MUSIC OF THE
EARLY NINETEENTH CENTURY

Of some significance in the history of Russian music of the early
nineteenth century is that of Alexander Alexandrovich Alyabyev
(1787–1851). Alyabyev was born in Tobolsk of aristocratic parentage. After a period as an official at the Petersburg (and later
the Moscow) Mining College, he became an army officer.
Having served at the front in the Napoleonic Wars, during
which he made the acquaintance of the poet Denis Davydov,
he settled in St. Petersburg where he became intimate with
Griboedov and the Decembrists. His comic opera *Lunnaya
noch, ili Domovye* (Moonlit Night, or the House-spirits) was performed with success at the St. Petersburg Bolshoy Theatre in
1823 and together with Verstovsky he took part in the opening
of the Moscow Bolshoy Theatre in 1825, composing incidental
music for the prologue *The Triumph of the Muses*. In the same
year, however, he was arrested on an unsubstantiated charge of
murder and held in prison for three years awaiting trial, till
being sentenced to Siberia in 1828 with deprivation of all rights
and forfeiture of his nobility. During this period his music still
continued to be performed. Having a piano in his room, he

wrote a number of works, including the well-known song 'Solovei'. While captive in Tobolsk in Central Siberia, he continued to compose, producing some of his finest *romances*, as well as organizing concerts and stimulating musical life. In 1832 he received permission to travel to the Caucasus for medical treatment, where, inspired by the magnificent scenery beloved of Pushkin and Lermontov, he collected Georgian, Armenian, and Azerbaijan folk music, which he incorporated in his *Kavkazskii pevets* (Caucasian singer). He also began a collection of Ukrainian songs, published in 1834 under the title *Golosa ukrainskikh pesen*, which received high praise from Gogol. Upon being posted to Orenburg in 1833, he occupied himself with the writing down of Bashkir and Kirgiz melodies (incidentally being the first person to do so), which he arranged for voice and piano. His last years were spent in Moscow. Though forbidden to appear in public, he wrote his last major work—the opera *Ammalat-Bek*, based on a story of A. Bestuzhev-Marlinsky, which is said to incorporate Caucasian themes written down by himself, though it seems that the opera was never completed.

Of Alyabyev's operas little is known, though much new light on his work and personality has been thrown by the musicologists B. Dobrokhotov and B. Shteynpress. (13) From the few fragments available, however, the music appears to be of a light sentimental nature, coloured with typical Romantic harmonies. His works comprise sacred pieces, symphonies, string quartets, the incidental music to many vaudevilles, orchestral compositions, piano, chamber and choral works, and over 200 songs.

ALYABYEV'S ORCHESTRAL WORKS

One of his best orchestral works is the overture to the tragedy *Otstupnik, ili Osada Korinfa* (The Apostate, or the Siege of Corinth), which was written as incidental music to a drama of the same name by the composer's brother, V. A. Alyabyev. According to an introductory note by V. Dobrokhotov, the music was composed on Alyabyev's return to the province of Moscow after his long exile and was his first attempt to write music to a tragedy. The manuscript of the score, which is preserved in the Glinka Museum, Moscow, bears the inscription: '20 February 1837, the village of Ryazantsy'. Stylistically the overture, which is scored for woodwind, two horns in F, two horns in D, two trumpets, three trombones, timpani and strings, shows the influence of Beethoven and Weber. It is preceded by a slow introduction, which makes reference to some of the themes heard later in the work. One peculiarity is that the overture is rounded off by a short coda concluding in a 4-bar *Lento*. Despite the number of instruments employed, the orchestration is conservative and shows no remarkable innovations.

Another overture to come down to us is in F minor, but as the original manuscript possesses neither signature nor date, it has been ascribed to Alyabyev through comparison of his handwriting and the nature of the musical content. Belonging most probably to the year 1829 it is likewise scored for the same combination as the *Siege of Corinth* overture, with the exception of the horns, which are all in F. The overture, which opens with a slow introduction leading into an *Allegro*, is a well-written work and has some fine orchestral sounds. Its most remarkable feature is the constantly recurring syncopation and the sense of urgency. The second subject has a feeling of 'Russian song'.

Among Alyabyev's works is a movement of a symphony in E minor. According to a note on the manuscript, it was commenced on 30 October 1830 in Tobolsk. It is scored for woodwind, four horns, two trumpets in Bb, a single trombone, timpani, and strings. The symphony commences with a slow introduction, leading into an *Allegro*. A curious feature is that the recapitulation is preceded by an *Andantino* section of 11 bars followed by a *Largo* of 8 bars. The work is interesting harmonically and certainly deserves an occasional performance.

ALYABYEV'S CHAMBER AND VOCAL WORKS

Before passing on to a brief examination of Alyabyev's songs, mention must also be made of his first string quartet in Eb major, which was written in 1815 and is one of the earliest examples of a quartet by a Russian composer. It is not known whether the work was performed in the composer's lifetime. Cast in four movements the work is conventional in design with the exception of the last movement. A slow introduction leads into an *Allegro vivace* rondo bearing the unusual signature 2/4 6/8 and this contrast of duple and triple time plays a prominent role. The texture is eminently playable, the part writing adventurous, and the composer is not afraid to let his instruments run the whole gamut of their musical range.

Mention may also be made of the Trio in A minor for piano, violin, and cello, which is regarded by some critics as one of the best Russian chamber works to be written before Glinka.

As a writer of more than 200 songs, Alyabyev must surely be one of the most prolific among Russian composers. His chief contribution lies in his psychological enrichment of the subject matter, his subtle treatment of the words and his gradual assimilation of the characteristic features of the folk idiom. His first efforts are written in the style of 'Russian song' and the sentimental *romance*, where, turning to the poetry of Pushkin, Delvig, and Vyazemsky he underlines the charm and simplicity of the words. Typical of these pieces are the graceful melodies, the somewhat unenterprising piano accompaniments, and the 'catchiness' of the tunes, which, needless to say, were immensely popular at the time. Indeed, his setting of Delvig's 'Solovey' (The Nightingale) was transcribed by Liszt for the piano, and Glinka even wrote a set of piano variations on it, as well as orchestrating the accompaniment. It is this tune which forms the basis of the slow movement of Alyabyev's Third Quartet. However, with increasing maturity, his work began to assume greater profundity, the peak of his creation being reached during his years of exile with such songs as 'Irtysh' (the middle of which depicts the noise of the river), 'Vecherniy zvon' (The Evening Chime) based on Moore's 'Those evening bells', 'Dva vòrona' (Two Ravens), &c., and there is little doubt that these songs, with their impression of solitude, yearning and dreams of freedom, are to a large extent autobiographical. Of particular interest are his ventures into the Oriental idiom, of which Alyabyev is one of the earliest exponents. Among his Eastern songs outstanding are the 'Kabardinskaya pesnya' (Kabardinian Song) and the lyrical 'Gruzinskaya pesnya' (Georgian Song). Harmonically the 'Georgian Song' seems oddly reminiscent of Rimsky-Korsakov (Mus. Ex. 3).

The sustained pedal drone, the nostalgic E♮ in bars 4 and 6 and the long flowing melody, with the characteristic drop of the

Mus. Ex.3

Andantino poco sostenuto

ALYABYEV

Pla-chet, pla - chet de - va gor: _____ rus-skiy, day tvoy vstre - tit vzor: _____ tam gde da - vyat vi - no - grad, _____ per-viy vstre - ti - la ya vzglyad;

fifth at the cadence, are all common features in the work of the Nationalist composers.

Although much of Alyabyev's music is derivative, it deserves to be remembered not only for the charm of its melodies and its ingenuous appeal, but for its powers of craftsmanship. His last songs, written in the 1840's, are remarkable for their revelation of peasant life, and like his comic-satirical songs anticipate the work of Dargomyzhsky and Musorgsky.

ALEXANDER EGOROVICH VARLAMOV (1801–48)

Another vocal composer of some importance was Alexander Egorovich Varlamov, who was born in Moscow in the year 1801 in the family of an official. His father had served till 1791 in the Guards and left the army as a lieutenant, but since he had not served as an officer on active service, he held noble rank only during his lifetime, the nobility being non-hereditary. As a child Varlamov was passionately devoted to music and taught himself to play the violin, for which he arranged 'Russian songs' by ear. So great were his musical talents that his father enlisted him at the age of ten in the Imperial Boy's Chapel, where he remained till 1819. In the Boy's Chapel, however, music was not studied systematically, so Varlamov continued to work at the viola in his spare time, his favourite pieces still being 'Russian songs'. When on one occasion the Director of the Chapel, Bortnyansky, heard him playing, he took an immediate interest in him and, encouraged by the distinguished composer, Varlamov taught himself to play other instruments, among them the guitar and the piano. His singing was also exceptional and he began to sing solos in the choir. Varlamov held Bortnyansky and the Italian style of his music in particular reverence and the smooth-flowing lines of Italian music together with 'Russian song' subsequently became chief features of his own compositions.

In 1819, when his voice broke, Varlamov left the Imperial Chapel and was appointed Choirmaster at the Imperial Russian Church at the Hague, Holland. His four-year stay in the Netherlands had great influence on his musical development and he found his visits to operas and concerts and his friendship with French opera-singers particularly profitable. Varlamov himself frequently appeared in concerts as a singer and guitarist while abroad.

Returning to Russia in 1823 Varlamov settled in Moscow where he taught in private homes and in academic establishments. However, strained financial circumstances caused him to make a second attempt to get into the Imperial Chapel and in the beginning of 1829 he was readmitted as a 'major chorister', at the same time being entrusted with the tuition of the best boy-singers. To this period (the end of the 1820's) belong his first attempts at composition—two sacred choruses, written in connection with his application to regain admission to the Chapel.

His work in St. Petersburg, however, was far from satisfying financially and in the quest for more remunerative work (and to rid himself of his accumulation of debts) he obtained a post at the Moscow Imperial Theatres as an assistant Kapellmeister, also teaching singing at the theatrical *uchilishche*. In 1834 he was recognized in the theatre as 'a composer of music'.

It was with his removal to Moscow that his real work as a composer began. As the result of his theatrical activities he made the acquaintance of the leading Muscovite musical celebrities, including Zagoskin, Verstovsky, the actor Mochalov, and somewhat later, Alyabyev. The interest of all these figures in national music confirmed Varlamov in his ideas and he began to compose numerous vocal works, his favourite genre being that of 'Russian song'. He also wrote music for theatrical productions at the Maly Theatre—music to Shakhovskoy's drama *Roslavlev* (based on the novel of Zagoskin), to Shakhov-skoy's *Dvumuzhnitsa*, later to Khomyakov's tragedy *Ermak*, and to Shakespeare's *Hamlet*. At the end of 1833 he began to publish a musical magazine entitled *Eolova arfa* (The Aeolian Harp), in each number of which were printed four or five vocal or piano pieces by Verstovsky and other composers. This magazine lasted only a little more than a year and terminated its existence at the beginning of 1835 with the issue of the tenth volume. Nevertheless, Varlamov's work was becoming well-known as the result of his teaching at private houses, his work at the theatre, and through the frequent performances of his own songs. However, despite his popularity, Varlamov never became a rich man. His way of life was Bohemian, he sold his composi-tions to his publishers at a loss, and he often failed to turn up for lessons.

In 1840 he made an attempt to sum up his work as a vocal teacher in his *Shkola peniya* (School of Singing), in the preface of which he underlined the significance of the declamatory element in singing, characteristic of the French school, and his indebtedness to Bortnyansky's style of writing. Varlamov re-garded his work (the theoretical part of which owed much to a book by Professor Andrade, of the Paris Conservatoire) as the foundation 'of a Russian school of singing', based on an analysis of Russian folk melodies and the peculiarities of their performance. In the introduction he wrote:

> I hope in the future to publish a special work in which our folk melodies will be examined in detail and I am sure that the Russian public, which hitherto has always approved my efforts as a com-poser, will find in it some new thoughts about the art of singing in Russia, which at the same time may serve as a supplement to the history of singing in general.

Unfortunately, this promise was never fulfilled and the work on folk melodies never came into being.

In 1844 Varlamov left the Moscow Theatre and the next year again travelled to St. Petersburg hoping to gain the post of Assistant Director of the Imperial Chapel. His efforts, however, were not crowned with success and he somehow managed to eke out a sparse existence by selling *romances* to Bernard the publisher and through giving lessons. The concerts organized each year were some help to him, despite the fact that his health had deteriorated and his voice had almost completely disappeared. In St. Petersburg he made the acquaintance of a group of *littérateurs*, including the young poet Apollon Grigoryev, who subsequently became known as a literary critic and was a great lover of Russian and gypsy song.

In his last years Varlamov made one last attempt to found a music journal. Published under the name of *Russkiy pevets* (The Russian Singer) it consisted of arrangements of Russian and Ukrainian folk-songs for voice and piano, made by Varlamov himself, together with piano variations on each of these songs by the Kapellmeister and composer V. Kazhinsky. Of the intended 100, however, Varlamov succeeded in arranging only 43 and these were later made into a separate collection.

Varlamov died suddenly in 1848. In its obituary column the paper *Severnaya pchela* wrote:

> On 15 October, to our great regret, passed away our renowned folk composer Aleksandr Egorovich Varlamov.

ASSESSMENT OF VARLAMOV'S WORKS

As opposed to Alyabyev, who wrote music of various genres, Varlamov devoted himself largely to vocal music, his output consisting of about 150 *romances* and songs for one, two, or three voices with piano accompaniment, several sacred compositions, piano pieces, ballets and incidental music. His music is essentially lyrical in nature, permeated by sincere and simple emotions. Varlamov's masterpiece was, of course, his song 'Krasnyi sarafan' (The Red Sarafan), which he published in his 'Musical Albums for 1833'. As N. A. Titov recalls in his 'Reminiscences':

> Varlamov's 'Krasny sarafan' caused a *furore*, was sung everywhere and by everyone—in a word, became a song for all. It

was sung by all classes—in the drawing-room of the great lord and in the chimneyless hut of the *muzhik*.

In some of Varlamov's songs, written in the folk idiom (e.g. 'Akh ty, vremya, vremyachko') one detects the influence of Russian 'protracted' song, particularly in the nature of the long-flowing melody. Other folk features apparent in this are the unison opening, the typical cadences with the ascending octave leap, and division of the song into contrasting sections— A minor and C major. Not all of Varlamov's songs are in slow tempo, however. The song 'Chto mne zhit i tuzhit', for instance, is of an animated nature (reflecting the determination of the deserted girl to pursue her lover), in which a realistic touch of colour is provided by a women's chorus echoing the sentiments of the soloist. Dance rhythms are encountered. In many cases Varlamov uses the words of actual folk-songs or the 'Russian Songs' of Tsyganov, Koltsov, Timofeev, and other poets who wrote in the folk idiom. Among other features of his style may be mentioned the influence of gypsy music, (14) and the Schumannesque (or perhaps, more accurately, guitar-like) accompaniments, of which Mus. Ex. 4 is a typical example.

Apart from the above-mentioned genres, Varlamov also wrote a number of ballads, such as the 'Pesn razboynika' (Robber's Song), which is based on A. F. Veltman's 'The Forests of Murom', or the three songs of Ophelia, written as incidental music to *Hamlet* in 1837, which he combined later into a single 'Ballad'.

Varlamov's music is still in a state of reassessment but judging from the musical fragments published by Glumov, it seems that the composer may well have been more gifted than is generally supposed.

Mus. Ex. 4
Allegretto
A. VARLAMOV

V nikh o - gon ne zem - noy zhar-che soln - tsa go - rit

ALEXANDER LVOVICH GURILËV (1803–58)

Alexander Lvovich Gurilëv was born in Moscow in 1803 the son of a serf musician belonging to Count Orlov. His father, Lev Stepanovich, was a composer, a pupil of Sarti, who, for the most part, composed liturgical works in the Italian style fashionable at the period. Lev Gurilëv was almost the only teacher Alexander ever had, though he did study for a short while with John Field. Gurilëv started his musical career as a violinist in the serf orchestra of Count Orlov. Soon, in addition to his regular commitments, he began to give lessons in piano-playing and singing in private houses. According to some accounts he often played the viola in the amateur musical gatherings organized by Prince Golitsyn. With the death of Count Orlov, Gurilëv and his family received their freedom and became members of the Moscow guild (*remeslennoe obshchestvo*). From about the 1830's Gurilëv began to pay greater attention to composition, writing songs, piano pieces, *romances*, mazurkas, waltzes, *galops*, and other pieces then in vogue. He also wrote a number of virtuoso piano variations, one of them being on a theme from the terzetto 'Ne tomi rodimyi' from Glinka's *A Life for the Tsar*. However, by far the most important were his *romances*, of which he wrote about one hundred, and so great was their success that within a very short time he became one of the most popular composers of the era, his best *romances* being written in the 40's and early 50's. What is remarkable is that some of his songs were adopted by gypsies and became folk-songs in their own right. Thus, his song 'Matushka-golobushka', first published in 1845, appeared again in 1850 in a 'Collection of Songs and Romances, Sung by the Moscow Gypsies—*Tsyganskiy tabor*' in a simplified form and without the composer's name.

Gurilëv was much influenced by the music of Varlamov, which he rated highly, indeed, he even wrote some quite elaborate variations on one of Varlamov's songs, 'Na zare ty eë ne budi'. After Varlamov's death he composed a *romance* 'Vospo-minanie o Varlamove' (Reminiscence of Varlamov) to words of Lensky, in which he imitated the melancholy character of the richly ornamented style of Varlamov's 'Russian song'. It was probably after Varlamov's example that Gurilëv undertook the arrangement of forty-seven folk-songs for voice and piano, which were published in 1849 entitled *Izbrannye narodnye russkie pesni* (Selected Russian Folk-songs). In his last years he suffered a mental disorder and was struck helpless by paralysis. He died in Moscow in 1858.

CHARACTERISTICS OF GURILËV'S VOCAL MUSIC

The chief place in Gurilëv's work is occupied by the sentimental *romance* and 'Russian song'. The composer confined himself to these two genres and made no attempt to write dramatic ballads. In style his music is melancholy, lyrical, and elegiac and is not affected by that passion and restlessness characteristic of Varlamov, though he does sometimes avail himself of the pathetic lyricism of gypsy song. His vocal lines are filled with delicate figurations, while the harmony and piano accompaniments are much influenced by Varlamov. A good example of his rhetorical style is afforded by the following excerpt from his song 'Razluka' (Parting) (Mus. Ex. 5):

Mus. Ex. 5 — A. GURILËV

RUSSIAN OPERA IN THE EARLY NINETEENTH CENTURY

The year 1800 saw the Moscow première of an opera which enjoyed prolonged success throughout the first decades of the nineteenth century—*Starinnye svyatki* (The Old Yule-Tide) by Blýma. (15) In its general style Blýma's opera adheres to the traditions of the eighteenth century and illustrates the folk customs and rituals much in the manner of *The St. Petersburg Bazaar*. The stage life of *Starinnye svyatki*, however, falls un-doubtedly into the nineteenth century, and when given in St. Petersburg on 13 January 1813, it was received with great enthusiasm. (16) Zhukovsky and Zagoskin, two of the leading writers of the period, saw it as a Romantic idealization of their native land in the manner of Scott. Although the music of the opera is of very mediocre quality, it is of some interest in that it makes use of at least one genuine folk tune—the well-known 'Slava' which is heard in Act III (No. 12)—besides containing several songs written in the town folk-song idiom. The melody of 'Slava' is identical with the folk-song as it appears in Prach, but the tune has been transposed into another key and has been given a new harmonization. During the course of the number, which is of considerable length, the main theme is interspersed with passages in a similar style. On the whole, however, the development is rather amateurish and in com-parison with Rimsky-Korsakov's and Musorgsky's arrange-ments, the harmonizations are unenterprising.

A sequel to *Starinnye svyatki* appeared a month and a half later (in 1813) entitled *Maslenitsa*, the music of which was by A. N. Titov.

OPERAS OF A. N. TITOV (1769–1827)

A prolific composer in the first two decades of the nineteenth century was A. N. Titov, (17) whose operas are of interest in that they sometimes make use of town folk-song inflections and, occasionally, of genuine folk melodies. However, by far the most remarkable number—indeed, for that matter in the whole of Titov's many attempts at creation in the folk idiom—is an unaccompanied female chorus in the first act of the opera *Devichnik* (1808). (18) The song, which might well be an original melody, shows the influence of Ukrainian folk-song and clearly belongs to the genre of wedding songs (Mus. Ex. 6):

Mus. Ex. 6

TITOV

Uzh ty mat mo — — ya ma — — tush — — ka,

Uzh ty mat go - su - da - — - — - ryn -ya.

When one considers the usual dreary, repetitive style of Titov's writing, it must be confessed that this wedding chorus, with its deliberate attempt to reproduce the characteristics of 'podgo-losnaya' polyphony, is a remarkable page in his musical creation. (19)

DAVYDOV'S RUSALKA

Of greater importance is the work of Davydov, which gives a good insight into the process of 'Russification' of foreign materi-al and its transformation in the hands of Russian musicians. Davydov was one of the most gifted Russian composers at the beginning of the nineteenth century and his output includes incidental music, several ballets, *divertissements*, and the music to two parts of the opera *Lesta, dneprovskaya rusalka*, which be-came one of the most popular operas of the period. (20) The source of the first part was the Austrian composer, Kauer's, celebrated *Singspiel, Das Donauweibchen*, based on an Austrian folk tale, which was performed successfully in Vienna between the years 1798–1839. Having attracted the attention of the Russian writer, Krasnopolsky, it was rewritten and presented in St. Petersburg in 1803. There are three Russian continuations of *Lesta* and for convenience they are given here in table form, indicating the librettist, composer and year of performance in St. Petersburg and Moscow (21):

	Librettist	Composer	Place of performance
Part I	N. S. Krasnopolsky	Kauer & Davydov	St. P. 1803; M. 1806
Part II	N. S. Krasnopolsky	Kauer & Cavos	St. P. 1804; M. 1805

	Librettist	*Composer*	*Place of Performance*
Part III	N. S. Krasnopolsky	Davydov	St. P. 1805; M. 1807
Part IV	Shakhovskoy (complete new text)	Davydov	St. P. 1807; M. 1824 (revived St. P. 1829 and 1852-4)

From its very inception *Lesta* achieved unprecedented success, which is confirmed by contemporary accounts. (22) The subject matter is very slight and is closely connected with de la Motte Fouqué's *Undine*. (23) The opera itself is a mixture of stage effects, intriguing situations and stage magic, and in its final version Shakhovskoy, the librettist, preserved the essential *Singspiel* features of the original, though transferring them to a Russian setting in which not only the names of the places were changed, but the characters also. The music to the first part of *Lesta*, being largely Kauer's, employs very little folk material, the only genuine folk-song introduced by Davydov being the Ukrainian melody 'Ekhal kazak za Dunai', which serves as the basis of Lesta's song in Act III 'Vy k nam vernosti nikogda ne khotite sokhranit'. The arietta is set in variation form and contains additional music of his own composition in a similar idiom. The second parts of *Lesta* (music by Kauer and Cavos) makes slightly more use of folk music, notable in the opera being the presence of Ukrainian musical intonations. The third part, however, is by far the most interesting. Whereas in the first two versions of *Lesta* the principal vocal form was the couplet song, duets being employed but rarely, the third part was of a more elaborate nature and included both solos and ensembles. Only the fourth part of the opera (which makes little use of folk music) has a real overture, but the introduction to the third part is an excellent piece of programme music and probably owes something to the opening of Gluck's *Iphigénie en Tauride* (1779). The orchestral introduction opens with an *Adagio* followed by a fiery *Allegro vivo*, which leads directly into the first scene, representing a mountainous district covered by dense forest. A storm rages accompanied by thunder and lightning, during which Prince Vidostan and his servant Tarabar seek in vain for shelter, till they are rescued by a group of passing hunters. The music describing this scene is most dramatic in its Romantic colouring and shows clearly the great strides made by Russian music in the first few years of the nineteenth century. Apart from the expansion of the musical forms and the enrichment of the harmonic texture, Davydov also makes use of folk-song, drawing his inspiration both from *bytovye* town song and peasant music. Thus, one of Lesta's arias in Act III 'Ya tsyganka molodaya' is based on a folk dance melody 'Za dolami, za gorami' and is set in ternary form with a coda. The middle section and the coda are a development of the folk-song itself. Lesta's daughter, Lida, is represented musically by the lively folk-song 'Kapitanskaya doch', which, with the exception of a few passages, is identical with the tune as it appears in Prach. Of particular interest in this number, however, is the penultimate bar of the operatic version in which, in the true Romantic spirit, Davydov has introduced some colourful ornamentations (Mus. Ex. 7):

Mus. Ex.7

Use is also made of Ukrainian music and 'Russian song'. A curiosity for the period is a trio based on the folk-song 'Sredi dolini rovniya', which is set in the form of a canon.

Davydov's *Lesta* is essentially a product of the Romantic era. Apart from orchestral innovations such as a passage for glass harmonica, the use of four horns in different keys to obtain four-part harmonies (a device obviously borrowed from Sarti), and the enterprising orchestration (in Vidostan's aria in Part I of *Lesta*, Act I No. 3, the accompaniment consists of harp and piano), Davydov's music is permeated by a Romantic spontaneity, which is remarkable considering the period. As regards the treatment of folk-song, he deserves a special mention among the early Russian composers of the nineteenth century. Not only does he draw material from varied sources—from both town and peasant genres—but he uses the folk material freely in conjunction with Romantic forms and harmonies, thus evolving a highly personal, sympathetic musical language, with a definite Russian colouring. It is not impossible that Glinka himself, who certainly was familiar with *Lesta*, as he tells us in his memoirs, was influenced by Davydov's skilful blending of folk music and counterpoint, and in his use of harp and piano in *Ruslan*.

OPERAS OF CAVOS (1776–1840)

One of the most diverse composers of the early nineteenth century was Catterino Cavos (1776–1840), who in the course of his long life did much to assist the development of the Russian theatre and Russian music. (24) Even in his very first operas Cavos displayed a lively interest in Russian subjects, and this is clearly in evidence in the early national opera *Knyaz-nevidimka ili Licharda-volshebnik* (The Invisible Prince or Richard the Magician) (1805),[1] which was Cavos's first effort in this genre. His subsequent productions included many based on Russian themes, such as the opera *Ilya-bogatyr* (Ilya the Bogatyr) (the words of which were by Krylov), the patriotic vaudeville *Kazak-stikhotvorets* (1812), (25) and others, most of which abounded in all manner of fantastic devices, and the weighing down of the action with every conceivable contraption that an enterprising stage mechanic could muster.

Of his many operas, however, the most outstanding is his *Ivan Susanin*, which was written in 1815 and, curiously enough, is the only one that appears to employ folk music. Written to a libretto by Prince Shakhovskoy, it may be regarded in its subject

---

[1] Licharda is a corruption of Richard.

matter as a direct reflection of the patriotic spirit which surged through Russia after the events of 1812. The plot is basically the same as that of Glinka's *A Life for the Tsar* except that in Cavos's version the opera is given a happy ending: Susanin, having led the Poles by a devious route to his village is about to be killed by the enemy, when he is saved by the unexpected arrival of a detachment of Russian soldiers.

Cavos's *Ivan Susanin* is close to the 'rescue' operas of Cherubini, Méhul, and others, and, like them, makes use of spoken dialogue. On the negative side it may be criticized for its lack of movement, the absence of individuality, the sharp divisions into 'good' and 'bad' characters, the exaggeration of the dramatic situations, &c. At the same time there are moments of excitement, the music is often vital and dynamic and there is also a skilful employment of folk music.

Ivan Susanin is preceded by a full-scale overture, which introduces the most important themes of the opera. In the opera itself the ensembles predominate, and although their length produces an impression of immobility, some are outstanding in their monumental power. *Ivan Susanin* well illustrates Cavos's skill in the composition of music in the folk idiom and was the result of many years practical experience in the arrangement of folk melodies and work in the Russian theatre. Outstanding in this respect is the first chorus of peasants (No. 1) in Act I 'Ne bushuyte vy, vetry buynye', which is based on a 'protracted' song, found in Prach (Mus. Ex. 8).

This chorus appears as a kind of frontispiece to the opera and determines the subsequent tone of the work. It undoubtedly had influence on Glinka, both in its polyphonic and contrapuntal treatment of a folk melody, the crude imitation of folk polyphony, the grandioseness of the introduction and the sturdiness of the harmony. Historically it is important as the first attempt (with the possible exception of Fomin's chorus 'Vysoko sokol letaet' from *The Post-drivers*) to use a folk-song in Russian opera in a large choral form. Particularly effective is the climax, followed by a peaceful coda, with which the chorus concludes.

Less successful is the employment of a folk-song in the duet of Masha and Matvey (No. 2), where the use of a 'Kamarinskaya' type of folk dance seems out of keeping with the Romantic nature of the words (a love duet). In this is discerned the

Mus. Ex. 8

Romanticization of folk life, characteristic of so many productions of the period (Mus. Ex. 9).

Nevertheless, the chromatic passages of Matvey's part (after the fermata) are interesting as an anticipation of many later composers' work, in which the voices move in contrary motion over a sustained pedal, the upper part being the folk tune.

Cavos also makes use of town folk-song.

ALEKSEY NIKOLAEVICH VERSTOVSKY (1799–1862)

The last important figure in Russian opera up to the time of Glinka is Aleksey Nikolaevich Verstovsky (1799–1862). (26) Verstovsky was a Romantic in the fullest sense of the word. Not only was he a composer, but a musical historian, translator, actor, and writer. As a composer he wrote incidental music to plays, melodramas, dramatic cantatas, vaudevilles, *divertisse-*

Mus. Ex. 9   CAVOS

ments, intermezzi, and, indeed, attempted most forms of musical composition.

The most decisive year in Verstovsky's life was that of 1823, since it marked his removal from St. Petersburg to Moscow, which was connected with the re-organization of the Moscow Imperial Theatres, and the appearance of some of his finest

ballads—'Nochnoy smotr' (Midnight Review), a translation by
Zhukovsky of Zedlitz's *Die nächtliche Heerschau,* 'Chërnaya shal'
(The Black Shawl), 'Tri pesni' (Three Songs), (after Uhland's
Die drei Lieder), and 'Bedny pevets' (The Poor Singer), which
were virtually the first successful examples of the dramatic or nar-
rative ballad (of the Zumsteeg-Loewe type) in Russian music.
The song 'Chërnaya shal' was performed in Moscow in costume
and with scenery and was also sung to orchestral accompaniment. Previous to this period he had occupied himself with
vaudevilles, many of which had achieved great success, (27)
but after a time, the superficialities of vaudeville ceased to
attract him and he began to contemplate compositions of loftier
dimensions. The ballads of 1823, with their greater emotional
range, were undoubtedly of assistance in developing the necessary qualities for the accomplishment of such a task. In 1825
Verstovsky entered the service of the Imperial Theatres in the
capacity of theatrical inspector, and from that time onwards
played a leading part in Moscow theatrical life. His association
with the leading literary and artistic figures served as a constant
inspiration to him, and his music may be regarded as completely typical of the time, with its ever-increasing interest in
the Russian people on the one hand, and its preoccupation
with the exaggerations of Romanticism on the other. (28)

The interest manifest in the 1820's among the Moscow *littérateurs* towards Romantic art also extended to the theatre. At
the end of the 20's melodrama had established a firm hold on
the Russian stage, in which typical were the abundance of stage
effects, unharnessed passions, elemental cataclysms, and shatter-
ing *dénouements.* Performances of this nature were enhanced by
the acting of such artists as Mochalov, Lavrov, Repin, Bulakhov,
Bantishev, and others, who, though possessing only slender
musical technique, found the music of Verstovsky excellently
suited to their musical and histrionic gifts. (29)

Verstovsky's gradual self-imposed apprenticeship through the
crafts of vaudeville, ballads, incidental music and melodrama
culminated in the writing of his first opera *Pan Twardowski,*
which was performed with great success in Moscow on 24 May
1828 with a libretto by Zagoskin. (30) The music was much
influenced by Weber and its interesting to note that, two years
before the appearance of the opera, Verstovsky clearly expressed

his opinions as to what he considered to be the acme of musical art in an article devoted to the history of opera. In this he gave pride of place to the creations of Méhul and Cherubini at the time of the French Revolution, and, as a direct consequence of their work, the German Romantic operas of Weber. It was inevitable that he should also be influenced by the work of Cavos, his senior by twenty-three years. *Pan Twardowski*, like all of his operas, still employs spoken dialogue and is essentially linked with the traditions of 'opera-vaudeville'. The overture incorporates some of the subject matter later appearing in the opera. From the national point of view the most important phenomenon is the appearance of gypsy music, which was fashionable at the period. The song 'My zhivëm sredi poley i lesov dremuchikh', like many other individual items in Verstovsky's operas, has remained popular to the present day, and as in the case of a number of Varlamov's and Gurilëv's songs, became a folk-song in its own right. (31)

Verstovsky's second opera *Vadim, ili probuzhdenie dvenadtsati spyashchikh dev* (Vadim, or the Awakening of the Twelve Sleeping Maidens) appeared in 1832, with libretto by Shevyrëv, a well-known Moscow poet, historian, *littérateur*, and journalist, and was based on the ballad by Zhukovsky. Stylistically *Vadim* is close to *Pan Twardowski*, folk music making only one solitary appearance.

VERSTOVSKY'S ASKOLD'S TOMB (1835)

On 16 September 1835, one year before the appearance of *A Life for the Tsar*, Verstovsky's finest opera *Askoldova mogila* (Askold's Tomb) was produced on the stage of the Moscow Bolshoy Theatre, with a libretto by Zagoskin, taken from his own story published two years before. (32) The opera obviously owes a great deal to Weber's *Der Freischütz*, which was performed in St. Petersburg in 1824, and it cannot be doubted that, in Weber's opera, Verstovsky found the epitome of his own ideals. (33) *Askold's Tomb* is a Romantic opera with a Russian flavour, the national element being represented by such scenes as the chorus of fishermen, the revelry of the Kievites, the feast of the Prince's bodyguard, and the rustic life in the village of Predslavino. Against this are opposed the fantastic features, in particular, the Hoffmannesque scene with Vakhrameevna the

Witch, with her folk incantations, and the attributes of her profession—the broomstick, the owl, the black cat, the pot with the mysterious brew! The musical similarities between the two operas are endless, but the comparisons may be extended to the dramatic aspects also. Both operas make use of spoken dialogue; the musical-dramatic action is concentrated mostly in the finales, taking the form of freely constructed ensembles. In the fantastic scenes there is the familiar use of melodrama. Characteristic also are the two-section arias, in which a slow introduction leads into a lively *Allegro* (the Italian *cavatina* and *cabaletta*), and the ballad songs—a logical outgrowth of Verstovsky's earlier efforts in that field. Of even greater similarity is the overture, which, though lacking the proportions of *Der Freischütz*, also introduces the main themes of the opera.

Of major importance is the national element, which is represented not only by the employment of folk melodies, but in the characters themselves, who, for perhaps the first time in Russian opera, are clearly drawn and distinguished by national characteristics. Outstanding in this respect is the person of Toropka-Golovan, the *gudok*-player, who figures prominently in the opera. Toropka is a true descendent from the *skomorokhi* and doubtless Verstovsky had such a figure in mind when he composed the music. Another national figure is Nadezhda, a typical Russian girl, sensitive, dignified, and passionate. Like Toropka she is the prototype of many other similar Russian operatic heroines. Neizvestniy (lit. 'The Unknown') is essentially a product of his period, though possessing international rather than national significance. Of interest on account of his constant appearance in nineteenth century Russian opera is the comic Varangian *mechnik* Frelaf, who is the model for Glinka's Farlaf. Frelaf's patter songs, like those of the Miller in *Melnik-koldun* and Farlaf's aria in *Ruslan* (Act I No. 7) belong to a type common in Russian opera.

Notable in *Askold's Tomb* are the folk choral scenes, which, like those in Glinka's *A Life for the Tsar*, form the mainstay of the whole opera. Perhaps the finest of all Verstovsky's choruses is 'Goy, goy, ty Dnepr' (Act I No. 2), which is remarkable for its writing in the manner of folk polyphony (Mus. Ex. 10). Apart from the fact that the first bars are based on a sustained pedal, a typical folk effect, the choral parts break into a most

Mus. Ex.10

effective unison at bars 6, 15, and later at bars 23–24. Predominant also is movement in parallel thirds, while even the ending, with its octave leap, bears the mark of authenticity.

Another attempt to suggest folk polyphony occurs in the chorus 'Svetel mesyats' (Act I No. 5). In its use of an opening solo phrase, sung by the sopranos, then continued by the remainder of the voices, first in unison, then in harmony, the chorus shows similarity to authentic folk performance. Mention should also be made of Toropka's ballad 'Blizko goroda Slavyanska' (which abounds in folk-song phrases), the Russian colouring of the chorus 'Akh, podruzhenki', and the chorus 'Gey! Zhgi!', which is of interest in that the accompaniment suggests the sound of folk instruments. Toropka's aria, which follows this chorus almost immediately, well reproduces the lively features of town dance song, perhaps with a touch of gypsy influence.

OTHER OPERAS BY VERSTOVSKY

After *Askold's Tomb*, Verstovsky wrote other operas, among them *Toska po rodine* (1839), *Son nayavu, ili churova dolina* (1844), and *Gromoboy* (1857). His later operas, however, added nothing to what had already been said.

SUMMARY

Verstovsky's prime importance is that he succeeded in achieving a coalescence between German Romantic opera and Russian folk music. While not completely abandoning spoken dialogue, he paved the way for continuous musical development by the greater use of recitative, so that the action was advanced almost entirely by the music. The fact that he was able to write convincingly in the folk idiom and to imbue his work with essentially Russian content, to say nothing of his expansion of musical forms and harmony, make him a worthy predecessor to Glinka. (34)

With *Askold's Tomb* of 1835 the second period of Russian opera comes to a close, a fitting year since it stands on the eve of the first Russian opera to dispense with spoken dialogue and fully to transcend the bounds of vaudeville and melodrama—Glinka's *A Life for the Tsar*.

CHAPTER 6

M. I. Glinka (1804-1857)

SIGNIFICANCE OF GLINKA IN RUSSIAN MUSIC

The chief significance of Glinka in the history of Russian music is that he was the formulator of the Russian musical language, just as Pushkin was the formulator of the Russian literary tongue. Indeed, the parallel between the two great men is even closer, for whereas Pushkin's work arose out of the creation of Lomonosov, Derzhavin, Karamzin, Batyushkov, Zhukovsky, Krylov, and others, so did Glinka's music spring from that of his Russian precursors—Verstovsky, Cavos, and a whole host of *romance*-writers too numerous to mention. In comparison with the works of his predecessors, Glinka's music is outstanding in its absolute professionalism. For the most part his mature compositions are beautifully constructed and free from the all-too-obvious links and joins characteristic of the Cavos-Verstovsky school. Apart from his role as a harmonic and orchestral innovator, he is also remarkable for his thorough knowledge of Russian folk music.

GLINKA'S BIOGRAPHY: EARLY YEARS

Mikhail Ivanovich Glinka was born on 20 May 1804 in the village of Novospasskoe in the Province of Smolensk on the small estate of his father, Ivan Nikolaevich, a retired captain and a wealthy landowner. His childhood and adolescence were spent in the usual kind of village environment in close contact with folk-song and folk life. (1) From his earliest days the songs and folk tales of his peasant nurse, Avdotya Ivanovna, attracted his attention and stimulated his imagination. As well as this, the events of 1812 must have made some impression on the young Glinka, for the Glinka's country house was situated near the Smolensk road not far from Elnya. In 1812 the region was the scene of intensive military operations and the centre of the partisan movement, in which the peasants of Novospasskoe participated. In the winter of that year, when the Glinka family moved to Orël to save themselves from the French invasion, their peasants defended the house from the enemy, and, on the family's return, Glinka must undoubtedly have heard stories of these activities, which roused his sense of patriotism.

Glinka was affected by music from an early age—indeed, his words 'Music is my soul' (reputedly uttered at the age of ten or eleven) have become famous. (2) In particular, he was attracted by the serf orchestra of his uncle Afanasiy Andreevich, who lived not far away, and which often visited Novospasskoe. As Glinka recounts in his *Memoirs*:

> During dinner they usually played Russian Songs, arranged for two flutes, two clarinets, two horns and two bassoons. These sadly tender sounds were completely comprehensible to me . . . and perhaps it was these songs, that I heard in my childhood, that were the main reason that I began to dwell primarily on Russian folk music later on.

Each visit of the serf musicians was a real holiday for Glinka. Taking in his hands a violin or a piccolo he would play with the musicians by ear—'imitating the orchestra'. As he again describes in his *Memoirs*:

> Father often grew angry with me for not dancing and leaving the guests, but at the first opportunity I again returned to the orchestra.

It was through the performances of this serf orchestra that he first became acquainted with examples of European music in the form of opera overtures (e.g. Boïeldieu's *Ma Tante Aurore*, Kreutzer's *Lodoïska*, Méhul's *Les deux aveugles*), excerpts from symphonies and other works popular at the time such as Steibelt's rondo *The Storm*, which he played quite well on the piano.

It was at the age of about ten that the future composer began to study music more seriously. A governess named Varvara Fëdorovna Klammer, who arrived from St. Petersburg, gave him piano lessons, while a serf musician from the orchestra gave him instruction on the violin, though, as Glinka himself observes he unfortunately introduced him to habits of bad bowing.

Shortly afterwards he received a more systematic education, for in the winter of 1817 he was sent to the capital, where he was enrolled in the newly opened Boarding School for Noblemen's Sons at the Main Pedagogical Institute—an establishment at which he was to study for four years, from 1818 to 1822. These years played a great part in the formation of Glinka's personality, for the teachers included such people as Wilhelm Karlovich Küchelbecher (1797–1846), a friend of Pushkin and later a participant in the Decembrist movement, who was the composer's personal tutor. At school he also met Pushkin, whose brother Lev Sergeevich, was likewise a pupil there. Doubtless Pushkin must often have met the young musician when visiting his brother and his friend Küchelbecher.

At the same time as his scholastic undertakings Glinka continued his musical activities. Among his several teachers were the celebrated pianist and pedagogue, John Field (from whom, unfortunately, he received only three lessons), and Charles Mayer, who subsequently became a close friend. The distinctive character of Field's Romantic music, the contemplative, elegant style of his playing must undoubtedly have had influence on the young composer's early compositions. Some idea of the standard of Glinka's own level of performance as a pianist is gained from the fact that he played Hummel's Concerto in A minor in public in 1822, with Mayer at the second piano.

Whilst studying at the Boarding School Glinka did not neglect orchestral music and his summer holidays were spent at Novospasskoe, where he worked with enthusiasm with his uncle's serf orchestra, acting both as performer and conductor. In his own words, it was through his practical work with the orchestra that he slowly began to master orchestration and we learn from his *Memoirs* that the works they performed (though at a slightly later date) included symphonies and overtures by Beethoven, Mozart, and Cherubini.

In St. Petersburg Glinka often took part in musical evenings as a pianist, violinist, and singer. He first took singing lessons at the age of about twenty and subsequently became an extremely good performer. Possessing a tenor voice he paid special attention to vocal technique and later many famous Russian singers such as Petrova-Vorobëva, S. S. Gulak-Artemovsky, D. M. Leonova, and others profited by his advice.

FIRST ESSAYS IN COMPOSITION

On leaving school in 1822 Glinka gave himself up entirely to music, and it is at this period that he also first began to compose. On the advice of his teachers (especially Charles Mayer), he wrote a cantata, a piano trio, two overtures, a sketch for a symphony in B♭ major (1822–6), three cycles of variations for piano (1822), and several *romances*. In his own words: 'Passion for composition decisively distracted me from practice in performance'. However, his first efforts in the field of composition were little more than skilful imitations of Western works popular at the time, though greater originality was displayed in his vocal works. As is only to be expected, his first piano pieces were very much determined by the tastes of the time, comprising *contredanses*, waltzes and *galops*, though two other genres are also encountered: the slow, lyrical pieces (redolent of Field and his nocturnes) similar in style to the sentimental *romance*, and the brilliant variations on motives from operas by Weigl, Mozart, and Cherubini or on original folk tunes.

INTELLECTUAL ASSOCIATIONS

Another decisive part at this period (i.e. from 1822–30) was played by his friendship with intellectuals. At the end of the 20's he often met Pushkin (after the poet's return from exile), Griboedov, Odoevsky, Zhukovsky, and Mickiewicz, as well as taking part in musical evenings in the home of Delvig. He was especially fond of Russian folk-songs and wrote many 'Russian songs' to Delvig's words—e.g. 'Akh, ty, noch li, nochenka' (O Night, Oh, Gentle Night), 'Ne osenniy chastyi dozhdichek' (Not the Heavy Autumn Shower), &c.—all of which were performed at Delvig's parties, in which also participated M. L. Yakovlev, a gifted singer and composer of *romances*. By the beginning of the 1830's Glinka had a number of fine *romances* to his credit, including the elegy 'Ne iskushay' (Do Not Tempt), written in 1825, the *romances* 'Bednyi pevets' (The Poor Singer), 'Skazhi zachem' (Tell Me Why), 'Gruzinskaya pesnya' (Georgian Song), and several chamber works—the Sonata for Piano and Viola, two Quartets—and numerous piano pieces.

INTEREST IN FOLK MUSIC

Apart from Russian folk music Glinka was also interested in the national music of other peoples inhabiting Russia and shortly after leaving school he was sent by his father in the summer of 1823 to undertake a mineral water cure at Pyatigorsk in the Caucasus. Whilst in the Caucasus he studied attentively the Georgian folk games and dances and took a keen interest in the life of the North Caucasian *auls* (villages). His impressions were reflected later in his opera *Ruslan and Lyudmila*.

FIRST TRIP ABROAD

In 1830, on his doctor's advice, Glinka was at last given permission by his father to travel abroad. His stay was of no less than five years duration, three years of which were spent in Italy, visiting Milan, Rome, Naples, and Venice, and one year in Vienna and Berlin. Whilst in Italy he studied vocal music, visited the opera, made the acquaintance of Bellini and Donizetti and even went to the extent of taking lessons in composition from Italian pedagogues. Among them was a certain Professor Basili, the head of the Milan Conservatoire, but so dry and pedantic did Glinka find his new mentor that he quickly discontinued his lessons.

Like most Russians Glinka was fascinated by the warmth and brilliance of Italy. The Italian operatic cantilena, the sweet *bel canto* were congenial to his Romantic nature and were quickly assimilated into his style. Italian instrumental writing also left its mark and whilst in Italy he wrote a series of works on popular themes from the operas of Bellini and Donizetti, the 'Pathetic Trio' in D minor for Clarinet, Bassoon, and Piano, the Piano Sextet in E♭ major (1832), several *romances*, all of which were clearly influenced by impressions of Italian life and the Italian countryside—e.g. 'Venetsianskaya noch' (Venetian Night), 'Pobeditel' (The Conqueror), and other works.

Nevertheless, despite his love of the Italian countryside and its people (Glinka could never resist a pretty face!), at the end of his third year he began to experience a strong sense of conflict between the surrounding world and his inner life. In particular he felt an ever-increasing awareness of his Russian nationality and in his *Memoirs* he wrote:

I did not compose but thought a great deal. All the pieces written by me in honour of the citizens of Milan, and which were published extremely nicely by Giovanni Ricordi, only convinced me that I was not following my own path and that sincerely I could not be an Italian. Longing for my native land led me constantly to the idea of writing something Russian.

The winter of 1833–4 was spent in Berlin in steady, unremitting labour. In particular he undertook a course in composition with the well-known theoretician Siegfried Dehn (1799–1858), himself a pupil of Cherubini, which undoubtedly did a great deal to assist him. In his own words:

There is no doubt that I was more obliged to Dehn than to all my other *maestri*; he . . . not only put my theory into order, but all my ideas about art in general, and through his lectures I began to work not from intuition but from knowledge.

Together with the improvement of his technique, the national tendencies in his music also began to mature, and to this period belong a series of works on Russian folk motives, which were largely written under Dehn's guidance. These include a Capriccio on Russian Themes for Piano Duet (which he calls a 'Potpourri' in his *Memoirs*), a sketch of a Symphony-overture on a folk-song, Piano Variations on the theme of Alyabyev's song 'Solovey', and several fragments, which were later included in his opera *A Life for the Tsar* (e.g. Vanya's song, the first theme of the *Allegro* of the Overture, and others).

RETURN TO RUSSIA: 'A LIFE FOR THE TSAR'

Immediately on his return to Russia in April 1834 Glinka set to work in order to realize a long-seated ambition—the creation of a large-scale national opera, a task in which he was supported warmly by his friends Pushkin, Odoevsky, and Melgunov. After several attempts to find a suitable subject, he settled (on the poet Zhukovsky's advice) on the historical legend of Ivan Susanin—the story of the Russian peasant, who saved his Tsar and country by leading the Polish invaders into the depths of the Russian forest, though at the sacrifice of his own life. As Glinka himself wrote:

The scene in the wood fixed itself firmly on my imagination. I found in it much that was original, characteristically Russian.

One of the sources of the opera was the *duma* (ballad) of Ryleev, the Decembrist poet, where the scene in the wood is the heroic culmination of the entire poem. In setting to work on the opera Glinka himself wrote the *scenario* and worked out in detail a plan of composition. At first Zhukovsky agreed to write the necessary verses, but later he withdrew and entrusted the task to Baron Rosen—a *littérateur* occupying a prominent position at Court as Secretary to the Tsarevich. Not that Rosen had an easy task, for so fervent was Glinka's enthusiasm that the music was frequently written before the words. As Glinka describes it:

> My imagination, however, anticipated the industrious German; as if by magic the plan of the entire opera came into being and the thought of contrasting the Russian music with the Polish; finally, many themes and even details of the development—all this flamed up in my head at once.

Glinka worked for about a year on the opera and at the beginning of 1836 *Ivan Susanin* was completed and in the autumn of the same year accepted for performance by the St. Petersburg Bolshoy Theatre, the conductor being Catterino Cavos. Rehearsals commenced in which the composer took an active part and to this period also belongs the friendship between Glinka and O. A. Petrov and A. Y. Vorobëva—the first performers of the roles of Susanin and Vanya. Tsar Nicholas I took a personal interest in the opera, and at his request the title of the work was changed to that of *A Life for the Tsar*. On 27 November the opera was given its première and for the most part was successful. Although the opera had its critics (one person claimed that it was 'la musique des cochers'), it was well received on the whole, Gogol regarding it as 'a wonderful beginning' to the approaching era of Russian music. (3)

DOMESTIC PROBLEMS

After the première of *A Life for the Tsar*, Glinka ran into difficulties. As a sign of the Emperor's favour he was appointed Kapellmeister of the Court Chapel under A. F. Lvov (1798–1870), who was its Director from 1837–61 and composer (in

M

1833) of the Russian National Anthem.[1] Glinka and Lvov seem to have been diametrically opposed in their personalities and their frequent arguments led to a complete break in 1839, when Glinka was obliged to resign his post. His position in society was further worsened by the fact that, in 1835, he had married the daughter of a poor noble family, Maria Petrovna Ivanova. Glinka's wife was incapable of sharing her husband's world and was frivolous and empty-headed into the bargain— indeed, the parallels between Glinka's marriage and that of the unfortunate Pushkin are regrettably close. In a short while the position became intolerable, husband and wife lived apart, and the whole tiresome operation of separation proceedings began, a divorce only being obtained in 1846. In all fairness, however, it must be stated that there were grave faults on both sides and Glinka himself was far from blameless in the matter. Somewhat ostracized by society, and himself ignoring such aristocratic friends as Prince Odoevsky or Count Vielgorsky, the composer sought solace either in the company of women or in the collection of writers, artists, and musicians gathered round Nestor Kukolnik, a connoisseur of art and man of letters. Kukolnik's gathering was a typical Bohemian circle in which the service to art was accompanied by abundant libations to Bacchus, and which acquired among contemporaries the somewhat contemptuous nickname of 'The Kukolnik Brotherhood'. (4) Nevertheless, the Kukolnik circle probably had a propitious effect upon him aesthetically, even if it were injurious physically and morally. Among the regular visitors were the famous artist Bryullov, the writer Belinsky, and many other *littérateurs* and members of the young aristocratic intelligentsia. Great interest was shown in the Romantic tendencies of the West, along with folk art and national themes, Glinka's work, in particular, being held in high esteem.

TRIP TO THE UKRAINE

A valuable event in Glinka's life was the trip that he undertook to the Ukraine in the spring of 1838, where he was sent in order to select singers for the Imperial Chapel. The whole Ukrainian

---

[1] Before Lvov's composition, the British national anthem 'God Save the King' was often played (see M. Montagu-Nathan. 'The Composer of the Russian Anthem'. *The Musical Times*, 1 February 1915, pp. 83–4).

ambiance, with its picturesque scenery, its lively folk dances and happy people all left their impression upon him, and on the Kachanovka estate in the Province of Poltava he wrote several Ukrainian songs, performing the first excerpts from *Ruslan* with the aid of his host's private orchestra. In listening to the many singers, Glinka noted the outstanding gifts of Semën Stepanovich Gulak-Artemovsky (1813–73), a fine baritone and the future composer of the Ukrainian national opera *Zaporozhets za Dunaem*. On Glinka's request Gulak-Artemovskiy was sent to St. Petersburg, where Glinka supervised his musical education in person.

INTERMEDIATE YEARS

The years between the première of *A Life for the Tsar* and the completion of *Ruslan and Lyudmila* were also fruitful from the point of view of composition. In the interim period he wrote the incidental music to *Prince Kholmsky* (1840), a cycle of *romances* entitled *Proshchanie s Peterburgom* (Farewell to Petersburg) (1840), and the songs 'Somnenie' (Doubt), 'Nochnoy smotr' (The Midnight Review), 'Ya pomnyu chudnoe mgnovenie' (I Remember a Wonderful Moment), and a host of piano pieces, among them the *Vals-fantaziya* (Waltz-Fantasy), which he later orchestrated.

'RUSLAN AND LYUDMILA'

Glinka's chief work over the period was, of course, his opera *Ruslan and Lyudmila*, which took nearly six years to come into being. And this was not only because of the unpropitious conditions of his life, but on account of the enormity of the task. As in the case of *A Life for the Tsar* the outline of the opera was formulated by Glinka and worked out in detail in his letters to V. F. Shirkov, his librettist. The text of the opera, however, was composed fragmentarily and in haphazard order by numerous figures, some scenes being written by friends such as Kukolnik, Markevich, and Gedeonov. The very music was composed in short bursts and during frequent removals, several fragments from it being performed to the general public at concerts. In the spring of 1842 the score of *Ruslan* was completed and the opera accepted for performance, the première taking place on 27 November 1842 in the St. Petersburg Bolshoy Theatre.

Ruslan and Lyudmila, however, was not a success, opinions about the opera being strongly divided. The general public received it coldly, the aristocracy did not accept it and Nicholas I left the theatre before the end of the performance. Indeed, *Ruslan and Lyudmila* was considered so tedious by Court circles that the Tsar's brother, Mikhail Pavlovich, was in the habit of sending officers guilty of misdemeanours to the opera instead of to the guardroom! The unusual and unfamiliar nature of the music brought forth outspoken criticisms, though some writers were wholehearted in their support. Odoevsky, for instance, concluded one of his articles on *Ruslan* with the following words:

> O, believe me! In our Russian soil has arisen a luxurious flower
> —it is our joy, our glory. Let the worms climb up its stem and soil
> it—the worms will fall to the ground, but the flower will remain.
> (5)

Nevertheless, after its bad beginning, the success of the opera gradually increased, a prominent part being played by Petrova-Vorobëva, the excellent performer of Ratmir, who had been unable to take part in the première. *Ruslan* continued to be performed for some time thanks to its fantastic setting and was eventually withdrawn only on the insistence of the Court. From 1843 an Italian troupe prevailed on the stage of the Petersburg Bolshoy and three years later the Russian opera company was transferred to Moscow. The revival of *Ruslan and Lyudmila* took place in the capital in 1858.

PERIOD OF DISILLUSIONMENT

Glinka himself was particularly upset by the opera's apparent failure. The interminable process of divorce, the constant attacks upon him in the press, still further sapped his vitality. Even in letters penned on 8 March 1841 he had written:

> For me there can be no happiness in Russia. Carry me from here . . . I have had enough of this vile country . . . They have taken everything from me, even enthusiasm for my art—my last resort.

The poor reception of *Ruslan* did little to alleviate this mood of depression and in 1844 he again went abroad for three years, being first in Paris (1844–5), and then in Spain (1845–7). (6)

SECOND STAY ABROAD

Glinka's stay in Paris was not without consequences. He was fascinated by the Parisian musical life and made the acquaintance of Berlioz, with whom he set up a warm friendship. Berlioz performed some of Glinka's music at one of his concerts and shortly afterwards a concert was given for Glinka's benefit, in which were played extracts from *A Life for the Tsar* and *Ruslan and Lyudmila*. Before this time (in 1842, and again in 1843), Glinka had met Liszt, who likewise recognized his gifts. Glinka's and Berlioz's concerts undoubtedly did much to make Russian music known abroad and in a letter from Paris Glinka wrote to his beloved mother not without a touch of pride:

> I am the first Russian composer, who has acquainted the Parisian public with his name and with his works, written in Russia and for Russia. (7)

It is worth noting that Glinka was also impressed by Berlioz's own compositions. In his own words:

> Study of Berlioz's music . . . brought me extremely important results.

It is significant, therefore, that at this period of his life he became interested especially in the question of orchestral music, doubtless the outcome of his examination of Berlioz's brilliant orchestration and symphonic technique. Of these proposed orchestral works ('picturesque fantasias' as he called them), having a national character, he stated that he wished them to be comprehensible not only to connoisseurs but also 'to the ordinary people'—a phrase that has a prophetic ring about it in view of the demands made of twentieth century Soviet music.

In May 1845 Glinka at last crossed the border to Spain—a country which had long fascinated him by the individuality and wealth of its folk music. There he spent two years, travelling through different towns, writing down Spanish folk melodies and making detailed observations on the life of the people, their dances and the art of the folk-singers. In September 1845, as a direct result of his impressions, he wrote the first of his two Spanish overtures—*Jota Aragonesa*.

YEARS OF RESTLESSNESS

In 1847 he returned to Russia and the next decade was spent in almost incessant movement. Glinka could never live anywhere for a prolonged time and creation appeared only in short brilliant outbursts. Although his gifts were still in full flower, the determination and concentration necessary for major undertakings were absent. His constitution ravaged by disease and excess, the composer was already a sick man. Twice Glinka visited Warsaw (in 1848 and 1849–51), where he wrote two of the most important works of the last years of his life: the second Spanish Overture *Noch v Madride* (Night in Madrid), based on four Spanish themes collected by himself, and the brilliant *Kamarinskaya* (1848). In Warsaw, too, he composed several of his best late *romances*—'Pesn Margarity' (Song of Margaret), 'Finskiy zaliv' (The Gulf of Finland), 'Zazdravnyi kubok' (The Toasting Cup), and others. Another visit to Paris took place from 1852–4.

DISTINGUISHED CONTEMPORARIES

The last years of Glinka's life coincide with an interesting period of Russian musical history, for it was this era that saw the flourishing of Dargomyzhsky's art (the première of *Rusalka* occurred in 1856), the first activities of Balakirev, and the writings of Stasov and Serov. To all these Glinka's music was a constant source of inspiration. Glinka valued in particular the gifts of Balakirev—then a young musician, who arrived in St. Petersburg from the provinces at the end of 1855.

The composer was also visited frequently by Dargomyzhsky. While working on his opera *Rusalka*, he acquainted Glinka with excerpts from the music. Extracts from the work were performed at Glinka's house by Dargomyzhsky himself and the gifted amateur singer, L. I. Belenitsyna.

ROLE OF GLINKA'S SISTER

A faithful supporter of Glinka in the last years of his life was his devoted sister, Lyudmila Ivanovna Shestakova (1816–1906), who did everything in her power to foster his genius. After his death she did much to publish and propagandize her brother's work and took an active interest in the musical affairs of the *Kuchka* (the Russian 'Five').

FINAL PROJECTS

Glinka never managed to accomplish his last intentions. At the beginning of the 50's he contemplated a symphony on Ukrainian themes—*Taras Bulba*, but abandoned it at the second movement as he was dissatisfied with the lack of any Ukrainian colouring. Another project was the opera *Dvumuzhnitsa* (The Bigamist) on a dramatic subject popular at the time by Shakhovskoy. These, however, were worked out only in sketches and the last years of his life were spent mostly on the editing and orchestration of his previous compositions. In 1854–5, on the advice of friends, he wrote his *Memoirs*, which are a frank and illuminating account of the life of the times as well as being the most important source of information as to the composer's biography. (8)

FINAL TRIP ABROAD

In the spring of 1856 he again went abroad—to Berlin, again with the intention of studying strict counterpoint (notably that of Palestrina, Lassus, Bach, and Handel) with his old teacher, Dehn, and of hearing the operas of Gluck (incidentally, one of Glinka's favourite composers), whose works at that time had never appeared on the Russian stage. In particular he was much concerned with the question of Russian polyphony, and with that aim worked hard on the harmonization of ancient *znamenny* melodies, examining their modal structure. He was inspired by the thought of creating a 'national counterpoint' with large polyphonic forms on a folk basis. Referring in a letter to his sister to the idea 'of connecting the Western fugue with the terms of our music through the ties of a legal marriage', he wrote:

> I have here a purpose—a lofty purpose . . . Shall I achieve this aim?—that's another matter—I shall strive towards it continually, if not quickly. (9)

On 3 February 1857, as the result of a heavy cold, Glinka died and in May of the same year, on his sister's request, his corpse was brought to St. Petersburg and interred in the Alexander Nevsky necropolis.

The first biography of the composer, based on authentic

materials, was written by V. V. Stasov in 1857, and with this task the young critic entered the lists as champion and literary spokesman of the Russian Nationalist School.

GLINKA'S OPERAS: 'A LIFE FOR THE TSAR' (1836)

To all extents and appearances Glinka's first opera—*A Life for the Tsar*—is very much in the traditions of French Grand Opera, comprising as it does the typical 5-Act structure, the Romantic development of the action, based on contrasts of scenes and moods, the large number of choral and ensemble episodes, ballet *divertissements* and, finally, the grand finale and apotheosis. However, *A Life for the Tsar* is largely free from the complexities which are found in the operas of Auber, Meyerbeer and Halévy. The first two acts introduce the main participants in the action—the Russian people and Susanin's family in Act I, the Poles in Act II. The Third Act shows the meeting of Susanin and the Poles—an especially effective act since the happy preparations for the wedding of Susanin's daughter, Antonida, in the first part clash violently with the sudden irruption of the Polish forces in the second. The Fourth Act provides a dramatic *dénouement* with the ever-increasing agitation of the Poles and the death of Susanin, while the Fifth Act smoothly rounds off the whole action. (10) The basic idea of the opera—that of patriotism and the heroism of the Russian people—is expressed in the two massive folk choruses, which frame the opera in the form of an introduction and epilogue, particularly striking being the decisive opening of the first chorus (Mus. Ex. 1).

That the composer desired to give the opera a national colouring is clearly illustrated by the plan of the first three acts of the opera, which is still preserved. (11) The following are two relevant extracts, referring to the opening chorus and the scene featuring Susanin, Vanya, Sobinin, and the peasants:

PLAN
Of the First Three Acts of the Opera
'Ivan Susanin'
A native heroic-tragic opera in 5 acts or parts.

Part One

The setting is a Russian village scene; in the stage background a river.

Mus. Ex. 1

No. 1. *Introduction.* 'In the distance is first heard a chorus of men, later, on the opposite side, a chorus of women, which, on approaching, are combined. This chorus, which leads into a fugue, must be written in a Russian metre [*sic*.] and the similes must be borrowed from rural subjects. The men go out first, soon followed by the women and when the voices and then the orchestra decrease in sound, a boat appears on the river with oarsmen who sing a protracted song *unissono*. This chorus must express the same feelings as the chorus *en fugue*, but the similes must be taken from topics relating to the river, the boat, &c. When the boat reaches the middle of the theatre and the chorus is *FF*, the orchestra plays a dance, which, as it grows in volume, gradually drowns the singers—and from the dance emerges a *khorovod* . . .'

No. 10. Part 3. '. . . This number, expressing the quiet, blissful feelings of family life, must undoubtedly be written in the Russian style in imitation of old songs'.

From this it is apparent that Glinka sought to give his opera Russian colouring, and this factor was immediately seized upon by critics after its first performance on Friday 27 November 1836. (12) It is worth noting that Glinka's opera marked an advance over its predecessors in that it was the first Russian opera to dispense with spoken dialogue—a factor that favoured a high level of musical development.

USE OF AUTHENTIC FOLK-SONGS

A Life for the Tsar is especially remarkable from the point of view of folk music. It makes use of only two authentic folksongs, and Glinka has left us an account of the manner in which he obtained them and the means by which he incorporated them in the opera:

> In the course of work, I was greatly obliged to the advice of Prince Odoevsky and to a certain extent to Charles Mayer. Odoevsky was extremely pleased with the theme which I took from the song of the Luga coachdriver, namely (Mus. Ex. 2):

> He advised me to recall this theme, with which the part of Susanin opens, in his last scene in the forest with the Poles. I managed to use it; after the words 'Tuda zavël ya vas' (I have led you here) is a progression based on a fragment from the theme given me by the coachman, namely (Mus. Ex. 3):

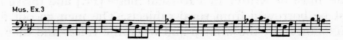

> In the composition of the beginning of Susanin's replies, I had in mind our well-known robbers' song 'Vniz po matushke, po Volge', using its beginning with a repeated movement in the accompaniment, like this (Mus. Ex. 4):

Glinka certainly used the two tunes as described, the song of the Luga coachman forming the basis of Susanin's melody in No. 3. But there are a number of differences between the song as it appears in the *Memoirs* and the form that it takes in the opera. The key has been changed and also the shape of the melody. In the circumstances it is impossible to tell how much of the tune was borrowed from the coachman and how much was Glinka's own composition. Nevertheless, of interest is the fact that the melody, as it now stands in the opera, shows close resemblance to a number of existing folk-songs, both in its unusual modal structure and in its cadential features.

The second folk-song 'Vniz po matushke, po Volge' is first heard in the entr'acte to Act IV (No. 16) and later serves as the accompaniment to Susanin's aria 'Tuda zavël ya vas' in Act IV No. 20c.

CREATION IN THE FOLK IDIOM

A Life for the Tsar abounds in folk intonations and no better example of this can be found than the opening chorus 'V buryu, vo grozu'. Of particular significance, not only in this number but in Glinka's creation as a whole, is the melodic pattern V—I—VI, which recurs throughout the opera (see Mus. Ex. 1). This progression is also common in folk-song. The similarity between the opening chorus and many actual folk melodies is shown from the following illustration (Mus. Ex. 5):

Ex. 5a is the theme as it appears in Glinka; Ex. 5b is part of the folk-song 'Letal golub', taken from Part I, No. 37 of Kashin's collection; Ex. 5c is a fragment from the folk-song 'Ty molodenkiy molodchik' (also taken from Kashin, Part I, No. 6); Ex. 5d is the opening of the folk melody 'Akh, ty, pole'.

There is likewise a resemblance between the minor variant of the Glinka theme and the folk-song 'Vspomni, moy lyubezniy' (Kashin's collection Part I, No. 22).

Two other melodies resemble the opening chorus. These are the folk-songs 'Ne bely snegi', which appears in N. Afanasev's collection (13) and 'Ty vzoydi, solntse krasnoe', which appears in Listopadov's. Mention should also be made of the similarities between Glinka's chorus and choral versions of soldiers' songs—in particular the song 'Chto za pesni raspevaet nasha Rus' as it appears in Popov's collection and other variants. (14)

The second section of the opening chorus in *A Life for the Tsar* is sung by women's voices and this too shows close resemblance to *khorovod* songs—notably to the song 'Belolitsa, kruglolitsa' (15)—as is illustrated by the following example (Mus. Ex. 6):

The opening theme of the first chorus (Mus. Ex. 1) sounds as a patriotic reminiscence motive throughout the opera, reappearing again in Susanin's part in Act III No. 12 ('I tak ya dozhil, slava Bogu'), in No. 21 (Epilogue), and, to some extent, in No. 23 ('Vsë ta-zhe toska, pechal v dushe'). It is possible that the opening motive is based on the folk-song 'Molodka molodaya', which appears in Rimsky-Korsakov's collection (p. 248). Nevertheless, all this serves to illustrate the manifold origins of Glinka's music. The source of any one particular melody may be found in no single folk-song, but in the inflections and intonations of folk-song in general.

For the musical characterization of the Russian people in *A*

Life for the Tsar, of particular significance is the chorus of oars-men in Act I 'Lëd reku v polon zabral', the sources of which might lie, according to the Soviet musicologist Vladimir Protopopov, (16) either in the folk-song 'Chtoy to vo pole', or in Glinka's own song 'Noch osennyaya, lyubeznaya', where the similarities of individual phrases, melodic turns and cadences are very close.

A little later in the same act is introduced the heroic theme of Sobinin (Antonida's fiancé), echoes of which are heard in the choral parts. The origin of these melodies is probably to be found in lively *molodetskie* songs,[1] or possibly in lyrical songs. An excellent illustration is the folk-song 'Snegi belye', where whole phrases coincide with the Glinka theme. (17) Balakirev observed a connection between lyrical songs and Sobinin's part when he wrote in a letter to Stasov (Mus. Ex. 7):

'I have been listening to the hauler's songs. One sang:

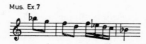

Mus. Ex.7

which struck me in the extreme'. (18)

The similarity between this, Sobinin's theme and the folk-song 'Snegi belye' is revealed in (Mus. Ex. 8):

Mus. Ex.8

(a) Ekh, kog-da zhen-nikh k ne-vest-e bez po-dar-ka pri-ez-zhal. Ya s mo-ey dru-zhi-noy v mes-te vrazh-yu shay-ku ra-zog-nal!

(b) Sne-gi be-ly-e pu-shis-ty-po-kry-va-li vse po-lya Od-no-vo lish ne po kry-li go-rya lyu-ta mo-e-vo.

---

[1] *Molodetskie*—heroic songs.

One of the most remarkable of all the melodies composed by Glinka in the folk idiom is the wedding chorus in 5/4 time, which brought forth excited comments from Glinka's critics and admirers, and which, incidentally, is the first known example of quintuple time in Russian classical music. (19) The pentatonic phrases of the melody instantly connect it with ancient wedding songs (c.f. the folk-song 'Elychka, vyalisya', taken from N. D. Berd's collection). (20) The whole of Glinka's chorus centres on the three notes C—D—E with the addition of the notes G above and below it. Such an organization is typical of wedding songs (c.f. 'Ne verba v pole shataetsya', of which a transcription by a collector is preserved in the Rimsky-Korsakov archive in the Saltykov-Shchedrin Public Library, Leningrad). (21) The resemblances between Glinka's melody and the archive transcription—the similarity in structure, the pentatonic framework, the constant return to the pivot G, the initial leap of the sixth, &c.—are clearly revealed in the following example (Mus. Ex. 9):

Mus. Ex.9

(a)

(b)

Ne ver - ba v po - le sha - ta — et - sya, knya - gi - nya

mo - lo - da — ya bla - go - slov - lya — et - sya.

Further similarities to other wedding songs may likewise be detected.

The theme of the chorus concluding Act III also shows links with folk-song, although the connection is not so close here as in the wedding chorus. The structure is more that of a town song, dividing into two distinct periods. The opening shows resemblance to the folk melodies 'U vorot sosna raskachalasya' (a song which is encountered in the nineteenth century collections of Villebois, Rubets, and others), and the song 'Ty chervonaya kalina', which is quoted in the *Bolshaya sovetskaya entsiklopedia*, Vol. IV, 2nd Ed., p. 522.

Of particular interest in Act IV is Susanin's aria, which not only contains many of the chief elements of Glinka's style but also is connected with folk music. Reference has already been made to the frequent use of the progression V—VI—IV—III—I, common in folk music, which occurs not only in Susanin's aria, but in the opening chorus, Antonida's *romance* and elsewhere. The fact that the melody has strong links with actual folk music is attested by its structural similarity to the Belorussian folk tune 'Dzya uchynenka', and to a Ukrainian melody 'Tyazhko tuzhit'.

Notable in the Epilogue is Vanya's melody 'Akh, ne mne bednomu'. There are several theories as to the origins of this theme. Serov, for example, considered that Glinka had adapted it from the folk-song 'Luchinushka'. However, a closer comparison may be found in the lyrical song 'Akh, razmolodenki', the content of which was described by the collector, P. V. Shein, as 'mournful thoughts of imminent parting with one's beloved'. The song was written down in 1855. (22) The melody has much in common with Glinka's theme and is a typical example of the melancholy 'protracted' songs found in the collections of Rupin and Kashin. Glinka's melody also shows resemblance to a song by Varlamov 'Ne znaval ya rodu', written as music to Shakhovskoy's drama *Dvumuzhnitsa* (The Bigamist). (23) The melody of this particular number was taken from another song 'Smolkni, ptashka', published by Varlamov in *Eolova arfa* (The Aeolian Harp), No. 6, 1834. The song is a typical illustration of a 'protracted' melody in its town variant and might well have been based on an original tune. There is also some resemblance between Vanya's aria and heroic *molodetskie* songs—for instance, the song 'Akh, ty Volga'. (24) The use of heroic songs in this context fully accords with the heroic character of Vanya. The origins of Vanya's music, therefore, may be found both in 'protracted' *molodetskie* songs and in quiet lyrical songs of the *romance* type. Vanya's theme is also connected with Susanin's aria 'Tuda zavël ya vas', though whether it is possible to read a deeper meaning into this (e.g. the fact that Glinka was trying to unite the work on a 'family' basis) it is impossible to tell.

Lastly, mention should be made of the chorus 'Slavsya', with which the opera concludes, and which has acquired the status of a folk hymn. (25) There is evidence to suggest that the main components of this chorus are foreshadowed by themes heard earlier in the work. (26) However, despite the fact that there are no immediate connections between folk melodies and the chorus, the modal structure of the piece and certain characteristic melodic turns betray the influence of folk music, in the form of leaps of the sixth, typical rhythms and the folk cadence with the falling fifth.

From the foregoing analysis it will be apparent that the folk element plays a far greater role in *A Life for the Tsar* than was previously considered. Glinka only rarely employs existing folk tunes; rather he has taken the characteristic intonations of Russian, White Russian, Ukrainian and even Siberian folk melodies and introduced them into arias, choruses, and recitatives, so that, as Melgunov expressed it:

> He has not restricted himself to close imitations of a folk melody . . . he has studied intently the structure of Russian songs, their performance by the people . . . In a word he has revealed the whole system of Russian melody and harmony inherent in folk music itself. (27)

OTHER OBSERVATIONS

So much, then, for the role of the folk element in *A Life for the Tsar*. In what other ways is Glinka's first opera remarkable?

Firstly, there is the use made by Glinka of the contrast between the Russians and the Poles. Generally speaking, the music of the specifically Russian scenes is set in duple or quadruple time, while that of the Polish scenes is represented by dances such as the polonaise, the mazurka, the waltz, and the krakowiak. An interesting feature is the transformation of the mazurka theme in the course of the action (c.f. the theme as it is heard at the Polish ball in Act II, and in the scene in the wood). (28)

Secondly, there is the excellent characterization of the Russian peasants, and, in particular, Susanin himself. Nowhere is Susanin's character better revealed than in the scene in the wood, which is the tragic culmination of the whole opera. In this scene Glinka does not give Susanin a 'heroic aria' but a simple melody (which is related to a theme in the Overture in a minor variant) in ternary form with an introductory recitative. (29) Brilliant touches in the aria are where Susanin recalls his children and his family, whose themes are ingeniously referred to in the orchestral accompaniment (the themes of Vanya, Sobinin, and Antonida).

The other characters are also revealed to some extent—particularly Vanya, who acquires special significance in the Epilogue and in the trio 'Akh, ne mne bednomu'.

A special part in the opera is played by the ensembles in which outstanding are the Trio in Act I and the Trio in the Epilogue. From them stem many similar vocal ensembles such as those in *The Tsar's Bride*.

Lastly, mention may be made of Glinka's brilliant orchestration and musical imitation of folk instruments, notably of the *balalaika* in No. 1 and No. 3, of pipes in No. 11 ('Miliye deti'), and possibly of the *gusli* in No. 20b ('Ty pridësh, moya zarya').

RUSLAN AND LYUDMILA

Glinka's second opera *Ruslan and Lyudmila* is a logical continuation of the means employed in *A Life for the Tsar*, with which it shares many common features. Thus, both operas are framed by massive folk choruses, both employ introductions, which furnish motives developed later in the course of the opera, and both are permeated by folk-song inflections and characteristic folk-song rhythms, intervals, and cadences. *Ruslan and Lyudmila* differs, however, in that, in addition, it makes use of exotic folk music—from Turkey, Persia, Arabia, Georgia, and Finland. (30) Unlike its predecessor it is a fantastic opera and portrays a scene set in Russia's legendary past. (31) Its inspiration was Pushkin's poem of the same name. However, the libretto, which is perhaps the opera's chief weakness, follows the original only loosely. (32) The final stage of the opera's composition is picturesquely described in the diary of N. Kukolnik (entry dated 10 September 1841):

Yesterday we had a very happy dinner with Glinka with a most curious finale; we—i.e. myself, Mikhail Gedeonov, Shirkov, *en tout* with our host—numbered 8 people. The conversation, of course, was for the most part about *Ruslan*. Misha [Glinka] expounded the whole plan with his clarifications; we discussed, debated, argued, jested; all of us, including Misha, are aware of

N

the bittyness, the fragmentariness of the separate scenes. There is
no continuity in the opera, no common link. And so we decided
to pool our resources to make that link. I undertook to write the
verses for the finale of the opera and for the scene of Ratmir in the
Third Act—the aria 'I zhar, i znoy'; Gedeonov, Shirkov and
Markevich also selected places according to their tastes; even
Misha will compose some lines. It appears then that the opera
Ruslan and Lyudmila will have 6 fathers from the poetic point of
view: Pushkin, Markevich, Shirkov, M. Gedeonov, Misha and I,
while with Bakhturin, who thought out the plan of the opera it
amounts to 7. According to folk wisdom 'with seven nurses a child
is without a head' . . . But this could not happen with us. Indeed
no; no matter how we transgressed, the genius of Misha would
smooth and cover our sins.

GENERAL OBSERVATIONS

Ruslan and Lyudmila, therefore, is an opera of the most motley
construction, the action whisking one from the princely court
in Kiev to the far North, to the mysterious forest or to the distant
magic kingdom of Chernomor. The opera is united, however,
by the overture and the two big folk scenes which open and
conclude it, the final chorus being based on the main theme
from the overture. Whereas in *A Life for the Tsar* the Russians
are contrasted with the Poles, in *Ruslan* the group of themes
connected with the heroes of Kiev are contrasted with the themes
depicting the followers and agents of Chernomor, the world of

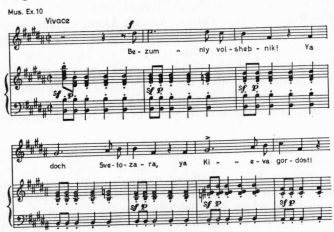

Mus. Ex.10

reality being opposed to the world of fantasy. The characters themselves, though, are real enough. The heroic Ruslan, the noble Svetozar, the tender Lyudmila, the languishing Gorislava, the cowardly Farlaf and the ardent Ratmir are all living people, and from them spring a whole host of subsequent persons such as Prince Igor (Ruslan), Yaroslavna (Lyudmila and Gorislava), Konchak and Konchakovna (Ratmir). In the opera itself prominent parts are played by Ruslan's aria, which is

Mus. Ex.11

really the centre-piece of the whole work, and the arias of Lyudmila, particularly that in Act IV, with its striking rhythm Mus. Ex. 10.

An additional character in the opera is Gorislava, who plays hardly any part in Pushkin's poem. Gorislava's cavatina was one of Glinka's favourite creations and in its 'yearning' antici- pates many similar arias at a later date, such as that of Yaro- slavna in *Prince Igor*, Lyubava in *Sadko*, Kupava in *Snegurochka*, Tatyana in *Evgeniy Onegin*, &c. Mus. Ex. 11.

Nearly every aria in the opera has a distinctive form. Thus, the fast part of Ruslan's aria is in sonata form, that of Finn in ballad form, and that of Farlaf in rondo form. Remarkable, too, is the canonic quartet in Act I (the scene of Lyudmila's abduc- tion), which takes place above a sustained pedal point, thus brilliantly suggesting the condition of enslavement embracing all those held in Chernomor's power. Chernomor himself does not sing a single note, but is represented instead by the famous whole-tone scale passage and by other typical Glinkan progres- sions (Mus. Ex. 12):

Several motives are employed systematically throughout the opera—in the Overture, in the scene of Lyudmila's abduction, and finally in Act IV in the scene of the battle of Ruslan and Chernomor, where the chorus of Chernomor's slaves sing: 'Pogibnet, pogibnet nezhdanniy prishlets' (He will perish, the unexpected newcomer will perish), the descending whole-tone scale motive symbolizing the flight of the evil magician. Particularly effective, too, is the famous March of Chernomor in Act IV.

Eastern colouring to the opera from the instrumental point of view is provided by the use of the cor anglais in Ratmir's aria and the nasal sounds of the oboe in the famous *Lezginka*. A peculiarity of Glinka's orchestration is that he favours solo instruments in accompanying the human voice. Thus, he uses a violin solo in Lyudmila's aria in Act IV, a bassoon counterpoint in Gorislava's aria and a solo clarinet in the finale of Act IV (Ruslan's arioso over the sleeping Lyudmila).

A special place in the opera is occupied by the Overture, which juxtaposes Ruslan's theme with that of Chernomor. (33) The Overture, which, to use Glinka's own words, opens with 'blows of the fist', is written in sonata form, with a short introduction and an extended coda. As opposed to the usual classical scheme the first subject is in D major, the second in F, while in the recapitulation the first subject is in D major, the second in A.

USE OF AUTHENTIC FOLK MELODIES

As in *A Life for the Tsar* Glinka uses several authentic melodies, some of which appear on more than one occasion. The provenance of these is partly described by Glinka in his *Memoirs*. Thus, in relation to the Finnish theme used in Act II, one reads the following, which refers to a holiday spent in Finland in 1829:

> One of the Finnish drivers sang a song which pleased me very much; I asked him to repeat it over and over again and, having learnt it by heart, used it later as the main theme of Finn's ballad . . .

In this number, therefore (the ballad of Finn), the folk tune is repeated with occasional modifications against constantly changing harmonic and orchestral backgrounds. (34) Glinka's alterations to the melody are governed entirely by the sense of the words, which they reflect with great skill (viz. the changing emotions of Finn, ranging from anger and mockery, gaiety and pathos, to remorse). The variation method used in this number is most successful, and there could be no greater tribute to Glinka's powers of ingenuity than the fact that, although the same tune is repeated time and time again, at the end it still retains its freshness.

The only Russian folk melody to be found in the opera is the folk-song 'Vo sadu li, v ogorode', which occurs in No. 16. (35) The song itself is somewhat grotesque in nature and its employment in this context as an accompaniment figure gives a weird touch of colour to the chromatically and canonically moving chorus. The folk tune serves as the basis for a series of variations.

The chief exotic theme is that of the Persian chorus in Act III (No. 12). The question of the origin of the melody of the Persian chorus, despite Glinka's statement to the effect that he

> heard at Shterich's a Persian song sung by the secretary of the ministry of foreign affairs—Khezrev-Mirza

which he used as the motive for the chorus 'Lozhitsa v pole mrak nochnoy', has roused much curiosity among Soviet musicologists in recent years. Some investigators have shown that Glinka could have known the melody from other sources—for example, from a collection published in St. Petersburg at the end of the 1820's in which were included six Persian songs (*mugams*), one of which was very close to the theme of the Persian chorus. (36) Others have refused to accept the Persian origin of Glinka's melody. (37) Arakishvili, for instance, asserts that he heard the melody from Georgians; the Azerbaijan artist Biul-biul Mamedov is of the opinion that the chorus is an Azerbaijan melody (38); V. V. Protopopov mentions the existence of the 'Persian' theme in present-day Turkmenistan, (39) while A. Kozlovsky writes of the prevalence of the theme in Uzbekistan. (40) A piano piece by Alyabyev, based on the themes of Caucasian folk melodies and published in 1834, also makes use of the opening bars of the chorus. It is quite likely that Glinka was acquainted with this work. Again, in a volume by P. Siyalsky (41) published in 1861 (42) is printed a song 'Kaladan kalaya gërdium' (No. 9). According to the collector this was a song 'sung everywhere in Georgia by Tartars, Armenians, and Georgians. It is their favourite song . . .' (43) And, indeed, there is a close resemblance between the two. Glinka's method of treatment of the 'Persian' chorus is identical with that of Finn's ballad: the same tune, or fragments of it, is repeated continually against a changing background, which reflects the mood of the words. In its style of arrangement the chorus served as a prototype for many subsequent efforts of a similar genre, such as the Persian chorus in *Khovanshchina*, and other works.

No. 14 makes use of a Tartar melody, which forms the basis of the *Adagio* section of Ratmir's aria. The melody is first introduced on the cor anglais, then is given to the voice, where it is subjected to further elaboration. As opposed to his practice in the Persian chorus and Finn's ballad, Glinka here treats the theme itself as the germ for development, the subsequent variations being drawn from the basic theme, which changes constantly in appearance. In the *Moderato* section he introduces an Arab melody, from which is derived the beautiful 6/8 section, which includes some of Glinka's finest pages. In the *Moderato* section, colour is given to the melody by the use of the flattened sixth and this later becomes one of the aria's salient features. In the 6/8 section the main theme evolves from the Arab melody, of which it is a logical development rather than a close imitation. This process of evolving theme from theme is one of Glinka's favourite devices (c.f. his analogous procedure in *A Life for the Tsar*) and gives the work a sense of unity and homogeneity. The closing section of this number is the least satisfying, for from the languorous harmonies of the previous sections one is plunged abruptly into an almost Beethovenian coda. This sudden transition from one musical era to another is a characteristic of Glinka's music, which was remedied by his successors. In the treatment of Oriental melodies Glinka was still a pioneer.

The remaining Oriental themes are all of interest. The first of these—a Turkish theme—appears in the Oriental dances (No. 20a). It consists of only four bars, which are repeated and then continued in a similar style. Subsequently the same music is repeated in related keys and against changing backgrounds. The second dance (20b) makes use of an Arab tune, but Glinka treats this in a slightly different manner. The Arab melody is still subjected to variation, but on this occasion, each time it is played, it is preceded by a contrasting section having no relation to the principal melody.

The Arab dance leads into the famous *Lezginka* (20c). In his *Memoirs* Glinka tells us:

> Gayvazovsky, who often visited Kukolnik, gave me three Tartar melodies. I consequently used two of these for the Lezginka.

D. I. Arakishvili, however, strongly questions the nationality of the second theme of the *Lezginka*:

> If one may attribute the first part to *Lezginka* melodies, under no circumstances may this apply to the second part, as this is the melody of a 'Kazachok', which I heard many times as a child in Vladikavkaz. (44)

The *Lezginka* likewise appears in Siyalsky's publication and was written down in Armenia in the 30's of the nineteenth century. Both Glinka's and Siyalsky's arrangements have much in common, the principal difference being that Glinka has retained a pedal D all the way through. (45) (46)

The Oriental dances are also of importance in that two of the melodies are heard later in the work in modified forms, the Turkish theme reappearing in the final chorus and the second theme of the *Lezginka* serving as the basis for the opening chorus of the Finale, No. 27.

The national element in *Ruslan and Lyudmila* is further stressed by the use of choruses, which open and conclude the work, by the appearance of the prophetic ballad-singer, Bayan, whose music is set in the form of *byliny* ballads, and by the employment of reminiscence motives throughout the opera, derived from the first subject of the Overture. These motives are also connected with the figure and music of Bayan; indeed, Soviet musicologists go further and claim that *Ruslan and Lyudmila* is an 'opera within an opera', the second opera being set in the form of a *bylina* introduced by Bayan and featuring *byliny* characters —the old Prince Svetozar (who may be compared with the *bylina* Prince Vladimir Krasno Solnyshko), (47) the gallant Ruslan, the comic Farlaf, the faithful Lyudmila, &c. Both Bayan's and Svetozar's music is permeated by folk-song inflections, much of Bayan's music (especially his first two songs) being written in imitation of *byliny*. From the opening of Bayan's first song, (48) which also shows a relationship with folk-song, (49) are derived several other numbers, which may be enumerated as follows (Mus. Ex. 13).

Thus, Ex. 13a is Bayan's song; 13b is the first chorus; 13c Ruslan's aria (No. 8) in Act II; and 13d the Overture. (50) On the framework of Ex. 13a is constructed much of the music of No. 1.

Mus. Ex. 13

Svetozar resembles Susanin in *A Life for the Tsar* in that his music is clearly related to folk-song—a fact which is illustrated by his opening bars in the Finale to Act I (No. 3).

The folk element is also manifest in a number of choruses, some of which reproduce old folk customs. The opening of No. 27, for instance, suggests the funeral lamentations of the ancient peasant ritual.

FURTHER EMPLOYMENT OF CAUCASIAN MUSIC

There is evidence that *Ruslan and Lyudmila* in addition to the examples already given makes further use of Georgian folk music. One of the most outstanding illustrations is to be found in the triumphal chorus to Lel—No. 3. That it shows some similarity to a Georgian *Khorumi* (a folk dance) is illustrated in Ex. 14:

Mus. Ex. 14

USE OF TOWN SONG

To conclude this brief analysis of the folk elements in *Ruslan* mention must also be made of the manner in which Glinka has freely introduced elements of town song. Numbers such as Farlaf's aria are of dubious origin, stemming either from the *skorogovorka* or patter of folk music, or, more probably, from Italian *opera buffa*, but other numbers are indubitably of town origin. Such are Lyudmila's Cavatina (No. 2), which shows the influence of 'Russian song', Ratmir's music in No. 3, a large proportion of Lyudmila's aria in No. 18, Ruslan's music in the Finale to Act IV, the A minor theme in the Prelude to Act V (which occurs again in the Finale—No. 27), and much of the duet of Finn and Ratmir (No. 26), the last in particular being an excellent illustration of Glinka's powers of creation in the folk idiom.

SIGNIFICANCE OF GLINKA'S OPERAS

Like Glinka's first opera, therefore, *Ruslan and Lyudmila* also makes use of folk music, though its folk sources are more diverse, embracing themes (in addition to Russian) of Turkish, Arabian, Finnish, and Georgian origin. Despite the fact that Glinka uses a greater number of authentic melodies in *Ruslan* than in *A Life for the Tsar*, the music speech is not so strikingly Russian in character, the folk intonations being more subtly concealed. As in *A Life for the Tsar* unity is given to the opera by the repetition of certain melodies and a process of theme transformation in which one theme evolves from another. Of importance in this respect is the figure of Bayan, from whose music, which itself shows resemblance to the melodies of ancient *byliny*, is possibly derived the first subject of the overture. The folk element is likewise manifest in a number of choral scenes, some of which reproduce old folk customs.

Glinka's operas were of great significance in the development of Russian opera in the second half of the nineteenth century. From *A Life for the Tsar*, with its subject matter drawing largely on realistic, psychological drama, subsequently resulted 'heroic-epic' works such as *Boris Godunov* and *Pskovityanka*, while from *Ruslan and Lyudmila*, with its fantastic action and exotic harmonies, sprang a whole series of similar productions culminating in *The Golden Cockerel* and *The Snow Maiden*.

ORCHESTRAL COMPOSITIONS

Glinka began to write orchestral works in St. Petersburg as early as the 1820's. These included an *Adagio and Rondo*, and two Overtures. A Symphony-Overture, written in 1834 in Berlin, was completed and orchestrated in 1937 by Shebalin. However, in none of these works had Glinka reached artistic maturity and work was frequently abandoned on account of the fact that he was unable to rid himself of the conventional method of development. Among his better symphonic works are the orchestral fantasy *Kamarinskaya* (1848), the two Spanish Overtures *Jota Aragonesa* (1845) and *Night in Madrid* (1848: 2nd version 1851), and his incidental music to Kukolnik's tragedy *Prince Kholmsky* (1840). (51)

KAMARINSKAYA

Kamarinskaya is of interest in that it makes use of two folk themes—a wedding song 'Iz–za gor, gor vysokikh' (52) and the dance tune 'Kamarinskaya' (Mus. Ex. 15 (a) & (b)):

Mus. Ex.15

The piece is constructed in the form of double variations— A B A' B'. The tonal plan is also unusual—F major—D major —F major—B♭ major—D major, and the whole work consists of a free development of the folk themes, which in the course of performance undergo transformation. Particularly striking is the clarity of the orchestration and the use of the 'changing backgrounds' technique in the treatment of the 'Kamarinskaya' theme.

JOTA ARAGONESA

The *Jota Aragonesa* is a sparkling orchestral work of greater dimensions than *Kamarinskaya*, and employing a larger orchestra in which considerable attention is paid to the brass group and to harp and percussion. The percussion includes kettle drums, castanets, cymbals, and bass drum. The Overture is of somewhat hybrid construction, combining features of both Sonata and variation form. A short introduction, consisting of triumphant fanfares, sets up a mood of expectation. After the *Grave* section, the first subject (Mus. Ex. 16) is heard played by a solo violin against harp and *pizzicato* strings, which skilfully suggest the sound of Spanish guitars:

Mus. Ex. 16

The *Jota Aragonesa* itself is an actual folk melody, which Glinka wrote down from a Spanish guitarist. His *Night in Madrid* employs four authentic melodies.

PRINCE KHOLMSKY

One of Glinka's most important orchestral works is his incidental music to Nestor Kukolnik's tragedy *Knyaz Daniil Dmitrievich Kholmsky*, which was written during September–October 1840. Falling between the composition of *A Life for the Tsar* and *Ruslan and Lyudmila* it is remarkable in that it is unlike either of the operas in style and contains a number of individual features. (53) The music to *Prince Kholmsky* consists of an overture, four entr'actes and three songs (two songs of Rachel and a song of Ilinishna, the proprietress of Skhary's house). In this work, more than in any other composition, Glinka approaches the heroic style of Beethoven, though Beethovenian echoes may also be found in *A Life for the Tsar*. This likeness is no doubt conditioned to some extent by the similarity between Kholmsky—the strong, bold *voevoda*, consumed by conflict and suffering eventual tragedy—and Beethovenian heroes such as Egmont and Coriolanus. *Prince Kholmsky*, indeed, is particularly close to Beethoven's *Egmont*, (54) for both are music to dramas, and both contrast a manly hero with a devoted girl willing to sacrifice everything for love (in *Egmont*—Clärchen, in *Kholmsky* —Rachel). It is characteristic that whereas in Kukolnik's drama Rachel is only an episodic personage, in Glinka she is elevated to a position of importance.

The chief moment of *Prince Kholmsky* is the overture—a remarkable example of the composer's orchestral skill. In the short introduction (*Maestoso e moderato assai*) the figure of Kholmsky is depicted with a truly Beethovenian force. A concise, rhythmic march reveals the hero's imperiousness and foreshadows the tragic *dénouement*. Throughout the whole introduction there is a feeling of funereal gloom (Mus. Ex. 17):

Mus. Ex. 17

'PRINCE KHOLMSKY' OVERTURE.

The *Allegro* is based on two themes—the song 'Rachel's Dream' (first subject) (Mus. Ex. 18):

Mus. Ex. 18

Agitato vivace

'PRINCE KHOLMSKY'

and the song of Ilinishna (second subject) (Mus. Ex. 19):

Mus. Ex. 19

'PRINCE KHOLMSKY'

The greater part of the symphonic introductions (to the Third, Fourth, and Fifth Acts) are devoted to the characterization of Kholmsky. The introduction to Act III depicts Kholmsky's seduction by Adelheide, the main theme consisting of a lulling, barcarolle type of melody. The introduction to Act IV is a triumphal march with an abundance of fanfares, representing the procession of the *veche*; in the second half, in accordance with the development of the action, it acquires a sombre colouring (moving from C major to C minor). The final entr'acte is the most dramatic and depicts Kholmsky's despair. The coda signifies the Prince's acceptance of defeat.

The introduction to Act II is devoted to the figure of Rachel and is based on the theme of her first song ('Hebrew song').

CHAMBER MUSIC

It is true that Glinka did not achieve the same heights in chamber music as he did in vocal, symphonic and operatic music. The reason for this is that, whereas in the other genres there was already a well-developed school, in chamber music there was far less. All Glinka's chamber works were written between 1822-32 and he never returned to chamber composition later in his life.

The very earliest of Glinka's chamber works known to us is a short fragment from a String Septet (1823) of which he writes in his *Memoirs*:

> As to composition in general, of thorough-bass, counterpoint, and other conditions for a good ability to write, my ideas were so indefinite, that I took up my pen not knowing how to begin or how and where to go. I started to write at first a Septet, then an *Adagio* and *Rondo* for orchestra. (55)

His next attempt—the commencement of the First (unfinished) Quartet—is described in a similar manner:

> I remember that at this time in 1824 I wrote a quartet for two violins, viola and cello (D Major), but this attempt was no more successful than the previous ones. (56)

This quartet was edited and completed by N. Myaskovsky and V. Shirinsky and published in 1948. The first movement of the First Quartet is in the lyrical vein so typical of the composer. More successful, however, is the second movement—a theme with variations—which has some felicitous moments. The third variation, which is written in an improvisatory manner, is quite charming (Mus. Ex. 20). As another writer has observed, it is perhaps significant, that it was this variation, in essence the least traditional of them all, that Glinka was unable to complete.

Mus. Ex. 20

Of the last two movements the *Rondo* (which is Mozartian in nature) is better than the *Minuet*.

Of interest is the Sonata for Viola or Violin and Piano, begun by the composer in 1825, which Glinka himself singled out from among his early works:

About this time I wrote the first *Allegro* of a Sonata in D Minor for piano and viola; this work was neater than the others and I played it with Böhm and Liglya; in the latter instance I played on the viola. The *Adagio* was written later, but I didn't manage the *Rondo*, whose motive in the Russian style I remember to this day. (I used it in a children's polka recently.) (57)

In another place in the *Memoirs* Glinka again refers to the Sonata. Having spent a few days with N. A. Melgunov (1828), he continues:

I wrote the *Adagio* (Bb Major) of the D Minor Sonata and I remember that in that piece I had some fairly skilful counterpoint. (58)

The fact that the Sonata was written for either violin or viola is indicative of the type of audience for whom the work was intended, though that Glinka should have chosen a viola is unusual.[1] This Sonata, too, remained unfinished, the *Allegro* (1825)

[1] There are three versions of this work, all of which are printed in Vol. 4 of the Complete Works. Reference is made here to the score edited by V. V. Borisovsky.

and the greater part of the *Adagio* being the only movements to
be completed. The music of the Sonata is fully typical of the
period. The first movement consists of a string of graceful
melodies, of which the first subject is heard in turn on the viola
and piano (Mus. Ex. 21):

The first melody of the second subject (*Poco tranquillo*) is quite
Mendelssohnian in style. Throughout the movement the piano
plays a leading part. An elegiac feeling is present in the opening
of the second movement—the *Larghetto ma non troppo* (Mus.
Ex. 22):

But darker shades are evident in the middle section (*Più
mosso*).

In his next quartet—the Quartet in F major—there is a
strong feeling of Mozart, indeed, it was written at a time (1830)
when Mozart's fame was at its height in Russia. The Quartet
in F major was Glinka's first quartet to be completed and consists of four movements: *Allegro spiritoso, Andante con moto, Menu-
etto,* and *Rondo.* For the most part he adheres to the Classical
formal construction, though there are features typical of his
later work, such as the unification of the quartet thematically

PLATE 9

BURLAKI by I. REPIN (1844–1930)

PLATE 10

M. I. GLINKA in 1840

A. S. DARGOMYZHSKY (1813–1869)

(the first, third and fourth movements have intonations in common). A cyclical treatment of themes is encountered again in the 'Pathetic Trio' (where motives from the first movement are heard in the finale). The principal melodies of the first movement are all lyrical, though without great expressive power; the *Andante* is contemplative in style; the *Minuet* (marked *Allegro brillante*), both from the point of view of dynamics and the extensive use of chromaticism, is essentially Romantic rather than Classical. The weakest part is the Finale, which lacks the sparkle and vitality of the Viennese masters and demonstrates that Glinka's language was still in a state of flux. Nevertheless, it was an achievement to have even completed the work and there is no doubt that it served him as a useful vehicle for experiment.

During his stay in Milan in March 1832 Glinka wrote several pieces for chamber ensemble. The first was a piece called in his *Memoirs* 'Serenade on Themes from Bellini's *Sonnambula*', (59) while the second was a serenade on themes of *Anna Bolena* by Donizetti for piano, harp, viola, cello, bassoon, and clarinet. In the same year of 1832 he wrote the Sextet for piano, two violins, viola, cello, and bass, and the 'Pathetic Trio' for clarinet, bassoon, and piano. The 'Pathetic Trio' and the Sextet mark the acme of his chamber creation.

Both the fantasy-serenades on operatic themes stand apart in Glinka's work and were the result of his operatic experiences in Italy. Fantasies and variations on operatic themes were very popular at the time. According to contemporary accounts Glinka's own efforts in this genre were highly regarded in Italy, Ricordi, the publisher, considering Glinka equal to Bellini and Donizetti, but 'more skilful than them in counterpoint'. (60) To the 'Serenade' (or, more accurately, 'Divertissement on motives from *La Sonnambula*') were devoted the following remarks in the journal *Molva* (Rumour), No. 24, 1834:

> Glinka recently returned to Moscow after a four-year stay in foreign lands and the other day played for connoisseurs and music-lovers two large pieces for piano and quintet, written and published by him in Italy. We would not dare to pronounce judgement on Glinka's works on a single hearing, but it seemed to us that in them were united, apparently, the various qualities of contemporary music: colour, melody and counterpoint, and so

o

combined that they formed one inseparable whole and highly
original.

The 'Divertissement' or 'Divertimento' on motives from
Sonnambula is of substantial proportions, dominated by the
piano, the strings playing only a subsidiary role. Such concert
fantasies, written in a virtuosic manner, were common at the
time (one thinks in particular of works by Liszt, Thalberg, and
others), but to find such a combination of colour, harmony,
virtuosity and contrapuntal ingenuity as in Glinka's work was
exceptional. In Glinka's original version of the 'Divertissement'
the piano part so overshadows the rest that it may be regarded
not as a chamber ensemble, but as a concert piece for piano and
string accompaniment. The solo role of the piano is underlined
in the composer's arrangement of the work for two pianos,
where Glinka states:

> To achieve the required effect in performing this work on two
> pianos, it is necessary to choose instruments with a different
> sound: for the main part one with a brilliant tone, for the accom-
> paniment one with a soft.

The 'Divertissement' opens with a *Larghetto* introduction in
the key of A♭ major, a leading part being played by the piano
(Mus. Ex. 23):

Mus. Ex. 23
Larghetto

Then follows a *Moderato* episode in Ab major, which is based on the heroine's cavatina—the bride Amina (Act I), where she sings of her impending happiness. (61) This lyrical melody is enhanced by a wedding chorus, which is heard in the string accompaniment *piano staccato*. The next episode (*Allegretto*—G minor) is the duet of the bride and bridegroom, in character more agitated and passionate, and this leads in turn to the central section of the 'Divertissement' (*Andante cantabile*)— Amina's aria from the finale of Act III. This aria is the dramatic culmination of the opera, where Amina appears sleepwalking before the assembled peasants; at this point Elvino is convinced of her innocence. After Amina's aria follows the final section of the work (*Vivace*—Ab major), which commences with the stirring music from the choral finale to Act I. This is followed by themes employed in the first part of the 'Divertissement'— the duet of Amina and Elvino and Amina's cavatina—but which are presented in a new guise, thus bringing the work to a satisfactory conclusion. The order of movements *Larghetto— Moderato—Allegretto, Andante cantabile, Vivace* is dramatically successful and the combination of Sonata Form features with variation development shows similarity to the practices of Liszt. In comparison with Bellini's treatment, Glinka's is far more contrapuntal.

At the same time Glinka worked on his Sextet for Piano and String Quintet, which was begun in June and finished in October 1832. Like the 'Serenades' the Sextet was written very much under the influence of Italy, in which it may be compared with Tchaikovsky's 'Italian Caprice' or the *Souvenir de Florence*. Like the earlier ensembles the Sextet is essentially lyrical in mood, but the whole work is on a larger scale and is of greater maturity. Glinka tends to exploit the timbres of the lower strings, thus gaining greater warmth and emotional colouring. Of the three movements—*Allegro, Andante* and *Allegro con spirito*—the first (which is in Sonata Form) makes effective use of repeated notes in the piano part, a device doubtless stemming from the opera overtures of Rossini (Mus. Ex. 24).

The central movement (*Andante*, 6/8) is in the form of a barcarolle—one of the earliest and most poetic examples of its kind in Russian music (Mus. Ex. 25).

Glinka's last chamber work was the 'Pathetic Trio' for

claritnet, bassoon and piano, which was written in the winter of
1832–3 and is one of the most Romantic of all Glinka's chamber

Mus. Ex.24

SEXTET, 1st Movement

works. The underlying emotion of the work is suggested by the
epigraph:

'*Je n'ai connu l'amour, que par les peines qu'il cause*'.

The two instruments of the Trio—the clarinet and the bassoon
—are, as it were, the two personages of the action and from the
very beginning of the work, following the short 'pathetic' introduction, both instruments weave and intertwine, thus evoking a
picture of tender sentiments, with happiness mingled with
sadness (Mus. Ex. 26):

The second subject is marked *dolcissimo e legato assai*. The second
movement, a *Scherzo*, has a waltz-like middle section. The

monologues of the clarinet and bassoon in the *Largo* (which exploit the registers of both instruments to their full extremes) are quite remarkable, the writing for the clarinet being particularly sympathetic (Mus. Ex. 27):

Mus. Ex. 27

The Trio concludes with a lively finale, which is terminated somewhat unexpectedly by a tragic coda, in which a prime part is played by a syncopated chromatically descending bass line, reminiscent of the conclusion of the first movement of the Beethoven Ninth Symphony. When the work was finished, Glinka played it with musicians from the La Scala Theatre and the bassoonist was so struck by the coda that he exclaimed: 'Ma questo e disperazione' (Why that's a thing of despair). And, Glinka adds: 'At that time I was in despair'. (62)

The 'Pathetic Trio' is Glinka's most important chamber work apart from the Sextet. The melodic language is richer and more interesting and there is no hesitancy in the writing. As in the music of Mozart, every note can be heard. The melody of the *Largo*, which is spread over some twenty bars, is an outstanding example of its kind in Glinka's chamber creation. The form of the work, too, is free, the first movement being a rather unusual kind of Sonata *Allegro* without any real development, which leads directly into the second movement—the Scherzo. The third movement (*Largo*) is in ternary form and has an unusual key scheme. In the finale Glinka gathers up the themes from the first movements and after these have been heard in free alternation, the work culminates in a 40-bar coda. The Trio really resembles a one-movement fantasy with a cyclic structure. The leitmotive of the introduction, for instance, appears in the beginning of the work, is heard in the first subject of the exposition, and again appears in the finale. The finale itself is based on the first subject from the first movement.

PIANO MUSIC

As in the case of his chamber music, Glinka's piano works must inevitably yield in quality to his operatic, vocal, and symphonic music, even though his piano works are infinitely superior to those of his Russian contemporaries Kashin, Zhilin, Gurilëv, Alyabyev, Esaulov, Laskovsky, Genishta, and others. Glinka first studied piano playing with V. F. Klammer, who was a pupil of the Smolnyi Institute, and then with John Field and Charles Mayer. During his youth he wrote several sets of variations for the piano. Apart from variations on 'Russian songs' and *romances*, such as those on the folk tune 'Sredi doliny rovniya' and Alyabyev's 'Solovey' (The Nightingale), he also borrowed themes from Weigl's *Die Schweizerfamilie*, Mozart's *Zauberflöte*, Cherubini's *Faniska*, Bellini's *Montecchi*, and other works of Italian composers, to say nothing of composing variations on the Irish song ' 'Tis the Last Rose of Summer' and 'Variations on his own Theme'. Although space does not permit an exhaustive survey of all Glinka's sets of variations, (63) two are of particular interest—the variations on Alyabyev's 'Solovey' (1833) and the 'Variations on a Scottish Theme'.

Alyabyev's song 'Solovey' is written to a sentimental poem of Delvig describing hopeless love and it is the verses of the poem which serve as a programmatic basis for the whole work. The 'Variations' commence with a short, very expressive introduction, consisting of arpeggio chords, suggestive perhaps of the sound of a *gusli* (Mus. Ex. 28):

Mus. Ex. 28

This serves as an excellent preface. The theme itself is almost void of any ornament and the melody has a severer outline than in the Alyabyev. In the first variation the theme is presented in the middle voice against a graceful contrapuntal figure (Mus. Ex. 29):

Mus. Ex. 29

This kind of writing influenced Tchaikovsky, as may be seen by examining parts of his Nocturne in C♯ minor, where the theme is also presented in the middle voice, and with the same kind of plaintive harmony. In the second variation the tension increases, contrast being provided by a slow major *cantabile* section (variation three). The dramatic fourth variation provides the finale. This consists of several episodes which refer back to preceding material.

Glinka's last set of variations—those on ' 'Tis the Last Rose of Summer'—were written in 1847 and may well be considered one of his best piano works. The melody is, of course, Irish, not Scottish, in origin and was included in a volume *Irish melodies with symphonies and accompaniments by Sir John Stevenson mus. doc. and characteristic words by Thomas Moore esqr. New edition. Edited by professor Clover. Dublin.* The theme was also employed by Beethoven (in an arrangement for voice with piano, violin, and cello accompaniment), by Flotow in the opera *Martha*, by Mendelssohn in his *Variations on an English [sic] Theme 'The Last Rose of Summer'*, by Thalberg (*Variations on an Irish Song*, Op. 73), and others. Glinka was fascinated by Scottish culture and even as a young man toyed with the idea of writing an opera *Matilda Rokeby*, based on Scott's poem. There is a strong epic feeling about Glinka's 'Variations' which is revealed in the brief introductory opening bars. The theme likewise is heard in the spirit of a ballad, arpeggio chords suggesting the sound of a harp. In comparison with the original the melody has been slightly modified, thus giving greater smoothness. Of particular interest is the second variation, where a modal ring is given to the melody, most effective being the weak-to-strong ending (Mus. Ex. 30):

Mus. Ex. 30

Moderato

legato assai

The ballad element is even further stressed in the finale, which takes the form of a kind of fantasia on the preceding material.

Among Glinka's shorter piano works may be mentioned his *Razluka* (Parting)—the first Russian nocturne—which may be said to anticipate moments in Rakhmaninov in its 'pathetic' intonations, descending chromatic appoggiaturas, and poignant harmony.

Another piano work of high quality is Glinka's *Barcarolle* (1847), which was written after his second trip abroad and likewise found its inspiration in Italy. The piece opens with a few introductory chords, which lead directly into the barcarolle (Mus. Ex. 31):

Mus. Ex. 31

The sense of the song is revealed by a quotation from the Italian poet Felice Romani, which appears as an epigraph: 'Ah! Would that you were with me in the dark gondola', and it is interesting that Glinka also wrote a song ('Il desiderio') to words of this poem when he was in Italy. According to Serov, Glinka performed the barcarolle himself 'with a soft, tender, velvet touch, which recalled the manner of Field'. (64) One rather charming device is the use of tritonal demisemiquaver figures, suggestive of drops of water (Mus. Ex. 32):

Mus. Ex. 32

Contrast is provided by a middle section which is quicker in tempo, and perhaps describes the hero of the piece.

Glinka was also the composer of a number of polyphonic piano works and although these were sometimes only exercises, some of them are of merit. Such is the Fugue in A minor, which is perhaps the first piano fugue in Russian music. It is a double fugue and is thought to have been written about 1833–4. The first theme has the characteristics of a *romance* as is revealed by its typical intervallic structure (Mus. Ex. 33):

Mus. Ex.33

The second theme makes use of descending chromaticisms somewhat in the manner of Bach. Connections with vocal music can also be seen in the fugues in E♭ and D major, though these are less interesting in other respects.

About half of Glinka's piano works are written in the form of dances such as waltzes, mazurkas, polkas, *contredanses*, *cotillons*, the Andalusian dance 'Las mollares', and even a *Tarentella* (based on the Russian folk tune 'Na pole berezonka stoyala') which is an interesting transformation of a foreign dance movement into a Russian idiom. Some of the mazurkas show the influence of Chopin, whom Glinka admired, while others, such as the 'Souvenir d'une masurque', written in 1847, and having the sub-title (taken from Metastasio) 'without illusions, farewell life!', clearly have a personal significance.

In 1854 Glinka wrote his *Detskaya polka* (Children's polka), in the introductory section of which is used the popular song 'Ladushka'. The Polka was dedicated to Glinka's small niece, Olya, though, like Schumann's *Kinderszenen*, it is more a piece about children intended for adults.

Mention may also be made of his *Waltz-Fantasy* (1839), which, though better known in its orchestral version, was originally written for piano.

Glinka was probably the first Russian to compose duets and his *Capriccio on Russian Themes*, which was written in Berlin in 1834, is well worthy of study. The *Capriccio* is conceived on a fairly large scale, and, like the Piano Variations on Alyabyev's 'Solovey' and the Symphony-Overture on a Russian

Mus. Ex. 34

Round Theme (all of which came into being about the same time) makes use of folk themes—'Ne bely snegi', 'Vo sadu li, v ogorode' and 'Ne tesan terem.' As in the 'Divertissement' the tunes are developed both by variation and contrapuntally. The three themes are presented in the exposition, each of which is developed by means of variation. The development commences with a *fugato*, in which is employed all the preceding material. There is a recapitulation and the piece concludes with a festive coda. Some idea of the novelty of Glinka's style is revealed by the following comparison, showing firstly Glinka's version of the folk-song 'Ne bely snegi' and then as it appears in two sets of variations written respectively by Kashin at the beginning of the nineteenth century, and by Gurilёv in 1831 (Mus. Ex. 34). Glinka's harmonization is outstanding in that it makes quite a good attempt to suggest folk polyphony, both in the alternation of solo and choral passages, in the breaking into unison at the end, and in the movement in thirds. The coda is remarkable, too, on account of its representation of bells, which is certainly the first example of its kind in Russian 'classical' music (Mus. Ex. 35):

Mus. Ex. 35

Many parts of the work sound so orchestral that some Soviet scholars consider that it was conceived originally as an orchestral piece, and that it was only sketched out in the form of a piano duet. Indeed, it was orchestrated successfully by M. V. Vladimirov in 1908. There can be no doubt that the *Capriccio* served as a preparation for his other works on Russian folk themes, such as *Kamarinskaya* and his operas. (65)

VOCAL MUSIC

Vocal music plays an extremely important part in Glinka's work. Despite the fact that he wrote operas and orchestral compositions, he never regarded the *romance* as a form of minor significance—something to be dashed off on the spur of the moment. His sixty or more songs, most of them to words by Russian poets, were written at all periods of his life, (66) and often in their composition were solved musical and aesthetic problems, determining the direction of his later works. Thus, many of the new features of *Ruslan* were prepared by his vocal works written at the end of the 30's and the beginning of the 1840's. Under Glinka's care the *romance* was raised to unprecedented heights.

Glinka's songs cover an extremely wide range—from the sentimental lyric to the pensive elegy, the lively drinking song to the Eastern *romance*, the 'Russian song' in the folk spirit to the Romantic ballad. All of the songs, however, have the same distinctive harmony, the same clarity and formal perfection, Glinka usually preferring the A—B—A type of song, relying on periodic repetition, to the *'durchkomponiert'* or 'through-composed' variety. Many of the songs have a piano introduction and epilogue, and some have an instrumental *obbligato*. Most of all, though, the success of the songs depends on the skill of the soloist and his ability to feel himself into the mood of the piece in question. Glinka himself was an excellent performer and all his works were written with an aristocratic chamber audience in mind. As he himself wrote:

> Particularly in vocal music the resources of expression are infinite. The one and the same word can be given a thousand shades, without changing even a single note, simply by altering the accent, now giving the lips a smile, now a serious stern expression. (67)

Glinka's earliest *romances* were written at a time when the form was at its height and a good insight into their nature is provided by his *Memoirs*:

> In the evenings and in the twilight I loved to muse at the piano. The sentimental poetry of Zhukovsky pleased me in particular and moved me to tears (generally speaking, in my youth I was a lad of a romantic disposition and loved to weep with sweet tears of emotion).

Glinka's early *romances*, therefore, are of lyrical content and well reflect the moods expressed by poets such as Zhukovsky, Baratinsky and Batyushkov, with their sentimentality, elegance and sophistication. One of the best songs of the period (and one of his earliest) is 'Ne iskushay menya bez nuzhdy' (Do Not Tempt

Me Needlessly) (1825), with words by Baratinsky, while also of importance are 'Bednyi pevets' (The Poor Singer) (1826) and 'Razocharovanie' (Disappointment) (1828). At this period Glinka was also fascinated by 'Russian song', most of his songs being written to words of Delvig. A typical example is 'Akh ty, noch li, nochenka', where Glinka resorts to the simplest kind of guitar accompaniment. In such songs as 'Gorko, gorko mne, krasnoy devitse' (Woe is Me, a Pretty Girl) (1827) and 'Akh ty, dushechka, krasna devitsa' (Ah, You Darling, Lovely Girl) (1826), may be seen a frequent use of Russian folk intonations, and it is significant that it was at this time that Glinka made a setting of Delvig's 'Ne osenniy chastyi dozhdichek' (Not the Heavy Autumn Shower), which was subsequently transformed into Antonida's *romance* (with different words) in *A Life for the Tsar*. A skilful piece of folk characterization is found in the delightful song 'Dedushka' (Grandad) (1828), with its lively accompaniment in the Russian dance style.

Among Glinka's other early compositions may be mentioned his 'Gruzinskaya pesnya' (Georgian Song), which is his first 'oriental' *romance*. The melody of the song was given to Glinka originally by the dramatist Griboedov, which the composer harmonized and arranged. When Pushkin heard it performed, he was so struck by it that he wrote some verses to it, the song now being known to the words 'Ne poy, krasavitsa, pri mne' (Do Not Sing, My Beauty, For Me).

Glinka's first trip abroad had considerable influence on the development of his vocal music, and *romances* such as 'Venetsianskaya noch' (Venetian Night), 'Il desiderio', 'Pobeditel' (The Conqueror) show greater profundity and maturity. 'Venetian Night', written to words of Kozlov, has the rhythm of a barcarolle, while 'Desiderio' (1832) clearly shows the influence of Bellini, both in the nature of the melody and the style of the accompaniment. Quite a number of Glinka's songs were written to dance rhythms, such as the waltz or mazurka.

The period between 1836–42 may well be called Glinka's 'Pushkin' period, for not only was the composer completely under the poet's spell but some of his best compositions such as 'Gde nasha roza' (Where Is Our Rose) (1838),[1] 'Nochnoy zefir'

---

[1] The year of composition, 1838, is established in Vol. 10 of the Complete Works (Moscow, 1962, p. xxii).

(Nocturnal Zephyr), 'Ya pomnyu chudnoe mgnovenie' (I Remember A Wonderful Moment) (1840), 'Ya zdes, Inezilya' (I Am Here, Inesilla), (68) were written to Pushkin's verses. In the songs of this period one finds a desire to pay closer attention to the words. The piano accompaniment is extended and one finds the composer thinking in orchestral terms. The harmonic language is likewise developed. In some of the songs each

Mus. Ex. 36
Andante mosso

verse is varied in accordance with the demands of the text, but most of the *romances* of his maturity are written in more complex forms. Ternary form is frequently employed with a repetition of the second and third parts, resulting in the pattern A—B—A—B—A, a device which is found in the *romances* 'Nochnoy zefir', 'Somnenie' (Doubt), 'Usnuli golubye' (The Doves Have Gone To Rest) and 'Poputnaya pesnya' (Song of Travel). 'I Remember A Wonderful Moment' is a particularly moving song, completely sincere in its outpouring of feeling, while both in mood and harmony it is a cross between Schumann's 'Ich grolle nicht' and 'Wenn ich in deine Augen seh'. In the song 'Doubt' (to words by Kukolnik), Glinka employs a violin *obbligato*, which underlines the pathetic emotions, the bathos, the heroism, as well as providing an effective prelude and postlude (Mus. Ex. 36).

Mention may also be made of the ballad 'Nochnoy smotr' (The Midnight Review) (1836), with words by Zhukovsky. Not only is this dramatic ballad, having as its theme the ghost of Napoleon rising up from his grave and surveying his troops, an anticipation of songs by Dargomyzhsky and Musorgsky and even Schumann's 'Two Grenadiers', but it is a miniature masterpiece in its own right, with its eerie colouring and nervous atmosphere. The soloist does not sing, but describes the events in a hushed tone as if afraid to speak too loudly. The piano part, with its military signals and drum beats, is likewise restricted to a strict ostinato march rhythm, while, running through the whole song, is the striking refrain: 'V dvenadstat chasov po nocham' (At twelve o'clock in the night) (Mus. Ex. 37):[1]

Mus. Ex. 37

In 1840 was written Glinka's only song cycle *Proshchanie s Peterburgom* (Farewell to Petersburg), which consists of twelve

[1] Two orchestral accompaniments to this song are printed in Vol. 8 of the Complete Works.

PLATE II

IVAN SUSANIN
from a portrait in oils

A. A. ALYABYEV (1787–1851)

PLATE 12

A. M. LISTOPADOV RECORDING FOLK SONGS OF THE DON COSSACKS ON THE PHONOGRAPH

songs, written to words by Kukolnik, though none of them are linked together either thematically or in subject matter. Among some of the best numbers may be mentioned 'Song of Travel' (a lively patter song in the folk spirit), and 'Zhavoronok' (The Lark), whose beautiful melody was later made into a piano piece by Balakirev.

The period between 1847–57 was also fruitful from the point of view of vocal music, though the number of *romances* written was not large. Generally speaking, they may be divided into two categories—the lively epicurean songs in the best Pushkin traditions, such as 'Zazdravnyi kubok' (The Toasting Cup), and songs of a more serious nature, such as the dramatic 'Pesn Margarity' (Song of Margaret), 'Ty skoro menya pozabudesh' (You Will Soon Forget Me), or 'Ne govori, chto serdtsu bolno', Glinka's last song, written in 1856 and reflecting in its imitative opening his interest in contrapuntal techniques.

SUMMARY

Mikhail Ivanovich Glinka, therefore, is the first great figure in Russian music. Not only was he more skilful, more imaginative, more gifted than his predecessors, but he was the first to formulate the principles of the Russian musical language—a language that was to be used and developed by the majority of his successors and admirers throughout the remainder of the nineteenth century. In every form that Glinka touched, whether the *romance*, chamber music, orchestral music or opera, he infused something new and elevated it to a higher plain, though he had no desire for exaggerated effect. In Glinka, as in Pushkin, formal perfection is united with a Classical restraint, an Italian love of melody with Beethovenian counterpoint, the Russian folk idiom with the sophistication of Mozart and John Field. And yet Glinka is not a mere imitator of any one of these. As a man of genius and through a natural musical instinct he raised Russian music to unprecedented heights.

P

CHAPTER 7

A. S. Dargomyzhsky (1813-1869)

SIGNIFICANCE OF DARGOMYZHSKY IN RUSSIAN MUSIC

A unique place in the history of Russian music is occupied by Alexander Sergeevich Dargomyzhsky, who was born in 1813 and died in 1869. As a younger contemporary of Glinka, he was much influenced by the older man's music and ideals and in turn exercised considerable influence through his own theories and compositions on the members of the *Moguchaya Kuchka*— Balakirev, Cui, Rimsky-Korsakov, Musorgsky, and Borodin. To the young Musorgsky in particular he was 'the great teacher of musical truth'. Apart from his interest in folk music and his desire for realism, he was also the possessor of a highly original mind, though his innovations were by no means contradictory to Glinka's ideals. Rather they were essentially the outcome of the changed social and political conditions of the time. Whereas Glinka's works were created in the spirit of the elegant age of Pushkin, Dargomyzhsky's compositions were the product of the era of Lermontov, Nekrasov and Gogol and, later, of the young Dostoevsky and Tolstoy. An especially important document of the period was Chernyshevsky's *Aesthetic Relationship of Art and Reality,* which was published in 1855 and had as its thesis the premise that the main function of art was 'to explain life and comment on it'. Although Dargomyzhsky owed much to Pushkin's writings, he was at the same time interested in the fate of the 'little man', the petty official. This concern with everyday life and the fate of 'the people' (especially the peasants) is found equally in the literary productions of writers such as Gogol, Saltykov-Shchedrin and the young Dostoevsky, and in the genre paintings of artists such as Fedotov (1815–52).

BIOGRAPHICAL DETAILS

Dargomyzhsky was born on 2 February 1813 on the small estate of his father in a village in the Province of Tula, where his parents had taken refuge from the Napoleonic invasion. His father, Sergey, was the illegitimate son of a great lord of Catherine's time named Ribeaupierre. Sergey's illegitimate origin compelled him to obtain a position in society through government work, and he served first in the Moscow post-office and then in the Commercial Bank in St. Petersburg, receiving finally his hereditary nobility in 1829. It was doubtless through his government service that he developed the rather serious business-like and at the same time whimsical disposition that was passed on to his gifted son. Dargomyzhsky's mother, *née* Princess Kozlovskaya, was also a potent influence. A woman of the world she composed verses, which were published in magazines in the 1820's. Alexander even used some of these later for his own songs. To the education of her children she introduced a spirit of sentimentality and didacticism, as well as a taste for French culture. Perhaps it is significant that Dargomyzhsky never married and all his life would take only female singers as his pupils. In 1817, when Alexander was only four years of age, the Dargomyzhskys moved to St. Petersburg, and from that time onwards his life was spent mostly in the capital. The conditions of Petersburg life, its remoteness from the country, could not help but influence Dargomyzhsky's outlook, and the style of his work was essentially urban in nature.

From his early childhood Dargomyzhsky displayed an interest in music, his domestic musical education following the pattern obtaining in most noble families of the time. Young Dargomyzhsky took lessons in piano, violin, and singing. In his own words:

> My passion and zealousness for music were so great that, despite the innumerable lessons which one was obliged to prepare for the itinerant Russian and foreign teachers, I had already composed at the eleventh and twelfth years of my life, through self-instruction, various piano pieces and even *romances*. (1)

His teacher at the time, A. T. Danilevsky, marvelled at his attempts at composition, but felt that they distracted him from piano practice. He learned the elements of theory and singing from the singing-master Zeibig and completed his piano studies with Franz Schoberlechner (1797–1843).

At the age of 17–18 Alexander was a many-sided musician.

According to his own testimony he was renowned in St. Petersburg as a good pianist and often participated in amateur concerts, playing both violin and viola parts in quartets. His vocal sight-reading was impeccable. His first attempts at composition had commenced at the age of 11 or 12 and as he grew older he became more and more interested in that field. In his autobiography he wrote:

> When I was 18 or 19 I composed, though not, of course, without mistakes, many sparkling pieces for piano and violin, 2 quartets, cantatas and a host of songs.

Of these works (one of which is a *romance* to his Mother's words 'Kolybelnaya pesenka moey vnuchke' [Cradle Song to my Granddaughter] written in 1831), only a very small quantity of piano pieces and *romances* has survived; and, indeed, they are in no way musically remarkable, consisting of dances (mazurkas, *contredanses*, polkas, waltzes), virtuoso piano pieces (among them variations on a 'Russian song' 'Vinyat menya v narode'), and songs of a sentimental nature. Even at this tender age, however, may be distinguished occasional glimpses of a desire for originality. Thus, he wrote one piano scherzo with the title *Pylkost i khladnokrovie* (Ardour and Equanimity), adding by way of a sub-title: 'Written from a conversation on nature' [*sic*].

In 1834 Dargomyzhsky made the acquaintance of Glinka, who had recently returned from abroad. As he himself describes it:

> An identical education, an identical love for art immediately united us, and we quickly became sincere friends, despite the fact that Glinka was 10 years older than I. In the course of 22 years I was with him continually on the most amicable, most friendly terms. (2)

This meeting played an important part in Dargomyzhsky's life and determined the subsequent direction of his work. He was present at the first orchestral rehearsals of *A Life for the Tsar*, often played duets with Glinka, analysed with him the symphonies of Beethoven, and together organized concerts for charitable purposes. Most of all he was impressed by Glinka's technical mastery and in his autobiography he wrote:

> Glinka's example and the sensible advice of N. V. Kukolnik compelled me to work seriously on the study of musical theory.

Glinka sent me the manuscripts on theory of Professor Dehn, which he had brought with him from Berlin. I copied them out with my own hand, and soon acquired the supposed wisdom of thorough-bass and counterpoint, for I had been practically accustomed to them from childhood, and began to work at orchestration.

From his earliest days Dargomyzhsky was attracted by musical genres associated with the spoken word, and this tendency to fall back on a literary text (or, in the case of his orchestral works, on a programme) remained characteristic of the composer the whole of his life. Indeed, among his mature compositions it is the vocal works that predominate. As soon as he felt himself sufficiently technically equipped to write an opera, therefore, he set to work with zeal. He himself observed that 'the desire to undertake a more extensive labour' was fanned into flames after his meeting with Glinka and his studies with him. In choosing an operatic subject, however, he soon ran into difficulties. Glinka's national sympathies were at that time still alien to him and he was attracted more by French grand opera with its social subject matter and its dramatic conflicts. (3) At first he attempted to write something on Hugo's *Lucrèce Borgia*, but he was dissuaded by the poet Zhukovsky. Then, after further deliberation, he settled on the libretto of *Esmeralda*, adapted from Hugo's novel *Notre Dame de Paris*, which was in great vogue at the time (4); indeed, interest in the novel was so prolonged that in 1837 it was produced in dramatized form at the theatre and eleven years later, in 1848, as the ballet *Esmeralda*. Dargomyzhsky set to work with enthusiasm, using a French libretto, and by 1839 the score was completed. The composer himself translated the text into Russian and the opera was delivered to the Imperial Theatres. It was not till eight years later, however, that, at the end of 1847, it at last appeared in Moscow, its St. Petersburg première being in 1851. As Dargomyzhsky recorded in his memoirs:

Those eight years of waiting in vain, indeed the most fervent years of life, lay as a heavy burden on my whole artistic output.

Esmeralda was essentially the product of a young composer fascinated by the grand operas of Auber and Meyerbeer, and, indeed, it abounds in all the elements usually associated with that genre—dramatic tension, vivid mass scenes, furious en-sembles, monologues, ballet *divertissements*, and colourful orchestration. That Dargomyzhsky himself realized the opera's shortcomings is confirmed by his own severe, though legitimate, criticism of the work in a letter written twenty years later:

> The music [of *Esmeralda*] is commonplace, often banal, such as one finds in Halévy or Meyerbeer; but in the dramatic scenes may already be discerned that language of truth and strength, which I have since endeavoured to develop in my Russian music.

Apart from being an imitation of French grand opera, in *Esmeralda* may also be noted the influence of the Russian *bytovoy romance* and the town dance. Most remarkable in the opera are the dramatic climaxes and Dargomyzhsky has treated the mass scenes with considerable skill for so young and inexperienced a composer. Such are the scenes of the beggars, infuriated by Frollo's conduct in Act I, the scene of the place of execution on the Place de Grève, the crowd's mockery of Quasimodo in Act II. Mention may also be made of the Quintet and chorus con-cluding Act II (the scene of the Fleur de Lis), with its keen sense of drama. An attempt to give the opera unity is provided by the use of an instrumental reminiscence motive, which characterizes Esmeralda, the young gypsy girl.

The ordeal in awaiting the première of *Esmeralda* was a morti-fying experience for the highly sensitive young composer and in the years following Dargomyzhsky attempted no large-scale productions. Surrounded by numbers of attractive female ad-mirers, amateur singers, Dargomyzhsky was inspired instead to compose *romances* and in 1843–4 one of the St. Petersburg pub-lishers issued a volume containing some thirty of his songs. Most of these were in the style of the *bytovoy* lyric of the time and show the influence of Glinka. Among them may be mentioned the *romances* 'Vertograd', 'Odelas tumanami Sierra Nevada' (The Sierra Nevada was Covered with Mist), 'Shestnadtsat let' (Sixteen), 'Yunosha i deva' (The Youth and the Maid), 'Tuchki nebesnye' (Celestial Stormclouds), and others, in which may already be noticed the careful attention to the words, the declamatory nature of the melody. Like Glinka, Dargomyzhsky had definite ideas how *romances* should be per-formed and gave careful directions to his singers.

A significant event in Dargomyzhsky's life was his first trip abroad, mainly spent in Paris, which was prompted by his dissatisfaction with his life as an official and disappointment over *Esmeralda*. Retiring from government service, he left Russia in the autumn of 1844. Dargomyzhsky's foreign impressions are vividly described in his few letters home. Visiting the Parisian theatres he found Meyerbeer's *Robert le diable* 'far from nature'. Of *Les Huguenots* he commented:

The craftsmanship and intellect are incredible, but no craftsmanship or intellect can imitate the human heart. (5)

However, he was delighted especially by the French vaudevilles with their brilliant satire and mordant wit:

One has to see [them]—there is so much bite and intelligence in the vaudevilles here! One has to hear these caustic comments about the *littérateurs*, the new plays, the ministers, etc.

He was left completely unmoved by Félicien David's spectacular programme symphony *Le Désert*, which created a *furore* in the French capital. In it he found so little of the 'spirit of Araby', and so much 'French padding' that he advised calling it 'Parisian boulevards'. The study of humanity in all its forms, however, particularly attracted his attention. In one of his letters to his father he wrote:

What has interested me most of all has been the *cour d'assises*, where they judge criminals. I have been at six trials and, had I remained in Paris, would have gone to many more. One cannot imagine how fascinating all these dramas are in fact . . . It is very interesting to read novels, in which fictitious proceedings are described. But to be a witness of a real live episode, where human passions prevail, to witness the very actors and follow the developments of the action—for me it is the most absorbing thing in the world!

As in the case of so many Russians when removed from their native-land (and the parallel with Glinka is striking!), absence from Russia made Dargomyzhsky become more aware of his own national heritage, and shortly after his return to St. Petersburg, he wrote on 19 May 1845 to a friend, who was contemplating a foreign trip:

A 6-month journey will be sufficient to convince you that there
is no people better in the world than the Russians, and if elements
of poetry exist in Europe, then they are in Russia.

An immediate result of this sudden awakening of interest in
national culture was the writing down of folk themes, in which
he also enlisted the help of his friends.

On his return to Russia a new period of creation began in
Dargomyzhsky's life. As far back as 1843 he had attempted to
write a cantata to words of Pushkin's *Torzhestvo Vakkha* (The
Triumph of Bacchus), but work was terminated by his trip
abroad. Under the influence of his Parisian impressions, however, he decided to transform the cantata into a lyrical ballet-
opera and in 1848 (one year after the staging of *Esmeralda*) it
was completed. As regards its performance he was again unlucky and it was eventually given only in 1867, nineteen years
after the opera had been composed. *The Triumph of Bacchus* was
the final work to terminate the long early period of Dargomyzhsky's creative evolution. There is little dramatic content and
the music owes much to French opera and ballet and Russian
salon music, though the influence of Glinka may also be
detected. It is also of interest in that it is the first large-scale
ballet opera in the history of Russian music.

In the many songs written at this period, Dargomyzhsky endeavoured to deepen their psychological content and to create
a new kind of *romance*—a vocal monologue full of dramatic tension in which the music reflected the poetic speech. Such are
the songs 'I skuchno, i grustno' (It's Boring and Sad) and 'Mne
grustno' (I Am Sad) to words of Lermontov. Formerly Dargomyzhsky had been keenly interested in Pushkin's verse, but
now he availed himself of the writings of Lermontov and
Koltsov. Another new factor was his composition of songs in
the folk idiom. 'Ne skazhu nikomu' (I Shall Tell No One), for
instance, anticipates some of the songs of Tchaikovsky. The
genre of comic songs was also crystallized in these years: such
are 'Melnik' (The Miller), to words of Pushkin, 'Likhoradushka' (The Fever), with peasant words noted by the composer, and 'Okh, tikh, tikh, tikh, ty' to words of Koltsov.
Mention may also be made of his use of 'low' gypsy melodies
(which enjoyed great popularity in the town and were disdained

by most serious musicians) in such pieces as the two-part vocal arrangement of the melody 'Vanka-Tanka'.

All these tendencies are revealed in his opera *Rusalka*, on which he worked constantly at this period. Although progress on the opera was at first inconsiderable, an impetus was given him by the fact that his work was at the beginning of the 50's acquiring general recognition. In April 1853, on the advice and suggestion of Prince Odoevsky, Dargomyzhsky gave a grand concert in aid of the 'Society for the Visitation of the Poor' (founded by Odoevsky), in which took part O. A. Petrov, Polina Viardot-Garcia (Turgenev's great love), and Dargomyzhsky himself, as well as other artists. The concert included *romances* by the composer, excerpts from *Esmeralda*, *The Triumph of Bacchus*, and other pieces. In his own words the concert was 'a sparkling and unexpected success' and succeeded in firmly establishing his reputation as a composer.

After this concert, work on *Rusalka* proceeded at a much faster rate and in 1855 the opera was finished, it being performed on 4 May 1856 in the Marynsky Theatre with the participation of the Russian singers O. A. Petrov (as the Miller) and D. M. Leonova (as the Princess). The attitude of the Theatrical Administration towards *Rusalka*, however, was not a friendly one. The opera was but seldom performed and even then with only a weak cast. However, *Rusalka* was appreciated by some, as is revealed by the following informative letter. When Dargomyzhsky's favourite pupil, the talented amateur singer L. I. Karmalina, was upset that Russia had not recognized him, the composer wrote to her in characteristic vein:

It is true that the Theatrical Directors have always been hostile to me; that the aristocracy has not visited my operas; that several newspaper hacks have been disloyal to me, being ashamed, however, to sign their names. But all this must apply only to a chance temporary state of affairs, and everything taken in reverse could not be a truer reward for my labours . . . You ask: in what can I find compensation, in what? . . . In the sympathy of those called to understand all that is good, elegant, noble. In the unfeigned tears, which I have seen in the eyes of many of my dear listeners— tears, which neither the absence of the aristocracy, nor the scoundrelly staging of the opera, nor the stupid criticisms of semi-connoisseurs could prevent. Finally, at those evenings, which I some time spent with you and with others dear to my heart and hearing, and in much, much undiscovered to most people . . . You know that I always write for some-one; that I wrote especially for you, when you so desired. . . . And so, if you and the others for whom I wrote value my gifts, what does the adulation of the Directors, the upper classes and papers mean to me? As far as I am concerned, speaking as an artist, you and all the others constitute Russia: so it happens, from my point of view, that Russia has fully recognised me. Am I right? (6)

After *Rusalka* a new period began in Dargomyzhsky's life from the end of the 1850's. Notable events at this period were the founding of the 'Russian Musical Society' in 1859, of which he was one of the initiators, and the establishing of the St. Petersburg Conservatory in 1862 and the Moscow Conservatory in 1866. Dargomyzhsky himself played quite an important part in the formation of the new school of performers. Thus, in his diary he recorded:

. . . moving constantly in the society of male and female singers I managed to make a practical study of all aspects of the human voice, as well as the art of dramatic singing. I can boldly assert that there was not a single well-known singer in Petersburg society, who did not take lessons from me, or at least seek my advice. (7)

At the same time Dargomyzhsky moved in a circle of *littérateurs*, poets, and artists, who were gathered round the satirical journal *Iskra* (The Spark), to which he himself occasionally contributed. He was also on friendly terms with the young members of the *Kuchka* and with V. V. Stasov, before whom he played his latest works, besides taking part in the performance of Musorgsky's own compositions. Dargomyzhsky's name also began to be known abroad (he visited Berlin, Leipzig, Brussels, Paris, and London in 1865), his compositions being performed in Belgium with particular success, as well as being reported in the Belgian press.

To this late period belong a number of *romances*, orchestral works such as the *Ukrainskiy kazachok* (Ukrainian Kazachok) (1864), *Baba-Yaga* (1862), and *Fantaziya na finskie temy* (Fantasia on Finnish Themes) (1867), all of which in their variation development and dance melodies show their indebtedness to the orchestral works of Glinka, and the opera *Kamennyi gost* (The Stone Guest). The songs of this late period are remarkable for their pathos, satire and irony and are somewhat different from the more sentimental effusions of the previous era, particular attention in them being paid to the exact reproduction of the intonations of human speech. In a famous letter of the period written in 1857 to Karmalina, attacking the press critics who desired only 'melodies flattering to the ear', he wrote:

> I do not wish to write music for their amusement. I want the sound to express the word. I want truth. They are unable to understand this. (8)

In the last years of his life Dargomyzhsky was a sick man, suffering from attacks of aneurism. Nevertheless before he died he managed to write in only a few months the greater part of his experimental and revolutionary opera *The Stone Guest*, which was written to an almost unaltered text from Pushkin's tragedy of the same name. In his will he requested that the opera be completed by Cui and orchestrated by Rimsky-Korsakov. Its première took place in St. Petersburg in 1872, though the opera never enjoyed success. Dargomyzhsky died on 5 January 1869.

DARGOMYZHSKY'S OPERAS: RUSALKA

Of Dargomyzhsky's four operas *Esmeralda, Rusalka, The Stone Guest* and the unfinished *Rogdana, Rusalka* is outstanding on account of its wide use of the folk idiom, folk characters, and the employment of authentic folk music, in some cases written down by Dargomyzhsky himself. From his works and writings it is clear that Dargomyzhsky was not indifferent to folk music, although he was familiar with it chiefly in its town form— 'Russian song'. Dargomyzhsky's early essays in the treatment of folk melodies consisted for the most part of piano works such as *Cosaque*, which comprised variations on a Ukrainian folk dance (and which he used again in his orchestral piece *Kazachok*), or 'Vinyat menya v narode'—variations on a 'Russian song'. Before embarking on the composition of *Rusalka* in 1848, however, he made a careful study of folk life—a factor which is attested by his own writings. Thus, in a letter to Odoevsky dated 3 July 1853 he wrote:

> I am working here on my *Rusalka*. The more I study the elements, of our folk music, the more I discover new facets. (9)

Earlier in his autobiography he tells how 'he set about forming a plan for the collection of materials for the opera', (10) and he also describes his study of Sakharov's *Skazanye russkovo naroda* (Sayings of the Russian People), the first volume of which appeared in its third edition in 1841, and T. Tereshchenko's *Byt russkovo naroda* (Life of the Russian People), which appeared in 1848. (11) The libretto of *Rusalka* was based originally on Pushkin's poem of the same name, but was later modified considerably by the composer as the result of his further study of folk materials. Among Dargomyzhsky's alterations to the original may be mentioned the addition of an ending to the story (Pushkin's poem was left incomplete) and the development both of the peasant scenes and the episode of the marriage ritual. There are changes also to the characters: Olga is introduced into the opera in place of the Mother in the original; the Miller's daughter is given the name of Natasha; and the Prince, who in Pushkin is portrayed as an abandoned sensualist, is represented in the opera as a Romantic hero, helpless in the coils of fate. In the opera the libretto has lost much of its original virility. Although Dargomyzhsky frequently altered or borrowed his texts from already existing collections (e.g. Prach, Trutovsky, Chulkov, Kashin, &c.), he made little or no use of the melodies to these words, preferring to compose his own music in the folk idiom. (12)

It must not be imagined, however, that *Rusalka* is Russian in every sense of the word. Indeed, its kinship with French opera is revealed in the structure of its ensembles, the big choral scenes, in the ballet *divertissements* and the fairy scenes of the *rusalkas*, &c. The world of fairy tale did not lend itself easily to Dargomyzhsky and it is significant that work on the subject of *Rogdana* was abandoned at a very early stage. It is characteristic, too, that the imaginative chorus of enchanted maidens surrounding the sleeping Princess Rogdana was a direct imitation of the chorus of enchanted maidens in *Ruslan*. For the magic scenes in *Rusalka* Dargomyzhsky reverted to composition in the style of 'salon' or French ballet music. Thus, the chorus of *rusalkas* 'Svobodnoy tolpoyu' was borrowed wholesale from a *romance* which he had written earlier. Two 'magic' numbers, however, do shows signs of originality—the voice of the *rusalka* singing the words 'Tebya, knyaz miliy, ya prizyvayu' (I summon you, dear Prince) at the end of the opera (the music of which is used also in the Overture, *Tempo d'Allegretto*, 6/8), and the final part of the chorus of *rusalkas* in Act III ('Tishche, tishche'—A♭ major).

FOLK ELEMENTS IN RUSALKA

A valuable document for the understanding and assessment of Dargomyzhsky's use of folk music is the note-book containing twenty-one songs (mostly Russian), which furnished the composer with a supply of folk themes, which he employed both in his operatic and his non-operatic works. (13) Whether these songs were written down by Dargomyzhsky directly from folk-singers or whether they were given him by friends (14) it is impossible to tell, but from the fact that several of them are not encountered in any other anthologies before this time it seems that they are Dargomyzhsky's own. (15) Some of the songs included in the note-book were popular at the period (e.g. 'Ivushka', 'Kak po moryu', 'Vspomni, vspomni'), but, on the whole, Dargomyzhsky's songs differ from the usual versions.

Study of the songs enables one to form an opinion of the folk characteristics that appealed to Dargomyzhsky. Thus, the Russian songs all appear to be given in their town variant; all are marked by strong rhythms and, generally speaking, are of a lyrical nature.

The first authentic folk-song to be employed is the melody 'Idët koza rogataya', which occurs in the opening and closing scenes of the opera. The tune was sung to Dargomyzhsky by his nurse as a child and in his declining years he gave it to Rimsky-Korsakov, who included it in his *100 Russian Folk-songs*, Op. 24. (16) The song does not appear in any other collection before this period. Dargomyzhsky is not only fascinated by the song (he uses it in other works as well), (17) but seems to regard it as a

symbol of magic. (18) The following example is the tune as it
appears in Rimsky-Korsakov's collection (Mus. Ex. 1):

Mus. Ex.1

I – dët   ko – za   ro – ga – ta – ya   za   ma – ly –

– mi   re – bya – ti – mi;   kto   sos-ku   so – sët,   mo – lo – ka   mi

pët   to – vo   bu, pro – vo – du,   na   ro – ga   po – sa – zhu.

The tune is first heard in the Overture, where it plays a prominent part in the musical development, and its use in the context
may be compared with the employment of the whole-tone scale
motive in *Ruslan and Lyudmila*, which is likewise a symbol of
magic. Mus. Ex. 1 is heard in the overture in different keys and
in contrasting forms, and this system of development is repeated
on its reappearance in the Finale. In some respects in the Finale
it anticipates the harmonic treatment of Wagner or Tchaikovsky: the same motive is repeated incessantly, gradually increasing in tension and volume; however, whereas Tchaikovsky

Mus. Ex.2

Zhe v te – rem moy,   ya zhdu   te – bya   po – prezh – ne – mu,   i

accel. e cresc.

bu – dem ne – raz – luch –ny my   na – vek sto – boy,   pri – di   zhe,knyaz,pri – di!

accel. e cresc.

would have taken the motive higher and higher, until seeming to have reached the *ne plus ultra*, Dargomyzhsky is content to pass from one climax to another, thus avoiding a sustained prolongation of the tension (19) (Mus. Ex. 2).

The second authentic folk-song to be employed in *Rusalka* occurs in the chorus 'Kak na gore my pivo varili'. The melody, which is not found in folk-song collections prior to this date, is taken from the composer's note-book. (20) As may be seen from the following examples, in the note-book the tune is in the key of Eb major and is sung to the words 'Sredi dvora, iz pod dreva', but in the opera the melody is given a four-part harmonization, is in the key of F major and is sung to the words 'Kak na gore my pivo varili' (Mus. Ex. 3):

In comparison with Glinka's treatment of folk choruses, Dargomyzhsky's contrapuntal handling of the material seems poor, though there are occasional moments of inspiration.

The third authentic song used by Dargomyzhsky is found at the end of Act I where Natasha addresses 'Queen Dnepr'. This too appears in his note-book where it is sung to the words 'Kuda bezhat, tosku devat'. (21) In the opera the song, which commences with the words 'Dnepr tsaritsa', is in G minor and is sung by the heroine, Natasha, against a typical operatic background of choral interpolations. One curious and rather striking effect is obtained by the orchestra continually breaking into unison when accompanying a specific phrase (Mus. Ex. 4):

Mus. Ex.4

Dne — pra — tsa — ri — tsa, pre — da — yus, mo —

gu — — chey vla — sti ya tvo — ey pri —

Dargomyzhsky's treatment of the folk-song in this number is typical of his usual manner of approach. The tune is first sung in its entirety by the voice, is then divided between voice and orchestra, and is finally developed beyond recognition, only fragments of the original folk-song remaining. It is given a diatonic accompaniment.

Dargomyzhsky not only makes use of authentic folk music but writes freely in the folk idiom. Although his texts are frequently drawn from existing folk-songs, he ignores the old tunes and prefers to compose fresh music. Thus, for example, the tune of the song 'Akh, ty, pole moë, pole chistoe' bears no resemblance to the melody of the song of the same name as it appears in Trutovsky and Prach. Conversely, only rarely does Dargomyzhsky set new words to an old melody (apart from his employment of authentic folk melodies). (22)

FOLK CHORUSES

By far the most important from the point of view of music written in the folk idiom are the choruses, which owe much to Glinka's models in *A Life for the Tsar*. The third number of the opera is a typical illustration of Dargomyzhsky's attempts to evoke a picture of popular life. (23) It is introduced by a shepherd's pipe (*dudka*) (represented by an oboe) and this serves as an accompaniment to a chorus which, at this stage, is handled more in the manner of Verstovsky or Cavos than of Glinka. The oboe theme is played in variations (Mus. Ex. 5):

Mus. Ex. 5

This is close to the lyrical 'protracted' songs of Russian folk music and shows some similarity to the wedding song *Chto ne pava* given in Prach (No. 111) and Rimsky-Korsakov (R-K No. 78). Notable in Dargomyzhsky's melody is the insertion of a sharpened seventh, which clearly shows the preference for the town folk genre, even when attempting to depict village life. (24) Later he introduces a new rhythmic figure, containing characteristic folk features, which clearly stems from the choral introduction to *A Life for the Tsar*. There is also a modulation to A major, which prepares the way for the next folk chorus. This is sung to the words 'Zapletisya, pleten', (25) a folk text common at the time. The tune is Dargomyzhsky's own, however, and contains folk-song phrases typical of the town song tradition. The women's voices are heard largely in parallel thirds and often reproduce folk-song practices such as the breaking into unison or octave at cadences. Effective also are the sustained pedal A's and E's. Although the choral writing cannot be compared with Glinka's, it shows Dargomyzhsky's imitation of Glinka's methods of procedure, with their skilful combination of counterpoint and folk-derived features. The middle section modulates from A to F by way of C and leads into the third chorus 'Kak na gore', to which reference has already been made. The key relationship between the choruses may be tabulated as follows:

Chorus I	*Chorus II*	*Chorus III*
D minor—A major	A major—C major —F major	F major

Though contrasting in thematic material and tempo, unity is provided by an inter-relationship of key, F major being the relative major of D minor.

Two other choruses are deserving of comment, both of which occur in the second act. Act II opens with a theme heard previously in the overture, though in a different key. In its shape and structure it is reminiscent of an authentic folk tune and forms the basis of the wedding chorus 'Kak vo gornitse'. (26) The same tune is repeated in varying forms, in different keys, and against changing harmonic backgrounds in the manner established by Glinka. In comparison with the finely interlacing structures of the greater master, however, Dargomyzhsky's music seems clumsy and artificial.

The chorus to the Finale of Act II is also of interest, and is based on the folk text 'Svatushka'. The chorus is one of Dargomyzhsky's most successful ventures in the folk idiom and, in its opening at least, shows resemblance to the wedding song 'Da kak Fëdorova matushka', which appears in the collection of Istomin and Dyutsch. (27) It contains some of the composer's favourite features such as the repetition of certain phrases, characteristic leaps and rhythms, the whole being notable for its freshness and peculiar 'Russian-ness'. (28) The part writing has nothing in common with authentic folk polyphony apart from the abundance of parallel thirds, but as an essay in the folk idiom it is convincing. With each verse the melody is varied in accordance with the sense of the words, which brings it into line with actual folk procedure. The weakest part of the chorus is the ending: as a general rule Dargomyzhsky was incapable of concluding a piece without having recourse to the well-worn cadential clichés of his day.

INDIVIDUAL CHARACTERIZATION

Among the individual characters the Miller is outstanding both dramatically and because his music, like Susanin's, is permeated by folk-song inflections. Often his music seems to be based on a kind of dance song, of which the tempo 2/4 is typical, though unlike Susanin he is given no specific theme. The Miller's earthy character is well revealed in his first aria, which abounds in folk-song phrases. The following example is striking on account of its similarity to passages both from *A Life for the Tsar* and *Ruslan and Lyudmila* (Mus. Ex. 6):

Mus. Ex. 6

Okh   to - vo vse vy,   dev-ki mo-lo-dy - e, posmotrish ma -   lo tol-kov nas

Although the same kind of music is found in his part throughout the opera, it changes in accordance with the dramatic action, this being clearly in evidence in the famous 'mad-scene' in the Third Act.

Folk-song intonations are evident in the part of Natasha, though are more in evidence when she appears as a simple peasant girl than in her role as a *rusalka*. For the most part her music, like that of Antonida in *A Life for the Tsar*, is drawn from 'Russian song' and consists of a union of the Russian folk idiom with passages of coloratura.

USE OF DRAMATIC RECITATIVE

In writing *Rusalka* Dargomyzhsky claimed that he wished to lay stress 'on the development of the dramatic elements' which are mostly contained in the ensembles. This is true of the first two duets in Act I (the duet of the Prince and Natasha and the final duet of Natasha and the Miller) and the duet of the Prince and the mad Miller in Act III sc. 2. Particularly important is the part played by recitative, which likewise appears at the culminatory points of the action in the duet of Natasha and the Prince (beginning at Natasha's words: 'Stop, stop, I wanted to tell you'), and that of Natasha and the Miller (beginning at the words: 'I don't believe you, it cannot be!'). The same applies to the duet of the Miller and the Prince. As Tchaikovsky himself observed in an article on *Rusalka*:

> It is a fact that Dargomyzhsky's strength lies in his wonderfully real and at the same time elegantly singable recitative, which gives his marvellous opera the charm of inimitable originality. (29)

And, indeed, it is perhaps in the dramatic scenes and in this remarkably supple recitative that Dargomyzhysky's talent chiefly lies.

SUMMARY

To sum up, one may say that Dargomyzhsky is essentially a transitional composer whose language is in a fluid state. Like

Glinka he has still not found an entirely satisfactory means of developing folk-song, but occasionally phrases of pure folk origin make their appearance. In his treatment of folk music he broke no new paths but his music is worthy of attention by reason of its assimilation of the folk idiom and the ability to create and develop characters rooted in Russian soil. (30) Like Glinka he also makes use of reminiscence motives, but little attempt is made to develop them and their employment is mostly limited to literal quotation.

THE STONE GUEST

A unique place in music is occupied by Dargomyzhsky's uncompleted opera *The Stone Guest*, most of which was composed at great speed in the last months of the composer's life. Speaking of the opera in a letter dated 9 April 1868 he wrote:

> It is not I that am writing but some kind of power unknown to me. *The Stone Guest* came to my attention some five years ago, when I was completely fit, but I recoiled from this colossal work. And now, a sick man, I have written almost three-quarters of the opera in the course of two and a half months. (31)

In *The Stone Guest* Dargomyzhsky broke decisively with all former Russian operatic traditions, avoiding the division of the music into individual sections and numbers by using a continuous musical texture. There are no ensembles or choruses and the opera is built exclusively on dialogues. In composing the music Dargomyzhsky considered that for each phrase he had to find a new musical idea to fit it and, indeed, the whole work abounds in curious augmented and diminished intervals, which are the result of the composer's endeavour to find a faithful reproduction of the intonations of human speech. Although there may be detected in these aspirations some similarities to the Wagnerian 'endless melody', Dargomyzhsky's music is quite unique. The orchestra plays only a minor role, though there are, however, some exciting moments, such as that in Act II when Don Juan describes in minor detail his duel with the Commendatore and the latter's death—all of which are reflected in the orchestral accompaniment.

The Stone Guest is based on the poem of the same name by Pushkin, and although Dargomyzhsky claimed that he was 'writing music to scenes from *The Stone Guest* just as they are without changing a single word', there are in point of fact some slight alterations. In Act I sc. 2 of the original drama, in the scene with Laura, three visitors appear who are excited admirers of Laura and her art. In the original they are given no individual characteristics, though the first is more loquacious than the others. In the opera, however, there are only two visitors, each of whom possesses a distinct personality: the first is a connoisseur of art, a serious lover of music, while the second is a complete fool. In his excitement he can only repeat the same words over and over again (set to equally repetitive music), and despite its seeming insignificance Dargomyzhsky has treated the episode with great skill. For instance, after Laura's performance of the song 'Odelas tumanom Grenada' (Grenada was covered in mist), which is greeted by cries of admiration from the others, the second visitor is so overwhelmed that he cannot even finish the sentence:

'O, bravo, bravo! O exce . . .'

(a phrase which does not appear in Pushkin at all). The whole thing is a clever piece of characterization and in the original MS of the vocal score the composer wrote in brackets, referring to the second visitor: ('Aristocrat of limited intelligence'.).

The dominating figure in the opera is, of course, the Don himself, and he is given an appropriate musical portrayal. Leporello, his servant, is alarmed by his master's adventures and his character is ingeniously reflected in the music, as, for instance, in the following illustration when Leporello falteringly delivers to the statue his master's invitation to dinner (Mus. Ex. 7).

In *The Stone Guest* Dargomyzhsky also makes some use of reminiscence motives, though, unlike the Wagnerian *Leitmotiv* these are not developed to any extent. That of Donna Anna first appears in the orchestral accompaniment to herald the approach of the heroine in Act I sc. 1 and possesses an almost ethereal nature. In Acts II and III, where her qualities as a widow are underlined, the motif is slightly modified. However, when she becomes infatuated with the Don in the second half of Act III, this 'motif of virtue' disappears completely—a subtle touch!

Mus. Ex.7

Leporello (in excitement)

Moy ba-rin, Don Zhu-an vas pro-sit zav-tra prit-ti po-poz-he v dom su-pru-gi va-shey i stat u..... u dve-ri....

Of great interest in the opera is the motif of the Stone Guest himself, whose unearthly qualities are represented by a whole-tone scale (in which action Dargomyzhsky is clearly following the traditions of Glinka). The motif first appears discreetly in the orchestra in Act II at Don Juan's words: 'I think that the Commendatore must be lonely without her'. However, at the Commendatore's knock in Act III the whole-tone motif resounds FF, while the conclusion of the opera consists of a symphonic elaboration of the theme (Mus. Ex. 8):

Mus. Ex. 8

(Knocks)

ff

Despite its avoidance of conventional harmonies and progressions, *The Stone Guest* also contains a few elements of folk music, though these are restricted to occasional vocal inflections in the music of Don Juan, Leporello and Laura. Laura's music, however, falls more often into the pattern of the *bytovoy romance*. The only deliberate employment of folk material is the introduction of a Spanish *jota* melody in Act I sc. I—the same melody, incidentally, that Glinka employed in his own *Jota aragonesa* (1845).

SUMMARY

The appearance of *The Stone Guest* provoked varied reactions among the musical world. To members of the *Kuchka* it was a work of genius, a beacon illuminating new paths. To others, like the critic Laroche, its merits were dubious and even Tchaikovsky claimed that to him the opera was 'the sorry fruit of a dry, often rational process of invention'. Regarded in perspective a century later, *The Stone Guest* still remains a unique and absolutely Russian phenomenon, brilliantly original, enterprising to the highest degree, yet impracticable in performance. The final judgement must surely rest in Rimsky-Korsakov's own assessment of the opera:

A. S. [Dargomyzhsky] has shown that to compose by the means which he has chosen [in *The Stone Guest*] is harder than following the usual means of composition, because for every phrase he must find a new musical idea to suit it, whereas the conventional method consists in the development of two or three themes.

DARGOMYZHSKY'S ROMANCES

Dargomyzhsky wrote more than 100 *romances* in the course of his life, as well as numerous choruses and ensembles, though not all of these have been preserved. In some of his early works may be detected elements that became essential features of his later style, particularly in the question of character studies. Among his early works, which are clearly influenced by Glinka (indeed, in several cases, he sets the same poems) may be found examples of the lyrical *romance* sometimes having a *salon* character such as 'Golubye glaza' (Blue Eyes); sometimes a more sensitive nature, such as 'Privet' (Welcome) or 'Ona pridët' (She is

Coming); or, occasionally, having a feeling of nobility and restraint, such as 'Ya vas lyubil' (I loved You) to words of Pushkin, or 'Vlyublen ya, deva-krasota' (I Am In Love, Fair Maid) to words of Yazykov. Like Glinka, Dargomyzhsky turns also to the musical forms of Romantic Spain in his 'Odelas tumanami Sierra Nevada' (Covered with Mists was the Sierra Nevada) or to the Orient in his 'Lezginskaya pesnya' (Lezghin Song) and 'Vertograd.' The most original *romances* of the period, however, are those dealing with everyday life. Thus, the song 'Kayus, dyadya, chert poputal' (I own it up, Uncle, the Devil Tempted Me) to words of Timofeev (32) is filled with a light irony. In another song 'Baba staraya' (The Old Woman), also to words of Timofeev, the ardour and sorrow of 'the young man' are transmitted in a convincing manner, the melody having a folk-like ring about it. In Dargomyzhsky's vocal *fantaziya* 'Svadba' (The Marriage) to Timofeev's sombre words 'It was not in Church we married . . . but at midnight in the dark forest', the genre of the Romantic ballad undergoes a new treatment.

MIDDLE PERIOD

The greater part of Dargomyzhsky's *romances*, however (approximately one half), belong to the period of his maturity, among them being several of his best works. On some occasions Dargomyzhsky made settings of the same poems as Glinka—e.g. 'V krovi gorit ogon zhelaniya' (In my Blood Burns the Fire of Desire), 'Nochnoy zefir' (Night Zephyr), 'Slyshu li golos tvoy' (Do I Hear Your Voice) and others, even going to the extent of using the same forms as the Spanish bolero, the oriental idiom, &c.

An important part in Dargomyzhsky's work at this time was occupied by 'Russian songs'—i.e. vocal works to words by Koltsov, Timofeev, or to folk texts, freely developing the tradition of Russian folk-songs as they were performed in the town. Among his 'Russian songs' of the period may be mentioned the lyrical 'Ne skazhu nikomu' (I Shall Tell No One), 'Dushechka devitsa' (My Darling Girl), 'Bez uma, bez razuma' (With No Mind, No Reason) and the particularly interesting comic song 'Okh, tikh, tikh, tikh, ty'. Another song, 'Likhoradushka', is a lively yet bitter folk-song about an old and unloved husband;

the words are authentic and the melody admirably fits the text.

Mus. Ex. 9

In the mature *romances* of this period is also seen a desire on the composer's part to give greater intensity to the meaning and declamation of the words. This appears particularly in his setting of Lermontov's 'Mne grustno' (I am Sad), and 'I skuchno i grustno' (Both Bored and Sad), in which noticeable is the absence of melismata, the flexibility of the melodic line.

In the last period of Dargomyzhsky's creation this form of lyrical *romance* received continuation in such works as 'Rasstalis gordo my' (Proudly We Parted), 'Mne vsë ravno' (It's All the Same to Me), though Dargomyzhsky attempted new genres in the form of satirical and dramatic monologues. Such are the parodical 'Mchit menya v tvoi obyatiya' (I am Carried Into Your Arms), the Spanish *romance* 'Ya zdes, Inezilya' (I Am Here, Inesilla), and the oriental 'O deva, roza, ya v okovakh' (O Maid, O Rose, I am in Chains), both to words of Pushkin. Some of his 'Russian songs', such as 'Kak prishël muzh iz-pod gorok' seem to lead directly to Musorgsky, while the descriptive 'Pesnya rybki' (Song of the Fish), to words of Lermontov, and 'Na razdole nebes' (In the Expanse of the Skies) are clearly precursors of Tchaikovsky.

DARGOMYZHSKY'S SATIRICAL SONGS

Unique among Dargomyzhsky's late compositions are the satirical songs 'Chervyak' (The Worm) and 'Stary kapral' (The Old Corporal)—both translations by V. Kurochkin of poems by Béranger—and 'Titulyarny sovetnik' (The Titular Counsellor), to words by P. Weinberg, all of which seem to treat the vocal *romance* in a new manner.

'Chervyak' is conceived not only as a vocal work but as a dramatic piece of music and abounds in directions to the performer, such as 'very modestly', 'with complete respect', 'smiling and stammering', 'screwing up the eyes', &c. Through the simple but pliant melody, punctuated by expressive pauses, are brilliantly transmitted the intonations of a wretched minor official, willing to sacrifice anything for the sake of the Count's protection (Mus. Ex. 9). Of the other two songs 'Titulyarny sovetnik' is a brief ironical sketch, consisting of several expressive lines about a 'titular counsellor', whom 'a general's daughter' has rejected. 'Stary kapral', on the other hand, is a tragic and effective monologue about an old corporal, condemned to be shot by his comrades for insulting an officer, and having, as in Glinka's 'Nochnoy smotr', a similar march-like refrain. In these poignant intonations it is not difficult to see a direct link between the *romances* of Dargomyzhsky and some of the brilliant character sketches of Musorgsky. Mus. Ex. 10 reproduces the *romance* 'The Titular Counsellor' in full (Mus. Ex. 10).

FOLK ELEMENTS IN DARGOMYZHSKY'S SONGS

Folk elements are evident in Dargomyzhsky's vocal music; indeed, one of his earliest songs 'V tëmnu nochku v chistom pole' (published 1836), shows resemblance musically to a number of Ukrainian melodies. The influence of gypsy music is seen in songs such as 'Likhoradushka' (which was orchestrated by Glinka). Songs such as 'Kak prishël muzh iz-pod gorok', with its amusing sound effects in the accompaniment, or 'Melnik' (The Miller), lead directly to Musorgsky, and one need only compare 'Melnik' with the latter's 'Akh ty, pyanaya teterya' to realize to what extent this is true.

Dargomyzhsky may not have been brilliantly gifted like Glinka, but his role was an important one nevertheless; without his contribution the Russian Classical School could not have reached complete fulfilment.

Notes

(1) The names of some of the *byliny bogatyrs* are connected with real historical personages. The *bogatyr* Dobrynya Nikitich, for instance, has the characteristics of two figures. One of them was the uncle of the great Prince Vladimir Svyatoslavich, who temporarily ruled Russia for him while he was still a child, who later introduced Christianity into Novgorod (the memory of this event is preserved in the *bylina* about the struggle of Dobrynya with the snake and of his bathing in the River Puchay). Another prototype of a *byliny bogatyr* was Dobrynya Ryazanich, nicknamed 'the Golden Belt', mentioned in the Chronicles among the list of dead warriors in the battle against the Tartars at the River Kalka in 1223. In the description of this battle is mentioned Alexander Popovich of Rostov, who is known in the *byliny* under the name of Alësha Popovich.

(2) W. R. S. Ralston. *The Songs of the Russian People*. London, 1872, pp. 303–4.

(3) Some excellent descriptions of ancient Russian beliefs are given in Ralston. Op. cit. Not the least interesting are those that deal with the ancient deity Perun, the Thunderer, the supreme god of the Slavonians: 'In Kiev, it is said, Perun had a statue of which the trunk was of wood, while the head was of silver, with moustaches of gold, but little more is known about it, except that it bore among its weapons a mace. White Russian traditions describe Perun as tall and well-shaped, with black hair and a long golden beard. He rides in a flaming car, grasping in his left hand a quiver full of arrows, and in his right a fiery bow. Sometimes he flies abroad on a great millstone, which is supported by the mountain spirits who are in subjection to him, and who, by their flight, give rise to storms. Perun, in many respects, corresponds with Thor, and one of the points of similarity is the mace which he bears, answering to Thor's hammer, Mjölnir, the name of which may be compared with the Russian words for a hammer and for lightning, *molot* and *molniya*. Ukko, also, the Finnish Thunder-God, has his hammer, and the Lithuanians used to pay special honour to a great

hammer with which a certain giant—perhaps Perkunas—had freed the Sun from imprisonment.

In the spring, according to a White Russian tradition, Perun goes forth in his fiery car, and crushes with his blazing darts the demons, from whose wounds the blood is sometimes described as streaming forth. That is to say, the lightning pierces the clouds at that season of the year, and causes them to pour forth rain. . . .

After Perun's statue at Kiev had been flung into the Dnieper by St. Vladimir [with the official conversion of Russia to Christianity], and that at Novgorod had been cast into the Volkhof, and the people who used to worship him had accepted just so much of Christianity as left them what the chronicler called "two-faithed", then his attributes were transferred to a number of the personages whom the new religion brought into honour. In the minds of most of the people he became changed into the Prophet Ilya, or Elijah, from whose fiery chariot the lightnings flashed and the thunders pealed as they had done in days of yore from that of Perun. The fame of his battles with the demons survived in the legends about the Archangel Michael, the conqueror of the powers of darkness, and other traditions relating to him may be traced in stories told about the Apostle Peter, or about Yury the Brave, our own St. George' (Ralston. Op. cit., pp. 92–5).

(4) Ralston, op. cit., pp. 193–4.

(5) An interesting light on the role played by these early songs is revealed by the following anecdote. Professor Rubtsov, the Russian folklorist, told me that once he came across some folk singers in a remote district and asked an old man what they were singing. The old man looked most indignant. 'Singing? We aren't singing!'—'Now come, *batyushka*. What do you mean "you aren't singing". What are you doing, then?'—'We're calling in the spring. That isn't singing!'

(6) Ralston refers to the feast of Ivan Kupalo as follows: 'Of thoroughly heathenish origin is a custom still kept up on the Eve of St. John. A figure of Kupalo is made of straw, the size sometimes of a boy, sometimes of a man, and is dressed in woman's clothes, with a necklace and a floral crown. Then a tree is felled, and, after being decked with ribbons, is set up on some chosen spot. Near this tree, to which they give the name of Marena [Winter or Death], the straw figure is placed, together with a table, on which stand spirits and viands. Afterwards a bonfire is lit, and the young men and maidens jump

over it in couples, carrying the figure with them. On the next day they strip the tree and the figure of their ornaments, and throw them both into a stream. . . .

Both Kupalo and the similar mythical being called in the songs Yarilo appear to be intended at times for the Sun or the Spring, at times for Perun. According to a Bulgarian tradition, the sun, on St. John's Day, loses its way, and therefore a maiden appears who leads it across the sky, this maiden being the Dawn. The Bulgarians assert, also, that on the same day the sun dances and whirls swords about, that is, it sends forth specially bright and dazzling rays. In Lithuania it is supposed that on that day the sun, a female being, goes forth from her chamber in a car drawn by three horses—golden, silver, and diamond—to meet her spouse the Moon, and on her way she dances and emits fiery sparks. The Servians assert that the sun stands still three times on St. John's Day, and they account for its apparent pause at the time of the summer solstice by the fear which seizes on it at the thought of its downward career towards winter. The mixture of nuptial and funereal ideas connected with this Midsummer festival gives it a double nature; one set of its rites and songs being joyous, as if to exult over a marriage, and the other tragic, as if to lament for a death. In the former case it appears to be a mystical union between the elements of fire and water that is celebrated; in the latter the downward course of the sun towards its wintry grave' (Ralston. Op. cit., pp. 241–3).

It will be seen that the dates of the most important festivals were determined by the movements of the earth round the sun. Thus, the 'winter solstice' took place on the evening of 24 December, after which the days began to grow longer. The New Year festival was called 'Kolyada' and the songs that accompanied it 'kolyady' or 'kolyadki'. An example of a singing-game connected with the winter solstice is 'Uzh ya zoloto khoronyu', in which the participants, moving in a circle, search for a golden ring, which is passed surreptitiously from hand to hand. In this genre may be observed traces of pagan mythology, the golden ring representing the sun, the *khorovod* (round-dance) its circular movement, while the game itself depicts the sun disappearing out of sight during the winter.

The day of the vernal equinox was accompanied by rituals to celebrate the arrival of migratory birds and the meeting of spring. A common custom was the baking of effigies of birds on that day.

The summer solstice (22–24 June), when the heat and light are at their greatest intensity, was celebrated by the feast of Kupalo.

The spring-summer festival of 'Rusaliya', called also 'zelëniye svyatki' (lit. 'the green festival'), or 'semitskaya' week, was linked with the adoration of Mother Earth. In some customs of the 'rusalnaya' or 'semitskaya' weeks were preserved survivals of plant worship, with the weaving of garlands, the adorning of birch trees, and also of the remembrance of dead ancestors—the protectors of the family.

(7) It is remarkable that in Ancient Kievite Russia not only women lamented for the dead (as was typical of Russian folk life in the eighteenth–nineteenth centuries) but men too. In the ancient Russian chronicles one may find accounts of male laments, performed at the obsequies of a knight by his sons and *druzhina* (retinue). Judging by the fragments preserved in Russian chronicles, the laments performed at the funeral feasts of heroes often contained descriptions of their great deeds.

(8) In the 'play' songs or singing games ('*igrovye pesni*'), for instance, a favourite theme is that of a hare, in which one performer imitates the actions of the animal as it leaps over brooks and steams, racing across country, &c.

(9) A description of the effect produced by a protracted song is given in Chekhov's story 'The Steppe': 'Suddenly quiet singing was heard. Somewhere far away a woman was singing, but where exactly and on what side was difficult to judge. The song, calm, leisurely and mournful, like a lament and only just audible, was heard now on the right, now on the left, now above, now out of the earth, as if carried over the *steppe* and sung by an unseen spirit . . . it began to seem to him that the grass was singing: in its song the grass, half dead, already doomed, was plaintively and sincerely convincing some one wordlessly that it was not its fault, that the sun had scorched it in vain; it would have us believe that it passionately wanted to live, that it would still have been young and beautiful, had there been no intense heat and drought.'

(10) Folk polyphony is a peculiarity of Russia and only in the Ukraine, in Belo-Russia and Mordovia can one find analogous forms. (The folk polyphony of Georgia and some of the less developed forms of the peoples of the Northern Caucasus is of a quite different kind.) Differences in style in performance are found even in Russia—for instance there is the Northern style of polyphony belonging to Pskov-Novgorod, Arkhangelsk,

Vologda; there is the style belonging to the districts south of Moscow (Ryazan, Tambov, Voronezh, &c.), and there is also the South Russian style (the lower regions of the Volga, the Donshchina, with the employment of a *podgolos* in the highest voice).

Sometimes the term *podgolosok* has the sense of a long sustained part in the high descant or falsetto register, consisting of a single note.

CHAPTER 2

(1) Richard Charques. *A Short History of Russia*. London, 1956, p. 21.

(2) Judging from preserved evidence, the Eastern Slavs originally used Greek or Roman letters. The literary language of Old Russia is known as Old Church Slavonic and is based on a Bulgarian dialect. In the ninth century it became a literary and liturgical language through the efforts of Saints Cyril and Methodius, who created a special ancient-Slavonic alphabet, since neither the Latin nor the Greek alphabets had sufficient signs to produce the necessary sounds. As Professor Mirsky points out in his *History of Russian Literature* (New York, 1960, pp. 3–4), while the spoken language of Russia underwent transformation between the eleventh–fourteenth centuries, Church Slavonic remained unaltered. Church Slavonic, however, was not the only written language and towards the end of the fifteenth century the language of the Muscovite chanceries became the official tongue of the Empire. It was not till the end of the seventeenth century in the writings of the Archpriest Avvakum that the Russian vernacular was first consciously employed. During the reign of Peter the Great a new alphabet was introduced in which the Slavonic letters were altered to resemble Latin letters. Russia thus became the possessor of two alphabets—a civil one and an ecclesiastical one.

(3) The Pechersky Monastery, or 'Monastery of the Caves' as it is otherwise known, was founded in the middle of the eleventh century by the hermits Anthony and Theodosius and for 200 years was a major centre of ecclesiastical learning. Particularly famous among its scholars was the chronicler Nestor (*c.* 1080).

(4) Describing a battle in 1220 a chronicler from Tver records that in preparing for the storming of the walls of an enemy fortress, the Russian armies sounded *nakry* (twin side-drums) and *argany* (metal percussion instruments), while the signal to attack was provided by trumpets, *surny*, and whistles.

According to a note in another chronicle, in the army of Prince Yury Vladimirovich, fighting at the battle of Lipitsky in 1216, there were 60 trumpets and *bubny*, and in the army of his ally and brother, Prince Yaroslav, 40. In many of the chronicles, details are given as to the number of banners as well as the number of musical instruments, so that one can estimate the size of the forces involved.

(5) In *The Penguin Book of Russian Verse*, ed. Obolensky, London, 1962, pp. 1–2, the opening of the *Slovo* is translated as follows: 'Would it not be fitting, brothers, for us to begin in the manner of the ancient lays the grievous tale of the campaign of Igor, of Igor the son of Svyatoslav? But rather let this song begin in accord with the events of our own time, and not with the design of Boyan. For Boyan the wizard, if he wished to make a song for someone, would fly in thought through the tree, like a grey wolf over the earth, like a blue-grey eagle beneath the clouds. For he recalled, as he said, the wars of olden times. Then he would let loose ten falcons upon a flock of swans: whichever swan was overtaken was the first to sing a song—to Yaroslav of old, to valiant Mstislav who slew Rededya before the Circassian hosts, to fair Roman, the son of Svyatoslav. But, brothers, it was not ten falcons that Boyan would let loose upon a flock of swans—but he would lay his magic fingers upon the living strings, and of themselves they thundered glory to the princes.

Let us then, brothers, begin this tale from Vladimir of old to Igor of our time, who girded his mind with firmness and sharpened his heart with valour, and, filled with a warlike spirit, led his brave hosts against the land of the Polovtsy, for the land of Russia. . . .'

(6) The passage is translated in *The Penguin Book of Russian Verse*, pp. 18–19, as follows: 'On the Danube Yaroslavna's voice is heard: like a desolate cuckoo she cries early in the morning. "I will fly", she says, "like a cuckoo along the Danube, I will dip my sleeve of beaver-fur in the river Kayala, I will wipe the Prince's bleeding wounds on his strong body".

'Yaroslavna, early in the morning, laments on the rampart of Putivl saying: "Wind, O Wind! Why, O Lord, do you blow so hard? Why do you carry the Huns'(?) arrows on your light wings against the warriors of my beloved? Was it not enough for you to blow on high beneath the clouds, rocking the ships upon the blue sea? Why, O Lord, have you scattered my happiness over the feather grass?"

'Yaroslavna, early in the morning, laments on the rampart of the city of Putivl saying: "O Dnieper Slovutich! You have battered your way through the rocky mountains across the land of the Polovtsy. You have rocked Svyatoslav's boats upon your waters, and carried them to Kobyak's camp. Carry, O Lord, my beloved back to me, that I may no more send him my tears down to the sea, early in the morning".

'Yaroslavna, early in the morning, laments on the rampart of Putivl saying: "O bright and thrice-bright Sun! You are warm and beautiful to all. Why, O Lord, did you dart your burning rays against the warriors of my beloved? In the waterless steppe why did you shrivel their bows with thirst and stop their quivers with sorrow?"'

(7) Raids by *steppe* raiders, particularly the Cumans and the Polovtsy, had been common from the eleventh century till the thirteenth, when the Tartars first appeared in the Russian land in the year 1223. 'No one knows for certain' reads an ancient chronicle, 'who they are, or from where they come, or what their language is, or race, or faith, but they are called Tartars'. In the thirteenth century both Kiev and Moscow were laid waste and ravaged.

(8) In the *Zadonshchina* is found the following: 'The horses neigh in Moscow, the *bubny* rattle in Kolomna, the trumpets trumpet [*sic*] in Serpukhov.' In the *Povest o Mamaevom poboishche* (The Legend of the Rout of Mamay) there is the passage: 'The sound of trumpets is heard on both sides. The Tartar trumpets seem to grow dumb, the Russian trumpets resound all the more'.

(9) As a point of interest the Mongols came to the aid of Russia in 1399 by inflicting a crushing defeat on the Lithuanian invaders of Russia on the River Vorskla.

(10) George Vernadsky's excellent summary of the contribution of Fioravanti and his followers is well worth quoting in this respect:

'The greatest of the Italian artists engaged by Ivan III was Aristotle Fieravanti (or Fioravanti) of Bologna, who was equally skillful as architect and engineer. He came to Moscow in 1475 and was entrusted with building Moscow's main church, the Cathedral of the Assumption in the Kremlin. Definite instructions were given that the new cathedral was to be in the Suzdalian style, like the 12th-century Cathedral of the Assumption in Vladimir. Fieravanti studied the architectural forms of the cathedral in Vladimir as well as of the other churches in Suzdalia and found them congenial to his taste. The wonderful cathedral he built in the Kremlin—much larger in size than the Suzdalian churches—was not a mere replica of any of them but a re-creation of their spirit. Fieravanti also had a share in planning the rebuilding of the Kremlin's walls and towers. Another cathedral was built in the Kremlin by the architect Aloisio Novi of Milan, and a palace (the Hall of the Facets) by Pietro Antonio Solari and Marco Ruffo. The building of the third Kremlin cathedral was entrusted to Pskovian architects. Thus within a new period of about thirty years the inimitable architectural ensemble of the Kremlin was created' (George Vernadsky. *A History of Russia*. Yale University Press, 1961, pp. 110–11).

(11) This, of course, forms part of the conception in the reign of Ivan III of Moscow as the 'Third Rome', a theory first formulated by Abbot Philotheus—'Moscow is the third Rome and there will be no fourth'. Ivan III himself was the first Russian ruler to adopt the title of Caesar (Tsar).

(12) The mouth of the Northern Dvina was reached by an Englishman, Richard Chancellor, in 1553, where the foundations of what was later to become the port of Archangel were laid. Ivan IV even sought an alliance with England by marriage.

(13) Reforms likewise took place in the other arts. As Vernadsky observes: 'As regards architecture, the "tent" style, with variations, remained the preferred form until the middle of the century, when Patriarch Nikon came strongly out against it on the ground that it did not follow the patterns of Byzantine architecture. The result (which Nikon could not foresee) was an increase of Western forms in Russian architecture, and particularly of the Baroque style. The latter became especially popular in Ukraine, but many of its characteristics appeared in Muscovite architecture as well' (Vernadsky. Op. cit., p. 143).

(14) In 1631 a divinity college was created in Kiev, which became a great centre of learning, vying only with that of Moscow. Being in close proximity to Poland, the Ukraine was particularly receptive to Western influences and in the seventeenth century Russians first began to write rhymed verses. As the prosody they used, however, was Polish, the verses depended on the number of syllables employed, the position of the accent being of no importance.

In the Ukraine religious theatres began to be founded at the divinity colleges and a key figure in the writing of religious plays was the gifted Ukrainian scholar, Simën Polotsky, who, apart from ecclesiastical works, wrote also odes, comedies, and other compositions.

A divinity school was founded in Moscow in 1687 similar to the Kiev College, but laying more emphasis on the Greek language, and this became known later as the Slavo-Greek-Latin Academy. Although there were no schools for science and technology in Russia at that time, the knowledge of Latin acquired there was of immense value in opening the way to Western learning.

CHAPTER 3

(1) I am indebted for much of the information in this chapter to N. Findeisen. *Ocherki po istorii russkoy muzyki* Moscow-Leningrad 1928–9 and to an unpublished translation of the same work by S. W. Pring.

(2) Kammer-junker Bergholtz. *Dnevnik*. Third edition in four parts. Published by P. Bartenev. St. Petersburg, 1902.

(3) For information regarding Belyaev see S. F. Platonov's article 'Iz bytovoy istorii petrovskoy epokhi' in *Izvestiya Akademii nauk*, 1926, p. 673.

(4) The embassy communications received from B. P. Sheremetev (1697) and P. A. Tolstoy (1697–9), as well as Prince F. A. Kurakin's reports, provide very interesting material concerning their musical impressions. The first of them heard a great deal of music of various kinds: one Roman grandee 'gladdened him with much music'; at Malta a trumpeter was assigned to him by the Master of the Order and performed constantly during the ambassador's dinner. Sheremetev's appointment did not last long, but from his fragmentary information one obtains the formula for musical entertainments and trumpet fanfares at meals, which were soon adopted in Moscow.

Tolstoy, who spent sixteen months in Italy and visited many Italian cities, gives more details concerning music in his reports; he returned to Russia in January 1699, enchanted with Italian life. On his way to Italy he passed through Vienna, of which he gives his impressions: the instrumental music he heard in St. Stephen's Cathedral seemed to him at first extraordinary noise—the Muscovites, of course, were used to soft, unaccompanied chanting—but when shortly afterwards Tolstoy heard the organ in a Paduan church, he began to revise his ideas on the subject. Another interesting account is of the Italian theatres he visited in Venice, and of other social amusements. He says that Venice then had five opera houses—(these, of course, were the palmy days of Venetian opera; between 1637 and 1699 eleven opera-houses were opened in Venice; whilst Tolstoy was there, Legrenzi, Lotti, and Alessandro Scarlatti were the favourite composers)—and he writes: 'Nowhere in the world are there such marvellous operas and comedies'. He is amazed to find that in one opera there were upwards of 150 costumed actors and actresses; he tells also of the Venetian carnival, during which people in masks amused themselves 'shamelessly', &c. In Naples he was surprised at the Duke's small children, who entertained the ambassador with singing from the music and dances 'in the French style'. In the houses he saw clavichords and other instruments for domestic use. His reports also include information concerning music in other cities (see 'Puteshestviya stolnika P. A. Tolstovo' in *Russkiy Arkhiv*, 1888, Vols. I and II).

At the beginning of the eighteenth century Prince F. A. Kurakin visited Holland and made notes of his travels. In a Rotterdam square he saw the statue of Erasmus, which he describes. He enumerates the amusements of fashionable society at the Hague, including social gatherings of various kinds, and mentions the music he heard in the churches. The inhabitants of Amsterdam met for the performance of vocal and instrumental music, but strangers were admitted by invitation only. In both cities comedy and opera provided amusement for the public. Prince Kurakin attended the concerts of the Amsterdam musical societies. In Rome there was special music of another kind—'the serenade, i.e. music with singers, rather like an opera, but performed in chambers and not in a theatre'. He also heard oratorio performances by the congregation of St. Filippo Neri and others.

The historical value of these notes is beyond question. They show how the interest of the Russian people in the arts of the West at the end of the seventeenth century was gradually developed, and how they provided examples to be followed by the next generation. Everything mentioned in these reports by the Muscovite emissaries was by degrees transplanted to Russian soil.

(5) *Dnevnik Puteshestviya v Moskovyu* (1698–9). Published by A. S. Suvorin, St. Petersburg, 1906. The following excerpt from his diary is typical:

> 9 July 1698. 'The ambassador was pleased to pay a visit to the outskirts of the forest so often praised and thus to have an opportunity of seeing Izmailovo. He was accompanied by musicians, in

order to combine the agreeable rustling of the breeze through the tree-tops with their own even sweeter melodies. The Tsaritsa with the Tsarevich and the unmarried Princesses were in residence at the castle . . . They chanced to be walking when the delightful sounds of trumpets and flutes came to their ears and compelled them to stop for a while, though they were about to return to the castle. The musicians saw that they had an appreciative audience and began to vie with each other in their efforts to sustain the attention of their august listeners, who departed at the end of a quarter of an hour after bestowing their approval on all the performers' (Korb, p. 158).

Korb states elsewhere that Markwart von Prinz, the Brandenburg envoy brought with him seven young oboists, whom the Tsar purchased from their instructor for 1,200 ducats (Korb, p. 116).

(6) The fact that he should choose the German form for the name of the town—Peter's Burg—is itself significant.

(7) In those days, before there were any inns in St. Petersburg, the Post-house was used instead.

(8) According to Bergholtz the assemblies were held in the winter at the houses of different grandees; the date and place of the next assembly were announced to the guests by the Emperor, or, in his absence, by the chief of police; in Moscow the commandant performed this duty. Admission was free to everybody. The host was not obliged to meet and escort a guest outside the room, even though it were the Emperor himself. In the ball-room a table had to be prepared with pipes, tobacco and wooden spills for smoking as well as tables for chess and draughts; cards were not allowed. Everyone was free to do as he or she chose—dance, smoke, play, chat, or look on. The guests might ask for wine, beer, vodka, tea, or coffee, but the host must not press them to eat or drink; he merely had to inform them what refreshments were available. The assemblies began about 5.00 p.m. and ended not later than 10.00 p.m. 'What I dislike at these assemblies', writes Bergholtz, 'is, in the first place, that they smoke and play draughts in the room where there are ladies and where they dance, and, secondly, that the ladies sit apart from the men, so that not only is conversation with them impossible but one can hardly manage to speak to them; when they are not dancing they sit like dummies and simply stare at one another' (Bergholtz. Op. cit., Vol. II, p. 71).

(9) That the musicians often had a hard time is likewise revealed from Bergholtz's *Dnevnik*. For example, he mentions that at an evening party given by one of his chiefs, dancing went on from

5.00 p.m. till 5.30 a.m. (i.e. for more than 12 hours, though
the same musicians had probably played 'table-music' at
dinner); there was one interval of a quarter of an hour, when
the band had their supper! At another assembly, at Count
G. I. Golovkin's house, there were two Polish and English
dances in succession, followed by an endless dance lasting
more than half an hour: 10 or 12 couples tied themselves together with handkerchiefs and each couple had to go forward
in turn and invent a new figure. It was very hard luck on the
musician, probably the leader of the band, who, at each of
these changes, had to skip ahead, 'with the result that he was
utterly exhausted' (Bergholtz. Op. cit., Vol. I, p. 81). When it
was all over the dancers made for the garden, or crept away
into various rooms and even into the attic!

(10) The author of *Selo Novospasskoe. Dedenevo tozh i rodoslovnaya
Golovinykh vladeltsev onovo* (P. Kazansky. Moscow, 1847) says
that in Peter's time the Golovin family were remarkable for
their musicality and their European culture. V. P. Golovin's
son, Sergey (1698–1715), received a good education at home
and had a fine voice and a knowledge of music; and Countesses
Marya Ivanovna and Marya Alekseevna and Natalya Niko-
laevna (*d.* 1763) were only some of the musical Russian ladies
at Court; educated in Sweden, they were excellent singers and
played on the harp and the piano (pp. 137–8).

(11) Bergholtz's diary has a detailed description of a serenade
arranged by the Duke in honour of the Empress on 24 November. For it there was an orchestra of 17 or 18 musicians, including five belonging to the Duke's suite and ten obtained from
Count Kinsky's band. The conductor's place was filled by the
assessor, Surland, a member of the Duke's suite and a keen
lover of music. Two rehearsals were held on the previous day,
to which guests were invited. The scene of the serenade, which
took place in the early morning, was the courtyard of the then
Winter Palace in Millionnaya Street, by the Winter Canal (on
the site of the former barracks of the Preobrazhensky regiment),
and it provides an interesting picture of Court life in Old St.
Petersburg. The 'band' was ready at 6.00 a.m. on the appointed
day, because the Duke wanted the serenade to begin before
dawn, to the light of torches. The procession was headed by
a quartermaster followed by twelve soldiers carrying tables,
chairs, and candlesticks for the musicians; then came Bergholtz, 'to see that no time was lost in posting the torch-bearers
about the courtyard', and twenty men with torches in double

file; between them were the Duke and his suite and 'the rear
was brought up by the musicians'. On entering the courtyard the quartermaster hastily set up the music-stands opposite
the Empress's windows, and Bergholtz posted the torch-
bearers: fifteen of them wearing the Duke's full-dress livery
and holding big wax torches were lined up in front of the
musicians and facing the Imperial apartments; the rest, not in
livery, stood in the rear. The instruments were tuned outside
the gates, the music was distributed, the bandsmen took up
their places, and the performance began. 'It lasted for nearly
an hour and was the more enjoyable because the weather was
calm and clear. Both princesses, in morning costumes, stood
at the windows and listened most attentively. The elder clearly
showed on this occasion that she was fond of music, as she
constantly beat time with her hand and head. His Highness (the
Duke) often gazed in her direction and probably sighed in
secret. We could not look round, as the Emperor came out of
the house. He went up to his Highness and embraced him
firmly and then approached the band turning one ear towards
the tables, but after listening for a while he walked rapidly
away'. Presently General Yaguzhinsky came out and thanked
the Duke on behalf of the Empress. When the music was
finished, the Duke and his suite departed, followed by Bergholtz with the bandsmen and the torch-bearers. 'Vodka to the
value of 80 or 90 roubles' was dispensed to the bandsmen.
(Bergholtz. Op. cit., Vol. I, pp. 169–70).

(12) Ibid., Vol. II, p. 19.

(13) For a reproduction of the music see N. Findeisen. Op. cit.,
Tom II, Vol. 5. Also B. Volman. *Russkie pechatnye noty XVIII
veka*. Leningrad, 1957, pp. 28–9.

(14) During the 1730's there are many references to all manner of
'acts' performed at Courts. There were puppet comedies, per-
formances by Dutch acrobats, and in the *Sanktpeterburgskie
Vedomosti* (No. 40) there is even an advertisement by 'a famous
English contortionist who was born without legs who already
had the honour of diverting many sovereigns by his amazing
performances'. Another source of Court entertainment was the
Court jesters, the names of some of whom have been preserved.
Some were musicians (the violinist Mira, otherwise the jester,
Pedrillo, for instance), while others were even titled persons.
For them the order of St. Benedict was instituted, of which
Pedrillo was made a knight.

In January 1740 the climax of the jesting business was

reached when the jester Prince Golitsyn was married to a Kalmyk woman in an ice house on the Neva. This incident, which was the theme of a novel by Lazhechnikov, was a joke in dubious taste, since the bride and bridegroom were compelled to spend the night in the house and were nearly frozen to death. The many foreigners present were astounded. The proceedings ended with a concert, mentioned in the reports of the French ambassador, the Marquis de la Chetardie, who wrote of 'the dances and music as strange as new' and of his surprise at 'the agility and strength displayed by the Ukrainians in their dancing'. (See P. Pekarsky. *Markiz de la Shetardi v Rossii, 1740–1742*. St. Petersburg, 1862, p. 60.)

(15) MOOS I, pp. 50–1, 80–1.

(16) See *Rivista Musicale Italiana*, Vol. XLV, 1941, p. 270.

(17) The complete libretti will be found in V. N. Peretts. *Italyanskie komedii i intermedii predstavlennye pri dvore imperatritsky Anny Ioannovny v* 1733–1735. Texts. Petrograd, 1917.

(18) MOOS I, p. 116.

(19) The success of *The Power of Love and Hate* is confirmed by Stählin, who says that it was received with much applause and gave enormous pleasure; the parterre and all the boxes were filled to overflowing. It had to be repeated about 100 times and several times with equal success (Heigold's *Beilagen*. Vol. IV, p. 90). This appraisal, however, seems to be somewhat exaggerated. Stählin further informs us that instead of the *intermezzi*, the intervals were filled with ballets. After Act I, for instance, there was a dance of satyrs and gardeners; Act II was followed by a ballet in the Japanese style; and the opera ended with dances by no less than a hundred people who came down from the upper galleries, combined with singing by the actors and actresses and instrumental music by the orchestra. The music for this final ballet was probably written by Araja; the composers of the other two are unknown.

(20) The libretto of *The Power of Love and Hate* (the first to be printed in Russia) was on sale at the Academy's book-shop.

(21) For example, each of Araja's operas were given on 29 January, the day after Anna's birthday.

(22) The civil lists show that on the whole the artists were well paid and in addition apartments were provided free of charge. The male soprano Dreyer received the highest salary (1,237 roubles, 50 kopecks)—at that time castrati were in great demand. The rank and file were paid from 150 to 250 roubles per annum. This compelled artists to value their appointments and where

possible to express their gratitude, especially as this was correspondingly rewarded. Court musicians were also provided with free quarters.

(23) See R. A. Mooser. 'Giovanni Verocai' (*Riv. Mus. It.*, Vol. XLII, 1938).

(24) All the Russian and some Western musicologists confuse Luigi with another violinist, Giovanni Madonis. See R. A. Mooser. 'Luigi Madonis' (*Riv. Mus. It.*, Vol. XLV, 1941).

(25) See R. A. Mooser. 'D. dall'Oglio' (*Riv. Mus. It.*, Vol. XLVIII, 1946).

(26) Pietro Mira, a Neapolitan, born in Monte Scaglioso, arrived in Russia in 1733. Reference has already been made to his propensity for clowning. Legend has it that he found it very difficult to get on with the conductor, Araja, and transferred himself to the jesters about 1735 or 1736. Suffice it to say that Pedrillo (as he was now called) earned what was then a handsome income. His crowning joke, in which he passed a goat off as his wife, served as the subject of an illustration in a polemic treatise by Troemer, which also contains a portrait of Mira-Pedrillo with a violin. Anna was so fond of this jester and had such confidence in him that she chose him as her partner at cards; she even commissioned him in 1736 to correspond with the feeble-minded Duke of Tuscany concerning the purchase of the famous Tuscany diamond. After her death Mira was given leave (on 17 December 1740) to return to his native land, together with his servant, Francesco Picoli. Subsequently (*c.* 1747) he joined the Dresden band, but seems to have ended his life as a hotel-keeper in Venice (*Arkhiv kn. Vorontsova*, book 29, p. 220. Letter from Lafermière, Venice, to Count Vorontsov, 1782).

(27) According to the civil list for 1731, Verocai received the highest salary paid to a musician—1,000 roubles. He was in Russia from 1731–8.

(28) J. von Stählin. *Nachrichten von der Musik in Russland*, printed in J. Haigold's *Beilagen zum neuveränderten Russland*. Riga-Leipzig, 1769–70. Vol. II, p. 100.

(29) Johann Hübner was born in Warsaw in 1696 and his musical training began at an early age in his native city, where music was at the time highly developed. In 1714 he moved to Vienna, where he studied under Rosetter, a violinist and teacher. Six years later he went to Russia and became conductor of Count Kinsky's band—Kinsky was the Austrian ambassador to the Russian Court and had apparently met Hübner in Vienna.

The band attracted attention in Moscow and on Kinsky's
return to Vienna in July 1721 Hübner with the band, or
part of it, transferred their services to the Duke of Holstein.
Hübner was especially successful at the Coronation, when he
conducted an orchestra of 60 musicians. After the Duke's
departure for Kiel, Hübner joined the Russian service. During
Araja's stay as conductor and composer of the Court operas,
Hübner retired into the background, but on 10 January 1740
was appointed head of the music school mentioned above.
(Archives of the former Ministry of the Imperial Court
36/1629, No. 44.)

(30) There were quite a number of Ukrainian *bandurists* at Court,
the most famous being Timofey Belogradsky and his family
(*c.* 1739).

(31) A key figure in the arrangements for the opening was Anna's
favourite, Biron, who, being an ardent Lutheran himself, was
anxious that the occasion should be as magnificent as possible.
The President of the Academy of Sciences, Korf, was given the
following order: 'On the command of her Imperial Majesty
the Academy of Sciences is ordered: for the blessing of the new
organ in the German Church of Peter and Paul to print in the
German printing house 56 songs on good paper, 400 on ordinary, and to bind 2 copies in gold, and 4 in silver *moire*, 50 in
wavy, 400 in boards, to be charged to His Highness Duke
Kurlyandsky. . . .' By 'songs' were probably meant chorales
with German text. (B. Volman. *Russkie pechatnye noty XVIII
veka*. Moscow, 1957, p. 35.)

(32) Fëdor Volkov (1729–63) had founded an amateur theatre at
Yaroslavl. The success of its productions attracted the attention of Elizabeth and he was summoned to the capital in 1752.

(33) In pre-Revolutionary Russia one's name day (i.e. the feast of
the Saint from whom one's christian name is taken) was
celebrated as well as one's birthday.

(34) Some idea of the brilliance of these festivities is given by the
following: During supper at the New Year Festival of 1751, the
Court singers, who then sang in Italian, performed Italian
instrumental and vocal music on a balcony in the hall, while
her Imperial Majesty's singers rendered choruses. The hall was
lighted by as many as 3,000 candles of white wax in crystal
chandeliers, pyramids, and the like, and the flower-beds were
illuminated by a vast number of small lamps made of glass or
moulded wax. As these suppers occasionally lasted for seven
hours on end, during which the musicians and singers per-

formed without a break, it may be imagined that their task was not a light one, and that they must have had a huge repertoire (SPV No. 2, 1751).

(35) According to a report in SPV (1755, No. 18), none of the six principals was more than fourteen years old.

(36) Pekelis, the Soviet musicologist, suggests, with perhaps some justification, that the influence of Russian dance songs may be detected in the overture (see PIRM I, pp. 109–10).

(37) SPV 1745, No. 33.

(38) At one of the Hermitage concerts, while listening to a Haydn string quartet, she summoned Count Zubov and said: 'When anyone plays a solo I know that he should be applauded at the end, but in a quartet I get lost and am afraid of doing so in the wrong place; please give me a glance when I should applaud' (S. N. Glinka. *Zapiski*. St. Petersburg, 1895, p. 154).

(39) Two English companies visited St. Petersburg during Catherine II's reign. The first arrived in the winter of 1761 and the theatre was in the Galley Yard of a house occupied by a merchant named Ray. Arapov, in a brief notice of the company, mentions the remarkable talent of some of its members: Brooks, his wife, Miss Cook and Mrs. Ray. Its repertoire is unknown. The *entrepreneur* of the New English Theatre, near the Summer Garden, was a man named Fisher, who afterwards took up teaching. He ran a company in the 1771–2 season, but it was apparently unsuccessful, and it was disbanded in May 1772. The repertoire included Charles Dibdin's *The Padlock*, *Midas* (an English ballad opera based on popular airs) and *Love in a Village*. (For the productions at the English Theatre see SPV: 1771, Nos. 97–100 and 104; 1772, Nos. 4, 12, 33, and 36.)

(40) Among the foreign works performed were Handel's *Samson*, Pergolesi's *Stabat mater*, while foreign virtuosi included Abt Vogler and Lolli (PIRM I, pp. 127–8). During the summer concerts were given in the numerous 'vauxhalls'—public halls named after the famous Vauxhall Gardens in London.

(41) The first public concerts took place in St. Petersburg probably in 1748, being organized by the Italian violinist G. Passerini (see MOOS I, p. 200), but not in Moscow till thirty years later.

(42) The papers of the time have advertisements such as the following: 'A foreigner, who speaks and writes various languages, knows arithmetic, plays the harp, is an artistic singer of

Russian and German songs, and can play accompaniments, desires an appointment suited to his qualifications' (SPV, 1794, No. 93). Again: 'A foreigner who understands Russian, Polish, German, Latin, and necessarily French, also writing and arithmetic, and who can play the harp and the violin . . . desires to enter a manufacturer's office as a book-keeper [!], or to give monthly lessons on the harp' (SPV, 1794, No. 24).

(43) In Riga, for instance, Catherine had a wonderful reception. On the night of 9 July, 'the whole of the city was brilliantly illuminated, and the fountains facing the town hall ran with wine for the rejoicing people, who, nearly all night long, to the sound of trumpets and kettle-drums, filled the air with incessant "vivats" '.

The following account of one of Catherine's excursions is contained in the memoirs of Lord Hamilton, *My Yesterdays*, London, 1950, pp. 609–10:

'Students of history will remember how, on the occasion of Catherine the Great's visit to the Crimea, her favourite, Potëmkin, had "camouflage" villages erected along the line of her progress, so that wherever she went she found merry peasants (specially selected from the Imperial theatres) singing and dancing amidst flower-wreathed cottages. These villages were then taken down and re-erected some fifty miles further along the Empress's way, with the same inhabitants. It was really a triumph of "camouflage", and did great credit to Potëmkin's inventive faculty. Catherine returned North with most agreeable recollections of the teeming populations of the Crimea, of its delightfully picturesque villages, and of the ideal conditions of life prevailing there'.

(44) For example, one advertisement reads: 'Cook, gardener and conductor required' (*Moskovskie vedomosti*, 1794, No. 61).

(45) Conditions, in fact, were so bad, that serf musicians often took refuge in flight and papers in the 1780's and 90's contain advertisements for fugitive musicians. In 1792 Major-General Svechin announced that two of his domestic musicians had fled—Zakhar Petrov and Egor Rodionov; after describing them, he added: 'If they say that they are Polish emigrants, don't believe them' (SPV, 1792, No. 43).

(46) Johann Hinrichs. *Entstehung, Fortgang und ietzige Beschaffenheit der russischen Jagdmusik*. St. Petersburg, 1796. A more recent publication on horn music is K. Vertkov. *Russkaya rogovaya muzyka*. Leningrad-Moscow, 1948.

(47) Horn music was very suitable, since its sonority in the open air was quite incomparable. In 1763, on the occasion of Catherine II's coronation in Moscow, a 'Mount of Diana', 42 feet high and 280 feet in circumference, was built on enormous sledges drawn by 22 pairs of Ukrainian oxen. It represented a wood full of deer, boars, foxes, and hares, and amongst the trees a horn band was concealed, which played during the long procession through the Nemetskaya suburb, past I. I. Betsky's residence, where Catherine was dining.

Sarti generally made use of a horn ensemble in his festival compositions and his cantata 'Glory to God in the Highest' (1792) was written for two symphony orchestras, horn band, chorus, fireworks and a salvo of guns. (See GIRMA II, pp. 105–18.)

(48) For a more detailed account of the history of the horn band, see Gerald Seaman. 'The Russian Horn Band'. *Monthly Musical Record*, May–June 1959, pp. 93–9.

(49) See B. Volman. *Gitara v Rossii*. Leningrad, 1961.

(50) Khandoshkin played on a re-tuned violin, the *g* string being tuned to *a*, *b*, or even *c*. *Scordatura* was a favourite trick of the period and had been employed in the West in the seventeenth century by Biber.

(51) In the announcement of his concert in 1799 D. Kashin wrote: 'A Russian composer of music . . . has the honour to give a grand vocal and instrumental concert, compiled from the best purely Russian musicians numbering more than 200, conducted by the composer himself . . . Such a populous and enormous concert is the first of its kind to be made up of Russian musicians alone'. Kozłowski's polonaise *Grom pobedy razdavaisya* acquired at the end of the century the status of an official hymn.

(52) Some idea of the general naïveté is given by the following definition: 'Flute, *flauto*. Rarely used in music, but mostly with the drums in regiments'.

(53) Indeed, one of them 'My drug druga lyubim' (We Love One Another), with words by Sumarokov, is actually labelled 'Minuet'. This song with two other examples is printed in GIRMA I (pp. 15–22).

(54) This and other examples are printed in GIRMA I, pp. 356–60.

(55) Four songs of Kozłowski are printed in GIRMA II, pp. 15–21.

(56) Much new light has been thrown on the question of early Russian piano and chamber music by L. Raaben. *Instrumentalniy ansambl v russkoy muzyke*. Moscow, 1961, and A. D. Alekseev. *Russkaya fortepiannaya muzyka*. Moscow, 1963.

(57) A number of Court theatres were built during the eighteenth century, among them being those of Gatchina (from the beginning of the 1780's), at Oranienbaum (1756–7), at Pavlovsk (1783) and at Peterhof and Tsarskoe Selo (both about the middle of the 1780's).

CHAPTER 4

(1) One of the most interesting of the early manuscript collections is preserved in the Saltykov-Shchedrin Public Library, Leningrad (MS Q. XIV—150). Written during the 1770's it contains some 110 *kants* and folk-songs (see M. S. Druskin and Y. V. Keldysh. *Ocherki po istorii russkoy muzyki.* Leningrad, 1956, pp. 52–8).

(2) Mikhail Ivanovich Chulkov (1740–93), a well-known actor, writer, journalist, historian and publisher of satirical journals (e.g. *I to i sio*, St. Petersburg, 1769, in which he published many folk-songs, proverbs and descriptions of wedding rituals, &c.), and a concise mythological dictionary (*Kratkiy mifologicheskiy slovar*, St. Petersburg, 1767), which was reprinted in 1778 under the title *Slovar russkikh sueverii* (Dictionary of Russian Beliefs) and again in 1786 with the name of *Avebege*. This later furnished much material for A. N. Afanasev in his work *Poeticheskie vozzreniya slavyan na prirodu* (3 vols. Moscow, 1865–9). (See Druskin and Keldysh, op. cit., p. 59.)

(3) This edition had the following title: *Novoe i polnoe sobranie rossiyskikh pesen, soderzhashchikh v sebe pesni lyuobovnye, pastusheskie, shutlivie prostonarodnye, khoralnye, svadebnye, svyatochnye, s prisovokupleniem pesen iz raznykh oper i komedii. V Moskve v Universitetskoy tipografii u N. Novikova.* 1780–81. *Shest chastey.*

(4) Vasiliy Fëdorovich Trutovsky (c. 1740 to c. 1810), the son of a priest, was a Ukrainian by origin. In 1761 he became a servant at the Court of Peter III and in 1766 'for good behaviour and excellent playing on the *gusli*' was transferred to the apartments of Catherine II in the rank of 'chamber-guslyist'. Trutovsky was a good performer of folk-songs. Apart from his folk-song collections, he also wrote piano variations (including one on the theme 'Vo lesochke mnogo komarov urodilosya') and a 'zastolnaya pesnya' (drinking song) *Kruzhka*, to words by Derzhavin. Further details of his life are fragmentary.

(5) All references are to V. Belyaev (ed.). *V. Trutovsky. Sobranie russkikh prostikh pesen.* Moscow, 1953.

(6) As Findeisen observes, it is difficult to see how he managed to do this if he had to alter the text (see FOIM, Tom II, p. 316).

(7) All references are to V. M. Belyaev (ed.). *Sobranie narodnykh pesen s ikh golosami na muzyku polozhil Ivan Prach.* Moscow, 1955.

(8) Johann Gottfried Prach (177? to *c.* 1816) was a Czech by origin, but spent his whole life in St. Petersburg where he served in the manifold capacity of composer, pianist, and teacher. Between 1780–90 and 1791–5 he was a pedagogue at the Smolnyi Institute for Daughters of the Nobility. During his residence in the capital he became associated with the poet Nikolay Aleksandrovich Lvov (1751–1803), a friend of Derzhavin. The collection of folk-songs, edited by Prach, was compiled at Lvov's initiative. Prach selected the songs and arranged them according to Lvov's suggestions. It is for this reason that the volume is often referred to as the Lvov-Prach collection. There is a possibility that other people assisted in its formation, such as Fomin, who himself later made use in his operas of a number of songs which appeared in the collection. As Gerald Abraham observes, his collection of folk-songs was almost exactly contemporary with Haydn's harmonizations of Scottish folk melodies (see *A History of Song*, ed. Denis Stevens, London, 1960, p. 340).

(9) Melodies taken from Prach were employed by many non-Russian musicians, such as Beethoven and Rossini.

(10) In his preface Lvov confuses Russian folk-song with ancient Greek music. However, he is aware of the existence of choral polyphony, values highly Russian 'protracted' song, and recognizes the difference between peasant music and town folk-song, acknowledging the fact that the latter is based on the harmonic principles of Western music.

(11) All references are to I. D. Gerstenberg and F. A. Dittmar. *Russkie pesni XVIII veka.* (ed. B. Volman). Moscow, 1958.

(12) All references are to *Drevnye rossiyskie stikhotvoreniya sobrannye Kirsheiyu Danilovym* (ed. A. P. Evgeneva and B. N. Putilov). Moscow-Leningrad, 1958.

(13) The name 'Kirsha Danilov' is written on the manuscript but may be fictitious. So far the true identity of the compiler has not been discovered. It seems fairly certain that 'Kirsha Danilov' was a member of the services.

(14) Only five vocal scores were published in Russia in the eighteenth century—*Derevenskoy vorozheya, Fevey, Gore-bogatyr Kosometovich, Pesnolyubie,* and the ballet *Didona.* Of these, only one—*Fevey*—was the composition of a Russian composer. One opera

S

—*Nachalnoe upravlenie Olega*—was published in score. During the nineteenth century three more vocal scores were issued by Jurgenson—*Melnik-koldun, Fedul s detmi*, and *Amerikantsy*.

With regard to Maddox's theatre the following extracts, taken from the journal *The Dominant*, January 1928 in an article entitled 'An English Operatic Manager in Eighteenth Century Russia' by Victor Belaiev, are of interest:

'. . . There has recently been issued in Moscow a book by Mrs. Olga Chayanova on the Moscow theatre managed by Maddox from 1776 to 1805. This is the first of a series of volumes to be published by the Aleksei Bakhrushin State Theatrical Museum, Moscow.

Mrs. Chayanova's book deals with the history of the Moscow theatre for the last quarter of the eighteenth century. This is closely connected with the name of an Englishman, Mikhail Egorovich (as he was called in Moscow) Maddox, the builder and manager of the Petrovsky Theatre. In 1805 this building was destroyed, and on its ruins there was erected in 1825 the Great Theatre (now the State Opera House), famous in the history of Russian music; its centenary was celebrated in 1925 . . .

The end of the Italian composers' reign at St. Petersburg coincides with the period of Mikhail Maddox's managerial activity at Moscow. We have no accurate information as to the origin of this remarkable man. According to one of his grandsons,[1] he was born in England on 14 May 1747. A professor of mathematics at Oxford University, in 1776 he arrived in Russia and became tutor of mathematics and physics to the Grand Duke Pavel Petrovich, the heir-apparent to the Russian throne. More trustworthy information, obtained from contemporary publications, states that Maddox came to Moscow in 1772 in the quality of a juggler, and in 1776 gave "meritorious mechanical and physical displays to the Moscow public, who were favourably disposed towards curious things". Still earlier news of him is contained in an advertisement in the "St. Petersburg Gazette" (*Vedomosti*), announcing that on October 15 1767[2] the "famous English Equilibrist" would exhibit his skill to the St Petersburg public.

In 1776 this English "juggler" and "equilibrist" joined the company of Prince Petr Vasilievich Urusov, on whom Catherine the Great had conferred the privilege of "master of all stage performances in Moscow". Maddox's activity as a theatrical and operatic manager began from this time, first at the theatre in the Znamenka, and after this was burnt in 1780 at the Maddox Theatre, built by him, as already mentioned, on the site now occupied by the Great (i.e. Bolshoy—G.R.S.) Theatre.

[1] His nephew, according to MOOS II, p. 168.
[2] October 9, according to MOOS II, p. 168.

Maddox's house was second to no European theatre of the period in a mechanical respect, and was fitted with all the contemporary appliances for the production of the complicated stage effects which seem to have been inseparably connected with the theatrical performances of those days. The repertory of Maddox's Petrovsky Theatre during its existence, i.e., from 1782 to 1805, comprised 425 Russian and foreign pieces, of which one-third were operas and the rest comedies (rather less than half the repertory), tragedies, dramas, and ballets. The operas by foreign composers included such works as Cherubini's *Les deux journées*, Cimarosa's *Il matrimonio segreto*, Mozart's *Zauberflöte*, Grétry's *Les deux avares*, Méhul's *L'irato*, Paesiello's *Il barbiere di Seviglia*, and Salieri's *La scuola de' gelosi* . . .

It is evident that Maddox kept himself well informed concerning the Paris and Vienna repertoires, as he lost no time in staging operas at Moscow shortly after their production in those cities.

As regards the operas of Italian composers, such as Paesiello and Martini, who had settled in Russia, Maddox had no need to consult the repertoires of foreign theatres: he had only to turn to the St. Petersburg Opera, which commissioned works from these and other Italian composers. It is worthy of note that he staged Mozart's *Magic Flute* at Moscow not more than ten years after its première at Vienna (September 3 1791). The Petrovsky Theatre's repertory of foreign operas proves that it was in no case behind the times, though it does not appear to have shared with Paris and Vienna the dictatorship of taste in matters operatic . . .

Maddox . . . did . . . much for the development of the Russian theatre in general, and of Russian opera in particular. Owing to the great cost of erecting the Petrovsky Theatre, and to an unfortunate combination of external circumstances which involved the unforseen payment of large sums of money, his enterprise ended in bankruptcy, and in 1789 the theatre was handed over to the jurisdiction of the Council of Trustees, to whom he had previously mortgaged all his property for 110,000 roubles. Maddox then became director of the undertaking which he had once owned, and had to endure many unpleasantnesses, the climax being the destruction of the theatre by fire in 1805.

This remarkable man, who arrived in Russia as a "juggler" and "equilibrist" and subsequently became one of the most distinguished workers in the Russian theatrical world of his time, and who was awarded the hereditary dignity of a Russian noble—this man is gradually beginning to receive due appreciation from those of us who are interested in the destinies of the Russian theatre and Russian opera of the eighteenth century.' *Translated by S. W. Pring.*

(15) The majority of these scores are housed in the Gos.-Tsentralnaya muzykalnaya biblioteka pri teatre imeni S. M. Kirova,

Leningrad (TSMB), and in the archives of the library of the Academy of Sciences.

(16) More detailed information on the music of Russian operatic composers of the eighteenth and early nineteenth centuries is contained in the works of Livanova, Volman, Rabinovich, and Mooser (see Bibliography).

(17) Mikhail Vasilevich Popov (1742 to *c.* 1790), a native of Yaroslavl, was originally an actor in the troupe of F. G. Volkov, the founder of the Russian theatre, but after receiving education in St. Petersburg, he abandoned the stage and became a celebrated writer of plays and verse.

(18) The libretto of *Anyuta*, a comic opera in one act in verse, is printed in Popov's *Dosugi* (St. Petersburg, 1772), while the libretto of *Lyubovnik koldun* was printed in 1779 in Moscow. Both were reprinted in *Rossiyskiy teatr*, Vols. 18 and 22 (1788–9).

(19) Alexander Radishchev (1749–1802)—the writer of *A journey from St. Petersburg to Moscow*. During his stay in Leipzig he fell under the influence of the French *Encylopédistes*—Voltaire, Montesquieu, Rousseau, Diderot, and the philosopher Helvétius, whose opinions his works reflect. His principal thesis was that serfdom was the cause of all evils in Russia.

(20) As Rabinovich observes (RODG, p. 41), there are four reasons to support this: (i) Pashkevich was the only Russian (and, moreover, St. Petersburg) composer capable of handling a score of this nature; (ii) the subject of *Anyuta* was specially suited to Pashkevich's gifts; (iii) the smoothness of his first known stage work, *Neschastye ot karety* (1779), force one to the opinion that he must have had previous operatic experience; (iv) foreign composers resident in Russia at the beginning of the 1770's would have undertaken the composition of a Russian opera only if it were of a sentimental or pastoral nature.

(21) See MOOS II, pp. 205–26, 265.

(22) The plot describes the transformation of the elderly heroine into a beautiful maiden through the offices of an obliging magician—hence the title of the opera.

(23) Of the composer D. Zorin we know practically nothing. Most probably he was an orchestral player at the Maddox or Locatelli Theatres in Moscow, like Sokolovsky. The title page of the score reads: 'Pererozhdenie, comic opera in two acts. Music composed by Mr. D. Zorin in St. Petersburg 1779'. The date 1779, as in the case of the majority of dates on old non-autograph MSS, refers to the year in which the copy was made. There is also a possibility that the opera at its first Moscow

performance in 1777 was not based on Zorin's score but on music more primitive (see RODG, p. 43).

(24) The author of the *Dramaticheskiy slovar* (The Dramatic Dictionary) says that 'this opera was one of the first productions to be given on the Moscow stage with original Russian songs . . .' (see *Dramaticheskiy slovar ili Pokazaniya po alfavitu vsekh rossiyskikh teatralnykh sochineniy i perevodov.* Moscow, 1787).

(25) Prach No. 55; Trutovsky No. 2; Gerstenberg No. 16.

(26) MOOS II, pp. 205, 265.

(27) Vasiliy Ivanovich Maykov (1728–78) was the son of a Yaroslavl landowner. Part of his life was spent in Moscow, where he worked as translator, writer and subscriber to various journals. In his later years he wrote many odes, cantatas, and dramas with music. From the literary point of view he was a follower of Lomonosov and Sumarokov. Though writing in a classical style he made use of folk elements, dialects and realistic characterization.

(28) A number of the Kerzelli family were employed in Russia between the years 1770–1820, mostly in Moscow, whose identities have become somewhat confused. According to Mooser, Frantz Kerzelli (a cellist and Kapellmeister, who gave the première of Haydn's *The Seven Words of the Saviour on the Cross* in Moscow, 1789) had a brother Johann (a composer). Frantz was the father of I. F. and M. F. Kerzelli, who were jointly responsible for the first performance in Russia of Mozart's *Requiem* (1802) (see MOOS II, pp. 662–3).

(29) N. P. Nikolev (1758–1815), son of a nobleman, was brought up from the age of six by his relative, Princess E. R. Dashkova. After serving in the Guards till the age of twenty, he devoted himself to literary work, writing fables, satires, epistles and love songs. As a dramatist his best works are *Rozana and Lyubim* (1776), *Prikashchik* (1777), the comic operas *Tochilshchik* (1780) and *Opekun-professor* (1782), and the tragedy *Sorena i Zamir* (1784).

(30) For example, in Act II sc. 6 there is the following: 'Here he falls onto a hillock near a hut; the music commences *Adagio*, but suddenly changes to *furioso*, upon which Lyubim, springing to his feet, begins to sing'.

(31) F. J. Darcis was born in France in the year 1759, where he studied composition with Grétry. An opera by him was performed in 1774 in Paris. In 1776, his father sent his gifted but dissolute son to Russia in the hope of protecting him from the temptations of Parisian life. Shortly after the composition of the music to *The Clerk* (1778), Darcis committed suicide.

According to the *Dramaticheskiy slovar*: 'his life was cut short in the bloom of his youth, to the sincere regret of all lovers of music'. (MOOS II, pp. 257–8).

(32) RODG, p. 50.

(33) *The Dramatic Dictionary* informs us, for example, that this piece so captivated the people's interest that it was played time after time to packed houses. Later it was given on many occasions at the St. Petersburg Court, and at Knipper's Free Theatre where it ran for twenty-seven consecutive performances. Not only was it loved throughout Russia but it also won the affections of foreigners. In short, no other Russian opera had ever gained so much admiration or applause. Derzhavin likewise expressed his approval of *The Miller* in his *Rassuzhdenie o liricheskoy poezii* (Collected Works, ed. Grot, Vol. VII, p. 604) where, recalling some of the first Russian operas, he says: '. . . but most of all, Ablesimov's *Miller*, is preferred which is so natural in its design and development and its use of simple language'. Merzlyakov's *Vestnik Evropy* (European Herald) dedicated a whole article to *The Miller* in its March edition 1817. In this article the opera is referred to as 'a piece loved by people of every denomination despite the fact that it only seems to be written about simple folk and their way of life; but whether it is played at the Hermitage or in the public and private theatres, whether the players are good or indifferent, it never loses its charm. Everyone seems to know and sing it by heart . . .'. One must bear in mind, however, that (as Rabinovich observes in RODG, p. 51) to Merzlyakov and his Russian contemporaries, 'the libretto, as such, was the true opera, and the music, like the scenery and acting, was only an embellishment'.

(34) Its success was so durable that in the *Khronika Aleksandrinskovo teatra* (Chronicle of the Aleksandrinsky Theatre) for the second half of the year 1839, one reads of *The Miller* as 'an opera which has lived on our stage for half a century and which still appears at each Shrovetide festival'.

(35) Alexander Ablesimov (1742–83), contributor to many Russian journals and author of *Skazki v stikakh* (Tales in Verse), editor of the satirical magazine *Raskashchik zabavnykh basen*. Commencing his life as a copyist, he rose to the rank of army officer and later became a minor official. *The Miller-magician* decisively established his reputation.

(36) Charles Simon Favart (1710–92), author of many French *opéras comiques*, who is considered the creator of this genre in the French theatre.

(37) The plot is as follows: Ankudin, an old countryman, wishes to marry his daughter, Anyuta, to a peasant. His wife, Fetinya, who is related to an impoverished nobleman, dreams of marrying her into the nobility. But Anyuta, unknown to her parents, loves a young lad named Philemon. In despair Philemon approaches Faddey, the village miller, who, like most members of his profession, is reputed to have magic powers. The wily miller promises his assistance, assuring the lovers that he will both unite them and please the parents at the same time. Eventually it emanates that Philemon is not a peasant but an *odnodvorets* (a small landowner, who owns no serfs). At this startling revelation Ankudin and Fetinya are delighted and readily give their consent to the marriage. The opera concludes with the miller receiving their general thanks.

(38) Rousseau's opera possibly received its Russian première (with a Russian translation) in Moscow, 1778. However, there is no certainty of this. (See MOOS II, p. 223.)

(39) *Devichnik*—a party given by the bride-to-be to her girl friends on the night preceding the wedding. There are a whole series of songs in Russian folk music celebrating this important event in the wedding ritual.

(40) The confusion has arisen from the fact that *The Miller* was renovated in the middle of the nineteenth century, the music being completely re-written and 'modernized' by one of the St. Petersburg conductors. In 1884 Jurgenson published a vocal score of this version with the name of Fomin on the cover. However, there are a number of differences between the printed edition and the first surviving version—the MS of 1806 (which is probably fairly close to the original); in some cases the form and arrangement of the vocal numbers has been changed, while the orchestral accompaniment has been altered throughout. A number of the orchestral parts of the 1806 score are missing so that it is impossible to compile a complete score.

(41) There is no record of Sokolovsky ever having received instruction in composition, which seems to confirm Fomin's part in writing the music.

(42) As Rabinovich observes, a weakness of *The Miller*, particularly in the treatment of non-folk melodies, is the continual use of 2/4 time and 2-bar phrases which makes for monotony. This was further aggravated by the mid-nineteenth century arranger of the version afterwards published by Jurgenson, who deleted the few 3-bar phrases and replaced them with two- or four-bar structures (see RODG, p. 56).

(43) The stage direction reads: 'The scene is that of the same peasant house with girls sitting on benches. One is weaving, another sewing—each having some form of employment. They are singing wedding songs'.

(44) A stage direction reads: 'Miller, drunk and with a *balalaika* . . . First tunes the *balalaika* and sings'.

(45) See B. Volman. *Russkie pechatnye noty XVIII veka*. Leningrad, 1957, pp. 89–93. Vančura's symphony is printed complete, ibid., pp. 245 ff.

(46) Baron Vančura de Rehnit was born about 1750 and died in 1802. Arriving in Russia about 1783 from 1786–96 he was employed in the service of the management of the Court theatres in St. Petersburg and was Court 'pianist of the Hermitage company'. He enjoyed influence at Court. Apart from opera he composed at least six symphonies, quartets for piano, and other works. From 1790–4 he published the above-mentioned music journal. (See MOOS II, pp. 410–11.)

(47) The opera overture is printed in GIRMA I, pp. 161–8.

(48) In the words of the *Dramaticheskiy slovar*: 'It was given fifteen consecutive performances. No other play proved so lucrative in his [i.e. Knipper's] whole career'.

(49) Mikhail Matinsky, serf and illegitimate son of Count Yaguzhinsky, was born in 1750 in the village of Pokrovsk, Zvenigorod district, in the Province of Moscow. He received a general education in the 'gymnasium' for *raznochintsy* at Moscow University, after which he travelled to Italy at the Count's expense. Between the years 1779–1802 he was a teacher of geometry, history, and geography at the Smolnyi Institute for Daughters of the Nobility. He was widely gifted and in the course of his life was a dramatist, translator of scientific books and fiction, a pedagogue and an amateur composer. Of his work as a composer we know very little and of his occupation as a teacher even less. He was the first Russian musician (as far as we are aware) to write his own libretto. He was an excellent linguist. He died in the 1820's (see MOOS II, pp. 269–70).

(50) From the linguistic point of view the opera is outstanding. Some of Matinsky's phrases might easily be proverbs.

(51) The plot is as follows: A merchant, Skvalygin, is about to marry his daughter, Khavronya (lit. 'sow' or 'pig'), to a cold-blooded scrivener Kryuchkodey (lit. 'caviller'). Together with his prospective son-in-law he endeavours to be as unpleasant as pos-

sible. They forge bills of exchange, cleverly cheat their creditors, persecute the poor. Eventually justice prevails and the final chorus concludes with the words: 'Reign, holy truth, reign in our times'.

(52) See V. A. Prokofiev. 'Mikhail Matinsky i evo opera Sanktpeterburgskiy Gostiniy Dvor' in *Muzyka i muzykalniy byt staroy Rossii.* 'Academia', Leningrad, 1927, pp. 58–69.

(53) In the 'Foreword' to the second version of *The St. Petersburg Bazaar* Matinsky himself speaks of the changes brought about in the music: 'Some of the songs of this opera have been set to quite different melodies, and a much better harmony was provided by Mr. Pashkevich, a Court musician.' It appears, therefore, that Pashkevich was definitely involved in the performance of the revised opera in St. Petersburg in 1792 and that, in addition to composing some of the musical numbers and editing the remainder, he probably corrected the harmony and completed the orchestration.

(54) Although these *podgolosy* ('underparts') will hardly bear inspection from the point of view of authentic *'podgolosnaya'* polyphony, as Pekelis suggests, it is quite possible that the *devichnik* music was sung in the town in this manner and that Matinsky's transcriptions are authentic by the standards of the time (see PIRM, I, p. 149). The melodies (though showing only the first soprano part) are printed in A. S. Rabinovich. *Izbrannye stati i materialy.* Moscow, 1959, pp. 61–2.

(55) The plot is as follows: Firulin, a landowner, is a confirmed Gallomaniac and is anxious to buy an expensive Parisian carriage. In order to raise the money he orders his serf, Lukyan, to be sold as a recruit. Lukyan is in despair. Together with his beloved, Anyuta, he approaches the heartless nobleman, but in vain. However, an insignificant circumstance saves them. Lukyan has somewhere learnt a few words of French and addresses his master in that language. The landowner sheds tears of emotion: *peasants can speak French!* He liberates Lukyan and permits him to marry Anyuta.

(56) Of Pashkevich himself we do not know a great deal. He was born *c.* 1742. From 1763 he was a violinist in the second Court orchestra and later a 'composer of music'. In 1783 he became a chamber musician in Catherine's Court and on 1 March 1789 was appointed 'Court Kapellmeister of ball music'. 'For different musical compositions and labours outside his normal duties' he received in 1790 the sum of 1,600 roubles. He died *c.* 1800.

(57) Mikhail Kheraskov (1733–1807), author of the *Rossiad*, an epic poem describing the conquest of Kazan by Ivan the Terrible.

(58) Hermann-Friedrich Raupach (1728–78). German composer and conductor, who first visited Russia in 1754 to replace Araja as Court conductor at St. Petersburg in 1759. His second visit was in 1768, where he remained till his death. (MOOS I, pp. 234–5.)

(59) According to Findeisen the plot is as follows: The regiment to which Prolet belongs is to go on active service and he is anxious about his sweetheart, Plenira; this does not, however, prevent his intimacy with another woman, Svarlida, who is wealthy and not only entertains the soldier and his regiment at her own expense, but also interests herself in his career. To obtain his promotion to sergeant she presents his commanding officer, Zamir, with a snuff box. The matter is hung up and Svarlida steals the snuff box from Zamir! The soldiers have noticed her and in escaping from their pursuit she meets Plenira, who is looking for Prolet. To save herself she declares that she is a fortune-teller, hands the snuff box and her hooded cloak over to Plenira and makes for the camp. Plenira is apprehended for the theft; Prolet is at his wits' end and resolves to marry Svarlida. But the affair is explained, Svarlida admits her trickery, and the lovers are united.

(60) In 1789 P. Plavilshchikov composed 'a comedy with music' entitled *Melnik i Sbitenshchik—Soperniki* (The Miller and Sbitenshchik—Rivals). In his preface he wrote: 'Although *Sbitenshchik* was well received in the theatre, it made no difference to the popularity of *The Miller*, which always achieved success by reason of the charm and simplicity of its characters, but despite all the skill with which *Sbitenshchik* was cloaked, one could observe glimmers of foreign influences in its composition'. As Findeisen observes, there are in the opera many situations possible in Spain or France, but out of place in Russia. In this respect the professional *littérateur* (Knyazhnin) proved to be less adept than Ablesimov or Matinsky, who were more or less casual authors, but whose libretti were true to life. The success of Bullandt's opera was unusually durable and even as late as 1853 O. A. Petrov (the great Russian bass) took the leading role. (RODG, p. 76.)

(61) Catherine II was responsible for a number of libretti to Russian operas (e.g. *Fevey, Fedul and the Children, The First Government of Oleg*, &c.). However, it now seems certain that the part author of the libretti was Khrapovitsky, her private secretary, who

developed and embellished the Empress's ideas. Catherine herself, being of German origin, had an imperfect knowledge of the Russian language. According to Khrapovitsky, Catherine's reply, when he endeavoured to explain the rules for the composition of an operatic duet, was 'Na eto plevat!' ('I don't care a damn!') (see *Dnevnik A. V. Khrapovitskovo. 1782–1793*. St. Petersburg, 1874. Entry dated 7 December 1790).

(62) An edition of 'a comic opera for piano and voices' made by Prach was published in 1789 and re-printed by Jurgenson in 1895. Prach's arrangement is somewhat inaccurate.

(63) We have an actual account of a performance of *Fevey*, which was given at the Hermitage Theatre in 1791, written by Valentin Esterházy, who was Ludovic XVI's ambassador at the Russian Court: 'Yesterday I was at the Russian opera, all the music of which was composed of ancient native melodies. The accompaniments were performed behind the scenes. Among them were some very beautiful melodies, but also some very strange ones . . . The words were composed by Her Majesty. The setting was magnificent. The scene took place in Russia in ancient times. All the costumes were prepared with the greatest luxury from Turkish fabrics, identical with those which are worn there. There appeared a legation of Kalmyks, singing and dancing with Tartar harmonies, and Kamchadali who were dressed in national costumes and who also performed dances of Northern Asia. . . . The ballet concluding the opera was executed by Le Picq, Madame Rossi, and other good dancers. In it were represented all the different peoples inhabiting the Empire, each in his own peculiar dress. I have never witnessed a spectacle more varied and wonderful; on the stage were more than five hundred people. In the auditorium, however, although the young princes and the four noble princesses with their governors and governesses were all assembled there, there could not have been more than fifty spectators, so rigid is the Empress in the matter of access to her Hermitage' (*Lettres du comte Valentin Esterházy à sa femme. 1784–1792*. Paris, 1907, pp. 318 and 326).

(64) One involuntarily recalls Prokofiev's *The Love for Three Oranges*, where the part of the Cook is given to a bass.

(65) According to Findeizen the plot is as follows: A whirlwind has carried off the Tsarevnas Luna and Zvezda, daughters of Tsar Akhridey and the Tsaritsa Darya. The Tsarevich Ivan Akhrideich offers to seek his sisters. On the way he takes from the werewolves a cap of invisibility, automatic boots, and a

hospitable table-cloth, which they had found. Baba-Yaga tells Ivan Tsarevich that the magicians Medved-Molodets and Morskoe Chudo-Molodets have carried off his sisters and directs the Tsarevich to them. He finds them, is welcomed by both magicians and afterwards, on the advice of one of the girls, acquires Tsar-Devitsa for his wife, having first killed the twelve-headed serpent on the Kalinov bridge. The tale ends with the return of the Tsarevnas and the presence of his parents at the Tsarevich's wedding with Tsar-Devitsa.

The naïveté of much of the libretto is revealed by remarks such as the following. At one point Morskoe Chudo says: 'Ivan-Tsarevich, I'm glad that you've come to see us, but I must go and catch a couple of quiet whales to harness to the Tsarevna Zvezda's chariot'. No less absurd is the Tsarevich's enquiry when Zvezda tells him he will have to go to the end of the world that day. Taking out his watch (!), he exclaims: 'Can I do it in the time?'

(66) Findeisen says of *Fedul*: '*Fedul* enjoyed a measure of success on the public stage at Petersburg and Moscow. Its subject is most uninteresting. Fedul, a widowed peasant with fifteen sons wishes to marry a widow. His children, learning his intentions, are displeased. One of his daughters starts singing a song popular at the period (it was written by Elisabeth before she succeeded to the throne), whose words constitute a warning to her father. Then appears the widow and gay dancing begins. Here, as in *Fevey*, Pashkevich's music is a mixture of Russian colour and reminiscences of Italian comic opera'.

(67) The orchestral score was published in 1791 and was the only full score of a Russian opera to be printed in the eighteenth century. A vocal score was issued by Jurgenson in 1896.

(68) Carlo Canobbio (*c.* 1741–1822) was an Italian chamber musician, who arrived in Russia in 1779 and who later became leader of the Court orchestra. Apart from his work on *Oleg*, he composed two ballets and two symphonies, as well as several sonatas for guitar, violin, &c. Most of his compositions are conventional and show little originality (see GIRMA I, p. 446; MOOS II, pp. 250–2).

(69) Giuseppe Sarti (1729–1802), famous Italian composer, who arrived in Russia in 1784. On coming into contact with Russian artistic and musical thought, his style of composition underwent a transformation. His works include oratorios, cantatas, and French and Italian operas. For his services in the field of acoustics he was elected a member of the Academy of

Sciences. He was also important as a teacher, his pupils numbering Davydov, Kashin, Degtyarëv, and others. Among his compositions may be found devices, subsequently employed by Lesueur, Berlioz, and Wagner. In *Armida,* for instance, he uses muted trumpets and clarinets, makes experiments in unusual combinations of instrumental colour (see *Muzykalnoe nasledstvo,* ed. M. V. Ivanov-Boretskiy. Moscow, 1935, pp. 199–207).

(70) Valentin Esterházy in another of his letters has described the content of *Oleg* as follows: 'Sarti has imitated the Greek forms to such an extent that the work has become gloomy and rather boring . . . The *décor,* although beautiful, would have been incomparably finer in Paris, but inasmuch as the costumes are concerned, it is difficult to visualize their wonder. All the fabrics are Turkish and are embroidered with gold and pure silver. They say that the play has cost an unbelievable sum'. On the other hand Catherine wrote to Melchoir Grimm: 'The choruses of *Oleg* are the most beautiful in the world and are mostly by Sarti: all the Greek modes are assembled' (*Pisma Imperatrisi Ekateriny II k Grimmu,* 1774–1796, ed. Grot. Russkoe istoricheskoe obshchestvo. Vol. XXIII, St. Petersburg, 1878, p. 525).

(71) Vasiliy Alekseevich Levshin (1746–1826) was a prolific writer, and translator and a man of unusually wide tastes. To his pen are attributed the libretti of the operas *Korol na okhote* (which was borrowed from Monsigny's *Le Roi et le Fermier*), *Svadba Voldyreva, Mnimye vdovtsy,* and *Svoya nosha ne tyanet. Svadba Voldyreva* was by M. Kerzelli, the others by I. F. Kerzelli.

(72) Extract from the libretto of Levshin's *The Mock Widowers*: *The Countess's secretary Cherkalov is seated at the harpsichord, having been commissioned to write an opera. He is saying the words over to himself in the hope of finding inspiration. At the moment he is stuck at the word 'blessed'* :

'Blessed . . . No, no! It needs something different. Blessed . . . That's a church chant . . . Tral-lal-dra-ri-ra. That's something from Haydn. Ri-ra-ra-ra. That's from Pleyel. Where the devil do all these tunes come from! No matter where I try, whether it's the treble or the bass, it's still the same. I have all the best bits of their compositions in my head. Envious people will say that I copied them. On my honour, I am unlucky to be born after them. They've stolen all my best ideas.' (*He strikes the harpsichord and sings the word 'blessed' to a well-known Polish dance . . .*) 'Bravo! At last! Got it!

'Thou art blessed, thou art beautiful,
Now that thou art come to me'.

Splendid! I must get that down'. (*He begins to write and speaks
in the meantime.*) The taste is strange now. They prefer a
street song, or a folk-song, or a Polish melody, but then,
nothing *really* pleases them. The author and composer have
to write things so that every dairy-maid and *sbiten*-seller can
sing it right first time . . . Take a well-known tune, dress it
up and they all clap like mad . . .' (RODG, p. 114).

(73) Evstigney Ipatevich Fomin was born in St. Petersburg on
5 August 1761. His father was a gunner in the Tobolsk Infan-
try Regiment. At the age of six he was sent to the Petersburg
Academy of Arts, where he studied clavichord playing under
Buini and composition under Sartori and Raupach. Finishing
brilliantly at the Academy (it is learnt from surviving documents that on his completion he received a financial award
'for his outstanding achievements'), he was sent to Bologna,
where he studied under the famous composer and theoretician
Padre Martini. On 29 November 1785 he had the distinction
of being elected a member of the Bologna Accademia filar-
monica. The following year he returned to St. Petersburg,
where he worked till his death in 1800, being appointed
'*répétiteur* of opera parts' in 1797. Of the thirty or so compositions written by him, only ten can at present be attributed to
him with absolute certainty (see MOOS II, pp. 374–6).

(74) As Rabinovich comments: 'It is a pity that we cannot attribute
this music to Fomin with absolute certainty, owing to the fact
that it was the custom in those days for the ballet numbers in an
opera to be entrusted not to the composer of the opera, but to
someone else (usually less qualified). However, the music of the
dances in *Boeslavich* is so outstanding in depth and spontaneity,
that it is difficult to attribute it to any composer other than
Fomin' (RODG, p. 87).

(75) The plot is as follows: The post-drivers are assembling at the
coach station. Among them are a lively young driver, Timothy,
and his wife, Fadeevna. Their enemy, Filka Prolaza, a thief and
a sneak, tries by underhand means to sell Timothy as a recruit
and thus separate him from his attractive wife, whom he
(Filka) had courted unsuccessfully in the past. The situation
seems desperate until, by the help of a passing officer and the
other coachmen, the matter is solved: Timothy is released, as
two of his brothers already serve as soldiers, and Filka Prolaza
is conscripted in his place, having avoided military service

the previous year. All thank the officer for his assistance and the opera concludes with a lively chorus.

(76) The striking qualities of the post-drivers have been noted by several writers. One of the earliest European authorities to comment on their music was Madame de Staël, who visited Russia in 1808. In her *Ten Years of Exile* she writes: 'There are the coachmen, driving with lightning speed while singing songs whose words, I am told, are compliments and encouragements to their horses'. Linëva, however, mentions that coachmen's songs were used to frighten away wolves (see E. Linëva. *Velikorusskie pesni v narodnoy garmonizatsii*. Vol. I. Moscow, 1911, p. xli).

(77) The first really convincing imitation of Russian folk polyphony in Russian classical opera is the chorus of peasants in Act V of Borodin's *Prince Igor*.

(78) For further details of Fomin's operas see *Monthly Musical Record*, Vol. 88. No. 985, January–February 1958. Gerald Seaman. 'Evstignei Ipatevich Fomin: 1761–1800'.

(79) Copies of both scores are preserved in the British Museum.

(80) For further details of Bortnyansky's operas see *The Music Review*, Volume Twenty-one, 1960, pp. 106–13. Gerald Seaman. 'D. S. Bortnyansky (1751–1825)'.

CHAPTER 5

(1) The first three decades of the nineteenth century are often termed the 'Pushkin period'. Pushkin's influence is especially noticeable in the development of the vocal lyric, the *romance*, and later, opera—musical genres, which are all intimately connected with the spoken word.

(2) Regarding Degtyarëv see Druskin and Keldysh. *Ocherki* . . . pp. 154–67.

(3) The Moscow Bolshoy Theatre was opened in 1825.

(4) The famous performer, Dyur, creator of the part of Khlestakov in Gogol's *Revizor* (The Inspector General), was a *protégé* of Didelot, his balletmaster at the *uchilishche*, then became an opera-singer, and finally a comedy and vaudeville actor.

(5) The fact that Boïeldieu used Scottish folk-songs in his opera *La Dame blanche* (1825) may well have been the result of his making the acquaintance of eighteenth-century Russian opera while in Russia.

(6) Aleksey Fëdorovich Lvov (1798–1870), famous violinist, guitarist, composer of the Russian national anthem (1833), many

works for violin, and several operas, including *Undina, Russkiy muzhichok i frantsuzskie marodery* (The Russian Peasant and the French Marauders), &c. From 1837–61 was Director of the Imperial Chapel, where he succeeded his father, N. A. Lvov, the collaborator with Prach.

(7) Information on the theatrical and social life of the period will be found in Druskin and Keldysh. *Ocherki* . . . pp. 350–91.

(8) Josef Genishta—a Muscovite composer of the early nineteenth century, famed for his many popular *romances* and piano pieces.

(9) Two manuals for playing the *gusli* are advertised in the press of the period: 'Alphabet or the very easiest Means of Learning to Play the *Gusli* from Music'. Maksim Pomerantsev, Moscow, 1802; and 'The Newest Complete Manual or Self-teacher of the *Gusli*. Fëdor Kushenov-Dmitrievsky. St. Petersburg, 1808.

(10) Merzlyakov (1778–1830), Professor at Moscow University, follower of Karamzin and writer of wistful songs and *romances* greatly influenced by folklore. Some of his songs went the full circle and were adopted by the people (for instance, his 'Sredi dolin rovnikh').

Karamzin (1766–1836), author of *Letters of a Russian Traveller, Poor Lisa*, and a *History of the Russian State* (12 vols.). A key figure in the evolution of Russian literature, his work influenced Pushkin, Gogol and Tyutchev. An admirer of Rousseau he was 'the father of sentiment' in Russian literature, the chief aim of his works being to convey gentle emotions. He is also important in that he introduced many neologisms from French and German and was one of the first writers of the Russian short story.

(11) Danilo Nikitich Kashin (1769–1841) was born a serf and received his freedom in 1798. He studied with Sarti, who appreciated his gifts, later calling him his 'collaborator'. Kashin's musical activity was intensive and many-sided. Apart from composition, he organized public concerts, appearing as pianist and conductor, undertook the transcription and arrangement of folk-songs and published a Journal of National Music (*Zhurnal otechestvennoy muzyki*), including in the 1806–7 numbers some of his own folk-song arrangements, which later appeared in the collection of 1833–4. (Mooser's date of 1830 for this collection is not confirmed by any of the Russian sources consulted.) His compositions include operas, *romances*, a chorus with symphony orchestra and horn band accompaniment, and a large number of folk-song arrangements. His instrumental music, with the exception of a few cycles of variations on

'Russian songs', has not come down to us, although it is known that a concerto with orchestra (of his own composition) featured in his programmes in 1790 (see MOOS II, p. 491).

(12) Ivan Alekseevich Rupin (1789[?]–1850) was also a serf. From his childhood days he displayed musical abilities and sang as a boy in a church choir. After studying singing under Muschetti, a well-known vocal teacher, and composition with Zhuchkovsky, he was sent to Italy to complete his training where he spent six years, appearing with great success at La Scala, Milan. He retained the Italianized form of his name (Rupini) for the rest of his life. Upon his return to Russia he was given his liberty. Although possessing a fine tenor voice, he was handicapped by an unpleasing stage appearance, and this obliged him to abandon his career as an opera singer. Dedicating himself instead to the life of a concert artist, he soon established his reputation as a first-class performer of 'Russian songs'. Rupin was also a teacher of singing at the Imperial Theatres. His output as a composer is not large and is connected primarily with his main interests. His songs and *romances* (some to words of Pushkin and Delvig) enjoyed great popularity (one of the best known being the song 'Vot mchitsa troyka udalaya') and were often performed at concerts and in homes. (GIRMA II, p. 489).

(13) B. Shteynpress. *A. A. Alyabyev v izgnanii.* Moscow, 1959.

(14) An account of gypsy music nearer our own time is found in the memoirs of Lord Hamilton, *My Yesterdays*, London, 1950, p. 439.

'One of the younger members of the troupe would begin a song in waltz time, in a curious metallic voice with a ring in it of something Eastern, barbaric, and utterly strange to European ears, to the thrum of the guitars of the swarthy males in the background. The elderly females looked inexpressibly bored, and hugged their woollen shawls a little closer over their heads. Then the chorus took up the refrain. A tempest of wild, nasal melody arose, in the most perfect harmony. It was metallic, and the din was incredible, but the effect it produced on the listeners was astounding. The old women, dropping their cherished shawls, awoke to life. Their dull eyes sparkled again, they sang madly, frenetically; like people possessed. The non-European *timbre* of the voices conduced doubtless to the effect, but the fact remains that this clamour of nasal, metallic voices, singing in exquisite harmony, had about it something so novel and fresh—or was it something so immemorially old?—that the listeners felt absolutely intoxicated.

On the Russians it acted like hypnotism. After the first song they

T

all joined in, and even I, the dour and unemotional son of a Northern land, found myself, as words and music grew familiar, shouting the bass parts of the songs with all the strength of my lungs.
The Russian language lends itself admirably to song, and the excess
of sibilants in it is not noticeable in singing . . .'

(15) František Xavier Blýma, probably a Czech in origin, was born
in 1770. At the beginning of the 1790's he moved to Russia
and worked in Moscow in the capacity of conductor at the
Petrovsky Theatre. Leaving Moscow soon afterwards, he
entered the service of Count Komburley, Governor of Volin,
where he remained for the rest of his life. According to Findeisen (FOIM, Vol. 6, p. 238), his first symphony (1799)
was based on Russian themes. In 1803 his second symphony
was performed in Leipzig and he received flattering criticisms
from the press (see *Allgemeine Musikalische Zeitung*, Vol. V, p.
483 and Vol. IX, pp. 482–6). The title page of *Starinnye
svyatki* reads: Opera/Starinnye svyatki/music composed by Mr.
Blýma/in the year 1799. (See also Löwenbach. *Ceskoruské
vztahy hudební*. Prague, 1947, p. 13.) Mooser gives his death
as late 1811 or early 1812 (see MOOS III, p. 749).

(16) These sentiments found expression in an article printed in the
Moskovskiy Telegraf (December 1829) signed by the initials
'V.V.' (V. A. Ushakov):

The Old Yule-tide

'In the course of its thirty years existence on the operatic stage
the charming opera *The Old Yule-tide* has delighted us with its
simplicity, its fidelity in depicting a bygone age, and the unaffected
melody of the music, which is based on the tunes of simple folk, or
rather on the tunes of our forefathers, which, as the sacred property
of our ancestors, have been preserved among simple folk, who did
not change the customs of their fathers . . .

In the opera *The Old Yule-tide* the author has transported us
into that era when the laws of seniority led to quarrels among the
haughty *boyars*, quarrels which ensued in a truly Christian-brotherly
reconciliation; when these same *boyars* lived in inelegant but
durably built palaces of vast dimensions . . . when for the sight of
beautiful damsels, the daring lover had to penetrate the iron bars
of lofty *terems* [the women's apartments of a Russian house], and
through the dread vigilance of chamber maids and a stern mother.
The author of the opera conducts us into this same impenetrable
apartment. He resurrects our forefathers and bewitches us with
their simple, happy games. The pretty maids dance neither gavottes
nor mazurkas in the *terem* of *boyar* Simsky. Why no! The beautiful
Nastasya and her companion, in accordance with the old Christian
game, dance to the gay song 'Gaday, gaday, devitsa!' and the

gracious movements of the dancing girls with their rich sarafans and pearl frontlets, their smooth swan-like gait, the exuberant bobbing of their delectable little heads, the snow-white hands, which they majestically wave, compel us to forget the pretentious dances of the beauties of our time. Later, the composer lets us into a little secret of the ancient *terems*. He causes us to overhear our modest great-grandmothers talking about the common necessity for mortals of the need to love. He shows us the innocent charm to which, according to custom, the girls resorted in order to find out their betrothed. He does not fail to show us the cunning of elderly men, who, being too old for games of love, as if in joyful reminiscence of former years, assist the enterprising lovers. He causes the passionate fiancés to declare their love in the decent straightforward language of our ancestors, and after this delightful scene, the author frightens everybody with a yule-tide event. He introduces a *domovoy* [house spirit], he animates the statues and closes the mouth of a wicked nurse with a magic lock. All this sorcery is done in a very unaffected manner. Then the composer acquaints us with the old *boyars'* hospitality, their cordiality, their unshaken honesty and their innocent joys within the family circle . . . With unbounded pleasure I listen to the riddles and conundrums which *Boyar* Simsky and Prince Gagin put to the enchanting girls. As far as singing is concerned, with which this opera is lavishly adorned, not only I, a reverer of the past, but the most diffident spectator, visiting the theatre in order to enjoy his beloved Italian *'far-niente'* will be awakened from his mental lethargy and with delight will listen to the beautiful Nastasya when she sings 'Glory to the sun on high and glory to our Russian Tsar!'

(17) A. N. Titov (1769–1827) came from a rich, highly cultured family, and served in the horse guards, where he gained the rank of major-general. More than twenty of his compositions are preserved in score, the majority being written between the years 1799–1823. His works include at least thirteen operas (mostly comic), ballets, incidental music, and melodramas, most important of which is *Andromeda and Perseus* (1802).

(18) There is a curious direction in the score: 'This is a chorus of girls without orchestra. It begins softly behind the scenes but when they appear on the stage, it is sung loudly, and in the same way grows quiet again when they disappear'.

(19) It is also curious that Titov made no attempt to use music of this nature in any of his other operas. From the point of view of actual folk polyphony Titov's music compares so favourably, with its unison passages, characteristic intervals, rhythms and cadences, that one is compelled to presume that the chorus is an accurate record of real peasant singing.

(20) Stepan Ivanovich Davydov (1777–1825) was born in the Ukraine and educated in the Imperial Chapel, St. Petersburg. After working in St. Petersburg as teacher and conductor, he moved to Moscow, where he served in the capacity of 'musical director of the Moscow Court Theatres' (see Druskin and Keldysh. Op. cit., pp. 263–82).

(21) In Loewenberg's *Annals of Opera*, 2nd Ed. Geneva, 1955, columns 537–8, it is stated that Cavos was the composer of the fourth part of *Lesta*. This is incorrect, since the name of Davydov is written on the cover of the autograph score preserved in TSMB.

(22) For example, V. Ushakov wrote in the *Moskovskiy Telegraf*, XXX (1829), pp. 378–92:

> 'The first part of this opera was given its first performance in Moscow in 1804. It so delighted the public that young and old alike were obliged to visit *Rusalka* [i.e. *Lesta*]. The arias were sung by everyone, the ball music from *Lesta* was given at children's dances, then very fashionable, the charming *pas* ... were danced to the well-known tunes 'Pridi v chertog ko mne zlatoy' [this is referred to in Pushkin's *Evgeny Onegin*, Book 2, xii] and 'Polnote vzdorit, nachnite plyasat'. The piano teachers were obliged to instruct the ladies in the *Tema con variazione* from *Rusalka*, and even the servant walking under the swings would receive the reply from the flushed beauty of his own rank 'Mushchini na svete, kak mukhi k nam lnut'. We have no grand opera in Russia; at least, it appears on the stage very rarely. And thank God that it is not often. We still remember the endlessly tedious recitatives and cadences from artists of the Paris musical academy. Even the most ardent French music-lovers are bored by Grand Opera ... One may boldly warrant that *Rusalka, Nevidimka* [*The Invisible Prince*—an opera by Cavos] and other entrancing spectacles will always be preferred to the lyric tragedies of Quinault, Metastasio, da Ponte and others; the national melodies evenly utilised in the above operas, which Cavos and Davydov have employed so skilfully, are more pleasing to the taste of the average Russian theatregoer than the most highly skilled productions of Gluck, Sacchini, Salieri and a thousand more. The public possessing great critical powers is very small: the public wishing to be amused almost without number. The latter demand sparkling *décor*, stage mechanics, transformations, flights, choruses, ballets—in a word, everything that in plain speech is termed mystification. It is necessary to humour this public, which, in my opinion, on the score of entertainments, is no less intelligent than the most scientific hierarchies.' (RODG, p. 135).

(23) The plot of *Lesta, Dneprovskaya rusalka* is as follows: Vidostan, a young prince, falls in love with Lesta, a peasant girl. After

seducing her, he abandons her and she throws herself into the River Dnepr, where she is transformed into a water nymph. The prince still loves her, however, and commits suicide by also jumping into the river. Thus, they are united in death and the opera ends in jubilation. Against the main characters are opposed the comic figures of Tarabar[1] (Vidostan's equerry) and Kifar, the cup-bearer. There are also two negative personages—the villains Plamid and Zlomira.

(24) Cavos was born in Venice, the son of an operatic impresario. In 1797, at the age of twenty-two, he was taken to Russia, where he spent the next forty-three years of his life, associating with Russian literature and cultural circles. He was a prolific composer, writing and arranging music for vaudevilles, dramas, plays, ballets, and comic and dramatic operas. As a conductor he improved the condition of the orchestra and raised the standard of operatic performances. His efforts in the theatrical school resulted in the appearance of a pleiad of Russian opera singers, but his work as a teacher often assumed Gargantuan proportions, since he was frequently obliged to teach and rehearse complicated ensembles to actors, who could not read a note of music. The outstanding feature of his art is that he successfully availed himself of all that was best in contemporary foreign opera and reproduced it in Russian form.

(25) Vaudeville was of particular importance in the development of Russian opera. Originating in France in the seventeenth century, it penetrated into Russia at the beginning of the nineteenth century and was soon acclimatized, occupying a place between comedy and comic opera. Vaudeville features also appeared in the Viennese *Singspiels* and French *Opéras comiques*, adapted for the Russian stage. From the 1820's vaudeville became one of the favourite forms of entertainment. In Griboedov's comedy *Gore ot uma*, for example, Renetilov remarks: 'Vaudeville's the thing. As for the rest, it's all rubbish! The subject matter was taken almost exclusively from contemporary Russian life or domestic humour. From this period

[1] The name Tarabar has given rise to interesting speculations on the part of Russian musicologists. Rabinovich observes that in the original *Singspiel*, performed in the Leopoldstadt in Vienna, the name of the clown was Caspar Larifara. In the Russian version this became Tarabar. It is quite possible that Pushkin's Farlaf is an anagram of Larifara, in much the same way that Shakespeare's Caliban is held to be an anagram of cannibal. If Pushkin were familiar with the German original of *Lesta*, it is quite likely that he chose this name to characterize a more or less related person (see RODG, p. 136).

onwards each performance, whether opera, ballet or drama, contained at least one or more vaudevilles. In Russia, however, vaudeville lost much of its satirical element; dramatists such as Shakhovskoy, Khmelnitsky, Pisarev, and others began to write their own vaudevilles which incorporated fantastic elements, together with Russian folk lore and local colour (characters, place names, &c.). In some cases the music made use of Russian folk-song and this was especially true of those pieces, which dealt with peasant life. The varied subject matter of the vaudeville and its use of peasant themes and folk music were of great assistance in the formation of a national operatic style. Not only did the stage characters begin to acquire clearly expressed features of individuality, but the music also, a process which was likewise assisted by the performances in Russia of the new French and German Romantic operas.

(26) Aleksey Nikolaevich Verstovsky was born in 1799 on his father's estate at Seliverstov in the province of Tambovsk. His father had his own serf orchestra and a large music library, with the result that, like Glinka, he was able to familiarize himself with music from an early age. Proving to be extremely gifted, he appeared in concerts at the age of ten, playing piano sonatas of considerable difficulty. After the Napoleonic Wars he was sent by his parents to St. Petersburg, where he studied under Steibelt and Field. He simultaneously attended a course in communications at the Institute of Engineering in 1817. By the beginning of 1820 he had made a reputation for himself in artistic circles, associating with the leading theatrical representatives of the time—Arapov, Shakhovskoy, Khmelnitsky, Kokoshkin, Zagoskin. His first vaudeville *Babushkini popugay* (Grandma's Parrot), with libretto by Khmelnitsky, was performed at the Bolshoy Theatre, St. Petersburg, in 1819. He later made the acquaintance of Pushkin, Griboedov, and Odoevsky, who broadened his outlook and aided his creative growth. Pushkin, in particular, valued highly his abilities. In 1823 Verstovsky moved to Moscow, where he remained till his death in 1862.

(27) For example, *Karantin* (Quarantine), with libretto by Khmelnitsky, was one of the best known vaudevilles of the 1820's and was first performed in St. Petersburg on 26 July 1820.

(28) Pushkin's *Tales of Belkin* (like those of Hoffmann) are an excellent illustration of this. In *The Coffin-maker*, for instance, the element of fantasy and horror vies with the descriptions of peasant and bourgeois life.

(29) The simplicity and singability of Verstovsky's music is commented on by the critic Aksakov. Writing of the opera *Pan Twardowski*, he states: 'one finds neither *aria di bravura*, nor any of that learned noise and chaos of which some of the modern composers make so much use' (see supplement to *Moskovskiy Vestnik*, 1828, Nos. 1, 2).

(30) Loewenberg gives the librettist as Aksakov. Aksakov made a rough draft of the libretto, but the definitive text was written by Zagoskin.

(31) According to Yuri Arnold, this song was sung at a musical party given in Liszt's honour when he visited St. Petersburg.

(32) The plot of *Askold's Tomb* is as follows: The scene is set in Ancient Kiev in the pre-Christian era during the reign of Prince Svyatoslav Igorevich. Although a pagan kingdom, Kiev already contains many Christians, among them an old fisherman, Alexey. His daughter, Nadezhda, is the fiancée of Vseslav, an obscure orphan adopted by the Prince. There is also a strange figure named The Unknown, a purely Romantic character muffled in mystery, at odds with the established order. He exalts the past while denying the present and looks back nostalgically to his former life under Prince Askold, which was full of honour and military glory. He condemns Prince Svyatoslav, surrounded by his foreign supporters (Varangians), who have brought with them dissoluteness and debauch. The Unknown reveals to Vseslav the secret of his (Vseslav's) princely origin, how he is related to Prince Askold, and urges him to overthrow Svyatoslav and restore Russia to her former state. Vseslav, however, refuses to betray his benefactor. The Unknown determines to employ subterfuge and arranges for Nadezhda to be abducted by one of Svyatoslav's retinue as she returns from church. In attempting to defend her, Vseslav kills one of the Prince's henchmen and is obliged to flee for his life. Nadezhda is taken to Svyatoslav's *terem* in the village of Predslavino. Toropka Golovan, a *gudok*-player, appears on the scene. Bubbling over with kindness and good humour, he comforts Nadezhda with a song, in which he intimates to her that help is at hand. While Toropka is entertaining the household with a ballad, Vseslav creeps into the apartment and rescues Nadezhda. After seeking them in vain the Prince's steward, Boyarin Vyshata, approaches Vakhrameevna, an old witch, with a request to reveal the lover's hiding place. Summoning the spirits and even Chernobog himself, Vakhrameevna discerns the lovers on the cliffs overlooking the River Dnepr. The pur-

suers approach the lovers and the fugitives are about to leap into the swollen waters of the flooded river, when Vseslav's friend, Sternid the groom, tells him that they have been pardoned by the Prince. The Unknown appears on the river in a battered boat, having tried unsuccessfully to turn Vseslav against the Prince. Swamped by a huge wave, his boat sinks and he perishes. Assembled on the shore, the people conclude the opera with a triumphal chorus.

(33) In a letter to Odoevsky dated December 1836 Verstovsky wrote that his 'main desire was to put the character of national Russian opera into European form'.

(34) In point of fact *A Life for the Tsar* did not at first gain a fraction of the success of *Askold's Tomb*. As Findeisen observes: 'If *A Life for the Tsar* outstripped its contemporaries, then *Askold's Tomb*, on the other hand, captured their understanding, opinions, and sympathies'.

CHAPTER 6

(1) From his *Memoirs* we learn that his father was twenty-seven when the future composer was born and his mother only nineteen. The Glinkas' first child, Aleksey, had died soon after birth, and Mikhail was succeeded by eight other children of whom his sister, Lyudmila Shestakova, was to have great influence on him. As a baby Mikhail was entrusted to the care of his grandmother, who spoiled and pampered him to an absurd degree. It was probably due to this early molly-coddling that he was always of a highly sensitive disposition with a lively addiction to hypochondria and the attentions of the fair sex.

(2) In his *Memoirs* he describes how he was fascinated as a child of eight by the sound of bells, which he would imitate on two copper bowls. Later, with regard to his uncle's serf musicians, he mentions the effect that the playing of a clarinet quartet by Crusell had upon him at the age of ten or eleven:

> This music made an inconceivable, fresh and delightful impression upon me—after hearing it I remained for the rest of the day in a sort of feverish condition . . .

(3) Among the critics of the opera may be mentioned Bulgarin, who wrote in the journal *Severnaya pchela*. Even Pushkin was dragged in to the controversy and wrote the following laconic epigram:

Slushaya siyu novinku,	In hearing this innovation,
Zavist, zloboy omrachas,	Envy, clouded by hate,
Pust skrezheshchet, no uzh Glinku*	May rage, but Glinka*
Zatoptat ne mozhet v gryaz.	Can never be trampled in the dirt.

* 'Glinka' is the diminutive of *glina*, meaning clay.

The dispute over Glinka's opera did not diminish over the years and indeed gave quite an impetus to the development of Russian musical criticism. It is not surprising that the first outstanding articles about Glinka by Odoevsky, Melgunov, and Neverov served as the basis of the work of Stasov and Serov—the Russian musicologists who wrote in the 1850's.

(4) PIRM I, p. 339. According to some sources the meetings of the 'Brotherhood' ended in 'orgies', which, it is claimed, might well have done much to undermine Glinka's constitution.

(5) V. Odoevsky. *Izbrannye trudi.* Moscow, 1951, p. 66.

(6) Even before his departure for Spain he wrote to his mother: 'The thought of returning to Russia frightens me'.

(7) LITNAS II, p. 272.

(8) Glinka's *Memoirs* have recently become available in a translation by Richard B. Mudge (*Mikhail Ivanovich Glinka.* Translated by Richard B. Mudge. University of Oklahoma Press, 1963).

(9) LITNAS II, p. 638.

(10) During the Soviet period a number of changes have been made to the text, while the Epilogue has been extended into two scenes. The opera is now known as *Ivan Susanin*.

(11) LITNAS I, pp. 305–14.

(12) One must mention in particular an article by N. A. Melgunov, as it was not printed during Glinka's lifetime. Melgunov sent his article to Glinka, who was abroad at the time, through the offices of Y. M. Neverov, on the understanding that Glinka should pass it on to the *Moskovskiy nablyudatel* (The Moscow Observer) when he had examined it. However, the composer decided not to publish it, though he sent it to A. N. Strugovshchikov, with whom it remained till 1874. Strugovshchikov included the article in his memoirs under the heading 'Glinka and his musical compositions':

To express in all forms of music, particularly in opera, the lyrical side of the Russian national character—that is the task which Glinka has taken upon himself. He has grasped the meaning of the words 'Russian music', 'Russian opera' in a different sense from his predecessors. He has not restricted himself more or less to close imitations of a folk melody; no, he has studied intently the structure of Russian songs; their performance by the people—the cries, the sharp transitions from serious to gay, from loud to soft, the *chiaroscuro*, the unexpected . . . in a word, he has revealed the whole system of Russian melody and harmony inherent in folk music itself . . . His first major attempt, his opera *A Life for the Tsar*, shows to what degree he has realized his idea and intention.

(See 'Reminiscences of Glinka', *Russkaya starina*, April 1874; see also Gogol's celebrated article in *Sovremennik*, No. 2, May 1837.)

(13) N. Afanasev. 64 *russkie narodnye pesni*. Moscow, 1866.

(14) G. M. Popov. *Sbornik boevikh, bytovikh i plyasovikh soldatskikh pesen, v dvukh chastyakh*. Kharkov, 1888, pp. 110 and 111.

(15) The first performer of the role of Vanya, A. Y. Petrova-Vorobëva wrote:

> The reality of this chorus quite amazed me. While the men's voices were so calm, the crowd of peasant women cluttered like a lot of old hens. After Italian music it was so new and natural that I could hardly contain myself from delight.

(A. Y. Petrova-Vorobëva. 'On the 500th performance of *A Life for the Tsar*'. *Glinka v vospominaniyakh sovremennikov*. Moscow, 1955, p. 172.)

(16) V. Protopopov. *Ivan Susanin*. Moscow, 1961, pp. 186–7.

(17) Glinka used the folk-song 'Snegi belye' in his *Capriccio for Piano Duet* (1834). The folk theme was first published in the second volume of Rupin's collection of 1833 (see T. Popova's comments in the introduction to the modern edition of Rupin's collection, Moscow, (1955)).

(18) Letter from Nizhny Novgorod dated 20 August 1858. *Perepiska M. A. Balakireva i V. V. Stasova*. Vol. I. Moscow, 1935, p. 27.

(19) '. . . One hears next the women's wedding chorus, based on a most original Russian motive in 5/4 time, but a motive, mark you, borrowed from nowhere (like all motives in Glinka's opera) but which, should it be heard apart from the opera, would be termed a wedding song, so thoroughly has the composer grasped the principles of Russian melody.' (V. F. Odoevsky. *Izbrannye muzykalno-kriticheskie stati*, p. 29.)

The 5/4 time signature in Glinka's chorus is determined by the structure of the verse (assuming that the words were written before the music). Tchaikovsky wrote to Arensky:

> Glinka apparently could not write the chorus in any other time but 5/4: here there is a real 5/4 rhythm—i.e. a continuous and even alternation of 2/4 and 3/4.

(M. I. Tchaikovsky. *Zhizn Pëtra Ilicha Chaikovskovo*, Vol. III, p. 73. Letter dated 25 September 1885.)

(20) Quoted in E. Kann-Novikova. *M. I. Glinka*. Vol. I, p. 57.

(21) Gos. publichnaya biblioteka imeni M. E. Saltykova-Shchedrina. Rukopisnyi otdel, Arkhiv N. A. Rimskovo-Korsakova, shifr 185-b.

(22) P. V. Shein. *Velikoruss v svoikh pesnyakh, obryadakh, obychayakh*, &c. Vol. II, St. Petersburg, 1900, p. 830.

(23) When Glinka thought of setting *Dvumuzhnitsa*, in preparing the composition he used the song 'Ne znaval'. There is a reference to this in a letter to his sister: 'On Friday (20 May 1855) I accompanied Petrov with the song "Ne znaval ya" . . .' (M. I. Glinka. LITNAS II, pp. 528–9.)

(24) V. Protopopov. Op. cit., p. 207.

(25) Of the final chorus Serov wrote:

> In all operas existing up to this time there is no final chorus which could be so closely connected with the task of a musical drama and with such a mighty brush could have painted a historical picture of a given country at a given period. Here is Russia of the time of Minin and Pozharsky—in every sound.

See A. N. Serov. *Kriticheskie stati*. Vol. IV, St. Petersburg, 1895, p. 1699.

(26) See A. N. Serov. *Izbrannye stati*, Vol. II, Moscow, 1957, pp. 35–43. Stasov finds the origin of 'Slavsya' in ancient Slavonic church chants (see V. V. Stasov. *Mikhail Ivanovich Glinka*. Moscow, 1935, p. 151).

(27) See 'Reminiscences of Glinka', *Russkaya starina*, April, 1874.

(28) On one occasion when Susanin speaks of the Poles his music loses its Russian colouring and takes on the triple time of the Poles themselves.

(29) It is significant that Glinka wrote in his *Memoirs*: 'the role of Susanin to be written as simply as possible'.

(30) Glinka was by no means the first Russian composer to turn to the East for his inspiration. In the eighteenth century Pashkevich sought to give oriental colouring to his music in the opera *Fevey*. In the nineteenth century Glinka was forestalled by Alyabyev and Cavos. Interest in the Orient was widespread in Russia and Glinka's efforts at this period may be compared with those of Bryullov, Orlovsky and Gagarin in painting, and Lermontov and Pushkin in literature.

(31) The plot is as follows:

Ruslan and Lyudmila

Act I. A wedding-feast is in progress in the Palace of Svetozar, the great Prince of Kiev. Lyudmila, Svetozar's daughter, is being married to Ruslan, a brave knight. The only unhappy people are Ruslan's unsuccessful rivals—Farlaf, a cowardly braggart, and Ratmir, a passionate dreamer (contralto). But suddenly the noisy festivities are hushed, while all listen in rapt attention to Bayan, the minstrel. In prophetic words, Bayan foretells the fate of Ruslan and Lyudmila—how sorrow and anguish await them, but that all obstacles to happiness will be surmounted through the power of true love.

In another song Bayan looks to the future. Through the mist of ages yet to come he sees a singer, who will tell of Ruslan and Lyudmila and extol his country (a reference to Pushkin).

Sadly Lyudmila bids farewell to her father, to her native Kiev. Goodhumouredly she teases the unfortunate suitors, Farlaf and Ratmir, and with words of greeting turns to her beloved. Svetozar gives the young people his blessing.

The next moment thunder is heard, lightning flashes, and all are chained to the ground as if turned to stone. Gradually the mist disappears and all return to normal, but Lyudmila has vanished. Stricken with sorrow, Svetozar promises half of his kingdom and his daughter's hand to anyone who can find her—a mission which is gladly undertaken by the three knights.

Act II. Sc. 1. In his search for Lyudmila in the far north Ruslan approaches the cave of Finn, a kindly magician. Finn discloses to Ruslan that Lyudmila has been abducted by Chernomor, a wicked sorcerer, though it will be Ruslan's fortune to overthrow him. On Ruslan's request Finn tells him the story of his life.

Once Finn was a poor shepherd who fell in love with a girl named Naina, but she disdainfully rejected him. In turn he tried to win her by heroism, riches, and worldly success, but nothing would thaw her cold heart. And so he resorted to magic. But again fate laughed in his face. When, after years of anguish, the long-awaited moment arrived and Naina confessed her love, he discovered that she had become a terrible old woman, hump-backed, grey, and with a shaking head, and, moreover, one simply burning with desire as a result of his all-too-successful sorcery. Although he constantly fled from her, Naina (who was now also a sorceress) pursued him relentlessly. Ruslan was her particular enemy and Finn warns him to be constantly on his guard against her machinations.

Act II. Sc. 2. The cowardly Farlaf is already prepared to give up his search for Lyudmila, but is unexpectedly confronted by a formidable old woman. It is Naina, who promises to help him locate the princess, if he will return home and await her instructions. Greatly heartened, Farlaf consents.

Act II. Sc. 3. Ruslan travels further and further north and eventually is confronted by a desert plain, showing signs of a recent battle.

Everything reminds him of the shortness of life, of the vanity of all earthly things. Here and there lie suits of armour, the bones and skulls of fallen warriors.

Unexpectedly the mist clears and before the astonished Ruslan arises a huge living Head. On seeing the knight, the monster begins to blow with terrific force, raising a veritable storm. Ruslan, however, boldly throws himself on the Head and pierces it with his lance, discovering underneath it a sword. The Head, thus vanquished, tells Ruslan its amazing story: once there were two brothers—one, a giant, the other, Chernomor, a dwarf, of whom it was prophesied that both would die from the same weapon. Having procured a miraculous sword with the help of his brother, Chernomor cut off the giant's head and by his magic art compelled it to guard the sword in this distant desert. Now the sword belongs to Ruslan and the Head begs him to put an end to Chernomor's treachery.

ACT III. Naina, wishing to kill Ruslan, decides to lure him to her magic castle. Seductive maidens, in Naina's power, tempt weary travellers to rest in their arms. Seeking her beloved, Gorislava (who has been abandoned by Ratmir) appears at the castle, but though Ratmir is there, he is oblivious to her entreaties and is bewitched by the magic maidens.

Ruslan, likewise, has been attracted to the castle. Captivated by the wonderful visions and illusions, he is willing to forget Lyudmila in the embraces of Gorislava, when the scene is interrupted by the timely entrance of Finn. With a wave of his magic wand the castle disappears and Finn tells the knights of their fate—how Ratmir will love Gorislava and Lyudmila belong to Ruslan.

ACT IV. Meanwhile, Lyudmila is languishing in Chernomor's magic garden. Nothing can dispel her gloomy thoughts, her longing for Kiev and her beloved. She is even ready to die rather than submit to the magician, but when she is about to throw herself into the water, the *rusalkas* dissuade her. A march is heard and Chernomor, a dwarf with an enormous beard, appears. By way of entertainment he orders dances to commence. All at once a horn call resounds: it is Ruslan summoning the magician to a duel. Plunging Lyudmila into an enchanted sleep, Chernomor goes out, but in a few moments is deprived of his flowing beard, wherein lies his strength. But all Ruslan's endeavours to awaken Lyudmila are in vain.

ACT V. SC. 1. Moonlight. In a valley on the road to Kiev, Ruslan, the enchanted princess, Ratmir and Gorislava and the former slaves of Chernomor have all settled down for the night. Ratmir stands on guard. Suddenly, Chernomor's slaves bring terrible news— Lyudmila has again been abducted! Once more Ruslan gallantly throws himself in pursuit. Before the disheartened Ratmir now appears Finn, who gives him a magic ring, which will awaken Lyudmila, and bids him set out on the road for Kiev.

ACT V. SC. 2. The royal chamber. Lyudmila is still in an enchanted sleep, having been brought to Kiev by the cunning Farfaf. But although he has stolen Lyudmila with the help of Naina, he has not the power to waken her. The sorrowful groans of the father, the laments of the princely servants are all in vain: Lyudmila can not be roused from her slumber! But finally the sound of horses' hooves are heard: it is Ruslan, Ratmir and Gorislava. In Ruslan's hands is the magic ring, given him by Ratmir. On Ruslan's approach Lyudmila awakens and Farlaf runs away in terror. The long awaited moment of re-union has dawned at last. General rejoicing.

(Taken from V. A. Pankratova [ed.]. *Opernye libretto*. Moscow, 1962, pp. 32–5.)

(32) In his *Memoirs* Glinka tells us that Pushkin would in all probability have written the libretto himself had it not been for his untimely death (see LITNAS I, p. 180).

(33) Glinka said of the Overture: 'It flies with full sails'.

(34) Glinka's original piano harmonization of the melody is published in *M. Glinka. Polnoe sobranie sochinenii*. Moscow, 1958, Vol. VI, p. 77. In this version the G♯ in b. 2 is sharpened.

(35) It is also used by Glinka in his *Capriccio on Russian Themes* (for Piano Duet) written in 1834. (See *M. Glinka. Polnoe sobranie sochinenii*. Vol. V, p. xii.)

(36) E. Kann-Novikova. *M. I. Glinka. Novye materialy i dokumenti*. Vol. II. Moscow, 1951, p. 128.

(37) D. Arakchiev (Arakishvili). *Vostochnye napevi v proizvedeniyakh russkikh kompozitorov. Muzyka i zhizn*. 1908, No. 5; 1910, No. 12.

(38) 'Venok Glinke'. *Sovetskaya muzyka*. 1954, No. 6.

(39) V. V. Protopopov. *M. I. Glinka*. Moscow-Leningrad, 1949, p. 35.

(40) A. Kozlovsky. 'M. Ashrafi i uzbekskaya narodnaya muzyka'. *Sovetskaya muzkya*. 2nd Vol. articles, Moscow, 1944, p. 40.

(41) Siyalsky was a St. Petersburg music lover who spent two years in the Caucasus from 1832–4. Details of his biography are given in *Pamyati Glinki*. 1857–1957. Moscow, 1958, pp. 203–7. His friend, Danilevsky, who was the arranger of the music for pianoforte, was one of the first teachers of Dargomyzhsky.

(42) The transcriptions were published in 1861, but as Danilevsky died in 1844, one may assume that the piano arrangements were made in the 1830's or early 1840's (see *Pamyati Glinki*, p. 206).

(43) P. Siyalsky. 'Nechto o pesnyakh i muzyke v Zakavkazskom krae'. *Illyustratsiya*, 1861. No. 193. With a supplement: 'Vosem pesen aziatskikh i odna lezginka, sobrannye i opisannye s golosov i instrumentov v oblasti P. Siyalskim, polozhennye dlya fortepiano A. Danilevskim'.

(44) D. Arakchiev (Arakishvili). 'Vostochnye napevy v proizvedeniyakh russkikh kompozitorov'. *Muzyka i zhizn.* 1908, No. 5, p. 3.

(45) Siyalsky writes of the *Lezginka*: 'The *Lezginka* is the most lively music of the Aziyatsi, and is performed by two dancers in turn while the spectators clap their hands in time' (P. Siyalsky. *Illyustratsiya.* 1861, No. 193, p. 283). Serov wrote of the *Lezginka* in his article 'Ruslan and the Ruslanists':

> For those who have been in the Caucasus or even the Crimea, here commences something very familiar—the 'Lezginka', transported into the concert hall with a magical brush of musical colour and symphonically arranged with wonderful skill. It is a piece of Caucasian life, a scrap of Caucasian sky, taken from human life.

(A. N. Serov. *Kriticheskie stati.* Tom IV, p. 1699, St. P. 1895.)

(46) Gerald Abraham informs us that this section was always cut at the Marynsky Theatre, being considered too 'modern' by official ears even three-quarters of a century after it had been written (see Gerald Abraham. *On Russian Music*, p. 40).

(47) See Gerald Abraham. Op. cit., p. 22.

(48) Bayan's *gusli* is ingeniously suggested by the combination of a piano and harp, a combination also used in the accompaniment to Ruslan's music in the Finale, No. 27 (p. 328).

(49) For example, the *bylina* 'Ermak Timofeevich' (R-K, p. 20).

(50) The Overture to *Ruslan* was one of the last numbers to be composed. Thus, in a letter to Shirkov he wrote: 'The overture and entr'actes can wait till last' (LITNAS II, p. 159).

(51) Like Mozart, Glinka was able to hear his music mentally extremely well, and was not obliged to have recourse to an instrument in order to compose. This fact was noted by several of his contemporaries. Thus, P. A. Stepanov, who lived with him at one time, described the period when *Ruslan* was coming into being:

> Glinka, completely immersed in himself in his creative work, would wander about the rooms . . . now he would go to the piano, would take several chords, would hurry into his room and quickly write on large sheets of music paper scattered round his desk; again he would walk, again write down, often without the help of any instrument.

(See P. A. Stepanov. 'Vospominaniya o M. I. Glinke'. *Glinka v vospominaniyakh sovremennikov.* Moscow, 1955, p. 60.) Another account is by P. P. Dubrovsky, who knew the composer when he was writing *Kamarinskaya*:

M. I. did not make the final draft for a long time and constantly thought about his work. During this time he hardly touched the piano at all.

(See P. P. Dubrovsky. 'Vospominanie o M. I. Glinke'. *Glinka v vospominaniyakh sovremennikov*, p. 260.) The same author describes the work's composition in the following manner:

He sat down at a small table in the middle of the room in front of his birds and wrote something on a large sheet of paper . . . This was *Kamarinskaya*. It was completely ready in his mind: he wrote it down, like an ordinary mortal, with dexterous signs, at the same time talking and joking with me. Soon two or three friends arrived, but he continued to write during the loud laughter and conversation, being in no way upset: and meanwhile one of his most remarkable works was being created in music.

All the above accounts are printed in *Pamyati Glinki*, p. 229.

(52) It is also known to the words 'Iz-za lesu, lesu temnovo'.

(53) The plot is as follows: The action describes the struggle of the Muscovite State with the Livonians in the fifteenth century. Prince Kholmsky, the Muscovite *voevoda*, is besieging Pskov with a large army. The Livonian knights, seeing in Kholmsky a dangerous adversary, strive to win him on their side by treachery. As the means of intrigue the sister of one of the Livonian barons, Adelheide von Schlummermaus, is chosen, with whom Kholmsky is in love. With the assistance of the Jew Skhary, a magician and astrologer, Baron Schlummermaus prepares the wedding of Kholmsky to his sister. Adelheide, however, is in love with the Pskovite merchant, Knyazich, and will take part in the intrigue only under pressure from her brother and the Jew. Together with this, Prince Kholmsky is also secretly loved by Skhary's daughter, Rachel, who expresses her feelings only in the song 'Rachel's Dream'. (At the conclusion of the drama Rachel throws herself into the river in despair.)

Schlummermaus and Adelheide fire Kholmsky's ambition with the thought of separation from Moscow and the creation of an independent principality, friendly to Livonia. In spite of the warnings and persuasions of his faithful servant, the jester Foma Sereda, Prince Kholmsky declares to the Pskovite *veche* the establishment of 'a maritime power of Velikiy Pskov and Novgorod Velikiy'. The *veche*, however, rejects these treacherous proposals and disperses. The Prince, abandoned by all save his servant, places his hope for happiness in Adelheide, but this last illusion is also shattered: Adelheide does not love him and becomes the wife of Knyazich. In conclusion *boyars* arrive from Moscow bringing with them tidings of the Tsar's displeasure.

(54) This similarity was noted by Serov in an article entitled 'Little known works of M. I. Glinka' written in 1857.

(55) LITNAS I, p. 86.

(56) LITNAS I, p. 89.

(57) LITNAS I, p. 90.

(58) In the Mudge translation of the Glinka *Memoirs* (p. 41) the translator mistakes 'B' (the symbol in Russian for B♭) for B♮, which is represented (as in German) by the letter 'H'.

(59) First published by Ricordi. In 1951 it appeared in a Soviet edition. The May number of *Sovetskaya muzyka*, 1962, contained an article by B. Dobrokhotov, describing the re-discovery of the *Anna Bolena* Serenade in a library in Modena. (Complete Works, Vol. 4 Supp.)

(60) Letter of S. A. Sobolevsky to S. P. Shevyrëv dated 14 November 1832. *Sovetskaya muzyka*. 1937, No. 6, p. 83.

(61) The story of *La Sonnambula* is briefly thus: the wedding of a peasant girl, Amina, is about to take place in a Swiss village. Suddenly the festivities are thrown into confusion when Amina's bridegroom, Elvino, discovers his *fiancée* asleep in the room of a visiting Count. He immediately jumps to the conclusion that Amina has been unfaithful, but peace is restored with the discovery that Amina is a somnambulist, and the opera ends with the lovers' happy reconciliation.

(62) LITNAS I, p. 140.

(63) A detailed account of these is found in the article 'Variatsionnye tsikly Glinki dlya fortepiano' in *Pamyati Glinki (1857–1957). Issledovaniya i materialy*. Moscow, 1958.

(64) A. N. Serov. *Izbrannye stati*. Vol. I. Moscow-Leningrad, 1950, p. 161.

(65) Regarding this see V. Protopopov's article: 'Dva krupnykh sochineniya molodovo Glinki—Simfoniya-uvertyura i kaprichchio na russkie temy' in *M. I. Glinka. Sbornik materialov i statey*. Ed. T. Livanova. Moscow-Leningrad, 1950. The article also contains a detailed analysis of the 'Capriccio'.

(66) Stasov wrote: 'Each of his vocal works is a page or line from his life, a fragment of his delights, his joys, or sorrows'. (See V. V. Stasov. *Izbrannye sochineniya*. 'Iskusstvo'. Moscow, 1952, Vol. I, p. 396.)

(67) A. N. Serov. 'Vospominaniya o Glinke.' *Kriticheskie stati*. St. Petersburg 1895, Tome III, p. 1323.

(68) As Gerald Abraham observes in his chapter on vocal music in

U

A History of Song, referring to the Spanish serenades 'Nocturnal Zephyr' and 'I Am Here, Inesilla', it is rather ironical that all but one of Glinka's Spanish songs were written before he visited Spain, the one exception being 'Milochka' (Darling) (1847), based on a genuine *jota* melody (see *A History of Song*, ed. Stevens, London, 1960, p. 350).

CHAPTER 7

(1) *Kratkaya avtobiograficheskaya zapiska. Sbornik 'A. S. Dargomyzhsky. (1813–1869)'. Avtobiografiya. Pisma. Vospominaniya sovremennikov.* St. Petersburg, 1921, p. 2.

(2) *Sbornik 'A. S. Dargomyzhsky'* . . ., p. 4.

(3) St. Petersburg had already seen by this time Auber's *La Muette de Portici* and Meyerbeer's *Robert le diable*.

(4) I. I. Panaev wrote in his literary reminiscences:

> I learnt about *Notre Dame de Paris* from the *Moscow Telegraph*. Shortly after this everyone in St. Petersburg who could read French began to rave about Hugo's new work of genius. All the copies received in Petersburg were immediately bought up. (PIRM I, p. 411.)

(5) *Sbornik 'A. S. Dargomyzhsky'* . . ., p. 15.

(6) Ibid., pp. 53–4.

(7) Ibid., p. 7.

(8) Ibid., p. 55.

(9) Ibid., p. 41.

(10) Ibid., p. 7.

(11) In 1850 there appeared in the newspaper *Severnaya pchela* the following:

> In this concert we have learned fortuitously that our talented Russian composer Mr. Dargomyzhsky is composing a Russian opera: *Rusalka* on the subject chosen by Pushkin and that with this aim Mr. Dargomyzhsky is going this summer to Little Russia, in order to gather local folk melodies and acquaint himself with the district.

(See *Severnaya Pchela*, 1850, 15 April, No. 85, p. 339.) According to Pekelis, this trip never took place (see M. Pekelis. *Dargomyzhsky i narodnaya pesnya*, Moscow-Leningrad, 1951, p. 63).

(12) Some of Dargomyzhsky's best songs in the folk idiom were written before he started work on *Rusalka*. In a typically Russian manner his interest in his native land was not roused till he went abroad in 1843. He called his pieces that he had

written in Paris his 'songs of a Russian nightingale in a foreign land'. The parallel between Dargomyzhsky's expression and Glinka's feelings before composing *A Life for the Tsar* is striking.

The plot of *Rusalka* is as follows:

ACT I. Natasha is sitting on the banks of the Dnepr in deep meditation. She is apprehensive and listens to the admonitions of her father, the Miller, only with difficulty. For several days now she has not been visited by the Prince, her lover. The Miller instructs her how to conduct herself with the Prince. He would very much like to see his daughter a Princess, even if this is but an empty dream. At all events, one might at least get a fine present or even some money from the Prince.

The Prince arrives and Natasha greets him with trepidation. As always he greets her tenderly, but tells her that soon he must leave her. He appears embarrassed and Natasha observes in him a change. Even the expensive necklace which the Prince has given her will not rouse her from her gloomy premonitions. Having reached manhood he tells her of his impending marriage and the fact that they must part. Natasha freezes with horror. In torment she tells him that she is soon to become a mother. The Prince urges her to take care of herself and quickly goes away. Natasha is broken-hearted. In despair she seizes her jewelled necklace, tears it from her head and with vengeance in her heart throws herself into the Dnepr.

ACT II. The Prince's wedding. Everyone congratulates the young couple and wishes them joy. Only a single voice sings a sad song describing how a young girl has drowned herself in the river, abandoned by her beloved.

The Prince recognizes Natasha's voice. All happiness is destroyed. However, all endeavour to maintain the impression that they have noticed nothing. The guests raise their cups. The Prince kisses his wife, but at that moment a loud female groan rings through the hall. Everything is thrown into confusion.

ACT III. Sc. 1. The days of the Princess pass by in tedium and in constant waiting for the Prince, who is away hunting. She remembers the first happy days of their marriage, now gone for ever. A hunter returns and informs her that the Prince has stayed behind on the banks of the Dnepr. The Princess is alarmed.

Sc. 2. Evening. On the banks of the river emerge the *rusalkas*, but hearing steps, they plunge into the water and disappear. The Prince stops by the ruined mill and with sorrow remembers his past happiness with Natasha, whom he passionately loved.

Suddenly an insane old man appears, calling himself a crow, and with difficulty the Prince recognizes the old Miller. Wishing to help him the Prince invites him to the palace, but with a wild cry of 'Give me back my daughter!' the Miller flings himself upon him. The Prince is saved by his retinue.

ACT IV. SC. 1. The underwater home of the *rusalkas*. Twelve years have passed since Natasha threw herself into the Dnepr and was transformed into a *rusalka*, but the thirst for revenge has not left her. And her hour has now arrived—the Prince is here, close at hand. Summoning her daughter, Natasha commands her to go to the shore and lure the Prince into the Dnepr.

SC. 2. The Prince stands pensively on the banks of the river. The familiar places remind him of Natasha. Suddenly a child-*rusalka* appears. She tells the Prince of her mother, who has become Queen of the Dnepr and invites him to her palace on the river bed. Overwhelmed by supernatural forces the Prince obediently follows the *rusalochka*. From beyond the mill run on the Princess and Olga, an orphan devoted to her. They endeavour to restrain him, but the enticing voice of the *rusalka* draws him on. With a heave the old Miller pushes the Prince into the water and he is led by the *rusalkas* to the feet of their Queen.

(Taken from Pankratova. Op. cit., pp. 37–8.)

(13) This is preserved in the archives of the Leningrad Conservatory. It contains 16 Russian, 2 Ukrainian, 1 Turkish, 1 Greek, and 1 Serbian folk-songs. No. 20 ('Ukazhi mne, mati') is used in the B flat major section of the symphonic scherzo *Baba-Yaga*.

(14) Dargomyzhsky asked his friends to send him folk-songs that they had written down. L. I. Belenitsyna, for example, sent the composer some folk-songs in 1859, for on 16 September he wrote: 'I value highly the folk-songs that you have sent me' (*Sbornik 'A. S. Dargomyzhsky . . .'*, p. 62).

(15) The note-book also contains a sketch of the chorus of *rusalkas* to Pushkin's words ('Chto, sestritsa, v pole chistom'), which did not appear in the final version of the opera.

(16) In the collection Rimsky-Korsakov noted: 'This motive was sung to A. S. Dargomyzhsky by his nurse to the words "Idët koza rogataya" ' (see R-K, No. 25, p. 55).

(17) For example, in the opera *Rogdana*. Rimsky-Korsakov uses it also in *Snegurochka* (Act I) in the scene between Kupava and the Snow-maiden, and again in his piano composition *Parafrazy* (Paraphrases).

(18) The tune is used in the final act where the *rusalka* lures the Prince into her acquatic domain. As Keldysh observes, there is something fascinating about the song (KIRM I, p. 547).

(19) Dargomyzhsky also uses the folk-song 'Idët koza rogataya' as an accompaniment to the chorus 'Khor volshebnikh dev nad spyashchey knyazhnoy Rogdanoy' in the incompleted opera *Rogdana*, which he attempted to compose in the 1860's. His

further interest in short fragments of folk-song repeated almost as an incantation (sometimes with amusing effect) is illustrated by the song of Ratibor Kholmogradsky in the same opera (*Rogdana*).

(20) It is printed in Tchaikovsky's collection of children's songs, Vol. 2, [1877–8], No. 4, where it is sung to the words 'Kak vo lesu my dolgo gulyali'. The key (D major) is different, but the melody is identical.

(21) The tune was well known at the period and was adopted during the nineteenth century as a town song. It may be compared with the arrangement by Kashin 'Akh, devitsa, krasavitsa' (D. Kashin. *Russkie narodnye pesni*, Part II, No. 6), and with the folk-song *O maiden fair*, arranged by the Englishman, Benjamin Beresford (1750–1819), a University teacher at Dorpat, Kharkov and Berlin, who spent ten years in St. Petersburg from 1806–16. In his collection he included the most popular Russian and Ukrainian folk-songs of the time (see B. Beresford. *The Russian Troubadour or a Collection of Ukrainian and other national melodies, together with the words of each respective air, translated into English Verse by the Author of the German Erato interspersed with several favorite [sic] Russian Songs set to Music by Foreign Masters and translated by the same hand.* London, 1816).

(22) In the chorus 'Akh, ty pole, moë pole' (Act I, No. 6, p. 97), which is based not on a folk-song but on an early vocal work of Dargomyzhsky himself—'Peterburgskaya serenada', No. 1 ('Iz strany, strany dalëkoy').

(23) The stage direction preceding it reads: 'Peasants enter with rakes and scythes; one of them plays on a *dudka*'.

(24) It is quite possible that Dargomyzhsky was ignorant of the modal nature of folk-song, although some of his arrangements do preserve it. However, on each occasion that he uses a modal folk tune in *Rusalka* he gives it a diatonic accompaniment.

(25) The song 'Zapletisya, pleten' occurs in the collections of Bernard, Gurilëv, Afanasev, Rimsky-Korsakov, Voevodin, Listopadov, and others.

(26) This text is found in a number of collections (e.g. Dubuque, Rimsky-Korsakov, &c.), but the tune employed by Dargomyzhsky is quite different.

(27) F. M. Istomin and G. O. Dyutsch. *Pesni russkovo naroda.* Imperial Russian Geographical Society, St. Petersburg, 1894. Wedding Songs, No. 24, p. 135.

(28) An attempt is made in this chorus to imitate the sound of *balalaikas*.

(29) P. I. Chaykovskiy. *Literaturnye proizvedeniya i perepiska. Polnoe sobranie sochineniy*, Vol. II, Moscow, 1953, p. 149.

(30) The Prince's music in *Rusalka* is also permeated by folk-song inflections, though not to so great an extent as that of the Miller.

(31) The plot of *The Stone Guest* is as follows:

> Act I. Sc. 1. Don Juan has secretly returned to Madrid from exile with his servant Leporello. He yearns to see again his native town with its wonderful women—the joy and single aim of his whole existence.
>
> A monk approaches the fence of the monastery where Don Juan and Leporello are awaiting the fall of night. From him Don Juan learns that Donna Anna is soon to come there—the widow of the Commendatore, whom the Don had killed. Seeing Donna Anna in a black veil, Don Juan is consumed with the desire to know her.
>
> It begins to grow dark; the moon rises. Don Juan postpones his meeting with Donna Anna and hurries on to Madrid to his beloved Laura.
>
> Sc. 2. Laura, surrounded by admirers, is entertaining at her house. The guests beg her to sing. She gives an inspired performance, accompanying herself on the guitar, stating afterwards that the words were written by Don Juan, whom she loves and can never forget. The single mention of the Don's name, however, rouses an outburst of jealousy from Don Carlos. In order to prevent a quarrel the guests implore Laura to sing again.
>
> It is now late and time for all to depart. Don Carlos alone remains. He is happy. But their conversation is interrupted by the entry of Don Juan, on whom Laura throws herself with joy. Maddened beyond reason Don Carlos draws his sword, but in the duel that follows Don Juan is the victor. Don Carlos is killed and Laura and her lover surrender themselves to the joys of their reunion.
>
> Act II. Disguised as a monk Don Juan hurries to the statue of the Commendatore. The thought of seducing Donna Anna has still not left him. Donna Anna, taking him for a monk, chats with him kindly, but the Don confesses to her that he is not a priest and swears to her his passion. He manages to wring her consent to visit her at her house. Delighted at his success a new idea strikes him and he tells Leporello to invite the statue of the Commendatore to dinner also. The cowardly, superstitious Leporello is afraid but dares not disobey his master. In horror he notices that the statue nods its head in answer to the invitation. Even Don Juan is not quite himself when, in reply to his repeated invitation, the statue again bows its head.
>
> Act III. In her chamber Donna Anna receives Don Juan, who has now adopted the name of Don Diego. He decides to reveal to her the secret of his real name. But even when she knows that before

her stands the murderer of her husband, Donna Anna is helpless and instead of hatred in her soul there springs the fire of love.

A knock is heard. On the threshold stand the statue of the Commendatore. Don Juan is terrified but pulling himself together greets him courteously and in answer to his guest's request offers his hand. The stone hand seizes Don Juan in a deadly embrace and with a terrible cry the Don is dragged downwards to the nether regions.

(Taken from Pankratova. Op. cit., pp. 38–9).

(32) Aleksey Vasilevich Timofeev (1812–83) was a Romantic poet who acquired popularity in the 1830's. Senkovsky, the editor of the *Biblioteka dlya chteniya*, in which Timofeev's works were largely printed, called him a 'second Byron'. He was responsible for a number of 'Russian songs' and five of his texts were set by Dargomyzhsky.

List of Abbreviations Employed

BAL   M. BALAKIREV. *Russkie narodnye pesni*. Ed. E. V. Gippius. Moscow, 1957.

FOIM   N. FINDEISEN. *Ocherki po istorii russkoi muzykalnoi istorii*. Moscow-Leningrad, 1928–9.

GIRMA I   S. L. GINZBURG. *Istoriya russkoi muzyki v notnikh obraztsakh*. Vol. I, Moscow-Leningrad, 1940.

GIRMA II   S. L. GINZBURG. *Istoriya russkoi muzyki v notnikh obraztsakh*. Vol. II, Moscow-Leningrad, 1949.

KIRM I   Y. KELDYSH. *Istoriya russkoi muzyki*. Vol. I, Moscow-Leningrad, 1948.

LITNAS I   M. I. GLINKA. *Literaturnoe nasledie*. Vol. I, Moscow-Leningrad, 1952.

LITNAS II   M. I. GLINKA. *Literaturnoe nasledie*. Vol. II, Moscow-Leningrad, 1953.

LRMK I   T. LIVANOVA. *Russkaya muzykalnaya kultura XVIII veka*. Vol. I, Moscow, 1952.

LRMK II   T. LIVANOVA. *Russkaya muzykalnaya kultura XVIII veka*. Vol. II, Moscow, 1953.

MOOS I   R.-ALOYS MOOSER. *Annales de la Musique et des Musiciens en Russie au XVIII siècle*. Vol. I, Geneva, 1948.

MOOS II   R.-ALOYS MOOSER. *Annales de la Musique et des Musiciens en Russia au XVIII siècle*. Vol. II, Geneva, 1951.

MOOS III   R.-ALOYS MOOSER. *Annales de la Musique et des Musiciens en Russie au XVIII siècle*. Vol. III, Geneva, 1951.

PIRM I   M. S. PEKELIS. *Istoriya russkoi muzyki*. Vol. I, Moscow-Leningrad, 1940.

R-K   N. A. RIMSKY-KORSAKOV. *Polnoe sobranie sochinenii*. Vol. XLVII, Moscow, 1952.

RODG   A. S. RABINOVICH. *Russkaya opera do Glinki*. Moscow, 1948.

SPV   *Sanktpeterburgskie vedomosti*.

TIRM I   N. TUMANINA. *Istoriya russkoi muzyki*. Vol. I, Moscow, 1957.

TSMB   Gos.-Tsentralnaya muzykalnaya biblioteka pri teatre im. S. M. Kirova, Leningrad.

Selected Bibliography

ABRAHAM, G. *On Russian Music.* London, 1939.

ABRAHAM, G. *Studies in Russian Music.* London, 1936.

AGRENEVA-SLAVYANSKAYA. *Opisanie russkoy krestyanskoi svadby s tekstom i pesnyami.* Vol. I–III, Moscow, Tver and St. Petersburg, 1887–1889.

AFANASEV, A. N. *Poeticheskie vozzreniya Slavyan na prirodu.* 3 vols. Moscow, 1866–9.

ALEKSEEV, A. D. *Russkaya fortepiannaya muzyka.* Moscow, 1963.

ALENDER, I. S. and VERTKOV, K. A. *Atlas muzykalnykh instrumentov narodov SSSR.* Moscow, 1964.

ASAFYEV, B. *Glinka.* Moscow, 1950.

ASAFYEV, B. *Izbrannye trudy.* Vol. I, Moscow, 1952; Vol. II, Moscow, 1953; Vol. III, Moscow, 1954; Vol. IV, Moscow, 1955; Vol. V, Moscow, 1957.

ASAFYEV, B. *Russkaya muzyka ot nachala XIX stoletiya.* Moscow-Leningrad, 1930. (Translated Swan, A. J., *Russian Music from the Beginning of the Nineteenth Century,* Michigan, 1953.)

ASEEV, B. N. *Russkii dramaticheskii teatr XVII–XVIII vekov.* Moscow, 1958.

ASTAKHOVA, A. M. *Ilya Muromets.* Moscow-Leningrad, 1958.

BACHINSKAYA, N. *Narodnye pesni v tvorchestve russkikh kompozitorov.* Moscow, 1962.

BARENBOIM, L. A. and MUZALEVSKY, V. I. *Khrestomatiya po istorii fortepiannoi muzyki v Rossii.* Moscow-Leningrad, 1949.

BERKOV, P. N. *Russkaya komediya i komicheskaya muzyka XVIII veka.* Moscow, 1950.

BERNANDT, G. *Slovar oper vpervye postavlennykh ili izdannykh v dorevolyutsionnoy Rossii i v SSSR/1736–1959.* Moscow, 1962.

BERSHADSKAYA, T. *Osnovye kompozitsionnye zakonomernosti mnogogolosiya russkoi narodnoi pesni.* Moscow, 1959.

BESSARABOFF, N. *Ancient European Musical Instruments.* Harvard University Press, 1941.

BOKSHANINA, E. A. *'Sankt-Peterburgsky Gostiniy Dvor' Matinskovo-Pashkevicha i russkaya opera XVIIIovo veka.* Moscow, 1955.

Bolshaya sovetskaya entsiklopedia. 2nd Ed. Moscow, 1949–58.

BRAZHNIKOV, M. V. *Puti razvitiya i zadachi rasshifrovki znamennovo rospeva XII–XVIII vekov.* Leningrad-Moscow, 1952.

BUGOSLAVSKY, S. E. and SHISHKOV, I. P. *Russkaya narodnaya pesnya.* Moscow, 1936.

BUNT, C. G. E. *Russian Art, from Scyths to Soviets*. London, 1946.
CALVOCORESSI, M. D. *Glinka*. Paris, [no date].
CALVOCORESSI, M. D. *A Survey of Russian Music*. London, 1944.
CALVOCORESSI, M. D. and ABRAHAM, G. *Masters of Russian Music*. New York, 1944.
CHADWICK, N. K. *Russian Heroic Poetry*. Cambridge, 1932.
CHARQUES, R. *A Short History of Russia*. London, 1956.
CHESHIKIN, V. *Istoriya russkoi opery*. St. Petersburg, 1905.
COBBETT's *Cyclopedic Survey of Chamber Music*. 2nd Ed. London, 1963.
COOPER, M. *Russian Opera*, London, 1951.
DANILOV, K. *Drevnye rossiiskie stikhotvoreniya*. Ed. Evgenev and Putilov. Moscow-Leningrad, 1958.
DARGOMYZHSKY, A. S. *Kratkaya avtobiograficheskaya zapiska. Sbornik 'A. S. Dargomyzhsky'*. (1813–1869). *Avtobiografiya. Pisma. Vospominaniya sovremennikov*. St. Petersburg, 1921.
DARGOMYZHSKY, A. S. *Izbrannye pisma*. Ed. Pekelis. Moscow, 1952.
Memoirs of the Princess Dashkov. Trans. Kyril Fitzlyon. London, 1958.
Dnevnik A. V. Khrapovitskovo. 1782–1793. St. Petersburg, 1874.
DOBROKHOTOV, B. A. A. Alyabyev. *Kamerno-instrumentalnoe tvorchestvo*. Moscow-Leningrad, 1948.
DOBROKHOTOV, B. *Aleksandr Alyabyev. Tvorcheskii put*. Moscow, 1966.
DOBROKHOTOV, B. *E. I. Fomin*. Moscow-Leningrad, 1949.
DOBROKHOTOV, B. *A. N. Verstovsky*. Moscow, 1949.
DROZDOV, A. and TROFIMOVA, T. *Russkaya starinnaya fortepiannaya muzyka*. Moscow-Leningrad, 1946.
DRUSKIN, M. *Istoriya i sovremennost*. Leningrad, 1960.
DRUSKIN, M. and KELDYSH, Y. (ed.). *Ocherki po istorii russkoi muzyki 1790–1825*. Leningrad, 1956.
EVSEEV, S. V. *Russkaya narodnaya polifoniya*. Moscow, 1960.
FINDEISEN, N. *A. S. Dargomyzhsky*. Moscow, 1904.
FINDEISEN, N. *Ocherki po istorii russkoi muzykalnoi istorii*. Moscow-Leningrad, 1928–9.
FINDEISEN, N. *Aleksei Nikolaevich Verstovsky*. St. Petersburg, 1890.
FRID, E. L. (ed.). *Russkaya muzykalnaya literatura*. Vol. I, Moscow-Leningrad, 1965.
GARBUZOV, N. A. *Drevnerusskoe narodnoe mnogogolosie*. Moscow-Leningrad, 1948.
GARBUZOV, N. A. *Mnogogolosie russkoi narodnoi pesni*. Moscow-Leningrad, 1939.
GARDNER, VON J. and KOSCHMIEDER, E. *Ein handschriftliches Lehrbuch der altrussischen Neumenschrift*. Monaco, 1963.
GERSTENBERG, I. D. and DITMAR, F. A. *Russkie pesni XVIII veka*. Moscow, 1958.

GINZBURG, S. L. *Istoriya russkoi muzyki v notnykh obraztsakh*. Vol. I, Moscow-Leningrad, 1940; Vol. II, Moscow-Leningrad, 1949.

GINZBURG, S. L. *Istoriya violonchelnovo iskusstva*. Vol. II, Moscow, 1957; Vol. III, Moscow, 1965.

GINZBURG, S. L. *Russkii muzykalnyi teatr, 1700–1835*. Moscow-Leningrad, 1941.

GLINKA, M. I. *Sbornik materialov i statey*. Ed. T. Livanova. Moscow-Leningrad, 1950.

GLINKA, M. I. *Literaturnoe nasledstvo*. Vol. I, Moscow-Leningrad, 1952; Vol. II, Moscow-Leningrad, 1953.

Mikhail Ivanovitch Glinka. Memoirs. Translated R. B. Mudge. University of Oklahoma Press, 1963.

GLINKA, M. I. *Sbornik statey*. Moscow, 1958.

Glinka v vospominaniyakh sovremennikov. Moscow, 1955.

GLINKA, S. N. *Zapiski*. St. Petersburg, 1895.

GLUMOV, A. *Muzyka v russkom dramaticheskom teatre*. Moscow, 1955.

GORDEEVA, E. *Iz istorii russkoi muzykalnoi kritiki XIX veka*. Moscow-Leningrad, 1950.

GOSENPUD, A. *Muzykalniy teatr v Rossii; ot istokov do Glinki*. Leningrad. 1959.

GROUT, D. J. *A Short History of Opera*. 2nd Ed. New York and London 1965.

GURILEV, A. L. *Izbrannye narodnye russkie pesni*. Moscow, 1849.

HAPGOOD, I. F. *The Epic Songs of Russia*. London, 1915.

HARRISON, F. and RIMMER, J. *European Musical Instruments*. London, 1964.

HINRICHS, J. *Entstehung, Fortgang und ietzige Beschaffenheit der russischen Jagdmusik*. St. Petersburg, 1796.

IVANOV, G. K. (ed.) *Russkaya poeziya v otechestvennoi muzyke (do 1917 goda)*. Spravochnik. Vol. I. Moscow, 1966.

IVANOV-BORETSKY, M. V. *Muzykalnoe nasledstvo*. Vol. I. Moscow, 1935.

KANN-NOVIKOVA, E. *M. I. Glinka. Novye materialy i dokumenty*. Vol. I, Moscow-Leningrad, 1950; Vol. II, Moscow, 1951.

KARYSHEV, T. I. (ed.). *Iz istorii russkoi-ukrainskikh muzykalnikh svyazei*. Moscow, 1956.

KASHIN, D. *Russkie narodnye pesni*. Moscow, 1833–4.

KASTALSKY, A. D. *Osobennosti narodno-russkoi muzykalnoi sistemy*. Moscow-Petrograd, 1923.

KELDYSH, G. V. (ed.) *Entsiklopedicheskii muzykalnyi slovar*. Moscow, 1959.

KELDYSH, Y. *Istoriya russkoi muzyki*. Vol. I, Moscow-Leningrad, 1948; Vol. II, Moscow-Leningrad, 1947.

KELDYSH, Y. V. *Russkaya muzyka XVIII veka.* Moscow, 1965.

KHOPROV, T., KRYUKOV, A., and VASILENKO, S. *Ocherki po istorii russkoi muzyki XIX veka.* Leningrad, 1960.

KOLOTILOVA-KOLTSOV. *Pesni severa.* Arkhangelsk, 1947.

KOLPAKOVA, N. P. *Russkaya narodnaya pesnya.* Moscow-Leningrad, 1962.

KREMLËV, Y. *Russkaya mysl o muzyke.* Vol. I: 1825–1860. Leningrad, 1954.

LEHMANN, D. *Russland's Oper u. Singspiel in der zweiten Hälfte des 18 Jahrhunderts.* Leipzig, 1958.

LINËVA, E. *Velikorusskie pesni v narodnoy garmonizatsii.* Vol. I–II, St. Petersburg, 1904; 1909.

LIVANOVA, T. *M. I. Glinka. Sbornik materialov i statei.* Moscow-Leningrad, 1950.

LIVANOVA, T. *Ocherki i materialy po istorii russkoi muzykalnoi kultury.* Moscow, 1938.

LIVANOVA, T. and PROTOPOPOV, V. V. *Opernaya kritika v Rossii.* Vol. I. Part 1. Moscow, 1966.

LIVANOVA, T. *Russkaya muzykalnaya kultura XVIII veka.* Vol. I, Moscow, 1952; Vol. II, Moscow, 1953.

LIVANOVA, T., PEKELIS, and POPOVA. *Ocherki po istorii russkoi muzyki.* Vol. I, Moscow, 1940.

LIVANOVA, T. and PROTOPOPOV, V. *'Glinka'. Tvorcheskii put.* Voll. I and II, Moscow, 1955.

LOEWENBERG, A. *Annals of Opera.* 2nd Ed. Geneva, 1955.

LOPATIN and PROKUNIN. *Sbornik russkikh narodnykh liricheskikh pesen.* 2nd Ed. ed. Belyaev. Moscow, 1956.

LOZANOVA, A. N. (ed.). *Pesni i skazaniya o Razine i Pugachëve.* Academia, 1935.

LVOV-PRACH. *Sobranie narodnykh russkikh pesen.* 5th Ed. ed. Belyaev. Moscow, 1955.

MAROGER, D. (ed.). *The Memoirs of Catherine the Great.* Portsmouth, 1955.

MILIUKOV, P. *Outlines of Russian Culture.* Part III, Philadelphia, 1942.

MIRSKY, D. S. *A History of Russian Literature.* New York, 1927.

MONTAGU-NATHAN, M. *A History of Russian Music.* London, 1914.

ALOYS MOOSER, R. *Annales de la Musique et des Musiciens en Russie au XVIIIe siècle.* Vol. I, Geneva, 1948; Vol. II, Geneva, 1951; Vol. III, Geneva, 1951.

ALOYS MOOSER, R. *Opéras, intermezzos, ballets, cantates, oratorios joués en Russie durant le XVIIIe siècle.* 3e éd. Bale, 1964.

ALOYS MOOSER, R. *Violinistes-compositeurs italiens en Russie au XVIIIe siècle.* Turin–Milan, 1938–50.

ALOYS MOOSER, R. *L'opéra comique français en Russie au XVIIIe siècle.* 2e édition. Genève-Monaco, 1954.

MUZALEVSKY, V. I. *Russkaya fortepiannaya muzyka.* Moscow-Leningrad, 1949.

Muzykalnaya starina. Ed. Findeisen. Vol. I–VI, St. Petersburg, 1903–11.

Muzykalnoe nasledstvo. Vol. II, Part 1. Moscow, 1966.

OBOLENSKY, D. (ed.). *The Penguin Book of Russian Verse.* London, 1962.

ODOEVSKY, V. *Izbrannye trudy.* Moscow, 1951.

OLKHOVSKY, A. *Music Under the Soviets.* London, 1955.

PALCHIKOV, N. E. *Krestyanskie pesni.* Moscow, 1888.

Pamyati Glinki 1857–1957. Issledovaniya i materialy. Moscow, 1958.

PANKRATOVA, V. A. (ed.) *Opernye libretto.* Moscow, 1962.

PEKELIS, M. *Aleksandr Sergeevich Dargomyzhsky i evo okruzhenie.* Vol. I: 1813–1845. Moscow, 1966.

PEKELIS, M. *Dargomyzhsky i narodnaya pesnya.* Moscow-Leningrad, 1951.

PEKELIS, M. *Istoriya russkoi muzyki.* Vol. I, Moscow-Leningrad, 1940; Vol. II, Moscow-Leningrad, 1940.

POPOVA, T. V. *Russkoe narodnoe muzykalnoe tvorchestvo.* Vol. I, Moscow, 1955; Vol. II, Moscow, 1956; Vol. III, Moscow, 1956.

POUGIN, A. *A Short History of Russian Music.* Trans. L. Haward. New York, 1915.

PROKOFEV, V. (ed.). *Muzyka i muzykalnoi byt staroi Rossii.* Leningrad, 1927.

PROTOPOPOV, V. *'Ivan Susanin' Glinki.* Moscow, 1961.

Pushkin. Selected Verse. Translated John Fennell. Penguin, 1964.

RAABEN, L. *Instrumentalnyi ansambl v russkoy muzyke.* Moscow, 1961.

RABINOVICH, A. S. *Izbrannye stati i materialy.* Moscow, 1959.

RABINOVICH, A. S. *Russkaya opera do Glinki.* Moscow, 1948.

RAJECKY, B. (ed.). *Studia Memoriae Belae Bartók Sacra.* London, 1959.

RALSTON, W. R. S. *The Songs of the Russian People as Illustrative of Slavonic Mythology and Russian Social Life.* London, 1872.

RAZUMOVSKY, D. *Tserkovnoe penie v Rossii.* Parts I–III, Moscow, 1867–9.

REESE, G. *Music in the Middle Ages.* New York, 1940.

RICE, T. T. *A Concise History of Russian Art.* London, 1963.

RUBTSOV, F. A. *Osnovy ladovovo stroeniya russkikh narodnykh pesen.* Leningrad, 1964.

Article 'Russland' in *Die Musik in Geschichte und Gegenwart.* Band 11, Bärenreiter Kassel-Basel-London-New York, 1963, Columns 1129–1191.

SEAMAN, G. 'Amateur Music-making in Russia'. *Music and Letters.* Vol. 47, No. 3, July 1966.

SEAMAN, G. 'Evstignei Ipatevich Fomin: 1761–1800', *Monthly Musical Record*. Vol. 88, No. 985. Jan.–Feb. 1958.

SEAMAN, G. 'The Rise of Russian Piano Music'. *The Music Review*. Vol. 27, No. 3, August 1966.

SEAMAN, G. 'The Russian Horn Band'. *Monthly Musical Record*. Vol. 89, No. 993. May–June 1959.

SEAMAN, G. 'Russian Folk-song in the Eighteenth Century'. *Music and Letters*. Vol. 40, No. 3, July 1959.

SEAMAN, G. 'D. S. Bortnyansky (1751–1825)'. *The Music Review*. Vol. XXI, No. 2, May 1960.

SEAMAN, G. 'Verstovsky and *Askold's Tomb*'. *Monthly Musical Record*. Vol. 90, No. 1002. Nov.–Dec. 1960.

SEAMAN, G. 'The National Element in Early Russian Opera, 1779–1800'. *Music and Letters*. Vol. 42, No. 3, July 1961.

SEAMAN, G. 'The Influence of Folk-song on Russian Opera up to and including the Time of Glinka'. Nov. 1961. Thesis deposited in Bodleian Library, Oxford.

SEAMAN, G. Article 'Folk-Music (Russian)' in Supplementary Volume to Fifth Edition of *Grove's Dictionary of Music and Musicians*. London, 1961.

SEAMAN, G. 'Folk-song in Russian Opera of the 18th century'. *The Slavonic and East European Review*. Vol. XLI, No. 96, December 1962.

SEAMAN, G. 'The First Russian Chamber Music'. *The Music Review*. Vol. XXVI, No. 4, November 1965.

SERDYUCHENKO, G. *A. M. Listopadov*. Moscow, 1955.

SEROV, A. N. *Kriticheskie stati*. St. Petersburg, 1895.

SEROV, A. N. *Izbrannye stati*. Vol. I, Moscow, 1950.

SHEIN, P. V. *Materialy dlya izucheniya byta i yazyka russkovo naseleniya Severo-Zapadnovo kraya*. Vol. I, Part II, St. Petersburg, 1890.

SHEIN, P. V. *Velikoruss v svoikh pesnyakh, obryadakh, obychayakh*. Vol. II, St. Petersburg, 1900.

SHISHOV, I. and BUGOSLAVSKY, S. (ed.). *Russkaya narodnaya pesnya*. Moscow, 1936.

SHLIFSHTEIN, S. A. *Dargomyzhsky*. Moscow, 1960.

SHTEYNPRESS, B. *A. A. Alyabyev v izgnanii*. Moscow, 1959.

SIMONI, P. K. *Kamer-guslist V. F. Trutovsky i izdanny im pervy russkii notny pesennik*. Moscow, 1905.

SKREBKOV, S. S. 'Bortnyansky—master russkovo khorovovo kontserta'. (*Ezhegodnik instituta istorii iskusstv AN SSSR*.) Vol. II, Moscow, 1948.

SLONIM, M. *Russian Theater, from the Empire to the Soviets*. Cleveland, 1961.

SOLOVEYTCHIK, G. *Potemkin; a picture of Catherine's Russia*. London, 1949.

Sovremennik. No. 2, May 1837.

STASOV, V. V. *Izbrannye sochineniya.* Moscow-Leningrad, 1937.

STASOV, V. V. *Mikhail Ivanovich Glinka.* Moscow, 1953.

ŠTĚPÁNEK, V. and KARÁSEK, B. *An Outline of Czech and Slovak Music.* Part I. Prague, 1964.

STEVENS, D. (ed.). *A History of Song.* London, 1960.

STIEF, C. *Studies in the Russian Historical Song.* København, 1953.

STOLPYANSKY, P. N. *Staryi Peterburg. Muzyka i muzitsirovanie v starom Peterburge.* Leningrad, 1925.

SWAN, A. J. 'The Nature of the Russian Folk-Song'. *The Musical Quarterly.* Vol. XXIX, No. 4. October 1943.

SWAN, A. J. 'The Znamenny Chant of the Russian Church'. Parts 1, 2, 3. *The Musical Quarterly.* Vol. XXVI, 1940.

TERESHCHENKO, T. *Byt russkovo naroda.* 1848.

The New Oxford History of Music. Vol. II, London, 1954.

TROFIMOVA, T. and DROZDOV, A. (ed.) *Nachalo russkovo romansa.* Moscow, 1936.

TRUTOVSKY, V. F. *Sobranie russkikh prostykh pesen s notami.* New Ed. ed. Belyaev. Moscow, 1953.

TSUKKERMAN, V. *'Kamarinskaya' Glinki i eë traditsii v russkoi muzyke.* Moscow, 1957.

TSULUKIDZE, A. *Gruzinskaya muzykalnaya kultura.* Moscow, 1957.

TUMANINA, N. *Istoriya russkoi muzyki.* Vol. I, Moscow, 1957; Vol. II, Moscow, 1958.

USPENSKAYA, S. L. *Literatura o muzyke, 1948–1953; bibliograficheskii ukazatel.* Moscow, 1955.

USPENSKII, N. D. *Drevnerusskoe pevcheskoe iskusstvo.* Moscow, 1965.

USPENSKII, V. *Mikhail Ivanovich Glinka. 1804–57.* Leningrad, 1950.

VARLAMOV, A. E. *Russkii pevets.* St. Petersburg, 1846.

VARNEKE, B. V. *History of the Russian Theatre, seventeenth through nineteenth century.* Original translation by Boris Brasol, revised and edited by Belle Martin. New York, 1951.

VASINA-GROSSMAN. *Russkii klassicheskii romans XIX veka.* Moscow, 1945.

VERNADSKY, G. *A History of Russia.* Yale University Press, 1961.

VERNADSKY, G. *The Origins of Russia.* Oxford, 1959.

VERTKOV, K. A. *Russkaya rogovaya muzyka.* Leningrad, 1948.

VOLMAN, B. *Gitara v Rossii.* Leningrad, 1961.

VOLMAN, B. *Russkie pechatnye noty XVIII v.* Leningrad, 1957.

VVEDENSKAVO, I. (ed.). *Sochineniya Imperatrisy Ekateriny II.* St. Petersburg, 1893.

YAMPOLSKII, I. *Russkoe skripichnoe iskusstvo. Ocherki i materialy.* Vol. I, Moscow, 1951.

List of Operas Mentioned in Text

INTRODUCTION

Reference has been made throughout Vol. I to theatres in St. Petersburg and Moscow in the eighteenth and nineteenth centuries. Since these are sometimes referred to under more than one name by Russian and Western commentators, it is hoped that the following may serve by way of clarification.

Musical-theatrical life in Moscow is generally regarded as commencing in 1776 with the activities of the Englishman, Maddox, who staged numerous performances at Count Vorontsov's house in the Znamenka. When the Znamenka (or Russian Theatre as it was otherwise called) was burnt down in 1780, the theatre was transferred to a specially constructed stone (*kamenny*) building on the Petrovka. These performances are thus referred to as taking place in the *Kamenny Theatre*, the *Petrovsky Theatre*, or the *Maddox Theatre*. In 1805, however, this theatre, too, was burnt down, twenty years later the theatre now known as the Bolshoy being erected on the same site. This building was likewise damaged by fire in 1853, but in 1856 it was rebuilt by A. K. Cavos.

In St. Petersburg the main cultural activities in the eighteenth century revolved round the Court, though a part was played by establishments such as Knipper's Free Theatre. An interesting factor is that in 1777 Catherine II had expressed the wish not to be detained more than an hour and a half at the Court Theatre. This, of course, necessitated some abbreviation of foreign productions and explains why on occasion certain Italian and German operas appear to consist of only two acts. From 1783 operatic and ballet performances were held in the Kamenny Theatre (otherwise known as the Bolshoy). A new Bolshoy was opened in 1836. From 1855 some Russian operas were performed in the Theatre Circus, till this was reconstructed to form in 1860 the Marynsky Theatre (the present Kirov Theatre opposite the Leningrad Conservatory). The Aleksandrinsky Theatre was opened in 1832.

LIST OF OPERAS MENTIONED IN TEXT

(Comprising eighteenth- and early nineteenth-century Russian operas, operas by foreign composers written in Russia, and some performances of West European operas in Russia either in the original language or in translation.)

1. *Alcide. Dramma per musica* in 3 Acts with choruses and recitatives. Composer—D. S. Bortnyansky. Libretto—P. Metastasio. Première at Venice in 1778. [Russian performance ?]

2. *Amerikantsy* (The Americans). Comic opera in 2 Acts, 3 scenes with choruses and ballets. Composer—E. I. Fomin. Libretto—I. A. Krylov arranged by A. I. Klushin. Composed 1788. Première on 8 February 1800 in St. Petersburg in the Kamenny Theatre. Score—TSMB. Vocal score published Jurgenson, Moscow, 1895. Copy in Musical Library of University of Southern California.

3. *Ammalat-Bek.* Opera in 5 Acts. Composer—A. A. Alyabyev. Libretto—A. F. Veltman after story by A. A. Bestuzhev-Marlinsky. Composed 1842–7. Only fragments of score and sketches preserved, most of which may be found in Fond No. 40 A. A. Alyabyev. Gos. Tsent. muzei muzykalnoi kultury im. M. I. Glinki, Moscow. (For precise details see B. Dobrokhotov. *Aleksandr Alyabyev.* Moscow, 1966, p. 295.) TSMB has scores of other operas belonging entirely or partially to Alyabyev: *Igrushka [Zabavy] kalifa ili shutki na odni sutki; Lunnaya noch; Molodaya mat i lyubovnik v 48 let ili Domashny spektakl.*

4. *Anyuta.* Comic opera in 1 Act. Composer—unknown. Libretto—M. V. Popov. Première on 26 August 1772 at Tsarskoe Selo.

5. *Armida e Rinaldo. Opera seria* in 2 Acts. Composer—G. Sarti. Libretto—M. Coltellini. Performed in Italian at St. Petersburg most likely for the opening of the Hermitage Theatre, 15 January 1786.

6. *Artaserse. Opera seria* in 3 Acts. Composer—F. Araja. Libretto—P. Metastasio (Russian translation—P. M. Medvedyev; German translation—J. von Stählin). Première in Italian on 29 January 1738 in St. Petersburg Court Theatre (Winter Palace).

7. *Askoldova mogila.* (Askold's Tomb). Romantic opera in 4 Acts. Composer—A. N. Verstovsky. Libretto—M. N. Zagoskin. Première on 16 September 1835 in Moscow Bolshoy Theatre. The score of this and approximately eight other operas by Verstovsky are preserved in TSMB. The work is available in modern reprint. There is a score in the Music Library of the University of Southern California.

8. *Baba-Yaga.* Comic opera in 3 Acts with ballet. Composer—M. Stab[h]inger. Libretto—D. P. Gorchakov. Mooser [*Opéras, Intermezzos, Ballets* . . . Bale, 1964] gives the première as 2 December 1786, Moscow. Bernandt, however [*Slovar oper* . . .

x

Moscow, 1962] gives the première as 1784 in Kaluga 'in the barn of Shemyakin the merchant on the Zhirovka opposite the ale-house', and the Moscow première as 2 December 1786 at the Petrovsky Theatre. Score in TSMB.

9. *Babushkini popugay* (Grandma's Parrot). Opera-vaudeville in 1 Act. Composer—A. N. Verstovsky. Libretto—N. I. Khmelnitsky (translated from the French). Première on 28 July 1819 in St. Petersburg Free Theatre.

10. *Barbiere di Siviglia ovvero La precauzione inutile* (The Barber of Seville or The useless Precaution). *Dramma giocoso* in 2 Acts. Composer—G. Paisiello. Libretto—G. Petrosellini after Beaumarchais (Russian translation—I. Vien). Première in Italian on 15 September 1782 in St. Petersburg Court Theatre. Première in Russian on 16 August 1790 in St. Petersburg Derevyanny Theatre. Première in French (translated—N. E. Framery) at Gatchina 1797. Vocal score published Ricordi (no date).

11. *Boesla[e]vich* (see *Novgorodskiy Bogatyr Boeslavich*).

12. *Bûcheron, Le, ou Les trois souhaits. Comédie mêlée d'Ariettes* in 1 Act. Composer—F. A. D. Philidor. Libretto—J. F. Guichard (Russian translation—?). Première in Russian at the Moscow Vauxhall on 4 (or 11) July 1787.

13. *Calandro. Commedia per musica* in 3 Acts. [First opera to be given in Russia.] Composer—G. A. Ristori. Libretto—S. B. Pallavicini. Première in Moscow Imperial Palace on 30 November 1731.

14. *Cephalus and Procris* (see *Tsefal i Prokris*).

15. *Clemenza di Tito, La. Dramma per musica* in 3 Acts. Composer—A. Hasse (with additional music by L. Madonis and D. dall'Oglio). Libretto—P. Metastasio (German and French [?] translations by J. von Stählin; Russian translation—I. Merkuryev). Performed in Italian at the Imperial Theatre, Moscow, on 29 May 1742 (for the Coronation of Empress Elizabeth).

16. *Creonte. Dramma per musica* in 2 Acts. Composer—D. S. Bortnyansky. Libretto—M. Coltellini. Première at the Teatro S. Benedetto, Venice, on 26 November (New Style) 1776. Russian performance [?].

17. *Demofoonte. Opera seria* in 3 Acts. Composer—M. S. Berezovsky. Libretto—P. Metastasio. Première in Livorno, Italy, 1773 during Carnaval period. Russian performance [?].

18. *Derevenskoy vorozheya* (The Village Fortune-teller). Russian *intermezzo* in 1 Act. Composer—J. Kerzelli. Libretto—V. I.

Maykov (written in imitation of J. J. Rousseau's *Le devin du village*). Performed in Russian at Moscow *c.* 1777. Fragments of the score with text published in Moscow in 1778.

19. *Derevenskiy prazdnik, ili Uvenchannaya dobroditel* (The Village Holiday or Virtue Rewarded). Pastoral drama with music in 2 Acts. Composer—M. Kerzelli. Libretto—V. I. Maykov. Première *c.* 1777 in Russian at the Znamenka Theatre, Moscow.

20. *Der Freischütz* (see *Freischütz, Der*).

21. *Deux avares, Les. Comédie mêlée d'Ariettes* in 2 Acts. Composer— A. E. M. Grétry. Libretto—C. G. F. de Falbaire (Russian translation—V. Voroblevsky; Z. Kryzhanovsky; F. Gench). Given in Russian at Moscow on 22 February 1783 (or perhaps earlier at Sheremetev's Theatre, Kuskovo); and in French at the Kamenny Theatre, St. Petersburg, 7 November 1800.

22. *Devichnik* (*Devishnik, ili filatkina svadba*) (Devichnik, or Filatkin's Marriage). Comic opera in 1 Act with choruses and dances. (Sequel to *Yam* [*ili Pochtovaya stantsiya*], and *Posidelki.*) Composer—A. N. Titov. Libretto—A. Y. Knyazhnin. Composed—1808. Première on 13 April 1809 in St. Petersburg. The score of this and at least twelve other identifiable operas of A. N. Titov are preserved in TSMB.

23. *Devin du village, Le. Intermède* in 1 Act. Words and music by J. J. Rousseau (Russian translation by . . . [V. I. Maykov?]). Possibly given in Russian by pupils of the Moscow *Vospitatelnyi dom* (orphanage, *pietà*) in 1778; and perhaps at the Hermitage, St. Petersburg in 1797.

24. *Didone abbandonata. Dramma per musica* in 3 Acts. Composer— B. Galuppi. Libretto—P. Metastasio (French and German translations by [?]). Given in Italian at the Court Theatre, St. Petersburg, 3 March 1766.

25. *Dobrye soldaty* (The Good Soldiers). Comic opera in 3 Acts. Composer—H.-F. Raupach. Libretto—M. M. Kheraskov. Written in 1799. Première on 26 February 1799 by pupils of the Moscow *Vospitatelnyi dom*. St. Petersburg première at Knipper's 'Free Theatre', 17 February 1780. Score in TSMB.

26. *Donauweibchen, Das* (see *Lesta, dneprovskaya rusalka*).

27. *Don Giovanni, dramma giocoso* in 2 Acts. Composer—Mozart. Libretto—L. da Ponte. Given in German at the German Theatre, St. Petersburg, between 1793-5.

28. *Esmeralda.* Opera in 4 Acts and 7 scenes. Composer—A. S. Dargomyzhsky. Libretto adapted by the composer from Hugo's novel *Notre-Dame de Paris*. Written 1838–41. Première on

5 December 1847 in Bolshoy Theatre, Moscow. St. Petersburg première on 29 November 1851 in the Aleksandrinsky Theatre.

29. *Faucon, Le.* French *opéra-comique* in 3 Acts. Composer—D. S. Bortnyansky. Libretto—F.-H. Lafermière adapted from Boccaccio's *Decameron.* Première in French at the Palace Theatre, Gatchina, on 11 October 1786. There is a score in the British Museum.

30. *Fedul s detmi* (Fedul and the Children). Comic opera in 1 Act with choruses and dances. Composer—Martín y Soler and V. A. Pashkevich. Libretto—Catherine II and A. V. Khrapovitsky. Première in Russian at the Hermitage Theatre, St. Petersburg, on 16 January 1791. Score in TSMB. A copy of the Jurgenson score published in 1895 is preserved in the Music Library of the University of Southern California.

31. *Fevey.* Comic opera with choruses and ballets. Composer— V. A. Pashkevich. Libretto—Catherine II. Première in Russian at the Kamenny Theatre, St. Petersburg, on 19 April 1786; at the Hermitage Theatre, 22 April 1786. Vocal score published in 1789. MS score in TSMB. Copy of Jurgenson score published 1895 in Music Library of University of Southern California.

32. *Fils-rival, Le, ou La Moderne Stratonice.* French *opéra comique* in 3 Acts. Composer—D. S. Bortnyansky. Libretto—F.-H. Lafermière. Première at Palace Theatre, Pavlovsk, on 11 October 1787. There is a score in the British Museum.

33. *Finiks* (The Phoenix). Russian 'drama with songs' in 3 Acts. Composer M. or I. Kerzelli [?]. Libretto—N. P. Nikolev. Written in 1779. Première in Russian in Moscow [?] 1799[?].

34. *Finto Nino, (Il), ovvero La Semiramide riconosciuta. Dramma per musica* in 3 Acts with ballets. Composer—F. Araja. Librettist— P. Metastasio (Russian translation by P. M. Medvedev; German translation by J. von Stählin). Première in Italian on 29 January 1737 at the Theatre of the Winter Palace, St. Petersburg.

35. *Forza dell'amore e dell'odio, (La). Dramma per musica* in 3 Acts. Composer—F. Araja. Libretto—'Chevalier F. P.' [Francesco Prata] (Russian translation by J. von Stählin; French translation by . . .?). Première in 1734 in Milan. Russian première on 29 January 1736 in the new Imperial Theatre, St. Petersburg. [It is *not* the first opera to be given in Russia (see *Calandro*).]

36. *Freischütz, Der.* Composer—Weber. Libretto—F. Kind. Russian première at St. Petersburg in 1824.

37. *Gore-bogatyr Kosometovich* (Kosometovich, the Woeful Knight). Russian comic opera in 5 Acts. Composer—Martín y Soler. Libretto—Catherine II and A. V. Khrapovitsky. Première on 29 January 1789 in the Hermitage Theatre, St. Petersburg. Vocal score published in St. Petersburg 1789. MS score in TSMB.

38. *Gromoboy*. Grand fantastic opera in 4 Acts, 5 scenes. Composer —A. N. Verstovsky. Libretto—D. T. Lensky (after V. A. Zhukovsky). Première on 24 January 1857 in Moscow Bolshoy. Score in TSMB. Vocal score published Moscow, 1857.

39. *Gypsies, The* (see 101).

40. *Ifigenia in Tauride. Dramma per musica* in 3 Acts. Composer— B. Galuppi. Libretto—M. Coltellini (with Russian, French and German translations). Première in Italian on 21 April 1768 in Hermitage Theatre, St. Petersburg.

41. *Ilya Bogatyr*. Magic opera in 4 Acts with choruses and ballets. Composer—C. A. Cavos. Libretto—I. A. Krylov. Première on 31 December 1806 in Court Theatre, St. Petersburg. Score in TSMB.

42. *Iphigénie en Tauride. Tragédie-opéra* in 4 Acts. Composer— C. W. Gluck. Libretto—N. F. Guillard (with Russian translation by . . .?). Performed in Russian at the Sheremetev Theatre, Kuskovo, after 1786.

43. *Ivan Susanin*. National opera (*narodnaya opera*) in 2 Acts with choruses. Composer—C. A. Cavos. Libretto—A. A. Shakhovskoy. Première in Russian on 2 January 1822 in Moscow at the theatre on the Mokhovoy. Score in TSMB.

44. *Ivan Tsarevich* (see *Khrabryi i smelyi vityaz Akhrideich*).

45. *Kak pozhivësh, tak i proslivësh* (As you live, so are you judged). Russian comic opera in 3 Acts. (Second version of *Sanktpeterburgskiy gostinny dvor*, *q.v.*) Words and music by M. Matinsky and V. A. Pashkevich. Given in Russian at the Hermitage Theatre, St. Petersburg, on 2 February 1792. Score in TSMB.

46. *Kamenny gost* (The Stone Guest). Russian opera in 3 Acts, 4 scenes. Composer—A. S. Dargomyzhsky. Libretto taken almost *verbatim* from Pushkin. Written 1866-9. Completed by Cui and orchestrated by Rimsky-Korsakov. Première on 16 February 1872 at the Marynsky Theatre, St. Petersburg. Vocal score published by Bessel, St. Petersburg, 1872. A score published in 1932 may be found in the Music Library of the University of Southern California.

47. *Karantin* (Quarantine). Opera-vaudeville in 1 Act. Composer—

A. N. Verstovsky. Libretto—N.I. Khmelnitsky. Première on 26 July 1820 in St. Petersburg.

48. *Kazak stikhotvorets* (The Cossack Poet). Anecdotal opera-vaudeville in 1 Act. Composer—C. A. Cavos. Libretto—A. A. Shakhovskoy. Première on 15 May 1812 in the New Theatre, St. Petersburg, with the aid of the students of the Theatrical School. Score in TSMB.

49. *Khrabry i smelyi vityaz Akhrideich* (The Brave and Bold Knight Akhrideich). Comic opera in 5 Acts with choruses and ballets. Composer—E. Vančura. Libretto—Catherine II and A. V. Khrapovitsky. Première in Russian at the Hermitage Theatre, St. Petersburg, on 23 September 1787. [Given under the title *Ivan Tsarevich* at its performance on 15 January 1820 in Moscow.] Score in TSMB.

50. *Knyaz nevidimka, ili Licharda Volshebnik* (The Invisible Prince, or Richard the Magician). Comic opera in 4 Acts 'with a grand performance, embellished with pantomimes, military evolutions, battles, with 17 transformations'. Composer—C. A. Cavos. Libretto—E. Lifanov. Première in Russian on 5 May 1805 in the Court Russian Theatre (in 5 Acts). Score in TSMB.

51. *Koldun, vorozheya i svakha* (Magician, Fortune-teller and Match-maker). Comic opera in 3 Acts. Composer—E. I. Fomin. Libretto—I. Yukin. Première in Russian in 1791 (or perhaps 1789 in St. Petersburg).

52. *Korol na okhote* (The King at the Chase). Comic opera in 3 Acts. Composer—I. Kerzelli. Libretto—V. Levshin (perhaps borrowed from Monsigny's *Le Roi et le Fermier* or from Goldini's *Il re alla caccia*). Première in Russian in . . . (Moscow?) *c.* 1793–4.

53. *Lesta, dneprovskaya rusalka.* This consists of five different works, which may be enumerated as follows:

   (i) *Das Donauweibchen. Singspiel* by F. Kauer performed in Vienna *c.* 1750. This was followed by a second and third part with music by Kauer and Hensler, which were performed in St. Petersburg in the German language.

   (ii) First part. *Rusalka.* Magic-comic opera in Russian by F. Kauer in 3 Acts with additions (2 numbers) by S. I. Davydov. Libretto by K. F. Hensler, freely adapted from the German by N. S. Krasnopolsky. Première in Russian on 26 October 1803 in the Bolshoy Theatre, St. Petersburg. Score in TSMB.

   (iii) Second part. *Dneprovskaya rusalka.* Magic-comic opera in

Russian by F. Kauer in 3 Acts, with additional numbers by C. A. Cavos. Libretto—Krasnopolsky (adapted from the German). Première on 5 May 1804 in the Bolshoy Theatre, St. Petersburg. Score in TSMB.

(iv) Third Part. *Lesta, Dneprovskaya rusalka.* Magic-comic opera, with music by S. I. Davydov in 3 Acts. Libretto by N. S. Krasnopolsky (adapted from the German). Première on 25 October 1805 in the Bolshoy Theatre, St. Petersburg.

(v) Fourth part. *Rusalka.* Magic-comic opera by S. I. Davydov in 3 Acts 'with choruses, ballets and transformations belonging to it'. Libretto— A. A. Shakhovskoy. Première some time between 10 September and 31 December 1807 in the Bolshoy Theatre, St. Petersburg. Vocal score, St. Petersburg (no date). Score in TSMB.

54. *Love in a Village.* English comic opera in 3 Acts. Music arranged by T. A. Arne from various sources including popular airs. Libretto by I. Bickerstaffe. Given in English at the English Theatre, St. Petersburg, 28 April 1772.

55. *Lunnaya noch, ili domovye* (Moonlit Night, or the Domovye). Comic opera in 2 Acts with choruses. Composer—A. A. Alyabyev. Libretto—P. A. Mukhanov and P. N. Arapov on a subject borrowed from the French. Written 1821–2. Première, first intended for 19 July 1822, took place on 7 June 1823 in the Bolshoy Theatre, St. Petersburg. Score in TSMB.

56. *Lyubovnik—koldun* (The Lover-magician). Comic opera in 1 Act. Composer—M. Kerzelli (with music arranged from Russian folk-songs). Libretto—N. Nikolev. Première in Russian in Moscow *c.* 1777.

57. *Maslenitsa.* Opera by A. N. Titov. Performed in 1813 [sequel to *Starinnye svyatki*].

58. *Matrimonio segreto (Il).* Dramma giocoso in 2 Acts. Composer— D. Cimarosa. Libretto—G. Bertati. Given in Italian at St. Petersburg in 1794 or 9 February 1795.

59. *Melnik koldun, obmanshchik i svat* (The Miller-magician, Deceiver and Matchmaker). Comic opera in 3 Acts. Composed in 1778. Music arranged initially by M. M. Sokolovsky from Russian folk-songs. Music revised by Fomin at a later date. Libretto— A. O. Ablesimov. Première in Russian at the Znamenka Theatre, Moscow, 20 January 1779.

60. *Mnimye vdovtsy* (The Mock Widowers). Russian opera in 3 Acts. Composer—I. Kerzelli. Libretto—V. A. Levshin (translated from the German?). Première in 1794 in Moscow.

61. *Nachalnoe upravlenie Olega* (The Early Reign of Oleg). Russian historical spectacle, 'in imitation of Shakespeare, without observing the customary theatrical laws', in 5 Acts. Music by C. Canobbio, V. A. Pashkevich and G. Sarti. Libretto— Catherine II. Première in Russian at the Hermitage Theatre, St. Petersburg, 15 October 1790 (performance 'incognito') and 22 October (official performance). Public première at Kamenny Theatre, St. Petersburg, 27 October. Orchestral score—St. Petersburg, 1791; Vocal score—Jurgenson, Moscow, 1896; Copies in British Museum; Paris Conservatoire; and Music Library of University of Southern California.

62. *Neschastye ot karety* (The Misfortunes of Having a Carriage). Comic opera in 2 Acts. Composer—V. A. Pashkevich. Libretto—Knyazhnin. Première in Russian at the Court Theatre, St. Petersburg, on 7 November 1779. Score in TSMB.

63. *Nevesta pod fatoyu, ili meshchanskaya svadba* (The Bride under the Veil or the Bourgeois Wedding). Comic opera in 3 Acts 'without observation of the theatrical and poetic rules'. Music by . . . (Fomin?). Libretto . . . (?). Performed 1789(?) . . . in Moscow(?).

64. *Novgorodskiy Bogatyr Boeslavich* (Boeslavich, the Novgorod Bogatyr). Russian comic opera in 5 Acts. Composer—E. I. Fomin. Libretto—Catherine II 'compiled from fairy-tales, Russian songs and other compositions'. Written 1786. Première in Russian at the Hermitage Theatre, St. Petersburg, 27 November 1786. Score in TSMB.

65. *Novoe semeystvo* (The New Family). Comic opera in 1 Act. Composer—Freulich. Libretto—S. K. Vyazmitinov. Première in the private theatre of Count Z. G. Chernyshev at Yaropolsk *c.* 1781. St. Petersburg première 1808. Score in TSMB.

66. *Opekun-professor ili lyubov khitree krasnorechiya* (The Guardian Professor, or Love is more cunning than Eloquence). Comic opera in 1 Act. Composer . . . (?) Libretto—N. P. Nikolev. Première in Russian on 29 June (or 4 December) 1784 in the Petrovsky Theatre, Moscow.

67. *Orfey i Evredika* (Orpheus and Eurydice). Russian melodrama. Composer—E. I. Fomin. Libretto—Knyazhnin. Première in Russian at St. Petersburg perhaps in 1791, but more probably in 1792.

68. *Padlock, The.* English comic opera in 2 Acts. Composer— C. Dibdin. Libretto—I. Bickerstaffe. Given in English at the English Theatre at St. Petersburg on 6 December 1771 (perhaps 10 November).

69. *Pan Twardowski*. Romantic magic opera in 3 Acts, 8 scenes with choruses and dances. Composer—A. N. Verstovsky. Libretto—M. N. Zagoskin. Première in Russian 24 May 1828 in Moscow Bolshoy Theatre. Score in TSMB.

70. *Pererozhdenie* (The Regeneration). Comic opera in 1 Act. Composer or arranger—D. Zorin. Librettist—? Given on 8 January 1777 in the Moscow Russian Theatre (Znamenka Theatre). However, whether this is the same as the opera of the same title given in St. Petersburg in 1779 (?) is not clear.

71. *Pesnolyubie* (Melomania). Comic opera in 3 Acts. Composer— Martín y Soler. Libretto—A. Khrapovitsky. Given in Russian on 7 January 1790 in the Hermitage Theatre, St. Petersburg. A vocal score arranged by Prach was published in St. Petersburg in 1790.

72. *Prikashchik* (The Clerk). Russian 'bagatelle dramatique', *mêlée d'Ariettes* in 1 Act. Composer—F. J. Darcis. Libretto— N. Nikolev. Première at the Free Theatre, Moscow, in July 1778.

73. *Quinto Fabio*. *Dramma per musica* in 3 Acts. Composer—D. S. Bortnyansky. Libretto—A. Zeno. Given at the Court Theatre, Modena, Italy, 26 December (New Style) 1778.

74. *Rogdana*. Composer—Dargomyzhsky. Selections from this opera were published by Bessel, St. Petersburg, 1875. A copy is in the Music Library of the University of Southern California.

75. *Rozana i Lyubim*. Russian 'drama with songs' in 4 Acts. Composer—M. Kerzelli. Libretto—N. Nikolev. Première in Russian at the Znamenka Theatre, Moscow, 1778. St. Petersburg première at Knipper's Free Theatre on 6 December 1780. Score in TSMB.

76. *Rusalka*. Russian opera in 4 Acts. Composer—Dargomyzhsky. Libretto arranged from Pushkin by the composer. Written 1848–55. Première on 4 May 1856 in St. Petersburg in the Theatre-circus. Vocal score published—F. Stellovsky, St. Petersburg. 1851–8.

77. *Ruslan i Lyudmila*. Magic opera in 5 Acts with choruses and dances. Composer—M. I. Glinka. Libretto—V. F. Shirkov and others after the poem of Pushkin. Written 1837–42. Première on 27 November 1842 in the Bolshoy Theatre, St. Petersburg. Score ed. N. A. Rimsky-Korsakov, M. A. Balakirev and A. K. Lyadov, St. Petersburg, 1878.

78. *Russkiy muzhichok i frantsuzskie marodery* (The Russian Peasant and the French Marauders) or *Starosta Boris* (Boris the Head-

man). Grand comic opera in 3 Acts. Composer—A. F. Lvov. Libretto—N. I. Kulikov. Première on 19 April 1854, St. Petersburg, in the Aleksandrinsky Theatre. Vocal score published by M. I. Bernard, St. Petersburg, 1854, under the title: *Russkiy muzhichok i frantsuzskie marodery (epizod iz voyny 1812g)*.

79. *Sanktpeterburgskiy gostinny dvor* (The St. Petersburg Bazaar). Comic opera in 3 Acts. Words and music by M. Matinsky. Première in Russian on 26 December 1779 in St. Petersburg at Knipper's Free Theatre. Score in TSMB. [Edited by V. A. Pashkevich and performed subsequently under the title *Kak pozhivёsh, tak i proslivёsh*.]

80. *Sbitenshchik* (The Sbiten-seller). Comic opera in 3 Acts. Composer—A. Bullandt. Libretto—Y. B. Knyazhnin. Première in Russian at the Court Theatre, St. Petersburg, in 1783 or 1784 (perhaps at the Petrovsky Theatre, Moscow, 2 June 1784). Score in TSMB.

81. *Schastlivaya Tonya* (Lucky Tonya). Comic opera in 4 Acts. Composer—Stabinger (Stabhinger). Libretto—Prince D. P. Gorchakov. Première on 14 January 1786 in the Petrovsky Theatre, Moscow. Score in TSMB.

82. *Skupoy* (The Miser). Comic opera in 1 Act. Composer—V. A. Pashkevich. Libretto—Y. B. Knyazhnin. Subject borrowed from Molière's *L'Avare*. Given in Russian at St. Petersburg (or at the Moscow Vauxhall) in 1782 (or 1783). Score in TSMB.

83. *Son nayavu ili churova dolina* (A Day Dream or Churov's Valley). Magic opera in 3 Acts, 6 scenes with transformations, choruses and ballets. Composer—A. N. Verstovsky. Libretto—A. A. Shakhovskoy. Première in Russian on 28 November 1844 in the Bolshoy Theatre, Moscow. Score in TSMB.

84. *Sorochinskaya yarmarka* (Sorochintsy Fair) see Volume II.

85. *Starinnye svyatki* (The Old Yule-Tide). Opera in 3 Acts with choruses and dances. Composer—F. X. Blýma. Libretto—A. F. Malinovsky. Written in 1798. Première on 3 February 1800 in the private theatre of Pashkov, Moscow. St. Petersburg première on 13 January 1813. Score in TSMB.

86. *Svadba [Gospodina] Voldyreva* (The Marriage of [Mr.] Voldyrev). Comic opera in 1 Act. Composer—M. Kerzelli. Libretto—V. Levshin. Performed in Moscow (?) in 1793 or 1794. Score in TSMB.

87. *Svoya nosha ne tyanet* (A Burden of one's own choice is not felt). Comic opera in 2 Acts. Composer—I. F. Kerzelli. Libretto—V. Levshin. Première (1794)(?) in Moscow (?).

88. *Tochilshchik* (The Knife-grinder). Comic opera in 2 Acts. Composer . . . (?). Libretto—N. Nikolev. Première on 27 April (?) 1783 at the Petrovsky Theatre, Moscow.

89. *Torzhestvo Vakkha* (The Triumph of Bacchus). Lyrical ballet-opera in 2 Acts. Music and words by A. S. Dargomyzhsky (after the poem of Pushkin). Written 1848 (originally, in 1843–6, in the form of a cantata: première on 22 March 1846 in the St. Petersburg Bolshoy Theatre). Operatic première on 11 January 1867 in the Bolshoy Theatre, Moscow. Vocal score published—M. Bernard, St. Petersburg, 1867.

90. *Toska po rodine* (Longing for one's Native Land). Comic opera in 3 Acts with a prologue. Composer—A. N. Verstovsky. Libretto—M. N. Zagoskin after his own novel. Première on 21 August 1839 in Moscow Bolshoy Theatre. Score in TSMB.

91. *Tsefal i Prokris* (Cephalus and Procris). Opera in 3 Acts. Composer—F. Araja. Libretto—A. Sumarokov (after Ovid's *Metamorphoses*) (French translation by Henniger). [The first opera, chronologically speaking, to be composed to an original Russian text and to be sung in Russian.] Given in Russian at the Court Theatre, St. Petersburg, 27 February 1755. Score in TSMB.

92. *Una cosa rara. Dramma giocoso* in 2 Acts. Composer—Martín y Soler. Libretto—L. da Ponte (Russian translation I. Dmitrevsky). Given in St. Petersburg in Italian at the Hermitage Theatre in October 1788; in Russian at the Kamenny Theatre on 1 June 1789.

93. *Undina*. Romantic opera in 3 Acts with dances. Composer—A. F. Lvov. Libretto—V. A. Sollogub after de la Motte-Fouqué in verse translation of V. A. Zhukovsky. Première on 8 September 1848 in St. Petersburg Bolshoy Theatre.

94. *Vadim, ili probuzhdenie dvenadtsati spyashchikh dev* (Vadim, or the Awakening of the Twelve Sleeping Maidens). Magic-Romantic opera in 3 Acts with a prologue. Composer—A. N. Verstovsky. Libretto—S. P. Shevirëv and others. Première on 28 November 1832 in the Moscow Bolshoy Theatre. Score in TSMB.

95. *Vrazhya sila* (see Vol. II).

96. *Yamshchiki na podstave* (The Post-drivers). Opera in 1 Act. Composer—E. I. Fomin. Libretto—N. A. Lvov. Première in Russian in St. Petersburg on 2 January 1788. Score in TSMB.

97. *Zaporozhets za Dunaem* (see Vol. II).

98. *Zauberflöte, Die.* German opera in 2 Acts. Composer—W. A. Mozart. Libretto—J. E. Schikaneder (Russian translation . . . ?). Given in German at the German Theatre, St. Peters-

burg, 1793 (date not absolutely certain); in Russian at the Kamenny Theatre, St. Petersburg, in 1794; and at the Petrovsky Theatre in Moscow, 1801.

99. *Zhizn za Tsarya* (A Life for the Tsar). Russian opera in 4 Acts with prologue and epilogue. Composer—M. I. Glinka. Libretto—Baron Rosen. Written 1834–6. Première on 27 November 1836 in Bolshoy Theatre, St. Petersburg. Score published by F. Stellovsky, St. Petersburg, 1881.[1]

100. *Zolotoe yabloko* (The Golden Apple). Comic opera in 2 Acts with choruses and ballets. Composer—E. I. Fomin. Libretto— I. Ivanov. Première 15 April 1803 in St. Petersburg. Score in TSMB.

101. *Tsygany* (The Gypries). Russian opera. Composer—M. Y. Vielgorsky (1788–1856). Written 1838, orchestration incomplete. Première [?].

[1] When writing his doctoral thesis, the author had access to a vocal score of this work, kindly made available to him by Dr. Gerald Abraham, which bore the signature of a former owner—Sir Arthur Sullivan.

Bibliographical Sources

CHAPTER 1

The main sources of this chapter have been KIRM I (pp. 19–35); PIRM I (pp. 7–65); TIRM I (pp. 7–27); W. R. S. Ralston. *The Songs of the Russian People as Illustrative of Slavonic Mythology and Russian Social Life*. London, 1872; G. Vernadsky. *The Origins of Russia*. Yale University Press, 1961; K. A. Vertkov. *Atlas muzykalnykh instrumentov narodov SSSR*. Moscow, 1963; T. V. Popova. *Russkoe narodnoe muzykalnoe tvorchestvo*. Voll. I–III, Moscow, 1955–6; and A. D. Kastalsky. *Osobennosti narodno-russkoi muzykalnoi sistemy*. Moscow-Petrograd, 1923. When studying in Leningrad the author was kindly permitted to consult a then unfinished manuscript work of the Russian folklorist, Professor F. A. Rubtsov, since published under the title: *Osnovy ladovovo stroeniya russkikh narodnykh pesen*. Leningrad, 1964. The account of the Ryabinin family is taken from PIRM I pp. 61–3. Information on M. S. Kryukova, who died in 1953, and other ballad-singers, will be found in: A. M. Astakhova [ed.] *Ilya Muromets*. Moscow-Leningrad, 1958, pp. 519–29. An extensive bibliography, together with lists of folk-songs and other materials pertaining to this chapter will be found in Vol. II of the present work.

CHAPTER 2

Based on KIRM I (pp. 39–127); PIRM I (pp. 66–100); TIRM I (pp. 7–76); with additional materials (with some corrections) from Popova (op. cit.); Vernadsky (op. cit.); FOIM; MOOS I; K. Danilov. *Drevnye rossiiskie stikhotvoreniya*. Moscow-Leningrad, 1958; D. S. Mirsky. *A History of Russian Literature*. New York, 1927; and the *Bolshaya sovetskaya entsiklopedia*. An historical survey of Russian ecclesiastical music will be found in Vol. II of the present work. The author visited the Cathedral of Saint Sophia, Kiev, in 1961 and can attest to the excellent state of preservation of the musical murals. When employing FOIM the author has taken advantage of an unpublished translation of the work made by S. W. Pring, though corrections have been made wherever necessary.

CHAPTER 3

Based on KIRM I (pp. 131–65; 244–58); PIRM I (pp. 100–29); TIRM I (pp. 79–150); FOIM; GIRMA I; Druskin and Keldysh [ed.]. *Ocherki po istorii russkoi muzyki 1790–1825*. Leningrad, 1956; B. Volman. *Russkie pechatnye noty XVIII v*. Leningrad, 1957; K. A.

Vertkov. *Russkaya rogovaya muzyka.* Leningrad, 1948; P. N. Stol-
pyansky. *Staryi Peterburg.* Leningrad, 1925; Y. A. Dmitriev [ed.].
F. G. Volkov i russkii teatr evo vremeni. Sbornik materialov. Moscow,
1953; Finagin [ed.]. *Muzyka i muzykalnyi byt Staroi Rossii.* Vol. I.
Leningrad, 1927; T. Livanova. *Ocherki i Materialy po istorii russkoi
muzykalnoi kultury.* Vol. I. Moscow, 1938; Ivanov-Boretsky, M. V.
Muzykalnoe nasledstvo. Vol. I. Moscow, 1935 (containing Stählin's
'Izvestiya o muzyke v Rossii'); M. Slonim. *Russian Theatre from the
Empire to the Soviets.* Cleveland and New York, 1961; A. D. Alekseev.
Russkaya fortepiannaya muzyka. Moscow, 1963; V. I. Muzalevsky.
Russkaya fortepiannaya muzyka. Moscow-Leningrad, 1949; S. L.
Ginzburg. *Istoriya violonchelnovo iskusstva.* Vol. II. Moscow, 1957.
Two other volumes worthy of mention are I. M. Yampolsky.
Russkoe skripichnoe iskusstvo; ocherki i materialy. Vol. I. Moscow, 1951
(the violin counterpart of L. Ginzburg's *Istoriya violonchelnovo
iskusstva*); and B. S. Shteynpress [ed.]. *Iz muzykalnovo proshlovo;
sbornik statei.* Vol. I. Moscow, 1960. Vol. No. 12, December 1950 of
Sovetskaya muzyka contains materials on Khandoshkin. For an
account of Bortnyansky's choral composition see: S. S. Skrebkov.
'Bortnyansky—master russkovo khorovovo kontserta'. (*Ezhegodnik
instituta istorii iskusstv AN SSSR.* Vol. II, Moscow 1948). Examples
of early Russian instrumental music may be found in FOIM;
LRMK I and II; GIRMA I and II; and in the collections of:
Barenboim and Muzalevsky. *Khrestomatiya po istorii fortepiannoi
muzyki v Rossii.* Moscow-Leningrad, 1949; Natanson and Nikolaev
[ed.]. *Russkaya fortepiannaya muzyka s kontsa XVIII do 6okh godov
XIX v*; khrestomatiya. Voll. I–II, Moscow, 1954–6; Drozdov and
Trofimova. *Russkaya starinnaya fortepiannaya muzyka.* Moscow-
Leningrad, 1946. Bortnyansky's *Sinfonie concertante* is published as a
supplement to the seventh section of LRMK II. No survey of this
period is complete without reference to the works of Mooser which
comprise his *Annales* (MOOS I, II, III); *Violonistes-compositeurs italiens
en Russie au XVIIIe siècle* (which appeared originally in the *Rivista
musicale italiana*, Turin-Milan, 1938–50); *Opéras, intermezzos, ballets,
cantates, oratorios joués en Russie durant le XVIIIe siècle.* Bale, 1964; and
L'opéra-comique français en Russie au XVIIIe siècle. 2e éd., Genève, 1954.
At the time of writing a new volume by Keldysh has appeared
under the title *Russkaya muzyka XVIII veka.* Moscow, 1965, though
this has not yet come into the author's possession.

CHAPTER 4

Based on KIRM I (pp. 142–258); PIRM I (pp. 87–199); TIRM I
(pp. 89–150); FOIM; RODG; Druskin and Keldysh. Op. cit.;

with corrections from MOOS and from personal examination of autograph materials. Other sources include: Volman. Op. cit.; Dieter Lehmann. *Russland's Oper u. Singspiel in der zweiten Hälfte des 18 Jahrhunderts.* Leipzig, 1958; G. V. Keldysh [ed.]. *Entsiklopedicheskii muzykalnyi slovar.* Moscow, 1959 (though this is not completely reliable); new editions of the folk collections of: Lvov-Prach (ed. Belyaev, 1953); Gerstenberg and Ditmar (Moscow, 1958); and K. Danilov. An extensive survey of folk elements in Russian music is found in N. Bachinskaya. *Narodnye pesni v tvorchestve russkikh kompozitorov,* Moscow, 1962; and in the author's doctoral thesis, *The Influence of Folk-song on Russian Opera in the Eighteenth Century up to and including the Time of Glinka,* November 1961, deposited in the Bodleian. This, however, should be used in conjunction with the present volume, since a number of errors have since been rectified. Useful summaries of eighteenth-century libretti may be found in S. L. Ginzburg. *Russkii muzykalnyi teatr, 1700–1835.* Moscow-Leningrad, 1941; and in A. V. Kokorev. *Khrestomatiya po russkoi literature XVIII veka.* Moscow, 1956. Materials on Fomin will be found in B. Dobrokhotov. *E. I. Fomin.* Moscow-Leningrad, 1949; and in *Muzykalnoe nasledstvo.* Vol. II, Part 1, Moscow, 1966, pp. 9–43. Discussion of Sarti's activities will be found in M. V. Ivanov-Boretskiy [ed.]. *Muzykalnoe nasledstvo.* Moscow, 1935.

CHAPTER 5

Based on KIRM I (pp. 261–368); PIRM I (pp. 200–328); TIRM I (pp. 153–234); FOIM; RODG; with corrections from: MOOS II and III; R. A. Mooser. *Opéras, intermezzos, ballets, cantates, oratorios joués en Russie durant le XVIIIᵉ siècle.* 3e éd., Bale, 1964. G. Bernandt. *Slovar oper vpervye postavlennykh ili izdannykh v dorevolyutsionnoy Rossii v SSSR/1736–1959.* Moscow, 1962; and personal examination of autograph materials. Material on Russian musical criticism and musical life in the nineteenth century will be found in Asafyev. *Izbrannye trudy.* Voll. I–V, Moscow, 1952–7; and *Russkaya muzyka ot nachala XIX v.* Moscow-Leningrad, 1930 [translated by A. J. Swan under the title *Russian Music. From the Beginning of the Nineteenth Century.* Michigan, 1953. This translation, however, contains some errors and should be used in conjunction with the review appearing in *Notes* 12. 1954–5, pp. 93–5.] Among the numerous other works dealing with the early nineteenth century and utilized in this volume are: Druskin and Keldysh. Op. cit.; Slonim. Op. cit.; Kremlëv. *Russkaya mysl o muzyke.* Vol. I. 1825–60. Leningrad, 1954. An account of the Vielgorsky's activities may be found in S. L. Ginzburg. *Istoriya violonchelnovo iskusstva.* Vol. II. Moscow, 1957, pp. 278–330; a survey of vocal music is contained in V. A. Vasina-Grossman. *Russkii klassicheskii romans XIX veka*. Moscow, 1956; chamber music is discussed in L. Raaben. Op. cit.; piano music in the works of Muzalevsky and Alekseev. Details of Alyabyev's activities will be found in: B. Dobrokhotov. *A. A. Alyabyev. Kamerno-instrumentalnoe tvorchestvo*. Moscow, 1948; the most recent survey of Alyabyev's work is that of B. Dobrokhotov. *Aleksandr Alyabyev. Tvorcheskii put*. Moscow, 1966, though this was received too late for inclusion in the present volume. Some interesting details of Alyabyev's incidental music, including that to Shakespeare's *The Merry Wives of Windsor* (1838) and Pushkin's *Rusalka* (1838) will be found in A. Glumov. *Muzyka v russkom dramaticheskom teatre*. Moscow, 1955. An account of Verstovsky's work is found in N. Findeisen. *Aleksei Nikolaevich Verstovsky*. St. Petersburg, 1890; B. Dobrokhotov. *A. N. Verstovsky*, Moscow, 1949. New volumes of opera criticisms are currently appearing, an important one being: Vol. I. Part 1 of T. N. Livanova and V. V. Protopopov. *Opernaya kritika v Rossii*. Moscow, 1966. Livanova is also editor of another series of volumes currently appearing, concerned with musical bibliography of the Russian periodical press during the nineteenth century. A remarkable volume, giving details of a huge number of musical settings of Russian literary and folk poetry is G. K. Ivanov [ed.]. *Russkaya poeziya v otechestvennoi muzyke (do 1917 goda)*. Spravochnik. Vol. I, Moscow, 1966. New editions are available of the collections of Rupin (Moscow, 1955) and Kashin (Moscow, 1959). A copy of Varlamov's collection *Russkii pevets* (no date or reference number) is preserved in the archives of the Leningrad Conservatory, where it was consulted by the author. Music examples of the period may be found in GIRMA I, II, III, in the above-mentioned collections of Drozdov and Trofimova, and Barenboim and Muzalevsky, and in a number of modern reprints.

CHAPTER 6

Based on KIRM I (pp. 369–435); PIRM I (pp. 329–406); TIRM I (pp. 235–310). The author is particularly indebted to V. V. Protopopov's volume '*Ivan Susanin' Glinki*. Moscow, 1961. pp. 163–241, which contains a searching analysis of folk elements in Glinka's opera. An account of Glinka's employment of oriental themes, with music examples, may be found in an article by Kh. Arakelov in *Pamyati Glinki*. Moscow, 1958, pp. 203–23. Two comprehensive volumes are LITNAS I and II, which contain Glinka's *Memoirs*, letters and other materials. The *Memoirs* are available in an English translation. A volume on Georgian music is A. Tsulukidze [ed.].

Gruzinskaya muzykalnaya kultura. Moscow, 1957, from which has been taken the *Khorumi,* quoted in Mus. Ex. 14. Two useful surveys of Glinka's chamber and piano music are the already-mentioned works of Raaben and Alekseev, both of which have been utilized. Other principal studies consulted include: B. V. Asafyev. *Glinka,* Moscow, 1950; E. Kann Novikova. *M. I. Glinka. Novye materialy i dokumenty.* Vol. I. Moscow-Leningrad, 1950; T. Livanova. *M. I. Glinka. Sbornik materialov i statei.* Moscow-Leningrad, 1950; V. Uspenskii. *Mikhail Ivanovich Glinka, 1804–57.* Leningrad, 1950; A. V. Ossovsky [ed.]. *M. I. Glinka: issledovaniya i materialy.* Leningrad-Moscow, 1950; with corrections from the Complete Works. An extensive bibliography of Glinka and precise details of the Collected Editions (still incomplete) will appear in Vol. II.

CHAPTER 7

Based on KIRM I (pp. 436–67); PIRM I (pp. 407–54); TIRM I (pp. 311–46). The author is particularly indebted to M. Pekelis *Dargomyzhsky i narodnaya pesnya.* Moscow-Leningrad, 1951, especially pp. 36–7, 114–54, and 155–80, which contain valuable examinations of the employment of folk elements in his work. Other sources include N. F. Findeisen. *A. S. Dargomyzhsky.* Moscow, 1904; N. Findeisen [ed.]. *Kratkaya avtobiograficheskaya zapiska. Sbornik 'A. S. Dargomyzhsky'. (1813–1869). Avtobiografiya. Pisma. Vospominaniya sovremennikov.* St. Petersburg, 1921; Dargomyzhsky, A. S. *Izbrannye pisma.* [ed. Pekelis]. Moscow, 1952; S. Shlifshteyn. *Dargomyzhsky.* Moscow, 1960; V. A. Vasina-Grossman. Op. cit. At the time of writing the first volume of a new study of the composer by M. S. Pekelis (*Aleksandr Sergeevich Dargomyzhsky.* Moscow, 1966) has appeared, though, regrettably, too late for consideration in the present work. A detailed bibliography and a list of Dargomyzhsky's works will appear in Vol. II.

Sources of Music Examples

Page

Quoted in PIRM I, p. 388. (Complete Works, Vol. 7, p. 42)   189

(19) Glinka. Excerpt from Overture to *Prince Kholmsky*. Quoted in PIRM I, p. 388. (Complete Works, Vol. 7, p. 51)   189

(20) Glinka. Excerpt from second movement of First Quartet in D major. Quoted in L. Raaben. *Instrumentalnyi ansambl v russkoi muzyke*. Moscow, 1961, p. 110. (Complete Works, Vol. 3, p. 95)   191

(21) Glinka. Excerpt from first movement of D minor Sonata for Viola or Violin. Quoted in Raaben. Op. cit., p. 112–13. (Complete Works, Vol. 4, p. 3)   192

(22) Glinka. Excerpt from second movement of D minor Sonata. Quoted in Raaben. Op. cit., p. 113. (Complete Works, Vol. 4, p. 19)   192

(23) Glinka. Excerpt from *Larghetto* of 'Divertimento' on Motives from *La Sonnambula*. Quoted in A. D. Alekseev. *Russkaya fortepiannaya muzyka*. Moscow, 1963, p. 79. The misprint appearing in the second half of bar 4 of Alekseev's example has been corrected. (Complete Works, Vol. 4, p. 30)   194

(24) Glinka. Excerpt from first movement of Piano Sextet. Quoted with slight modifications in PIRM I, p. 336. (Complete Works, Vol. 4, pp. 94–5)   196

(25) Glinka. Excerpt from second movement of Piano Sextet. Quoted in Alekseev. Op. cit., p. 82. (Complete Works, Vol. 4, p. 124)   197

(26) Glinka. Excerpt from first movement of 'Pathetic Trio' (Clarinet part transposed). Quoted in PIRM I, pp. 334–5; Raaben. Op. cit., p. 123. (Complete Works, Vol. 4, p. 173)   197

(27) Glinka. Excerpt from *Largo* of 'Pathetic Trio' (Clarinet part transposed). Quoted in Raaben. Op. cit., p. 124. (Complete Works, Vol. 4, p. 200)   198

(28) Glinka. Excerpt from opening of Piano Variations on Alyabyev's 'Solovey'. Quoted in Alekseev. Op. cit., p. 91. (Complete Works, Vol. 6, p. 135)   199

(29) Glinka. Excerpt from First Variation of 'Solovey' Variations. Quoted in Alekseev. Op. cit., p. 92. (Complete Works, Vol. 6, p. 136)   199

(30) Glinka. Excerpt from Piano Variations on ''Tis the Last Rose of Summer'. Quoted in Alekseev. Op. cit.,

Index

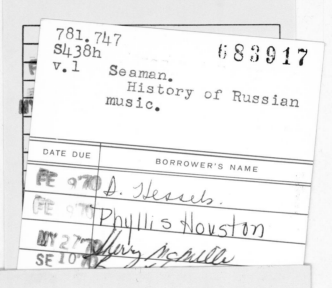